D1270902

Critical Essays on
A. R. AMMONS

CRITICAL ESSAYS
ON
AMERICAN LITERATURE

James Nagel, General Editor
University of Georgia, Athens

Critical Essays on
A. R. AMMONS

edited by

ROBERT KIRSCHTEN

G. K. Hall & Co.
An Imprint of Simon & Schuster Macmillan
New York

Prentice Hall International
London   Mexico City   New Delhi   Singapore   Sydney   Toronto

G. K. Hall & Co.
An Imprint of Simon & Schuster Macmillan
1633 Broadway
New York, NY 10019

Library of Congress Cataloging-in-Publication Data

Critical essays on A.R. Ammons / edited by Robert Kirschten.
p. cm. — (Critical essays on American literature)
Includes bibliographical references (p.   ) and index.
ISBN 0-7838-0044-4 (acid-free paper)
1. Ammons, A. R., 1926-   —Criticism and interpretation.
I. Kirschten, Robert, 1947- . II. Series.
PS3501.M6Z63 1997
811'.54—dc21   97-15750
                                                                        CIP

The paper used in this publication meets the minimum requirements of American National Standard for Information Sciences—Permanence of Paper for Printed Library Materials. ANSI Z39.48-1984. ∞™

10 9 8 7 6 5 4 3 2 1

for Barbara Kirschten,
her husband, James Feinerman,
and their daughter,
Anna Louise

Contents

General Editor's Note

◆

This series seeks to anthologize the most important criticism on a wide variety of topics and writers in American literature. Our readers will find in various volumes not only a generous selection of reprinted articles and reviews but original essays, bibliographies, manuscript selections, and other materials brought to public attention for the first time. This volume, *Critical Essays on A. R. Ammons,* is the most comprehensive collection of essays ever published on one of the most important modern poets in the United States. It contains both a sizable gathering of early reviews and a broad selection of more modern scholarship. Among the authors of reprinted articles and reviews are Wendell Berry, Helen Vendler, Nathan Scott, Willard Spiegelman, Geoffrey Hartman, and Cary Wolfe. In addition to a substantial introduction by Robert Kirschten, there are also two original essays commissioned specifically for publication in this volume, a new study by William J. Rushton offering an analysis of one of Ammons's "Tombstone" meditations, and an article by Robert Kirschten exploring the Sumerian songs. We are confident that this book will make a permanent and significant contribution to the study of American literature.

JAMES NAGEL
University of Georgia, Athens

Publisher's Note

◆

Producing a volume that contains both newly commissioned and reprinted material presents the publisher with the challenge of balancing the desire to achieve stylistic consistency with the need to preserve the integrity of works first published elsewhere. In the Critical Essays series, essays commissioned especially for a particular volume are edited to be consistent with G. K. Hall's house style; reprinted essays appear in the style in which they were first published, with only typographical errors corrected. Consequently, shifts in style from one essay to another are the result of our efforts to be faithful to each text as it was originally published.

Introduction

Robert Kirschten

In an unassuming manner, with virtually none of the self-promotion or politicking that marks many literary careers—indeed, until recently, he has seldom given poetry readings—A. R. Ammons has quietly amassed one of the most impressive bodies of work in postmodern American poetry. Author of more than 20 volumes of verse, Ammons has twice won the National Book Award, for *Collected Poems: 1951–1971* in 1973 and for *Garbage* in 1994. His book-length poem *Sphere: The Form of a Motion* won the Bollingen Prize in 1975; and, in 1981, his *Coast of Trees* won the National Book Critics Circle Award. In addition to receiving honors for specific books, Ammons has won a Guggenheim Fellowship, a MacArthur Prize Fellowship Award, the Levinson Prize, an American Academy of Arts and Letters Traveling Fellowship, an award from the National Institute of Arts and Letters, and a Lannan Foundation Award. In 1973, he was given the the degree of doctor of letters by Wake Forest University, and because of his distinctive overall achievement, Ammons has been awarded the title of Goldwin Smith Professor of Poetry at Cornell University, where he started as an instructor in 1964.

Notwithstanding this array of prestigious acknowledgments, Ammons began his career in obscurity and isolation with the publication of his first book of poems, *Ommateum,* which was privately produced in 1955 and sold 16 copies in five years. So thoroughly unnoticed was his first volume that, 18 years later, Ammons could joke that "[t]he royalties were so little that they used to send me postage stamps instead of a check. I remember one year I got two four cent stamps . . ."[1] As far as the literary world may be concerned, Ammons was born in even greater obscurity in a farmhouse, which his grandfather built, near Whiteville, North Carolina, on 18 February 1926. According to an interview in the *Cornell Daily Sun* in 1973, he attended grammar school in a small, rural, wooden schoolhouse, from which he was excused early in the spring to help with plowing and farm chores. His remarks about his country background provide significant insight not only into his youth but into his poetics as well:

> It was a time of tremendous economic and spiritual privation, even loneliness. . . . I never brought a book home. It was impossible. . . . the only book we had in our house was the Bible. . . . But all this privation was compensated for by a sense of the eternal freshness of the land itself. So I substituted for normal human experience, which was unavailable to me much of the time, this sense of identity with the things around me.[2]

Ammons served in the South Pacific in the navy during World War II and began to write during long stretches on a destroyer escort when there was little else to do. Ammons received his bachelor of science from Wake Forest, where he wrote few poems and showed them to virtually no one. In 1950, he was principal of a small grammar school in Hatteras, North Carolina, then briefly attended graduate school at Berkeley. There he met poet Josephine Miles, one of his greatest influences, to whom he dedicated his first book. From 1952 to 1964, Ammons lived in southern New Jersey, where he worked for a glass manufacturing company that specialized in laboratory equipment. As noted earlier, since 1964, Ammons has taught at Cornell University in Ithaca, New York, where he was offered a position in the English department after giving a poetry reading at the university.

The critical response to Ammons may be divided into three major phases: first, initial neglect in the mid-fifties; then a rise with *Expressions of Sea Level* to (perhaps) the highest point of his reputation in the mid-seventies after the publication of *Collected Poems, 1951–1971;* a falling off with the appearance of *The Snow Poems* in 1977; and finally, another, still continuous ascent, beginning with his award-winning *Coast of Trees* in 1981 and strongly reinforced by his National Book Award for *Garbage* in 1994.[3]

I

While he was working in business in New Jersey, Ammons managed to collect enough poems for his important first volume, *Ommateum* ("compound eye"), in 1955. Although its initial reviewing fortunes (or lack thereof) have been noted, it has since then received considerably more attention. Perhaps the early published criticism was scanty on this volume not only because Ammons was unknown but also because the volume was difficult and austere. In the very first review of Ammons's career in *Poetry* in 1956, Reuel Denney is less than positive about *Ommateum,* observing that Ammons's "tone-of-voice remains elusive." Further, this voice, according to Denney, does not seem to be "speaking to anyone. . . . The result is poetry that does not exactly . . . want to be listened to, not to say, 'understood.' "[4] Like Denney,

Alan Holder thinks that "the poetry is personal but abstract, intense but distanced. Taken as a whole, the volume is attenuated and unduly strange, coming to us from too far away." With regard to the speakers' shifting voices in this volume, Holder believes that at times "the book appears to be casting about for a style."[5] Frederick Buell agrees with Holder in claiming that a major limitation in these poems is that "[b]ehind Ammons's early work looms a desire too large and sometimes too corrupted by indefinite sin or decay to be able to find in nature an image for itself or to be able to make, going beyond nature, objects for itself."[6] Gilbert Allen thinks another limitation of the book is that the "social dimension [is] absent from *Ommateum*" and that its "poems renounce the everyday world and its rhetorical gestures."[7] In *Diacritics* in 1973, David Kalstone is also critical, noting that "there is surprisingly little sense of movement; action is arrested by the completed pasts into tableaux, characters in a frieze as they reach for or just attain transcendence." On the other hand, Kalstone is positive in observing that the poems of *Ommateum* are "[f]ull of ceremonies and rituals," employing "the simplest syntax to recount supernatural events."[8]

In disagreement with Holder, Richard Howard embraces the distancing aspect of *Ommateum,* calling the lyrics in the book "litanies . . . ways of looking at landscape, history, and deity" in "strange bug-eyed views wherein the world is refracted into various but adjacent fragments." Although Howard agrees with the negative critics in stating that *Ommateum* evinces certain weaknesses, at times "a wavering form" and "an uncertain voice," he also notes perceptively that the need to solve these technical problems leads Ammons to at least two of his early, major discoveries: first, an authoritative voice for these poems, which Howard identifies as a recreation of the biblical prophet Ezra; and second, Ammons's "tremendous theme: putting off the flesh and taking on the universe."[9] As to the identity of this early, seminal "authoritative voice," Harold Bloom identifies Ezra not as biblical figure nor as Ezra Pound but as "a suddenly remembered hunchback playmate from childhood, brought back to the poet's consciousness by a report of his death in war."[10] While Frederick Buell concurs with Bloom as to the identity of Ezra, Sister Bernetta Quinn, OSF, disagrees with Bloom and Buell about the meaning—or, at least, the major source—of this name. Citing the Good News Bible, she finds the formula "I, Ezra" in three places, for example, "I, Ezra, was on Mount Sion" (2 Esdras 2:42).[11] Janet DeRosa agrees with Bloom while also arguing for the "multiple associations" of the name "Ezra," for "its simultaneous allusiveness to the childhood companion, the poet, and most importantly, within the contexts of the poem and Ammons' poetic mission, the minor prophet Ezra."[12]

Whatever the final resolution for this central issue, a number of critics, through the years, have argued for the importance of *Ommateum* in Ammons's overall, poetic development. In *Diacritics* in 1973, Patricia Parker states that "[t]hese early poems are still the best introduction to Ammons' ongoing poetic enterprise." Parker justifies her claim by noting perceptively that it was in *Ommateum* that Ammons first dramatized one of the most recurrent topics in his poetic canon, namely, his penchant for revealing "the various strategies of mind in an alien environment . . . [and] to entertain . . . things that will not stay to the determination to fix some immovable center in the midst of constant change"[13] Likewise, D. R. Fosso argues for the importance of Ammons's first book insofar as *"Ommateum* . . . opens with 'So I Said I Am Ezra' and rightfully so, for everything that Ammons has published originates from and returns to that poem."[14] Further, in claiming that "Ammons' first poems" are "short, hieratic, and hard" with a "magically mobile" self who is "beyond the resolving power of merely human vision," Jerald Bullis says of these early lyrics that Ammons's "subsequent performance has justified their quality"[15] The poet himself is insistent on the importance of this first volume when, in an interview in 1989, he emphatically claims that *"Ommateum* remains a very powerful influence with me," that he believes it is still "very strong" and "may be my best book," and that the poems are "sometimes very rigid and ritualistic, formal and off-putting, but very strong." Finally, in no uncertain terms, he concludes, "Someone . . . said that I was a poet who had not yet renounced his early poems. I never intend to renounce those poems."[16]

Not until nine years after *Ommateum* did Ammons publish his second collection, *Expressions of Sea Level,* in 1964. In general, this book was favorably reviewed and marks the beginning of the critical ascent of Ammons's reputation, which continued to gain momentum, as noted earlier, from the mid-sixties directly through the late seventies. In the *Antioch Review* in 1964, Laurence Lieberman favorably compares Ammons with James Dickey and argues that both poets "treat language with special attention to tone, modulation, and breathing space: all are suavely managed."[17] In the *Nation,* also in 1964, Wendell Berry is enthusiastic about the volume, especially regarding Ammons's use of scientific diction: "[T]he energy of poetry . . . takes over the language of science only as a resource, and causes it to belong to a larger, more exuberant statement than the specialized vocabulary alone could make." Berry thinks the book "admirable," exhibiting "a wonderful eagerness" that "accommodates surprises and accidents" in the process of poetic discovery through which "[w]e see differently and better."[18] Alan Holder finds *Expressions* a major advance in Ammons's career. For, unlike *Ommateum,* this book, with poems occurring in specific settings with recollected characters, establishes "a past and concrete existence," as opposed to the realm of Ammons's earlier, "disembodied speakers." Like Berry, Holder also appreciates Ammons's poetic use of science in that he employs "scientific notation" to get emotionally and philosophically "beyond those terms."[19] Alfred Reid also thinks that *Expressions* is a watershed moment in Ammons's career insofar as it "represents a striking departure from the modernist sensibility [of *Ommateum*] in which the poem is artifice and man is cut off from his world."

According to Reid, Ammons's second book exhibits "a belief in an orderly world in which finite and natural boundaries reflect an immense universal order" with its "harmonious and wonderful operations."[20] Several critics have been even more positive about *Expressions*. Richard Howard calls the book "magnificent," while Nathan A. Scott Jr. thinks its title poem "extraordinary," "one of the central poems of [Ammons's] career."[21] Sister Bernetta Quinn echoes this enthusiasm while recognizing the religious impulse in Ammons, especially in his construction of "natural" landscapes through which he dramatizes a major feature of his voice; he is, she claims, "a Francis of Assisi, whom legend credits with an ability to read in the Book of the Creatures . . . to speak its language."[22] In *Poetry Magazine* in 1964, Josephine Jacobsen praises *Expressions* in the highest terms. While noting that Ammons "is writing a poetry of . . . essential optimism," "honesty," and "uncanny perception," she believes that he possesses "an originality and power which place him solidly in the front rank of current American poets."[23]

With the appearance of two books in 1965, *Corsons Inlet* and *Tape for the Turn of the Year,* Ammons's career gained considerable critical momentum. Yet, because of this larger exposure, his work also became a broader target for controversy. For example, of *Corsons Inlet,* Robert Pinsky claims that the book, like much of Ammons's work, is based on "a difficult marriage of poetics or epistemology with nature description. . . ." Pinksy finds Ammons's diction "strained" and "oddly garrulous," and he thinks the conclusion to the book's famous title poem "awkwardly argumentative" and presented in an "idiom" that has a "pinched quality."[24] Laurence Lieberman worries about "a tendency" in Ammons "to multiply abstract verbiage until it recoils upon itself." However, Lieberman also calls the title poem an "astonishing success," and, further, he finds Ammons to be an extraordinary technician. Of Ammons's development of form, Lieberman notes: the "poet, with extraordinary nimbleness, discovers and rediscovers the movement of his line—and nothing can be preconceived, all must emerge instantaneously from the flux of language and the interplay of lines."[25] Richard Howard is very positive. He notes that in the opening poem, "Visit," Ammons achieves a "perfected diction," marked by a "rhythmical certainty" that issues from "the speed and retard of words," from "the shape of stanzas," and from "rests" that "create the soft action of speech itself." Howard goes on to claim exceptional originality in this volume from Ammons: "a formality . . . which is new to American poetry."[26] Like Lieberman, Guy Rotella believes that the title poem is a masterpiece; "Ammons's most central poem [is] a kind of testament . . . by which much of his other work may be read."[27] John Elder values "Corsons Inlet" for the "way in which nature and the poet alike break open old orders . . . to liberate materials from which new orders may be 'grasped.' "[28] Willard Spiegelman thinks that the poem "Prodigal" represents "the singular hallmark of Ammons's poetic diction—its polysyllabic and abstract words laced with jaunty colloquialisms."[29] Finally, David Kalstone claims that the volume's concluding poem, "Gravelly Run," is "remarkable" for "the modulation of tone, the range of voices to which it is open."[30]

Over the period of approximately one month, from 6 December 1963 to 9 January 1964 (if we assume the dates in the poet's text and on the dust jacket are correct), Ammons wrote a book-length, 205-page "long/thin/poem" in 33 parts on a roll of adding-machine tape, approximately 100 feet long and 3 inches wide. While composing, the poet adhered to the margins set by the tape and concluded only when the tape ran out.[31] Insofar as *Tape for the Turn of the Year* was considerably more experimental than *Corsons Inlet*, it was also more controversial and challenging to assess. Richard Howard calls *Tape* "not so much a poem as the ground of a poem."[32] Harold Bloom is of two views; he judges *Tape* "a heroic failure that is Ammons's most original and surprising invention."[33] Although Helen Vendler admires much in *Tape*, calling Ammons's vision of "the fertile changingness of the external world . . . a very rich discipline," she also thinks that his method of including extensive, domestic detail "risks being merely fussy."[34] Alan Holder thinks that *Tape* had "some tensions and doubts" and more than its share of "blank or dull passages" and was an act of "slightly nutty labor" with no discernable plot. However, Holder also thinks the poem shows that our daily lives can be "touched with the wondrous" and, more poignantly, "how much, for Ammons, life *is* the act of composing verse, riding the stream of one's works."[35] Willard Spiegelman echoes this double-edged sentiment when he notes that, in *Tape*, "Ammons's greatest failing is the tedium of indiscriminateness" in what Spiegelman considers "a nervously experimental poem." Spiegelman also believes that the poem has several strengths, namely, that it is the best of Ammons's long poems in creating "the poem's meaning through the resonant harmonies of its music" and is especially valuable in reflecting "the way the mind in the act of proposing, and the reader in the act of viewing, the inscribed data can reinterpret the substance of experience."[36]

Tape for the Turn of the Year received numerous favorable responses, many of which center on assessments of the challenging issue of form in Ammons's work. In the *Hudson Review* in 1965, Laurence Lieberman thinks *Tape* "a daring book. It takes valiant risks." Lieberman values the work because, through the composition of the poem on an adding-machine tape, it is able to capture "the many sides of [the poet] that work at cross-purposes in life, and embrace them in the process of dynamic interchange and imbalance."[37] Philip Fried believes *Tape* a success because of the physical material of the tape itself, which, thus, determines the poem's form, for "the poem becomes an object in process," that is "mysterious" and "alive." Implying even larger implications for the contemporary poet, Fried observes that Ammons's method suggests that "the perfect work of art is not possible . . . as far as the long poem is concerned. The syntheses that make such a work possible are just not available to us. Therefore, the only honest thing to do is to confront the incomplete and fragmentary nature of our lives."[38] Jerome Mazzaro thinks *Tape* a major "breakthrough" in the development of Ammons's distinctive voice for his version of process poetry. "The very self-consciousness of *Tape*," according to Mazzaro, "allows it to assume a sense of process" that enables "the personality of the poet to come through" so successfully that its "persona . . . makes the figure of the later, more specialized essay poems, seem anemic."[39] Nathan A. Scott Jr. calls *Tape* a "great success," "an exemplary . . . case of Ammons's art and one of his more impressive accomplishments in the medium of the long poem."[40] Likewise, in the *Southern Literary Journal* in 1975, William Harmon judges *Tape* "possibly Ammons's very best long work so far" and "among the select group of large poems genuinely American and genuinely great."[41] Finally, Donald H. Reiman believes that *Tape*'s strengths underline a major, revolutionary element in contemporary lyric. Reiman locates this element in Ammons's choosing to break "away from the tight, thematic reticence of the high Modernists" while rejecting "stereotyped epic conventions" to fulfill his poem's "intentions" as "an epic of modern consciousness."[42]

Patrick Deane thinks *Tape for the Turn of the Year* a playful and representative "avant-garde" work "of the early sixties." In its preoccupation with surfaces and processes, *Tape* is valuable because, in its "spirit of fun," it radically alters the traditional, mimetic approach of making the content of a poem seem an organic outgrowth of its form. According to Deane, Ammons's "pointedly gratuitous form" frees the poem's content and its coherence "[b]eyond the control of the writer," making "both [him] and the reader . . . free to function" in a metaphysically "life-giving" experience.[43] Klaus Martens values *Tape* for its "method of unfolding, not with breaking out, but with breaking loose" from a traditional poetic of unified parts. Martens believes that "[s]equence and sequentiality do not constitute the form of the poem but rather the subject of the speaker's reflections. . . . The poem is merely a verbalization of immediate and transient conditions in a heraclitean state of flux, not even preserved, but simply left behind as the poem proceeds."[44] Matthew Wilson enthusiastically thinks *Tape* "a break-through poem" for Ammons in that it constitutes a "homecoming" or "return from his own early work, a return from states which have tempted and still tempt him, the 'haunted / lands and transformations' of *Ommateum*." In *Tape*, Ammons's voice comes home from "the stultifying 'dread' of the *Ommateum* poems," which are only "shard[s]" to the "balanced movements" [of *Tape*], which "embrace antithetical movement" in an integrating, structuring form.[45] In *Salmagundi* in 1973, Hyatt H. Waggoner thinks *Tape* "a wonderful poem" in an Emersonian or transcendental tradition insofar as it, like the tradition, "puts enormous emphasis on the single word, the single image, the discrete perception that may become an intuition."[46] Frederick Buell is very positive, calling the work "Ammons' essential poem of America . . . a remarkable achievement in a Whitmanian vein."[47] In the *South Carolina Review* in 1979, Alfred Reid feels this poem important enough to note that with it Ammons "explicitly joined the post-modernist movement begun ten years

earlier by Ginsberg and Lowell" insofar as they "advocated direct autobiographical treatment of reality and favored spontaneity over art."[48]

Published in 1966, *Northfield Poems* is an extremely strong volume of
brilliant, short lyrics—one to two pages—beautifully crafted in both comic
and serious modes. This book contains several of Ammons's most impressive
meditations, such as "The Constant," "One: Many," "Saliences," "Two
Motions," and "Muse." The collection brought mostly favorable responses
from critics, although a few also had negative things to say. In *Poetry* in 1967,
Hayden Carruth praises Ammons for his "sharp eye" and calls him "a very
good writer," but also complains that the book is "dull," "talky," and "pretentious," filled with "abstract talk" and "chatter."[49] In the *Hudson Review* in the
same year, Laurence Lieberman is extremely enthusiastic, pointing out that
one of Ammons's main virtues is his ability to dramatize ideas as "jointed
bodies colliding with each other and with observed natural phenomena"
through "the self-discovering rhythms" of poems that, at times, convey "an
astonishing impact." Yet Lieberman is also critical in that he thinks that some
of the poems suffered from "over-writing" such that, in "Sphere" and "Discoverer," "the subject . . . recedes as the dense filigree of language drives it
underground." Overall, however, Lieberman finds Ammons's work so "entic-
ing," "surprising," and technically risky that it "begin[s] poetic art afresh."[50]
Richard Howard notes recurrent themes for Ammons in this book. He claims
that the volume "enacts Ammons' now familiar insurgence against finitude"
and, more important, the poet's "transformation of process into words," what
Valery calls "*le changement des rives en rumeur,* the change of shores to sound."[51]
In the *Nation* in April of 1967, John Logan thinks the volume extremely
strong. Logan calls Ammons "one of the most . . . intelligent gifted poets of
recent years . . . a major talent . . . who has the courage and the heuristic
power to discover new form, as well as the eye and the ear and the mind to
hold us and to give us what [Dylan] Thomas called 'the momentary peace of
the poem.' "[52]

Published four years later in 1970, *Uplands* is another collection of
Ammons's finely crafted, brief lyrics, many of which—"Snow Log," "If Anything Will Level with You Water Will," and "The Unifying Principle," for
example—are as high in quality as the best poems in his previous book. In
addition, this book contains several of Ammons's brilliant, short pieces, such
as "Small Song" and "Love Song," which were collected in a later volume of
his short poems. Harold Bloom thinks very highly of *Uplands,* calling it "a
majestically sad book" and noting that "[a]ll the poems . . . have [a] new
ease" presented in a manner of "unmediated telling, a purely visionary
poetry" that "deals in a purer representation than even Wordsworth could
have wanted."[53] Alan Holder makes a major statement about a change in
Ammons's aesthetic direction when he notes that the treatment of nature in
the poem "Upland" indicates—contrary to Bloom's views—an antitranscen-
dentalist direction: "nature does not figure for Ammons as it often did in the

past: a generalized presence informed by a beneficent or at least significant spiritual force. He concerns himself with particular manifestations of the natural" that "continually engages his feelings" and "mind."[54] In the *New York Times Book Review* of 9 May 1971, David Kalstone is very positive about the volume, emphasizing Ammons's place in the American tradition of "solitary testings of the mind against a landscape. . . ." Kalstone then goes on to applaud the poem "Uplands" for its "tough wry explorations, as well as for the intensity and buoyancy with which Ammons makes a familiar kind of poetry his own."[55] Richard Howard praises the book, noting that *Uplands* is a volume of "sudden, attractive fits and starts" in which "the poet urges himself into a new economy, a bright particularity of diction entirely *gainful* to his panoply, a way of handling verse without giving up conversation."[56] In the *Yale Review* in 1971, Louis Martz also thinks *Uplands* strong, exhibiting "great critical vigor" in poems that "are primarily about the nature of human perception" and evincing a "subtle fusion of abstract and concrete [qualities]."[57]

A long book at 105 pages, *Briefings: Poems Small and Easy* (1971) is also one of Ammons's best. As the title suggests, *Briefings* contains finely chiseled, one-page poems with short titles, including "Cut the Grass," with its wonderful final line, "less than total is a bucketful of radiant toys," and the book concludes with Ammons's famous, much-anthologized lyric "The City Limits."[58] His topics consist of general archetypes such as circles and light; however, his characteristic method is to begin with a specific object or idea ("Center," "Cougar," "Crevice"), then build a dialectical progression out of classical opposites such as his favorite pair, the one and many, which may be found in "Early Morning in Early April." In general, critics looked at the book favorably, though a few had reservations. Robert Pinsky thinks that the conclusion of "The City Limits" revealed "a lamely rhetorical motive" for the "turning" of the poet's acceptance of even the darkest of nature's forces.[59] In the *Yale Review* in 1971, Laurence Lieberman is of two minds about this book when he notes that in many of the poems "either the sniper fire [of the poet's imaginative eye] has flown wide of the mark or the imagination picked too high or low a perch." However, Lieberman also believes that each poem contains "moments" of loveliness. And, further, "in the best poems, the whole delivery bursts forth with the surety and ease of a supreme word acrobat who can juggle the beautiful simplicities of the natural heart as though such artistry were mere play."[60] In 1971 in *Ringers in the Tower*, Harold Bloom thinks *Briefings* to be Ammons's "finest book."[61] In the *Southern Review* in 1978, Bloom reiterates his enthusiasm, claiming that the best poems in *Briefings* "celebrate a radiance, a light seen and held" in an Emersonian tradition, to which Ammons adds "a unique pride and saving comedy." Regarding "The City Limits," Bloom calls the poem an "extraordinarily . . . high song [of] triumph."[62] John Hollander is very enthusiastic, calling *Briefings* a "most important group of poems whose matter is in fact larger than their length, and whose meditative structure is rather harder than their syntax." Like many of Ammons's critics, Hollander notes the romantic interaction of speaker and terrain, which he claims is the "determining fiction" of "the interaction of his ordering mind with the givens of the world."[63] Helen Vendler is also positive; she thinks *Briefings* is the book in which "Ammons brought his difficult form of short poetry to perfection." In addition, Vendler notes that *Briefings* also exhibits one of Ammons's most interesting, general idiosyncrasies, namely, "[t]he poetry he is best able to write is deprived of almost everything other poets have used, notably people and adjectives."[64] In the *Partisan Review* in 1972, Richard Howard calls Ammons "a great poet," for "[o]nly Ammons . . . of all American poets today, has . . . the capacity to endow the moment of loss, the moment of metamorphosis and the moment of release with an equal light. . . ."[65] After reviewing *Briefings* in 1973, Hyatt H. Waggoner declares Ammons "a poet of religious vision who is as wary of intellectualist abstractions as he is of pious dogmas." Waggoner goes on to say emphatically "that of the 'new' poets I've read since Roethke's death, Ammons seems to me at or near the top."[66]

II

Winner of the National Book Award for Poetry in 1973, *Collected Poems, 1951–1971* is, thus far, Ammons's central collection and his best-known book. It is the volume that solidified beyond dispute his reputation not merely as a nationally recognized poet but as one of the truly distinguished lyric poets of the second half of this century. Although they found minor flaws with it, critics were virtually unanimous in praise of the collection's overall character. Nonetheless, the range of diversified reaction is instructive in attempting to delineate this poet's distinctive powers and limitations. In a major review in the *New York Times Book Review* of 19 November 1972, Geoffrey Hartman is exceptionally enthusiastic in calling the volume a "remarkable book" that proves Ammons to be "a major American poet." Hartman thinks that Ammons's long poems, such as "Hibernaculum" and "Extremes and Moderations," were "extravagant and beautiful" and that "no one in his generation has put 'earth's materials' to better use, or done more to raise pastoral to the status of major art."[67] In *Parnassus* in 1973, William Meredith is also extremely positive, calling *Collected Poems* an "enormously attractive and energetic book" by "one of the surest craftsmen of organic form." Like many critics, however, Meredith prefers Ammons's shorter verse. Unlike Hartman, he thinks the three long poems at the end of the volume ("Essay on Poetics," "Extremes and Moderations," and "Hibernaculum") are unsuccessful in that "they don't seem to represent any new risks" and in that they "indulge in familiar and easy discourse, relying on their charm to cover up a certain aimlessness."[68] In contrast to Meredith, Harold Bloom calls the Ammons of *The*

Collected Poems an Emersonian expounder of "true science," especially with regard to "Extremes and Moderations," which Bloom considers "Ammons's major achievement in the long poem": "More than Whitman, or even Thoreau or Dickinson or Frost, Ammons is the Poet that Emerson prophesied as necessary for America."[69] Regarding Ammons's long poems in this collection, Willard Spiegelman disagrees with Bloom by noting that two of the poet's self-conscious flaws—for example, in "Extremes and Moderations"—are "the dullness of prosaicisim and the airiness of abstraction," though both are "necessary risks of a scientific, discursive poet." However, Spiegelman also believes that Ammons's discursive aspect is one of his strongest features, for "[a]s an explainer," Ammons "is without peer."[70]

While enthusiastic about *Collected Poems,* Helen Vendler notes, in the spring of 1973, that Ammons's poetry is "severe . . . attempting the particularity of Hopkins with none of what Hopkins's schoolmates called his 'gush,' trying for the abstraction of Stevens without Stevens's inhuman remove from the world of fact, aiming at Williams's affectionateness toward the quotidian without Williams's romantic drift." In fact, Vendler thinks that, insofar as this book was written by a man in his mid-forties, Ammons may, through future experiments, succeed at having "written the first twentieth-century poetry wholly purged of the romantic."[71] On the important topic of Ammons's romanticism, David Kalstone disagrees with Vendler by claiming that Ammons is not only a modern romantic but that he seems "almost sentenced to write pastoral poems. . . . His *not* being purged is the problem. He has always had a gift for recalling romantic promises as if there were fresh ways for them to be fulfilled." In fact, this disposition leads to what Kalstone labels as one of Ammons's basic strengths: "[t]o devise in the face of that sense of nature an ample rhetoric has been Ammons's problem and finally his distinction."[72] In the *Partisan Review* in 1974, Paul Zweig is also concerned about Ammons's rhetoric and romantic vision. On the one hand, he observes negatively that *Collected Poems* contains "a great deal of tentative language" and that the poet's "gravest fault" is that "he fails to connect the conceptual framework of the poem with the local effects of his language," making the poetry "cold" and "thin." Even so, Zweig agrees with many critics that Ammons is a major poet whose "turn at the banquet table has come." According to Zweig, Ammons's real achievement is this: "the lyrical articulation of small moments of experience; his ability to organize shapes of language into an epiphany of movement, a frozen flood of perceptions which is visionary not because of any passionate metaphysics, but because of the sheer clarity of the poet's ability to recreate what he 'sees.' "[73] In *Boundary* in 1973, Richard Howard is exultant about this collection, recording his "stunned gratitude" for Ammons's work and calling him "a great inventor of forms" and "one of the largest [poets] to speak among us."[74] Finally, in the *New York Review of Books* in 1973, John Ashbery calls Ammons a great "American original" and argues that "the fascination of his poetry is not the transcendental but his struggle with it." Ashbery is impressed by the "austerity" and "sparse iconography" of Ammons's "palette," while, on the other hand, celebrating the "Wordsworthian splendor" of his work and noting how in Ammons's case the "regional [setting in upstate New York] has become universal."[75]

Sphere: The Form of a Motion appeared in 1974, and is the winner of the 1973–1974 Bollingen Prize in Poetry. Like *Tape for the Turn of the Year, Sphere* is a book-length poem. It runs 79 pages, and it is divided into 155 sections, each of which contains four three-line stanzas. Insofar as *Sphere* is one of Ammons's most ambitious projects, it aims high and encompasses much; it evoked a wide range of critical reaction, some severe. In *Parnassus* in 1975, Denis Donoghue is especially critical of Ammons who, he claims, "can at one glance evade the responsibility of history" and "circumvent the claims of other people. . . ." Further, he states, Ammons "protests that he is concerned with Nature, including human nature, but he rarely makes me feel that he cares much about any human nature but his own. His poetry is rural in the sense that you can walk for miles in it without meeting anyone; so the dramatic sense of life never appears." Even more acute: "I can remember nothing of *Sphere* but incidental felicities and . . . the degeneration of feeling in routines and postures. . . . Nothing in the poem convinces me that Ammons has anything comparable, so far as language is evidence, to the capacity of feeling which the finest of Eliot, Yeats, Stevens, and . . . Williams possesses."[76] In 1976, R. W. Flint calls *Sphere* "[a] rambling, confiding, button-holing poem," which he contrasts with the work of James Dickey but finds Ammons "cooler, more reflective, absorptive, and self-contained," Flint concludes with reservations about the poem, "asking if it *really* plays in New Haven."[77] Donald Reiman has a negative view of the poem. As opposed to the poet's earlier, successful long poem, *Tape for the Turn of the Year,* "*Sphere* sinks into bathetic anti-epic under the weight of its unstable mixture of factual reportage and unsupported (and only half-believed) assertions."[78]

Critics also expressed mixed views of *Sphere.* In the *New York Review of Books* in 1975, Donald Davie expresses both frustration and enthusiasm for Ammons's long poem: "How could I be anything but exasperated by [*Sphere*], profoundly distrustful, sure I was being bamboozled, sure I was being threatened? And how is it, then, that I was on the contrary *enraptured?* Have I gone soft in the head? . . . No. I am as suspicious as ever I was of Ammons's initial assumptions and governing preoccupations. . . . And yet I can't refuse the evidence of my senses and my feelings. . . ."[79] In the *New York Times Book Review* of 22 December 1974, Calvin Bedient also has mixed feelings about *Sphere,* calling it an " 'open' American counterpart of the closed Augustan verse essay." Bedient feels that the work "has scope, is original," yet it is "blandly imposing." And, further, "[a]lthough almost nothing in the poem moves or ravishes, almost everything interests and holds" because of Ammons's "intelligence," "crispness of . . . language," the "geniality of his tone," and "his *reasonable* approach to Romantic 'spirituality.' "[80] In the *Yale*

Review of spring 1975, J. D. McClatchey also finds "patches of tedium" in *Sphere,* along with invocations to the reader that he finds "forced and unconvincing." Yet, even though he thinks that *Sphere* is "unwieldy, absorbing" and "abstract," he feels very positively that its overall "ambition and accomplishment are rare."[81] Alan Holder finds a "strong religious strain" in *Sphere* that fuses the "mind and the divine" and "Creation and imagination." While he thinks the poem strong, he questions the poem's resolution, which "makes a presumption [of harmony] about the state of this nation and of the world that many of us cannot share."[82] In the *Georgia Review* in 1975, Jerome Mazzaro finds a few weaknesses in *Sphere;* for instance, "[w]hole deflections into biology or geology . . . sound flat and impersonal." However, Mazarro concludes by stating that Ammons's "revival of the poetic essay" reveals a "confidence" and "mastery" that places him "unquestionably among the best poets writing today."[83]

Many critics were unabashedly positive about *Sphere.* In *Parnassus* in 1981, David Lehman is extremely enthusiastic, noting that the book's "motion of a spiral" gives it a "renewing energy" and thus "the effect of a continuous present, a grand pageant of simultaneous 'events' " that make Ammons "indisputably large, multitudinous, and democratic."[84] Cary Wolfe finds a political implication to the poetic flow of *Sphere,* namely, that by focusing on "the making and not the made, the mechanism and not the substance, is to engage a poetics of the centrifugal, to consciously resituate poetry—and, by extension, culture."[85] Stephen Cushman values *Sphere* because it reveals one of the primary strengths of Ammons's use of poetic form, namely, its "richly self-reflexive passage" through, "extended qualification, variation, and apposition" that enables Ammons to avoid "complete dissolution of self into the alien world of nature . . . or poetic autism."[86] John Elder thinks highly of *Sphere* because of Ammons's capacity to observe nature precisely: "To observe the beautiful adjustments of the earth's stability, from the revolutions of air and water on a spinning planet to the coevolution of animals and plants in a given terrain, is to celebrate the integrity of motion's holding."[87] James E. Miller thinks *Sphere* "remarkably effective as a long, multi-faceted poem," written in the Whitmanian tradition of "the lyric-epic" that reveals a "genuinely democratic spirit."[88] In *Pembroke Magazine* in 1979, R. C. Kenedy favorably compares the Ammons of *Sphere* to the Roman poet Lucretius insofar as he claims that "[t]he passions of Ammons" are "great as well as noble," and they "pinpoint emblems of the mind against the ultimate terrors of the soul." In the final analysis for Kenedy, *Sphere* is best read in terms that are "ritual and festive," for the poet's vision evinces "the splendour . . . of a special, unique and radiant route."[89] With regard to one of its central driving mechanisms, Jerald Bullis perceptively notes that "[t]he ideational content . . . of the poem is so precisely dialectical that one is hard put to locate *any* assertion that is not 'complimented' by its contrary."[90] Steven P. Schneider thinks *Sphere* important because he believes that in Ammon's use of astronomy he has "rediscovered Whitman's spirit," a "spirit of integration and celebration that ultimately triumphs over feelings of isolation and loneliness." According to Schneider, the "ultimate benefit" of Ammons's vision "of widening scope is the breaking down of artificial barriers so that one can 'assimilate' the cosmic lights, the cellular whirlwinds, and the 'needful needless.' "[91]

Published in 1975, *Diversifications* is Ammons's 11th book of poems. It consists of what by this time had become characteristic Ammons lyrics: witty, finely crafted, disciplined, one-page poems, preceded by brief, often one-word titles, which centered on his traditional themes: transcendence, permanence, eternity, circular motion, and meditational landscapes. The volume is concluded by a remarkable 19-page lyric entitled "Pray Without Ceasing," its title most likely stemming from St. Paul's directive in 1 Thessalonians 5:17 and from Emerson's title for his first Unitarian sermon in 1827. In general, critics were positive, though some had reservations. Alvin Rosenfeld rightly identifies these poems as those of a "solitary," marked by a "[l]anguage" that "turns in precise and gentle motions, providing a 'small music' that echoes back the muffled sounds of our world in a way that seems almost too merciful for such an over-wrought and noisy age." Even so, Rosenfeld finds "Pray Without Ceasing," to be "voluble" and "undisciplined," "generally unchastened by form and diffuse in effect."[92] On the other hand, Alan Holder thinks this lyric "among Ammons' most interesting poems." While observing perceptively that the method of "Pray Without Ceasing" is a parody of "the patische technique of the modernist long poem" (such as *The Bridge* or *Paterson*), he feels that this work more fully and effectively expresses human pain in the face of personal and social change than did the more internally directed *Tape*.[93] Steven P. Schneider has mixed feelings about *Diversifications*. He thinks it "a modest volume with many good poems, but it lacked the energy, innovation, and exuberance of *Sphere*."[94] R. W. Flint finds the book full of "charm," "compactness," and "assurance," yet he expresses a tentative reservation about the long, concluding lyric "Pray Without Ceasing."[95] Helen Regueiro Elam thinks positively of the volume, finding in it "a resistance of mind . . . which places a different emphasis on the poetic enterprise, even when such resistance is considered a defeat and not a victory."[96]

Ammons published *The Snow Poems* in 1977. Of all of his books, this one is easily the most experimental and the most controversial, for he abandons almost all considerations of sequential narrative and argument in favor of a variety of typographic arrangements, lists, lyric moments, asides, voice changes, dirty jokes, word games, and other fragmentary tactics, which often infuriated reviewers. Consequently, this collection was met with considerable critical disdain when it appeared, and many readers were ready to write off Ammons as a poet. Marjorie Perloff is severe with regard to *The Snow Poems*. She finds the contents undisciplined and filled with excessive, useless detail.

She charges that, in this book, Ammons gives us merely "doodles drawn by eighth-grade boys during a boring math class," and she goes on to say that "[i]n playing such games, Ammons may be entertaining himself, but he can hardly be said to entertain his readers." So great a failure is this book for Perloff that at the end of her review she inquires sternly: "[A]re these failures temporary aberrations on Ammons's part or not?"[97] Echoing Perloff's concerns, Hyatt Waggoner claims that *Snow Poems* is "a thick book of dull, tired poems that prompt us to wonder, does Ammons write too much?"[98] Hayden Carruth notes, just as emphatically, that "[i]n spite of a bright, attractive technique, which could be used perfectly well in real poems, and in spite of lyric parts that remind us of earlier work, 'The Snow Poems' is a dull, dull book."[99] Gilbert Allen is "intrigued" by *The Snow Poems* but also finds them "insistently garrulous" and "diffuse," and his reaction to the book is "like my reaction to John Ashbery's work: I find it more enjoyable to talk about than to read. I am glad Ammons has written the book, but I hope that he doesn't write it again."[100] In the *Georgia Review* in winter of 1978, Peter Stitt thinks the book a "monumental failure," written in a "disastrous confessional voice" that is completely inappropriate for Ammons, who as a literary character does not evince the "tensions, neuroses, and self-destructive impulses" necessary for "[g]ood confessional poetry."[101]

Contrary to the opinions of Perloff, Carruth, Waggoner, and others, poet and critic William Harmon is much more positive in the *American Book Review* in December of 1977. Harmon claims that in *The Snow Poems* "Ammons' wordplay and typewriter games become increasingly salient as his experiments progress, and they deserve our most deeply sympathetic attention." Even more positively, he notes that "[t]he overall impression" of this book "is . . . one of heroic patience and courage." For, Harmon believes that Ammons begins "in a condition of outlandish solitude, isolation, and loneliness" and then "occupies himself with obsessive devotion to the making of pure poems dedicated . . . to hope."[102] Working from a distinctively postmodern point of view, Richard Jackson values *The Snow Poems* because it "deconstructs the idea of a book as simple linear progression of units," thus revealing that Ammons's is "a poetics of sudden gaps, chasms that are the source of discontinuous flux." For Jackson, Ammons's semantic deferment is one of the central strengths of the poet's language, which "is a parabolic discourse whose surface images are equidistant from a central meaning that always remains hidden, written over."[103] In a critical vein similar to Jackson's, William Doreski comes closer to describing Ammons's aesthetic than his negative readers by identifying his method as a struggle "against decisive closure as well as the afflatus of ecstasy, using the disruptive aesthetic of modern sequence. . . ." Furthermore, Doreski maintains that "irregularity is more than a principle of organization: it is the drama" and also that the book is organized "around a program . . . not of writing but of seeing."[104] Frank

Lepkowski finds a religious dimension—or rather the lack of one—as one of the central, impressive traits of *The Snow Poems,* which is "a descent to the underworld, an exploration of the abyss of mind and will . . . in isolation from God and His grace."[105]

Donald Reiman claims that *The Snow Poems* successfully reveals, especially in the poem "My Father Used to Tell of an," the Freudian theme of "the psychological trauma underlying Ammons' pervasive sense of alienation from others" that "originated in the fear and hostility his father had aroused in him during childhood."[106] Helen Vendler also thinks well of *The Snow Poems,* valuing Ammons's range of vocal styles, his "curious observation of the out-of-doors," and his "hard inquiry." She offers an interesting approach to reading this controversial book, an approach that may well answer many of Ammons's negative critics: "The book needs to be lived in for days, reread after the first reading has sorted out its preoccupations and methods, and used as a livre de chevet if its leisurely paths are to be followed in their waywardness." She then concludes with a strong statement on behalf of the poet: "How odd it remains that the solitaries who are bedeviled by the possibilities of words remain the chief chroniclers of the emotional history of mankind."[107] Finally, in the *Chicago Review* in the summer of 1981, like Jackson and Doreski, Michael McFee argues on behalf of *The Snow Poems.* McFee believes that it succeeds effectively in revealing the "deep antiformalism" of the poet and, further, "more of the man behind the poet than in any previous book." Instead of writing the "lofty, sublime" lyric "almost purified of human presence," Ammons offers a "garrulous . . . mode, full of humorous asides and wordplay" that, most importantly, "shows us the dark side of Ammons's radiant sublimity."[108]

III

After writing the explosively controversial *Snow Poems* in 1977, Ammons returned to a more conservative poetic mode of construction in one of his best volumes of verse, *A Coast of Trees,* in 1981. So strong is this book that it won the National Book Critics Circle Award for Poetry in the same year. Containing primarily single-page lyrics with one-word titles, in single columns flush against the left-hand margins, *A Coast of Trees* exhibits brief, carefully crafted meditations that have fully developed beginnings, middles, and ends. Ammons's return to the finely honed lyric also marks the third major movement in his critical reception, namely, an ascent that is still in progress. Steven P. Schneider thinks the book far stronger than *The Snow Poems* in that Ammons "is more consistently in control of his material. . . . [E]very single poem . . . is finely honed, as if the poet were signaling to his critics and readers that whatever had gotten into him in the previous volume was now gone."[109] Hyatt Waggoner echoes this sentiment by calling it "a volume of recovery" that "reads both like return and a fresh start, as though the poet had gotten his second wind."[110] Likewise, Nathan A. Scott Jr. argues that *A Coast of Trees* constitutes Ammons's return "to the short, hard lyric, and the song is simply stunning in its purity and grace."[111] David Lehman is extremely positive in claiming that *A Coast of Trees* contains "fresh poems bearing witness to the powers that make Ammons one of the indispensable poets of his generation."[112] In the *Yale Review* in 1982, Louis Martz also uses superlatives, calling *A Coast of Trees* "some of the best poems that [Ammons] has ever written: and that means some of the best that contemporary poetry can offer."[113] Several critics single out one lyric for special praise. Helen Vendler pronounces "Easter Morning" (about Ammons's deceased relatives) a "great poem" that is "a new treasure in American poetry."[114] Mark Soifer also thinks that " 'Easter Morning' . . . is one of our great poems," especially for its range of vocal tones that begins "with a slow movement of deep beauty and consequence about birth and death," then develops into "a fervent lament concerning loneliness and the lost."[115] Frederick Buell believe "Easter Morning" the best poem in the book because, among other things, unlike confessional poets such as Lowell, Plath, and Sexton, Ammons renounces "psychological and biographical sensationalism" in favor of "a far more lasting, profound, and universal self-revelation."[116] Irvin Ehrenpreis thinks highly of the entire book although focusing on another poem; he calls "Sunday at McDonald's" a powerful "outcry against the American addiction to living in a detached present."[117]

A thin volume of scarcely 50 pages, *Worldly Hopes* (1982) is the second of three books, appearing after *The Snow Poems,* in which Ammons returned, to use Nathan A. Scott Jr.'s terms, to "the short, hard lyric[s]" that had largely built his reputation. Though not as enthusiastic about this collection as they were about *A Coast of Trees,* critics were favorable. In the *Times Literary Supplement* in May of 1984, David Lehman likens Ammons to William Carlos Williams, Robert Frost, and Wallace Stevens in terms of Ammons's attention to minute detail, his dark vision of nature, and his considerable gift for abstraction. Claiming two of the book's poems, "Hermit Lark" and "Scribbles," the equal of Ammons's best lyric work, Lehman thinks that a major aspect of this poet's originality lies in poems that "manage to sound . . . so genuine and unforced" that "they compress observation into metaphor, identifying the poem's self with what he sees." According to Lehman, *Worldly Hopes* is "a most welcome book" with "transcendental tendencies" and "verbal gesture[s] of great intricacy."[118] In the *Library Journal,* Laurie Brown finds value in Ammons's "continuing attempt to pare away words" that produce an "[a]ustere" diction and "evoke a Chinese simplicity." For Brown, the book does not match the level of excellence of some of his earlier work, yet she thinks "there is comparable depth—and the same admirable lucidity."[119] Steven P. Schneider is also reserved yet positive, and like Brown, analogizes

Ammons's work to Asian models. He thinks this book a "continuation of Ammons's 'experiments in the minimal' " because of its "brief," haiku-like poems that "are content to achieve . . . a pleasing evocation of the natural event."[120] Of this book and of *Lake Effect Country,* James Finn Cotter believes both successful as continuities of Ammons's past searches of nature "for a pattern" that not only unites man and objects but also threatens to dissolve Ammons's lyric speaker into that pattern.[121]

Stronger than his previous volume, Ammons's *Lake Effect Country* appeared in 1983. The book contains a number of extraordinary, transcendental meditations featuring Ammons's characteristic, neo-Eastern vocabulary of terms such as "the Way," "the infinite," "nothingness," "bliss," and "emptiness." By singling out specific poems, the critics focused on this religious impulse in the book and on the tension implicit in Ammons's earthly longings for the "higher" movements of the human mind. D. R. Fosso thinks that the poem "Singling & Doubling Together" is "a remarkable work that in epitome focuses and resolves for a moment central concerns in [Ammons's] poetic metaphysic."[122] Nathan A. Scott Jr. also thinks "Singling & Doubling Together" a great poem that, like poems such as "Essay on Poetics" and "Vehicle," exhibits "how deeply religious his basic sensibility is" with its "attitude of such admiring gratitude and veneration [with which] he faces the manifold things of this world."[123] Wayne Eason finds the book "remarkably brilliant" because it effectively links mystical and metaphysical elements in "a 'philosophy' that is revealed through a metaphorical *tour de force* to translate a metaphysical union of the world of thought and the world of feeling." Eason believes that in *Lake Effect Country* Ammons is "a master at work," for it exhibits a particularly powerful "drama of speech" or "struggle" in which "archaic rhythms . . . begin a melding into shape" of "a Being born" of particulars, a process that forever alters "the poet and the reader/listener."[124] Shelby Stephenson also thinks highly of this book. He claims that Ammons's world is one of "endless motion and endorsement of creation." Of the most impressive literary elements that Ammons creates, "disembodied voices" are the "heroes" of his poems, for they "give dramatic tension through the playing and dallying flow [of nature], always offering alternative perceptions to the existing world of fact and necessary seriousness."[125] John Lang praises *Lake Effect Country* and finds in it one of Ammons's definitive tensions, namely, a "dialectical movement between nature and the supernatural and between speech and silence."[126] In *Poetry* in February of 1984, Penelope Mesic thinks "Yadkin Picnic" "a self-mocking but sweet pastoral"; however, she begins her review with a double-edged generalization about Ammons's prolific, perhaps repetitive output by observing that "[t]here are some people who can't get enough of A. R. Ammons, and then again there are some people who can."[127] In *Twentieth Century Literature* in 1994, Frank Lepkowski thinks the book strong because of its religious significance. Lepkowski likens

Ammons's piety in "Singing & Doubling Together" to the metaphysical humility of George Herbert insofar as Ammons recognizes "God's grace as a personal gift in his own human identity."[128]

Reiterating an interest in ancient Sumer that initiated his career, Ammons entitled his 20th book of poems *Sumerian Vistas,* which appeared in 1987. Divided into three sections, the volume begins with two extraordinary long segments entitled "The Ridge Farm" and "Tombstones," and it ends with a 70-page sequence of his characteristically short, tight lyrics called "Motions' Holdings." All sections are extremely strong, and the first two reveal a new "landscape" method for Ammons, namely, building long poems out of shorter lyric units of varying sizes and formal strategies. Perhaps Ammons's best book since *Collected Poems,* his *Sumerian Vistas,* nonetheless, received mixed reviews. In *World Literature Today* in the spring of 1988, Ashley Brown declares that Ammons's "sequence of meditations . . . called 'Tombstones' is one of his finest achievements."[129] In the *New Yorker* in February of 1988, Helen Vendler thinks highly of the collection, observing that Ammons's long poem "The Ridge Farm" reveals an intelligence capable of at least three impressive elements: a "joyful precision" noticing "natural fact," "fine-grained meditations on the mind's ways of being," and "an ethics founded on . . . cultural illumination and human concern."[130] Bonnie Costello believes the volume strong because, among other things, it reminds us of how Ammons linguistically looks "at nature not for itself but for what it can offer the imagination."[131] In *Poetry* in 1988, Alice Fulton calls Ammons's verse "luminous." According to Fulton, one of the prime strengths of Ammons's poetry is his "aesthetic of inclusion" by which his lyrics console us into "celebration" yet simultaneously force "us to educate ourselves anew."[132]

In the *Ohio Review* in 1988, working from a poststructuralist suspicion about the referential capabilities of language, Donald Revell is critical of *Sumerian Vistas'* long, introductory poem, "The Ridge Farm," "because of its stubbornly inauthentic conviction concerning the part of nature that is necessarily a dream of words" such that the poem "too often descends to the practice of a false mimesis. . . ." While one may object that Ammons's poem shares similar concerns about linguistic "substance," Revell nonetheless finds "profound, durable" moments in the lyric. He is, however, critical of the shorter pieces in the collection, finding them "limited and sometimes even marred by the poet's willful passivity in the face of his own observations." Yet for Revell, Ammons's short lyric "Memory" is first-rate and deserves "a collection by itself."[133] In 1988 in the *Hudson Review,* James Finn Cotter is critical of some poems in the volume in that he thought that Ammons's voice at times seems to disappear from his poems: "Ammons" is "so reticent that he risks retiring from his own lines," and thus leaves the reader feeling "left out." Nonetheless, Cotter believes that Ammons "makes even his faults work for him" in a vision of "gleams and glimpses" that gives his work "religious" and "transcendental" qualities "but with his own stance and creed."[134] Finally, Steven P. Schnieder calls this book "an important collection" that does not "parody or dully echo earlier poems" but "renew[s] himself and his readers through vigorous, imaginative language and creative poetic strategies," especially in the book's long, opening sequence, "The Ridge Farm."[135]

Published in 1990, *The Really Short Poems of A. R. Ammons* brings together 160 poems, none longer than a page, most 12 lines or shorter, and most previously published. Although the character of the collection reminds one of a "selected poems," the mixed responses of the critics are instructive because they deal with Ammons in one of his most basic formal modes, the minimal. In *Poetry* of November 1991, Steven Cramer is concerned that this "minimalist Ammons may disappoint as well as disarm" the reader used to Ammons's longer meditations. However, Cramer concludes positively in stating that these poems are "[u]napologetically slight." They "flicker into focus, exchanging minor mystification for minor enlightenment. They dawn on you."[136] In the *Southern Review* in 1992, Fred Chappell has good and bad things to say about *The Really Short Poems.* On the negative side, he charges, "[T]here are a number of trivial verses in the Ammons volume, as well as incomprehensible ones, silly ones, flat ones, and some that are so dumb it strains the mind to imagine they were produced by an organic entity." On a positive note, however, Chappell says of Ammons that "at his best, he is incomparable. No one else is so cheerfully quirky, so slyly sensible, so oxymoronically accurate."[137] In the *Hudson Review,* Robert Schultz thinks that "one should not expect to find Ammons' greatest work in these miniatures"; nonetheless, he thinks the book "a pleasure to browse for its striking perceptions and deeply humane knowledge."[138] In the *Library Journal,* Fred Muratori is positive in stating that "[t]he best short poems return much more than they demand" by encompassing "wit," "paradox," "*koan*-like mystery," and "an unusual understanding of nature's processes and politics."[139] Steven P. Schneider praises the volume, noting that, although Ammons's poems are brief, they have "once again demonstrated the expansiveness of his vision" by inviting us "to look anew, and through our looking redeem not only the world, but one another and ourselves."[140]

Winner of the National Book Award for 1994, *Garbage* was published in 1993 and is yet another of Ammons's ambitious, book-length poems, running 121 pages of pagewide, unrhymed, two-line units in 18 sections. *Garbage* is an extended seriocomic meditation on a subject that the poet calls "spiritual, believable enough to get our attention" and can "deflect us from the / errors of our illusionary ways."[141] In the *Kenyon Review* of fall 1994, David Baker is extremely positive. He calls *Garbage* "a brilliant book," perhaps "a great one" that "may be one of the central poetic accomplishments of our time." Among its many excellences, this poem reveals a voice that is "disarmingly direct"; it is "a dazzling dance of purposes and speculations, made of whatever material it finds at hand." Baker thinks that "the values of *Garbage*" are foregrounded in the "encouraging romanticism of Emerson," a realm in which the poet "enacts an Emersonian cosmology where the wastes of the contemporary soul are converted into consolation, connection, and even hope."[142] In the *Southern Review* in the same year, David Kirby believes *Garbage* to be an engaging and energetic "Dantesque ziggurat of steaming refuse" that represents "the antic aspect of the aging seer" and defeats "the world's sameness by paralleling it."[143] In the *Hudson Review,* James Finn Cotter calls the poem "discursive and intense, rambling and ordered, funny and serious. It's all trash and treasure, trivial and essential, public and personal." He praises it as a "thoughtful book" that "makes a good read and a great deal of sense."[144] Steven P. Schneider notes contrary qualities in the poem: abstraction and dullness, "risks" that Ammons had traditionally taken in his long poems, for "[h]e insists on inventing a form that enables him to 'dispose' of both the clutter in his life and its meditative re-collections." Moreover, for Schneider, Ammons's poem is important insofar as it is "penetrating *and* transcendental," for the poet fills it with significant "discoveries, and in so doing creates his own radical solution to the problem of waste in our lives."[145] In the *Library Journal* for August 1993, Fred Muratori thinks highly of *Garbage,* noting that it contains "wit" and "rhetorical grace" in a work that is "funny, elusive, enlightening, self-conscious, surprising, purposeful, and vertiginous."[146]

Books, Bibliographies, and Journals on A. R. Ammons

In the winter of 1973, *Diacritics* devoted an entire issue to A. R. Ammons. Though brief at 61 pages, the issue contains seven articles, all substantial, by distinguished poets and critics such as Harold Bloom, Josephine Jacobsen, Jerome Mazzaro, Linda Orr, Patricia A. Parker, David Kalstone, and Josephine Miles. There is also a significant interview, conducted by editor David Grossvogel, in which Ammons discusses his most important philosophic sources, especially Emerson and Laotse, in addition to his conscious employment of narrative, mythic structure, and the pathetic fallacy. The volume concludes with 14 new poems by Ammons, including "The Form of a Motion," which later became the opening 10 segments of *Sphere.* This is the first single issue of a journal dedicated entirely to Ammons's work.

A. R. Ammons by Alan Holder is the first book-length study of Ammons's poetry. Published in 1978, Holder's book begins with a biographical sketch of the poet, then surveys his work from the publication of *Ommateum* (1955) through *Diversifications* (1975). Although the study is organized chronologically to some degree, its chapters and their divisions are divided by topics central to Ammons's ongoing poetic projects. For instance, Holder's sixth chapter, entitled "Poetics," is divided into sections that include "Critical Discourse versus Silence," "Poetry and One: Many," "Limits of Poetry," " 'Configurations,' " and "Poetry and Motion," to name several. Even though the book contains perceptive readings throughout, its terminological organization is its strength, for the study strategically approaches Ammons's poetry through its often dense and difficult vocabulary. By defining the poet's central terms, both philosophically and contextually, Holder offers an extremely helpful ground for understanding individual lyrics and the larger issues involved in assessing Ammons's poetic methods. This book seems designed to be an introductory survey; however, it constitutes a first-rate inquiry into the complex materials of one of our most challenging contemporary poets. A serious reader of the criticism on A. R. Ammons may wish to begin with Harold Bloom's well-known articles, but he or she could also begin with Alan Holder.

Modern Critical Views: A. R. Ammons, edited with an introduction by Harold Bloom, appeared in 1986. This is the first collection of critical material on Ammons and encompasses major essays and reviews written from the late sixties to the mid-eighties. The collection employs one of Bloom's important, early essays on Ammons and Emerson as its introduction, then is organized chronologically, including pieces from the Ammons issue of *Diacritics* (Winter 1973), with significant articles by Patricia A. Parker, Linda Orr, David Kalstone, and Jerome Mazzaro. The volume also contains a substantial number of central reviews: positive responses by Richard Howard, a negative review of *Sphere* by Denis Donoghue, a negative estimation of Ammons's diction by Robert Pinsky, and another of Bloom's major essays, this one centering on Ammons's High Romantic quests. In addition, the book includes a chronology and a brief, but useful, bibliography. This book constitutes the first major stage in the collecting of Ammons criticism.

Also appearing in 1986, *Pembroke Magazine,* published at Pembroke State University in North Carolina, dedicated its 18th number almost entirely to Ammons. At 250 pages on Ammons, this substantial collection includes 21 essays of varying lengths by noted poets and critics such as Alice Fulton; Frederick Buell; Sister Bernetta Quinn, OFS; and Robert Hill. In addition to two interviews with the poet, there are over 30 poems by distinguished writers and scholars such as Ammons himself, M. H. Abrams, William Harmon, Kenneth A. McClane, and Henry Hart. The longest and perhaps the best discussion is the leading article by Jerald Bullis, entitled "In the Open: A. R. Ammons' Longer Poems." Few of the pieces in this edition of *Pembroke Magazine* have been reprinted since its appearance, making this copy of the journal one of the major sources of collected Ammons material.

A. R. Ammons: A Bibliography, 1954–1979 (1980) by Stuart Wright is the only extant bibliography of Ammons's work. The contents are divided into six sections: a listing of separate publications, primarily books, accompanied by a copy of each book's title page plus standard information such as press run, contents, typography, paper, and notes on the printing background of the particular volume; second, a listing of the first appearance of Ammons's contributions to books; third, a list of the first appearance of his poems in periodicals; fourth, a list of the first appearance of his prose pieces; fifth, interviews and published comments; and, finally, a section of miscellaneous items such as works edited by Ammons. For a student of the publishing history of Ammons, Wright's notes in his first section are especially interesting. For instance, one reads of *Ommateum*'s undistinguished appearance in June of 1955, namely, that " . . . of the 300 copies printed, only 100 were bound and, of these, approximately 40 were purchased by his father-in-law and mailed to business associates in South America."[147] This is a rich, comprehensive, and highly detailed overview of the literary career of A. R. Ammons, and it constitutes the first serious chronological record of this poet's publishing career. The delineation of the first appearance of each of his poems in periodicals is especially informative and valuable.

A. R. Ammons and the Poetics of Widening Scope (1994) by Steven P. Schneider is the most recent book-length study of Ammons's poetry. Schneider uses his own background and interest in science—he is the coauthor of a book on behavioral optics, entitled *The Athletic Eye*—to explore how Ammons's poems "evoke the possibilities and mysteries of sight, as his vision moves both outward into the world and inward . . . into the reflective self."[148] Schneider divides his study into chapters on different conceptions of science in Ammons's romantic ancestors such as Emerson and Whitman, on "distance vision and peripheral vision" in Ammons's long poems such as *Sphere* and "Essay on Poetics," and on how "the natural eye" provides a ground for Ammons's use of language, metaphor, and personal motivation. Then, shifting the scope of his own thesis considerably, Schneider finishes his inquiry with brief discussions of *Sumerian Vistas, The Really Short Poems,* and *Garbage.* Of all of the segments in this challenging book, Schneider's pairing of Ammons and Thoreau is the most fruitful.

The Plan of Critical Essays on A. R. Ammons

The purpose of this book is to celebrate Ammons's achievement by collecting a representative overview of critical response to his work. This collection is, accordingly, divided into two sections. The first consists of a survey of initial reviews of Ammons's poetry, beginning with the very first in 1956 by Reuel Denney, who gives a lukewarm reception to *Ommateum,* and ending with David Baker's enthusiastic appraisal of *Garbage* in 1994. In between, critical reaction—positive and negative—to Ammons's work constitutes a critical narrative that is controversial and in conflict with itself. This collection highlights the central areas of praise and contention by chronologically arranging a number of pieces in an alternating sequence that provides contrary points of view. If Geoffrey Hartman believes that the appearance of Ammons's *Collected Poems* is a major event in the literary world, Jascha Kessler does not. And, while Hayden Carruth has little use for *The Snow Poems,* Michael McFee argues persuasively for a reconsideration of this controversial book. By placing these conflicting views in proximity to each other, this collection hopes to define more clearly the central issues at stake in Ammons criticism and to enable the reader to choose in an informed way from among them.

The second section consists of full-length essays, none of which have been previously collected. Two of these essays are original: my own inquiry into Ammons's use of Sumerian mythology and William J. Rushton's incisive analysis of science and language in the 19th meditation from the poet's long sequence "Tombstones" in *Sumerian Vistas.* The essays are arranged more or less chronologically by subject matter, beginning with Sumer and ending, as noted, with *Sumerian Vistas.*

Notes

1. A. R. Ammons, "Poetry Is a Matter of Survival," interview by Nancy Kober, *Cornell Daily Sun,* 27 April 1973, 12.

2. Kober, 12.

3. I have chosen to survey only the major, single-volume collections in Ammons's canon, with the exception of *Collected Poems, 1951–1971* and *The Really Short Poems of A. R. Ammons.* I have excluded *Selected Poems, The Selected Poems, 1957–1977, Selected Longer Poems,* and *The Selected Poems, Expanded Edition* because the contents already appear substantially in books discussed by critics in my overview. I have also excluded *Highgate Road* because of its limited press run (36 copies) and because, consequently, of its limited critical reaction.

4. Reuel Denney, "Invitations to the Listener: Nine Young Poets and Their Audiences," *Poetry* 89 (1956): 50.

5. Alan Holder, *A. R. Ammons* (Boston: Twayne, 1978), 21, 27.

6. Frederick Buell, "To Be Quiet in the Hands of the Marvelous," in *Modern Critical Views: A. R. Ammons,* ed. Harold Bloom (New York: Chelsea House, 1986), 197.

7. Gilbert Allen, "The Arc of a New Covenant: The Idea of the Reader in A. R. Ammons' Poems," *Pembroke Magazine* 18 (1986): 91.

8. David Kalstone, "Ammons' Radiant Toys," rpt. in *Modern Critical Views,* 107.

9. Richard Howard, "The Spent Seer Consigns Order to the Vehicle of Change," rpt. in *Modern Critical Views,* 36.

10. Harold Bloom, introduction to *Modern Critical Views,* 2.

11. Frederick Buell, in *Modern Critical Views,* 197; Sister Bernetta Quinn, OSF, "Scholar of Wind and Tree: The Early Lyrics of A. R. Ammons," *Pembroke Magazine* 18 (1986): 237.

12. Janet Elizabeth DeRosa, "Occurrences of Promise and Terror: The Poetry of A. R. Ammons" (Ph.D. diss., Brown University, 1978), 19.

13. Patricia Parker, "Configurations of Shape and Flow," *Diacritics* 3 (Winter 1973): 26.

14. D. R. Fosso, "Poetic Metaphysics in A. R. Ammons," *Pembroke Magazine* 18 (1986): 158.

15. Jerald Bullis, "In the Open: A. R. Ammons' Longer Poems," *Pembroke Magazine* 18 (1986): 41.

16.   A. R. Ammons, "An Interview with A. R. Ammons," interview by William Walsh, *Michigan Quarterly Review* 28 (Winter 1989): 110.

17.   Laurence Lieberman, *Unassigned Frequencies: American Poetry in Review* (Champaign: University of Illinois Press, 1977), 250.

18.   Wendell Berry, "Antennae to Knowledge," *Nation* 198 (23 March 1964): 305, 304.

19.   Alan Holder, 33, 40.

20.   Alfred Reid, "The Poetry of A. R. Ammons," *South Carolina Review* 12 (Fall 1979): 4.

21.   Richard Howard, 50; Nathan Scott, "The Poetry of A. R. Ammons," *Southern Review* 24 (Autumn 1988): 729.

22.   Sister Bernetta Quinn, OSF, 244.

23.   Josephine Jacobsen, "A Poetry Chronicle," *Poetry Magazine* 105 (1964): 205.

24.   Robert Pinsky, "Ammons," in *Modern Critical Views,* 189–90.

25.   Laurence Lieberman, 255–56.

26.   Richard Howard, 44.

27.   Guy Rotella, "Ghostlier Demarcations, Keener Sounds: A. R. Ammons's 'Corsons Inlet,' " *Concerning Poetry* 10 (Fall 1977), 25.

28.   John Elder, *Imagining the Earth: Poetry and the Vision of Nature* (Champaign: University of Illinois Press, 1985), 144.

29.   Willard Spiegelman, *The Didactic Muse* (Princeton: Princeton University Press, 1989), 117.

30.   David Kalstone, in *Modern Critical Views,* 109.

31.   A. R. Ammons, *Tape for the Turn of the Year* (Ithaca, NY: Cornell University Press, 1965), 1.

32.   Richard Howard, 42.

33.   Harold Bloom, in *Modern Critical Views,* 23.

34.   Helen Vendler, *Part of Nature, Part of Us: Modern American Poets* (Cambridge: Harvard University Press, 1980), 331.

35.   Alan Holder, 118, 116, 120, 116.

36.   Williard Spiegelman, 116, 124.

37.   Laurence Lieberman, 255.

38.   Philip Fried, "Theodore Roethke and A. R. Ammons: The Modern and Contemporary Sensibilities," *Pembroke Magazine* 18 (1986): 121, 129.

39.   Jerome Mazzaro, "Reconstruction in Art," *Diacritics* 4 (Winter 1973): 43.

40.   Nathan A. Scott, Jr. 736.

41.   William Harmon, " 'How Does One Come Home': A. R. Ammons's *Tape for the Turn of the Year,*" *Southern Literary Journal* 17 (Spring 1975): 3.

42.   Donald H. Reiman, "A. R. Ammons: Ecological Naturalism and the Romantic Tradition," *Twentieth Century Literature* 31 (Spring 1985): 35, 37, 38.

43.   Patrick Deane, "Justified Radicalism: A. R. Ammons with a Glance at John Cage," *Papers on Language and Literature* 28 (Spring 1992): 207, 216.

44.   Klaus Martens, "Rage for Definition: The Long Poem as 'Sequence,'" in *Poetry and Epistemology: Turning Points in the History of Poetic Knowledge: Papers from the International Poetry Symposium Eichstatt 1983,* ed. Roland Hagenbuchle and Laura Skandera (Regensburg: Pustet, 1986), 350–65.

45.   Matthew Wilson, "Homecoming in A. R. Ammons' *Tape for the Turn of the Year,*" *Contemporary Poetry: A Journal of Criticism* 4.2 (1981): 60, 62, 72–73.

46.   Hyatt H. Waggoner, "Notes and Reflections," rpt. in *Modern Critical Views,* 67.

47.   Frederick Buell, in *Modern Critical Views,* 207.

48.   Alfred Reid, "The Poetry of A. R. Ammons," *South Carolina Review* 12 (Fall 1979): 5.

49.   Hayden Carruth, "Four Poets," *Poetry* 111 (1967): 44.

50. Laurence Lieberman, 63, 66, 69.

51. Richard Howard, 47.

52. John Logan, "Interior and Exterior Worlds," *Nation* (24 April 1967): 542.

53. Harold Bloom, in *Modern Critical Views,* 28, 26.

54. Alan Holder, 89.

55. David Kalstone, "Uplands," *New York Times Book Review,* 9 May 1971, 5.

56. Richard Howard, 51.

57. Louis Martz, "Recent Poetry: Visions and Revisions," *Yale Review* 60 (1971): 413.

58. A. R. Ammons, "Cut the Grass," *Briefings* (New York: W. W. Norton, 1971), 89.

59. Robert Pinsky, 191.

60. Laurence Lieberman, 72.

61. Harold Bloom, in *Modern Critical Views,* 29.

62. Harold Bloom, "Dark and Radiant Peripheries: Mark Strand and A. R. Ammons," *Southern Review* 8 (January 1972): 148.

63. John Hollander, "Briefings," *New York Times Book Review,* 9 May 1971, 5, 20.

64. Helen Vendler, *Part of Nature, Part of Us,* 330.

65. Richard Howard, 53.

66. Hyatt H. Waggoner, rpt. in *Modern Critical Views,* 70.

67. Geoffrey H. Hartman, "Collected Poems, 1951–1971," *New York Times Book Review,* 19 November 1972, 39–40.

68. William Meredith, "I Will Tell You about It Because It Is Interesting," *Parnassus* 2 (Fall/Winter 1973): 175, 183.

69. Harold Bloom, "The New Transcendentalism: The Visionary Strain in Merwin, Ashbery, and Ammons," *Chicago Review* 24 (Winter 1973): 36.

70. Willard Spiegelman, 114, 111.

71. Helen Vendler, "Ammons," *Yale Review* 62 (Spring 1973): 424.

72. David Kalstone, in *Modern Critical Views,* 100.

73. Paul Zweig, "The Raw and the Cooked," *Partisan Review* 4 (1974): 609, 608, 610.

74. Richard Howard, 54, 53.

75. John Ashbery, "In the American Grain," in *Modern Critical Views,* 58–59.

76. Denis Donoghue, "Ammons and the Lesser Celandine," in *Modern Critical Views,* 173–74.

77. R. W. Flint, "The Natural Man," in *Modern Critical Views,* 182.

78. Donald H. Reiman, 38.

79. Donald Davie, "Card of Identity," *New York Review of Books* (6 March 1975): 10.

80. Calvin Bedient, "Sphere," *New York Times Book Review,* 22 December 1974, 13.

81. J. D. McClatchey, "New Books in Review," *Yale Review* (Spring 1975): 430, 432.

82. Alan Holder, 152–53, 156.

83. Jerome Mazzaro, "*Sphere: The Form of a Motion,* by A. R. Ammons," *Georgia Review* 29 (1975): 516–17.

84. David Lehman, "Where Motion and Shape Coincide," in *Modern Critical Views,* 244.

85. Cary Wolfe, "Symbol Plural: The Later Poems of A. R. Ammons," *Contemporary Literature,* 30.1 (Spring 1989): 90.

86. Stephen B. Cushman, *Fictions of Form in American Poetry* (Princeton: Princeton University Press, 1993), 158, 150.

87. John Elder, 197.

88. James E. Miller, "The American 'Lyric-Epic' " in *Poems in Their Place: The Intertextuality and Order of Poetic Collections,* ed. Neil Fraistat (Chapel Hill: University of North Carolina Press, 1986), 298, 300, 299.

89. R. C. Kenedy, "His Subject Is the Universe," *Pembroke Magazine* 11 (1979): 218–19.

90. Jerald Bullis, 45.

91. Stephen P. Schneider, *A. R. Ammons and the Poetics of Widening Scope* (Cranbury, NJ: Associated University Presses, 1994), 135, 146.

92. Alvin Rosenfeld, "A. R. Ammons: The Poems of a Solitary," *American Poetry Review* 5 (July/August 1976): 41.

93. Alan Holder, 132.

94. Steven P. Schneider, 155.

95. R. W. Flint, 182.

96. Helen Regueiro Elam, "Radiances and Dark Consolations," in *Modern Critical Views,* 282.

97. Marjorie Perloff, "Tangled Versions of the Truth: Ammons and Ashbery at 50," *American Poetry Review* 7 (1978): 6.

98. Hyatt H. Waggoner, "On A. R. Ammons," in *Contemporary Poetry in America: Essays and Interviews,* ed. Robert Boyers (New York: Schocken Books, 1974), 622–23.

99. Hayden Carruth, "Reader Participation Invited," *New York Times Book Review,* 25 September 1977, 30.

100. Gilbert Allen, 102, 100.

101. Peter Stitt, review of *The Snow Poems,* by A. R. Ammons, *Georgia Review* 32 (Winter 1978): 944.

102. William Harmon, "*The Snow Poems:* A. R. Ammons," *American Book Review* (December 1977): 16.

103. Richard Jackson, "No Available Ground: A. R. Ammons and the Poem as Event," *Pembroke Magazine* 18 (1986): 172, 171.

104. William Doreski, "Sublimity and Order in *The Snow Poems,*" *Pembroke Magazine* 21 (1989): 69, 72.

105. Frank Lepkowski, " 'How Are We to Find Holiness?': The Religious Vision of A. R. Ammons," *Twentieth Century Literature* 40.4 (Winter 1994): 489.

106. Donald H. Reiman, 40.

107. Helen Vendler, *Part of Nature, Part of Us,* 369, 371.

108. Michael McFee, "A. R. Ammons and *The Snow Poems* Reconsidered," *Chicago Review* 33:1 (Summer 1981): 35–37.

109. Steven P. Schneider, 166.

110. Hyatt H. Waggoner, *American Visionary Poetry* (Baton Rouge: Louisiana State University Press, 1982), 172.

111. Nathan Scott, 740.

112. David Lehman, in *Modern Critical Views,* 250.

113. Louis Martz, "Ammons, Warren, and the Tribe of Walt," *Yale Review* 72 (August 82): 63.

114. Helen Vendler, *The Music of What Happens* (Cambridge: Harvard University Press, 1988), 328–29.

115. Mark Soifer, "The Precise Magic of A. R. Ammons," *Pembroke Magazine* 18 (1986): 210.

116. Frederick Buell, "The Solitary Man: The Poetry of A. R. Ammons," *Pembroke Magazine* 18 (1986): 144.

117. Irvin Ehrenpreis, *Poetries of America: Essays on the Relation of Character to Style,* ed. Daniel Albright (Charlottesville: University Press of Virginia, 1989), 236.

118. David Lehman, "Perplexities Embraced," *Times Literary Supplement* (25 May 1984): 573.

119. Laurie Brown, *Library Journal* 107 (15 April 1982): 815.

120. Steven P. Schneider, 176.

121. James Finn Cotter, "Poetry Encounters," *Hudson Review* 36 (Winter 83–84): 723.

122. D. R. Fosso, 162.

123. Nathan Scott, 741.

124. Wayne Eason, "Particulars/in words other: An Inquiry into Language and A. R. Ammons," *Pembroke Magazine* 18 (1986): 183.

125. Shelby Stephenson, "A. R. Ammons: The Dance of a Visionary," *Pembroke Magazine* 18 (1986): 202.

126. John Lang, "The Lore Song's Lost In," *Pembroke Magazine* 18 (1986): 233.

127. Penelope Mesic, *Poetry Magazine* (February 1984): 303.

128. Frank Lepkowski, 494.

129. Ashley Brown, review of *Sumerian Vistas,* by A. R. Ammons, *World Literature Today* 62 (Spring 1988): 283.

130. Helen Vendler, "Veracity Unshaken," *New Yorker* (15 February 1988): 103.

131. Bonnie Costello, "The Soil and Man's Intelligence: Three Contemporary Landscape Poets," *Contemporary Literature* 30.3 (1989): 424.

132. Alice Fulton, "Main Things," *Poetry* (January 1988): 364, 360.

133. Donald Revell, "The Deep En-leaving Has Now Come": Ammons, Matthews, Simic, and Cole," *Ohio Review* 41 (1988): 119, 122.

134. James Finn Cotter, "The Voice of Poetry," *Hudson Review* 41 (Spring 1988): 226.

135. Steven P. Schneider, 182–83.

136. Steven Cramer, "Paying Attention," *Poetry Magazine* 159 (November 1991): 101, 104.

137. Fred Chappell, "Brief Cases: Naked Enterprises," *Southern Review* 28 (Winter 92): 176–77.

138. Robert Schultz, "Poetry and Knowledge," *Hudson Review* 44 (Winter 1992): 675.

139. Fred Muratori, *Library Journal* 116 (1 April 1991): 122.

140. Steven P. Schneider, 218–19.

141. A. R. Ammons, *Garbage* (New York: W. W. Norton, 1993), 18.

142. David Baker, "Review," *Kenyon Review* 16 (Fall 1994): 172, 176.

143. David Kirby, "Is There a Southern Poetry?" *Southern Review* 30 (Autumn 1994): 872, 878, 872.

144. James Finn Cotter, "Poetry Preserves," *Hudson Review* 47 (Summer 1994): 314.

145. Steven P. Schneider, 221, 224.

146. Fred Muratori, *Library Journal* (15 September 1993): 108.

147. Stuart Wright, *A. R. Ammons: A Bibliography, 1954–1979* (Winston-Salem: Wake Forest University Press, 1980).

148. Steven P. Schneider, 12.

REVIEWS
◆

Invitations to the Listener:
Nine Young Poets and Their Audiences
[A review of *Ommateum* by A. R. Ammons]

REUEL DENNEY

Ammons['] tone-of-voice remains elusive. . . . The result is . . . that [he] does
not exactly seem to want to be listened to, not to say, "understood."

There is one poet here, Ammons, whose imaginary audience, and whose
tone-of-voice, remains elusive. If he is speaking to anyone, or anything, he
seems, as I have suggested, to be holding converse with the language itself.
The result is poetry that does not exactly seem to want to be listened to, not
to say, "understood." Yet, oddly enough, the rhythms of these poems seem
more individualized than that of the poems by the other writers here—and at
least one of his poems is compelling. In this experimental piece, he has taken
the treacherous model of Whitman's style—building loosely declamatory
additive sentence variations around a single visual symbol—and hammered
out a potent poem. The general effect is like hearing a symphony orchestra in
its shell, playing a resonant work from a great distance.

> "With ropes of hemp
> I lashed my body to the great oak
> saying odes for the fiber of the oakbark
> and the oakwood saying supplications
> to the root mesh. . . .

"Invitations to the Listener: Nine Young Poets and Their Audiences," by Reuel Denney, first
appeared in *Poetry* 89 (1956): 50, by the Modern Poetry Association, and is reprinted by permission
of the editor of *Poetry*.

Antennae to Knowledge
[A review of *Expressions of Sea Level* by A. R. Ammons]

WENDELL BERRY

There is a wonderful eagerness in this book. . . .

In this admirable book, Mr. Ammons' aim isn't beauty, though there are poems here that I think are beautiful, and it's not the suggestiveness which is sometimes meant by the word "poetic." His aim is knowledge, the getting of it and the use of it; the art of poetry is held out to the world like an antenna. A man who is concerned with knowing must necessarily be concerned with what he does not know; and one of the principles here is an honesty which insists on clarifying the difference and will then consider what is unknown or unaccountable: "I admit to mystery / in the obvious. . . ." The suggestive is confined to what is authentically mysterious. These poems take place on the frontier between what the poet knows and what he doesn't; perhaps that explains their peculiar life and sensitivity. They open to accommodate surprises and accidents. The poet's interest is extended generously toward what he didn't expect, and his poems move by their nature in that direction.

The poems are worked out, not by the application of set forms to their materials, but in an effort to achieve form—in accordance with a constant attentiveness to, a hope for, the possibility of form—the need of anything, once begun, to complete itself, meaningfully. Mr. Ammons' way in this can be seen in the poem called "Mechanism." The movement begins with a goldfinch lighting in a bush:

>   the yellow
> bird flashes black wing bars
> in the new-leaving wild cherry
>   bushes by the bay. . . .
>
> flitting to a branch where
>   flash vanishes into stillness. . . .

Originally published in the *Nation* 198 (23 March 1964): 304–6. Reprinted by permission.

And then there's a consideration of the multitudinous biological dependences of the goldfinch—all the minute causes and effects of digestion, sex, instinct, habitat, etc., almost inscrutably complex, and involving a kind of miracle: "mind rising / from the physical chemistries. . . ." The poem then returns to the bird itself, a model of the world, both containing and caught up in the natural workings, ignorant of all of them, singing on its perch: the

> goldfinch, unconscious of the billion
> operations
>   that stay its form, flashes,
>   chirping (not a
> great songster) in the bay cherry
> bushes wild of leaf.

The form here is circular; we wind up where we started. But by the time we've come all the way around, though the bird hasn't changed, we have. We've learned something. We see differently, and better. We've seen the world working, which is not only informative but dramatic. This gives a fair idea of how Mr. Ammons goes about his task. He attempts to mediate, make or discover an intelligible continuity between the complex and the simple, the vast and the small, the overruling laws of creation and the creatures.

In several of the poems there's a large proportion of scientific language. In the following you can see how the scientific talk is broken into, made flexible, by the commoner language of everyday:

> Honor a going thing, goldfinch,
>   corporation, tree,
>   morality: any working order
> animate or inanimate: it
>
> has managed directed balance,
> the incoming and outgoing energies
>   are working right.

However, in lines where the language is predominantly or purely scientific the effect the poet's ear can have on it is extremely limited:

> honor the chemistries, platelets,
>   hemoglobin kinetics,
> the light-sensitive iris, the
>   enzymic intricacies
> of control. . . .

That language is by nature stiff, like a wooden shoe. No conceivable amount of use would limber it up. Except for the word "honor," the poet is taking the scientific vocabulary pretty much as it comes. About all he can hope to do with it, as a poet, is to place it exactly within the larger rhythm of his poem—everything seems to depend on that.

"Mechanism," I believe, makes more use of this kind of language than any of the others. But so many of the poems include lines or passages that have the cadences of prose that I assume it must be deliberate, part of Mr. Ammons' usual method. The only near-equivalent or precedent for this, so far as I know, is the gathering in of prose quotations, statistics, etc., in such modern poems as *Paterson* and *The Cantos*. And it works, I think, the same way: the prose detail is admitted raw into the poem, not to be transformed into poetry by it but to be illuminated or nearly clarified by the energy with which the poem surrounds it—and to serve the poem in some way in which only prose can serve it. This use of prose in poems may be justified by the poet's conviction that poetry might legitimately deal with subject matter which is customarily the subject matter of prose—his realization that some of the things he knows and is concerned about are new, and haven't been prepared for poetry by any considerable period of association or usage. What I'm indicating here is that Mr. Ammons aims to bring science into his poems as *subject matter,* not just to borrow words or images from it.

The poet attempting to lay hold of such materials is up against the possibility of enlarging the powers and working spaces of his art at the risk of weakening it. The effort is experimental in the purest sense of the word, and involves the risk of experiment. The only measure for it is: Does it work? Can the reader take it in?

I think that Mr. Ammons makes it work often and well. The poetry doesn't inhere consistently in the verbal texture of the poems, but in the forms, the arrangements of the contents. Sometimes the reader is unsure that what he's reading is poetry until he has read all the way through. But when he comes to the end of a poem like "Mechanism"—which attempts to bring to bear on the image of the singing bird, and to bring under the control of that poetic image, all that the poet *knows* about it—he's conscious that a unifying exciting energy has been released among the subject matters; and he knows that it's the energy of poetry, which takes over the language of science only as a resource, and causes it to belong to a larger, more exuberant statement than the specialized vocabulary alone could make. "Mechanism" isn't a biologist's poem; it's the poem of a poet who knows biology.

There's a nearly opposite kind of Ammons poem, represented here by "Nelly Myers," "Hardweed Path Going" and "Silver." These poems recollect the poet's country boyhood. Again the use of prose, this time a kind of narrative prose, is characteristic. And again the necessity for prose seems one of the conditions imposed by the materials. Here the subject matter is not difficult because, like the scientific, it has been kept pure of emotional or literary associations; it's difficult because it has been too much and too poorly written about—too much condescended to, you could say, by the conventions that claim to have been invented for it. I'm talking about all the oversweetening, distortion, falsification that have been left sticking to rural things by the pastoralizers, sentimentalizers and folksifiers since God knows when. Such things are usually both written and read about in a kind of institutional blindness to the sweat, crap, blood, and biting insects which are as much a part of the real experience as white lambs and new-mown hay. Mr. Ammons' poems of this life manage an honesty about it which is an achievement. He proceeds in these as he does in the poems of scientific lore, keeping a respectful loyalty to what he knows, refusing to think of it or write about it in any falsifying rhetoric. It must be given to the reader in the most direct way, otherwise there can be no meeting of minds.

The poem "Nelly Myers" is about a simple-minded woman of that name, a maker of brooms, who lived with the poet's family during his boyhood. The difficulty of writing this poem must have been Mr. Ammons' sense both of the uniqueness and the meaningfulness of her life, the presence of her life in his life. The two would, I imagine, have tended to cancel each other out: her uniqueness would have threatened to overpower her meaningfulness, make it incommunicable; or to emphasize the meaningfulness might have reduced her to a stereotype. Mr. Ammons' solution is to be openly personal. Some of the details of the poem are given with the directness, not even of prose fiction, but of biography:

> my grandmother, they say, took her
>   in
> when she was a stripling run away
>   from home
> (her mind was not perfect
>   which is no bar to this love song
>   for her smile was sweet,
> her outrage honest and violent)
> and they say that after she worked
>   all day her relatives
> would throw a handful of dried peas
>   into her lap
>   for her supper
> and she came to live in the house
>   I was born in the
> northwest room of . . .

The poem is an elegy, and the relaxed passages of description or narrative support and give their specificness of feeling to an elegiac lyricism which is authentic and powerful, and which charges not just the passages in which it occurs purely, but the whole poem:

> oh I will not end my grief
> that she is gone, I will not end

```
        my singing;
        my songs like blueberries
        felt-out and black to her search-
        ing
            fingers before light
        welcome her
        wherever her thoughts ride with
            mine, now or in any time
                that may come
        when I am gone; I will not end
            visions of her naked feet
        in the sandpaths: I will hear her
            words
```

We're moved by Wordsworth's solitary highland lass because she's seen at a distance, and the poet is left free to suppose and suggest. We're moved by Nelly Myers because we're brought very close to her. She's not idealized, nor idealizable—she's too much present, we know too much about her. The power of the poem is that we're made to know her as she was, and to care for her as she was. Only the sympathy approaches some kind of ideal.

There is a wonderful eagerness in this book, a whetted appetite for the phenomena of seashores and farms and landscapes and factories. And the interest is not directed at things as objects or appearances, but at their ways—how they act, how they mix. The excitement of anything is that it moves, changes, influences other things—"boundless in its effect, / eternal in the working out / of its effect. . . ." Each poem is, in a way, an ecology—the revelation of a harmony which is both found and made.

A. R. Ammons: Of Mind and World
[A review of *Northfield Poems* by A. R. Ammons]

LAURENCE LIEBERMAN

Not the least of A. R. Ammons' virtues is that he is an original philosopher in his poetry. . . .

NORTHFIELD POEMS

Not the least of A. R. Ammons' virtues is that he is an original philosopher in his poetry, though often he parades in the guise of poet-as-anti-philosopher, much as Plato wore the guise of philosopher-as-anti-poet. In "Uh, Philosophy," he cuts deeper into the subject the more he pretends, with graceful offhandedness, to dismiss its importance:

> I understand
>   reading the modern philosophers
> that truth is so much a method
>   it's perfectly all
> right for me to believe whatever
>   I like or if I like,
> nothing:
>   I do not know that I care to be set that free:

He comes at each idea a little from the side, obliquely, with a chuckle of ridicule in the voice of the poem every time the meandering river of the speaker's mind inclines to become trapped by any one idea or perspective, or threatens to take ideas in and of themselves as having supreme consequence:

Reprinted from *Beyond the Muse of Memory: Essays on Contemporary American Poets* by Laurence Lieberman (Columbia: University of Missouri Press, 1995), 231–39. Reprinted by permission.

> philosophy is
> a pry pole, materialization,
>   useful as a snowshovel when it snows;
> something solid to knock people down with
>   or back people up with:
> I do not know that I care to be backed up in just that way:
>   the philosophy gives clubs to
> everyone, and I prefer disarmament:

The irony masterfully saves the poem, always reminding the reader that ideas are so many disinterestedly linked events in the circuitous drama of the poem's argument, which ends exactly where it began:

> what are facts if I can't line them up
>   anyway I please
> and have the freedom
>   I refused I think in the beginning?

The poem's secret, which is revealed subtly and implicitly in its movement, is that the mind finds truth, is truest to itself, when it is released into the self-discovering rhythms of a good poem. To be true to the voice and line of the poem, an ever-changing field of play, always captures the speaker's first allegiance, never the ideas themselves. Most ideas would remain inert if not for the vivid life the poem's artistry imparts to them.

Ammons' knack for self-mockery saves the studiedly philosophical poems from self-conscious straining, as in "Zone," in which matter-of-fact remarks about the time of day, and such, interrupt the flow of formal scientific discourse. Ideas, in the poems, are quantities of form, shape, design; they are not vehicles for conveying logic, truth, validity. Ideas have texture, color, size, weight. To Ammons, they have the quality of physical objects:

> A symmetry of thought
> is a metal object:
> is to spirit
> a rock of individual shape . . .
> a crystal, precipitate

Ammons treats ideas as so many jointed bodies colliding with each other, and with observed natural phenomena, interchangeably. Conversely, actual objects may be decomposed into substanceless vapors by the intense play of the mind. The interchange of form between ideas that have grown solid and objects that have turned gaseous, or bodiless, may have been suggested to Ammons by Einstein's formula $E = mc^2$, demonstrating the relation between energy and matter. (Ammons, indeed, has been schooled in the sciences, and this background broadened the scope of his poetic imagination from the start.) Whatever the source of his idea/thing inversion, one may more profitably inquire into the use he makes of it, the way he fits it to his unique sensibility. I see it as a particularly apt formula for embodying Ammon's original view of the relation between mind and world, between inner and outer reality. Though ideas and things may exist separately, they can have no importance or vitality, for Ammons, unless they disturb each other, interact. When this interaction is carried to the point of total engagement, the poet achieves his vision, a state in which elements of thought and elements of nature mix freely, and exchange identities, in a kind of ecstatic flux of poetic imagination, as in "Peak" (I quote the poem entire):

> Everything begins at the tip-end, the dying-out,
>   of mind:
> the dazed eyes set and light
> dissolves actual trees:
>   the world beyond: tongueless.
> unexampled
> burns dimension out of shape,
> opacity out of stone:
> come: though the world ends and cannot
> end,
>   the apple falls sharp
> to the heart starved with time.

The peak experience is defined and demonstrated. Mind stretched to its utmost limits (the "tip-end" of consciousness), after acute concentration on particulars of concrete experience ("actual trees"), casts into "the world beyond." Paradoxically, a scrupulous attention to the thing itself, its precise identity, begets a mental state in which the most solid things lose their form, become dimensionless, apparitional ghosts in the poet's vision (trees dissolve, stone loses its opacity). Ammons' genius is most evident in the transition into the final stanza: "come, though the world ends and cannot/ end." Invitation to the reader to take the final step, to throw himself fully into the world of the poem without holding anything back, is a frequent device; in this poem, it is perfectly timed and has the disarming simplicity of a handshake. The reader was at the point of recoiling from the experience, since the poem had shown that mind's peak is a sort of mindlessness in which the lovely things of this world fade away into shadows of themselves, but Ammons now assures us that we shall return from the "peak" (as Frost swings back on his birches) to find a world of things more solid for having undergone his visionary dissolution: "the apple falls sharp." One must be willing to sacrifice the world completely, in faith, if one is to get it back whole, regain it to the peak of mind's embrace.

Ammons, the craftsman, often declares that he will risk everything, technically, to avoid the temptation to take refuge in the safety of pre-given forms; and, from time to time, he discards methods, devices of his own, that have proven successful, as in "Muse":

> . . . how many
> times must I be broken and reassembled!
> anguish of becoming,
> pain of moulting,
> descent! before the unending moment of vision:

In learning to write all over again, he stumbles, gropingly, the lines of the poem "inching rootlike into the dark." Since he must slog through many failed poems "to find materials/for the new house of my sight," he takes his place beside D. H. Lawrence and Whitman in the Anglo-American free verse tradition of blessedly "uneven" poets. Probably that sort of unevenness will always be the sacred trademark of the most gifted and revolutionary poets, since most of our good writers seem satisfied, if not compulsively driven, to maintain a constant of external polish in everything they write.

Ammons is pursuing a theory of poetry that radically departs from the theory advanced by the poetry of Yeats and the criticism of Ezra Pound. Ezra occurs as an advocate to be resisted or revolted against in a number of poems in this book and in the previous collection:

> I coughed
>   and the wind said
> Ezra will live
> to see your last
>   sun come up again . . .
> the wind went off
>   carving
> monuments through a field of stone
>   monuments whose shape
> wind cannot arrest but
> taking hold on
> changes
>   (from "The Wind Coming Down From")

If Ezra is a monument of stone, Ammons chooses to identify with the lowly weed. If Ezra advocates the poem of permanence, the indestructible art-object, Ammons prefers the poem as a way of being, of being in touch. While Ezra affirms what is most tough and enduring in man, the ruthless will to immortality of the conventional major poet, Ammons reveres a delicate, sensitive transitoriness of being. The best of Ammons' poems point, finally, away from themselves, back to the most evanescent motions and vicissitudes of wind, leaf, stream, which first enchanted the poet and finally stole his heart away. The gentlest motions of things touch him most deeply, speak to him with a sort of ultimate, if non-human, intimacy. He is vulnerable, nakedly exposed, receptive to the touch of feather, pebble, birdsong—in fact, these phenomena have such command over him as to leave him looking helplessly struck (or struck dumb), as by indecent or obscenely overpowering forces:

> I turned (as I will) to weeds and . . .
> weedroots of my low-feeding shiver

So far is Ammons from forcing or contriving his vision, his awakening, in the best poems—in "The Constant" he struggles to resist, even to suppress, the *onset* of revelation, with the air of a man who has been used overmuch, exploited, by his admittedly favorite mistress:

> When leaving the primrose, bayberry dunes, seaward
> I discovered the universe this morning,
>   I was in no
> mood
> for wonder,
>   the naked mass of so much miracle
> already beyond the vision
> of my grasp:

If formerly the mistress of experience (of miracle) consented to be a passive, supine guest to his advances, in "The Constant" she has become the aggressor: the poet, helpless and reluctant, allows himself to be overpowered by her mastery.

In a number of poems, Ammons unleashes surprising resources of power in himself by a sort of feminine submission to experience. In "Kind," "Height," and "The Wind Coming Down From" there is a fierce insistence on lowliness and passivity ("preference sends me stooping/ seeking/ the least"). This is his answer, his refusal, to the male challenge addressed to him by the massive antagonist in each poem—the giant redwood, the mountain, the wind; in each case, he recoils. Like St. Francis (and unlike Ezra!), he savors the strength of weakness. Strangely, all three poems seem facile, the dialectic merely clever and fanciful, perhaps archly whimsical. The poems are all statement, all philosophy, despite the illusion they try to advance of drama and dialectic. I don't believe the wind or redwood as antagonists because their *being* in the poems lacks the solidity of a felt presence. They exist only as foils to the persona, and the poems never extend beyond direct emission of "message." They desperately need extension into the world of substance and event.

The weakest poems in the book suffer from over-writing. "Sphere," like "Discoverer," is all writing: the subject—a voyage through the dark waters of the womb—recedes, as the dense filigree of language drives it underground. The subject is so self-limiting, the language so overtaxed, a reader has no sense of traveling any distance across its sinuous contour. Only the agility of Ammons' rhythms can induce a reader to proceed from one end of the poem to the other. A succession of weighty phrases, strung like clothes on a line, smothers the poem's life-breath: ". . . amniotic infinity . . . boundless in circularity . . . consistency of motion arising—annihilated . . . infinite multiplicity, in the deepening, filtering earthen womb. . . ."

"The Constant" succeeds precisely where the other poems fail because the poet's experience of the world, even though felt to be a "drab constant," is so intense it forcibly invades the poet's mind and takes possession of the landscape of the poem. Though the opening and closing lines (quoted above) are clung to by the speaker's intellection, those lines are the feeble, defeated cries of a lover ravished by his mistress, who inhabits the dominant central section of the poem's battlefield. The war between mind and world, though a losing battle for mind, yields fantastic life to the poem. The mind's defeat is the poem's victory. And yet, the speaker's dissatisfaction of mind, resentment even, at the end of the poem, is a valid redirection in itself. In "Corsons Inlet" and "World," poems of the previous volume, Ammons had already fully mastered the plateau of experience successfully revisited in "The Constant": the apocalyptic stroll along the dunes, the Blakean discovery of an entire universe in a clamshell-enclosed "Lake," the sense of totality and self-containment balanced by the sense of fragility and temporariness, likening the clamshell universe to the poem:

> . . . a gull's toe could spill the universe:
> two more hours of sun could dry it up:
> a higher wind could rock it out:
>
> the tide will rise, engulf it, wash it loose:
> utterly:

Perhaps the only distinctly new element in "The Constant" is the recognition that the poet has been here before and is anxious to break out of the enclosure of old experience, to escape into a fresh territory. I suspect there is a hushed cry of frustration at the heart of *Northfield Poems*. The author senses that most of the good work in the book is a repetition of past success.

Some of the very short poems indicate a remarkable new direction in Ammons' work. At first reading, there is no clue to a significance beyond the purely pictorial and imagistic. Suddenly, one word or line will touch off an astonishing number of overtones. In "Trap," one is at first merely enticed by the visual clarity of the mating butterflies:

> . . . they
> spin, two orbits
> of an
> invisible center:
> rise
> over the roof
>
> and caught on
> currents
> rise higher
>
> than trees and
> higher and up
> out of sight,
>
> swifter in
> ascent than they
> can fly or fall.

The poem's surprising force comes from the last lines. The spareness, clean-ness, sharpness—the absence of ambiguity or overtones—all contribute to the astonishing impact of the finish, which transforms the entire poem, at a single stroke, into symbol. The reader is left stunned: where did all the hidden propulsion spring from? The restraint with which most of the poem is rendered allows the body of the piece to serve as a perfect conductor of the charge that travels between the two poles—title and last lines—as swiftly as lightning takes the tree.

The most impressive poem in the volume is a long one which achieves a new scope emerging unexpectedly in the familiar setting of the best former poems: the shore. In "One: Many," after the slightly stilted and heavy-handed philosophy of the opening lines, Ammons resumes his favorite technique of cataloging brilliant ephemera along the creek bank: "When I tried to summarize/a moment's events along the creek. . . ." Following a delicious summary, the sentence concludes: "I was released into a power beyond my easy failures." At this point, the mind leaps into a new dimension of world, as the catalog extends suddenly from the familiar imagery of shore to the free-ranging geography of the American continent. Ammons finds himself, for the first time, in the company of Whitman's wayfaring and wandering, or that of Roethke's last North American meditations. But the imagery is uniquely Ammons'; it has been revived and re-tuned to his most sinuous lines and rhythms:

> I think of California's towns and ranges,
>   deserts and oil fields;
> and of Maine's

    unpainted seahouses
     way out on the tips of fingerlands,
lobster traps and pots,
freshwater lakes; of Chicago,
     hung like an eggsac on the leaf of lake
Michigan, with
its
Art Museum, Prudential Building, Knickerbocker Hotel
(where Cummings stayed);
of North Carolina's
     sounds, banks, and shoals,
     telephone wire loads of swallows,
of Columbus County
       where fresh-dug peanuts
       are boiled
         in iron pots, salt filtering
in through the boiled-clean shells (a delicacy
true
as artichokes or Jersey
asparagus): and on through villages,
along dirt roads, ditchbanks, by gravel pits and on
     to the homes,
inventions, longings:

He started in his own back yard, and fumbled into the impossibly new ground, into "unattainable reality itself." At his best, Ammons is willing to stake everything on the full health of the single imagination, cut loose from history and the genius that labored the language into monuments, to begin poetic art afresh.

Review of *Collected Poems: 1951–1971*

GEOFFREY HARTMAN

With these "Collected Poems" . . . [Ammons's] distinction as a major American Poet will now be evident.

With these "Collected Poems" a lag in reputation is overcome. A. R. Ammons's 400 pages of poetry, written over the space of a generation, manifest an energy, wit and an amazing *compounding* of mind with nature that cannot be overlooked. Even with the omission of Ammons's longest continuous work, "Tape for the Turn of the Year" (1965), this is a remarkable book, enriched by three long poems (together almost 80 pages) that must have been composed since "Uplands" (1970) and "Briefings" (1971). Indeed, with "Hibernaculum," 112 stanzas in length, a high point of the poet's delayed career is reached. His first book, "Ommateum" ("Compound Eye"), caused no stir when it appeared in 1955; and even the mid-sixties' explosion of "Expressions at Sea Level" (1964). "Corsons Inlet" (1965) and "Northfield Poems" (1966) did not make of him an inescapable presence. Ammons snared some academic admirers, but many remained suspicious of this prolific nature bard who kept turning it out like prose. His distinction as a major American poet will now be evident.

There is a problem of bulk. Ammons is a poetic Leviathan, "Created hugest that swim the Ocean stream." The intrepid mass and inner paradoxes of his verse delight and alarm at the same time. Perception is enough, Ammons seems to say, or too much. Nature-news flashes all around us, "bends and blends of sight," "the news to my left over the dunes. . . ." The ticker-tape effect is especially remarkable in such poems as "Saliences" or the microcosmic "Corsons Inlet." It bespeaks, however, no simple vitalism, for nature's plenty makes us feel poor.

Originally published in the *New York Times Book Review,* 19 November 1972, 39–40. Reprinted by permission.

Ammons yields to every solicitation from nature only to find he has no identity left, or no firm power of naming. "So I said I am Ezra," he begins his first poem, conjoining saying and naming. But, he continues, "the wind whipped my throat/gaming for the sounds of my voice." Ammons's best poems about this loss of self and voice to nature are "Gravelly Run" and the late and very beautiful "Plunder." In the latter, reality accuses the mind of "stealing" from it to create language, and the punishment for this strange new Prometheanism is, clearly enough, that the poet cannot collect himself, even in these "Collected Poems."

A man, says Emerson, "cannot be a naturalist until he satisfies all the demands of the spirit. Love is as much its demand as perception." This clarifies, perhaps, the difficulty of all nature-poetry, but especially that of Ammons. For he subdues himself totally to *love of perception,* refusing all higher adventure. "No arranged terror: no forcing of image, plan, /or thought: /no propaganda, no humbling of reality to precept: /terror pervades but is not arranged, all possibilities /of escape open: no route shut, except in / the sudden loss of all routes" ("Corsons Inlet"). Nature herself, as in Wordsworth, must lead to a loss of the way.

This means, however, that Ammons can only extend the Wordsworthian revolution: emptying lyric poetry of false plots, then keeping the emptiness open for a confluence (always gracious or chancy) of event and significance. Hence his "eddies of meaning" or "swervings of action /like the inlet's cutting edge," which produce an essayistic type of poem of variable length and tenuous meter; hence also those fine, organic minglings of mind and nature, or interlacings of figure and ground. But what is often given up is the formal, graduated perfection we still feel in many poems like "Gravelly Run," "Laser," "The City Limits" and "Periphery."

Undeceived poets like Ammons are aware that nature cannot suffice even when they claim that "somehow it seems sufficient / to see and hear whatever coming and going is." Their nature poetry is an almost religious kind of discipline: it acknowledges the mind's defeat, chastens self-concern, and tempers the philosophical quest for meanings. At some point, then, the "Overall" or "sum of events" must be reckoned with. This is what happens preeminently in "Essay on Poetics," "Hibernaculum" and "Extremes and Moderations," which revive modern poetry's quest for the long poem.

In these extravagant and beautiful poems—verse essays really—Ammons maintains a virtuoso current of phrasing that embraces all types of vocabulary, all motions of thought, and leads us back now to Whitman and now to the accumulative (if hopefully cumulative) strain of Pound's "Cantos" or Williams's "Paterson." Building on a non-narrative base, that is, on a will-to-words almost sexual in persistence, he changes all "fleshbody" to "wordbody" and dazzles us with what he calls "interpenetration"—a massively playful nature-thinking, a poetic incarnation of smallest as well as largest thoughts.

Let me quote two sequences from "Hibernaculum" to show the difficult integrity of these longer poems. Here is Ammons at his worst:

>   I see
> Aggregates of definition, plausible
>   emergences, I see
> reticulations of ambience . . .
>
> what do I see: I see a world made,
>   unmade, and made again
> and near crying either way: I look
>   to the ground for the
> lost, the ground's lost: I see grime,
>   just grime, grain
> grist, grist. . . .

This is not improved by the Hopkinsian bumps and grinds. There are too many words: inspiration becomes inflation, "invents vents" and destroys adequate form.

At his best, however, Ammons, like Rilke and Stevens, addresses "the empty place" that threatens his power of speech. A poet, says Rilke in the "Sonnets to Orpheus," cannot but celebrate: "nie versagt ihm die Stimme am Stauber" ("his voice never fails him, though it is choaked by dust"). Nature's indifference, or even the uselessness of speech in the face of that indifference, provokes Ammons to bursts of astonishing celebratory power:

>   if the night is to be
> habitable, if dawn is to come
>   out of it, if day is ever
> to grow brilliant on delivered
>   populations, the word
>
> must have its way by the
>   brook, lie out cold all night
> along the snow limb, spell by
>   yearning's wilted weed till
> the wilted weed rises, know
>   the patience and smallness
>
> of stones: I address the empty
>   place where the god
> that has been deposed
>   lived. . . .

It is not always easy to appreciate an imaginative project of such scope, especially when it is fragmented in so many ways, scattered over so much verbal space. Even the essay-poems, "on course but destinationless," seem occasionally all periphery and no center. Ammons's nature chit-chat can bring him closer to William Cowper's "The Task" than to Wordsworth's "Prelude" or to Coleridge in his streamy "Notebooks."

The poet knows the problem, of course; he hints that he wants to do away with the traditional center-plus-frame kind of lyric in favor of one that respects the principle of entropy. Like nature's energy, poems should run down into an "ideal raggedness: the loose or fragmented or scopy," even as they release imagistic bursts, "airy avalanches, sketchy with event . . . overspills, radiances."

Yet because Ammons expresses everything in casual or pastoral terms, because he "lies low in the light as in a high testimony," there is a danger his achievement will remain self-limited. Instead of a true "saying, binding" he may be creating only an *objet trouvé* art—full of delightful nuggets of perception and self-perception, veined stones found on the beach of the mind which the child prefers to the rare or terrible crystal. But no one in his generation has put "earth's materials" to better use, or done more to raise pastoral to the status of major art.

Exteriors
[A review of *Collected Poems: 1951–1971* by A. R. Ammons]

JASCHA KESSLER

. . . if you want the source of such poetry, if you can call it poetry, do read the scientists rather than this stuff.

If one were obliged to discourse on the American poetic imagination today and its relation to what some call the "tradition," and had to derive one's formulations from the work of one of our most recently prominent poets—A. R. Ammons—one might find it hard to avoid saying that this period, however productive and interesting it seems, is a desperate one. Even though our great, terrible present may be such that it defies description, penetration and habitation by the humane spirit, still one hopes that the poetic imagination will persist in its task: that of carrying us into our own present, if not the future. At least that much, since without the present we may as well forget the future, even if the poets of that time are already nascent. I say *we*, for when our voices fail us, or fail themselves, we are in real trouble. It has happened before, in our own history. Judging from Ammons, this may well be our case. Nevertheless, the failures of poetry are more precious than most kinds of success, even a trace of its element being essential to our existence. What is most startling about this failure is to find Ammons locatable somewhere between 1810 and 1850, and not even in the present really; and though those were no doubt good enough times, they are nevertheless ours no longer.

Imagine, for example, Thoreau, his sensibility, his powerful attention to the natural fact, his feet on his rural threshold, his mind contemplative of the newspapers, the *Bhagavad-Gita,* the Harvard Library (with more than 75% of its holdings composed of old sermons and Calvinist treatises), and the behavior of the micro-macro-cosmos, notebook ever in hand. Resurrect him in 1950, and you have, very loosely and maunderingly incarnated,

Originally published in *Kayak* 32 (July 1973): 64–66. Reprinted by permission.

A. R. Ammons as he appears in his *Collected Poems: 1951–1971*. But much diminished though, perhaps by entropic processes. Recall Thoreau as Yankee mystic, poet-manqué devolving into obsessive observer, losing, perhaps necessarily, the grand drift in weltering detail, but having already achieved the metamorphosis of fact into hard, beautiful prose pregnant with wit and probity—and intellectual power. Whereas Ammons, having begun as fervent initiate to the landscapes of the Southwest, and whose voice on the page refracts Pound and W. C. Williams, sometimes also echoing what seems Amerindian poetry as translated by Gibran, ends in this recent decade writing garrulously on the universal quotidian, and (and this is a bad sign) poetics. A specimen of his early mode, when still the lyrical solitary seeking his vision:

> So when the year had come full round
> I rose
> and went out to the naked mountain
> to see
> the single peachflower on the sprout
>
> blooming through a side of ribs
> possibly a colt's
> and I endured each petal separately
> and moved in orison with the sepals
> [pp. 39–40]

This sort of thing is more or less what Ammons is for a decade, the simple-portentous prosy way of Williams long ago, not his voice though nor his own really, and not Dickinson's either, though more like her than anyone else since, in manner if not content . . . though not that either, for Dickinson tells her passions slant, her multiple vision composed of the ineffable as fact, fact as numinous apparition, while Ammons has no passions. What he has is daydreaming arrested adolescence in the form of wondering at the wondrousness of things. Still, what's interesting for 200 pages is his religiosity, after all: Ammons talks to the wind and to the mountain, to a "you" that is perhaps Manitou, perhaps our absconded "Thou," and they, He, It, talk back in the seminarian prose of a cuneiform translator. As he gains strength, he leaves that mix of Gibran-McKuen-Sumerian behind (I can't burden these pages with it), dedicates himself to observations, and begins his long rambles about the Northeastern littoral and riparian scenes, the molecular-galactic, organic-cellular landscapes, chatting about the Creation, as might have Cowper, Goldsmith, Wordsworth, Whitman, were they writing today. Removed from the desert, he has been taken also from the voices of the winds. Instead, he makes his daily American rounds about lawn and meadow, wood, hill, stream, in an easy, articulate, flat, utterly uneventful expository syntax. Altogether unlike Thoreau's sinewy, exacting, apothegmatic prose, and unlike that suavely undulant later Stevens from whom he borrows some of his stanza structures or envelopes, transmogrifying the Master of Imagination into a freshman-text writer who uses the colon for endless, undigestible linkages, never daring Stevens' comma, or venturing Thoreau's period.

As for Ammons' communications? The Scop traditionally conveyed poet-lore until Wordsworth relinquished his *Excursion*. (MacDiarmid and Pound in their long works, Marxist and Fascist bards, both lost bardry, willingly, to the extent they dignified pamphlets of propaganda). Ammons' world-lore, however, is much better conveyed to us each month by *The Scientific American*. For this poet has by and large done little more than to act as a plain-speaking redactor of such reading matter. That he can summarize our contemporary scientific interests when gazing at the worlds of summer and Ithacan blizzard-winters, or walking the tidal swamp or the maze of geological times, is his chief skill; but it is far, far less interesting, alas, than reading the journals and the science writers themselves, and doing the imaginative work for oneself while strolling and watering one's own lawn. At the end of 20 years and 400 pages, Ammons is lecturing endlessly, mostly on himself writing: he has subsumed flower and storm, flood and glacier to the analysis of himself as provider of the facticities—like the later Thoreau, a failed mystic. For critics and readers who can't meet general science as it comes to us on the newsstand in *Science,* Ammons must seem the very image of a major poet. But there's more *poetry* to be found in a year's subscription to the *Scientific American* than in all of Ammons, more clear evidence of immense imaginative *work* getting done by smart people in the labs, non-writers who write better about the things of this world than this poet does. What, Athena and Apollo preserve us! is this pseudo-science, pseudo-poetics:

> poem are verbal
> symbols for these organizations: they imprint upon the mind
> examples of integration in which the energy flows with maximum
>
> effect and economy between the high levels of oneness and the
> numerous subordinations and divisions of diversity; it is simply
> good to have the mind exposed to and reflected by such examples:
>
> it firms the mind, organizes its energy, and lets the controlled
> flows occur: that is simple good in itself: I can't stress that
> enough: it is not good for something else
>
> [pp. 314–315]

and so on *ad infinitum.* Five years from now, when they change the communications-engineering jargon again, what will Ammons' efforts at postulating a poetics of the cerebral networks that form the cultural-historical-linguistical-existential anastomosis of conscious-cum-unconscious-consciousness appear to be? Vacuous, as they are to me now. Shoot me quick! but don't talk about major poetry in the central line down from Emerson: this poet is Erasmus Darwin reborn as J. B. Watson! And, by remaining on the exterior of the scientists' descriptions of the exterior side of matter, Ammons has remained exterior to the phenomena of the imagination too. Neither the "Thou" he once cried to in the Southwest, nor we ourselves are likely to be grateful for such a concern and such a printout of toneless, mechanical work. If you like your nature and your nature poetry in hypostasis and at 3rd hand, fine. But if you want the source of such poetry, if you can call it poetry, do read the scientists rather than this stuff.

Cards of Identity
[A review of *Sphere: The Form of a Motion* by A. R. Ammons]

DONALD DAVIE

> How could I be anything but exasperated by [*Sphere*] . . . and how is it . . . I was on the contrary *enraptured?*

I am way behind, getting to A. R. Ammons only now. And I know why; everything I ever heard about him said that he wasn't my cup of tea. (The Britishness of that idiom is much to the point.) He was, I gathered, a poet who said "Ooh" and "Ah" to the universe, who had oceanic feelings about the multiplicity of things in nature, and the ubiquity of nature's changes; a poet enamoured of *flux,* therefore; and so, necessarily, a practitioner of "open form"—which last comes uncomfortably close for my taste to being a contradiction in terms. In short, he was one whom Harold Bloom had applauded as "a major visionary poet"; and if that doesn't raise my hackles exactly, it certainly gives me goose-pimples.

And everything that I heard is true. Imagine! A poem 1,860 lines long, with only one full stop in it, at the end of the last line; and put before *me,* who like to think of myself as Doctor Syntax, all for demarcations, a devotee of the sentence! Whatever the opposite of an ideal reader is, I ought to have been that thing so far as this poem is concerned. How could I be anything but exasperated by it, profoundly distrustful, sure I was being bamboozled, sure I was being threatened? And how is it, then, that I was on the contrary *enraptured?* Have I gone soft in the head? Have I suffered a quasi-religious conversion? Shall I drag myself on penitent knees to the feet of the saintly Bloom? No. I am as suspicious as ever I was of Ammons's initial assumptions and governing preoccupations. I still hunger for sentences and full stops, and for a

Originally published in the *New York Review of Books* 22 (6 March 1975): 10–11. Reprinted by permission.

colon that has precise grammatical and rhythmical work to do, instead of being the maid-of-all-work that Ammons makes it into. The cast of his temperament is as alien to me as I thought it would be. And yet I can't refuse the evidence of my senses and my feelings—there wasn't one page of his poem that didn't delight me.

To start with, this visionary is a comedian:

> ...at
>
> clarity of zooming, I'm unpassed in Cayuga Heights, unparalleled
> (nobody hanging on that wing, baby) possibly: at easing
>
> into orbit grease, nuzzling right in there with not a touch
> till the whole seal smacks: at that I'm unusually salient,
> gritless in curvature with withal enthralling control,
>
> perfection of adjustment, innocence of improvisation beginners
> and old strumpets of the spirit know: I don't want shape:
> I'll have water muscles bending streams (recurrences of
>
> curvature): wind sheets erect, traveling: lips accommodating
> muscle glides: identity in me's a black, clear bead: I've
> strongboxed and sunk it, musseled and barnacled with locks ...

This is Ammons characterizing himself, as a poet of the sublime, a rhapsode; and whatever one's suspicions of that poetic posture, how can they not be disarmed when the smiling rhapsode himself admits the windy self-aggrandizement it lets him in for—or would, if he didn't keep his comic wits about him? Supply the rest of the first line, and we have here, complete, one of the 155 sections of this poem. And they are absolutely uniform: each of them, like this one, consists of twelve lines, arranged in threes, in a measure that is not free verse but normally accentual hexameter. "I don't want shape," he says; and sure enough, these sections are not "shapes" but insistently only units, repetitions of one rigid module, uniform therefore, and essentially, deliberately arbitrary. Ammons for instance gives as much care to getting each section syntactically open at both ends as most poets would give to getting a satisfying entry to each, and to each a satisfying closure. And this is entirely logical: there is only one "entry" to this poem, its first line, and only one "closure," its last.

We tend to think that a poetry which celebrates Becoming will find itself in organic or expressive forms; but it is more logical for it to use, as it does here, a form that is inorganic, rigid, mechanical, and arbitrary. Of course this makes for difficulties; the poem is too long, also too dense and exuberant, to be read at a sitting, and yet these open-ended sections provide no resting places, where we can break off and later resume. If, like me, you roughly and provisionally mark places where one stage of the argument is completed and another starts, what is startling and—given the scheme of the whole—very impressive is that these breathing spaces virtually never coincide with the spaces between sections. As for "argument," does it have one? Didn't poems stop having such things, quite some time ago? Apparently not: this poem has an argument; in fact it addresses itself to that hoariest of all arguments, the problem of the Many and the One, no less!

The exuberance, the inventiveness (though always within a rigid frame, and serving a rigid conception) are what is winning. When the exuberance is comical, as it blessedly often is, it recalls nothing so much as late Auden—an Auden, one might dare to say, beaten at his own lexicographer's games, and ultimately much more serious, because convinced of a much more exalted role for the imagination than late and chastened Christian Auden could believe in. But the exuberance comes in other modes than the comic. For instance:

> when the grackle's flight shadows a streak of lawn, constellations
> of possibility break out, for example, the multitude of
> grassblade shadows subsumed in a sweep . . .

or (of the identity of the man extinguished in death, as distinct from the identity of the man-as-poet):

> . . . then the small
> self will taste the ruin that has been my only food . . .

(This one can't be registered out of context; restored to it, in section 79, it can move to tears.) And in the end, for "exuberance" one has to read "elation" or "vitality" or, most simple, just "hope":

> the safety engineers complain that the people are numb
> along the fault line and will not survive if they do not
> respond to warning signals: maybe so: but how
>
> have we survived at all but by numb nonchalance: to know
> and care is to take victory out of the moment when a
> moment's victory is what everything is for, apparently: . . .

I'm not sure that I'm persuaded by this, when I'm away from Ammons's poem; so long as I'm *with* the poem I'm persuaded, and exhilarated and grateful. Put this poem beside John Hollander's "Reflections on Espionage" (so much more melancholy, yet like this in its controlled fluidity, and the inventive ease of its diction), and I begin to think that the genius of American poetry persisted undeterred under all the revolutions and counter-revolutions and personality cults of the tedious Sixties. And how long has Ammons been writing as well as this? I've a lot of homework to catch up on.

Reader Participation Invited
[A review of *The Snow Poems* by A. R. Ammons]

HAYDEN CARRUTH

"The Snow Poems" is a dull, dull book.

No matter how they deny it—and many do—what writers want is communion; not communication, communion. They want the reader right in there with them, soul to soul. It's a hunger. (And by no means, says the voice at my shoulder, limited to writers alone.)

Once writers could solve their problem by making a story, an allegory, some invented world, into which they invited or enticed the reader, so that both could live there together for a while, soul to soul, in the "willing suspension of disbelief." It worked; it worked for a couple of thousand years. But more and more in our century writers came to feel that the suspension of disbelief was failing, was downright fraudulent, and they turned to formalistic means. They thought, if you can just make the reader participate in the *technique* of writing, then you will have him caught, a willing (but nicely subservient) collaborator in the artistic process. Hence Modernism in all its aspects. Today some poets even publish random words or lines and ask the reader to make his own poem. Conceptualists, I believe, is what they're called.

A. R. Ammons has not gone that far. But he does lay his procedures open to view, often ingratiatingly, so that when he has second thoughts about a word, for instance, he does not cross out the original and substitute the new, he leaves them both there. The correction, amplification, set out in repetition, is not laziness but a real way to make us see how poetic language moves toward intensity and precision. At other times, when he writes a longer piece that isn't quite satisfactory, he puts a paraphrase or counter-thought in the margin. And it's true, afterthought adds to forethought, stylistically and

Originally published in the *New York Times Book Review*, 25 September 1977, 30. Reprinted by permission.

substantially, a resonance that lets us see the poet's mind in process. It's like reading Emerson's journals, the gathering fragments that became the essays.

Which brings us to Ammons's topic. Emerson's mind was focused on something—many things, tough, resistant things. Ammons writes about anything, randomly. "The Snow Poems" is a long sequence in diary form, even though the poems are undated. I have never read so much verse about the weather in my life; also about decay of consciousness, separation from nature, the sorrow of knowledge; in short, the trivia of a professorial mind in daily academic and domestic life. Often passages of simple word-play intervene, like infantile regressions ("egad, gasso, glorybe"), or invented or half-invented proverbs ("intercourse is better than no course at all"). Much of this incidentally is bright and attractive. But how it does go on!

Why? He says,

> hello from one who knows
> nothing
> (and never lets you hear
> the end of it)

But we all know nothing, and we all talk of it endlessly, and this is the human condition; there is value, indubitably, in establishing its presence in art, much value. The poet, ignorant and agonized, at least establishes his existence; he survives. But what of us, his readers? Do we survive, too, by attending to this random scribbling? Ammons doesn't say.

As readers I think we can survive, sometimes. The key is passion, a transcendent passion that elevates writer and reader alike to a plane of subjective freedom; apart from the determined world. Millions have found survival in Wordsworth's passionate early poems, but not one (except W. W. himself) in his later maunderings. Ammons is famous now, celebrated, a prize-winner, with lots of good poetry behind him, real created poems. But he has begun to maunder. He thinks he is inventing himself in these new poems; but he is only reporting himself. And that is not enough.

In spite of a bright, attractive technique, which could be used perfectly well in real poems, and in spite of occasional lyric parts that remind us of earlier work, "The Snow Poems" is a dull, dull book. The best a reviewer can do for everyone concerned, including the poet, is to say so.

A. R. Ammons and *The Snow Poems* Reconsidered

Michael McFee

The Snow Poems shows us the dark side of Ammons's radiant sublimity.

For many critics, the only good poet is a dead poet. Then we can shape his career, even his eccentricities, into some comfortable pattern which fixes his place in the cast of literary history. Of course, we can try the same trick with a contemporary poet, though if he is worth his salt he is likely to be uncooperative.

A. R. Ammons is an excellent example of the latter. The popular critical pacifier, as manufactured by Bloom and others, was that Ammons had come into the world to fulfill the Romantic Transcendental heritage, to realize the promise of Organic Form. It is hard to deny the basic truth of this approach, and the substance of Ammons's work seemed to confirm it, as the poet himself acknowledged in several poems *for Harold Bloom.* During the process of Ammons's canonization, his prosody was not much remarked upon, probably because it appeared less significant or important than the mind behind the poems. But an interesting thing happened: as Ammons became more prominent, the form of his poetry became more conservative, taking on a more orderly and regular appearance. This is best seen in his long poems, which are the fullest measure of Ammons's singular enterprise. After the radical experimentation of *Tape for the Turn of the Year* (written 1963/64), Ammons turned toward stanzaic form and increasingly elaborate structures in his next extended pieces, written between 1970 and 1973—*Essay on Poetics* (tercets, with interludes), *Extremes and Moderations* (quatrains, with an interlude), *Hibernaculum* (112 sections of three tercets each), and *Sphere: The Form of a Motion* (155 sections of four tercets each). It was the best of all possible worlds

Originally published in *Chicago Review* 33:1 (Summer 1981): 32–38. Reprinted by permission of *Chicago Review.* Copyright (c) 1981 by *Chicago Review.* All rights reserved.

for the critics, yoking conceptual purity with formal complexity, and the poet was rewarded with the National Book Award and a Bollingen Prize. A pattern had been established: collections of high hard lyrics balanced by longer, more circuitous poems.

Then came *The Snow Poems* (written 1975/76), and trouble in paradise:

> imagine!
> writing something that never forms a
> complete thought, drags you
> after it, spills you down, no barrier
> describing you or dock lifting you up:
> imagine writing something the CIA would
> not read, through,
> a mishmash for the fun-loving,
> one's fine-fannied friends!
>   imagine, a list, a
> puzzler, sleeper, a tiresome business,
> conglomeration, aggregation, etc.
> nobody can make any sense of:
>   a long poem, shindig,
> fracas, uproar,
> high shimmy uncompletable, hence like
> paradise, hellish paradise,
> not the one paradise where the points
> & fringes of
> perception sway in and out at once
> in the free interlockings of
> permanence
>   (*The Snow Poems,* pp. 17–18)

Judging from the testy reception of *The Snow Poems,* most readers did not appreciate having the formal ladder jerked out from under them and being spilled on their fine fannies. But Ammons knew they wouldn't even as he wrote the poem ("imagine!" he begins): people want poems that form complete thoughts (a *Sphere*-like "Form of a Motion"?), that make sense, that preserve the illusion of permanence in a pageful of lines. What he wants to offer us instead is provisional and piecemeal, not finished—a mishmash, a shindig, a high shimmy uncompletable, an infernal chaos rather than a unified paradise. Ammons paid the price for his audaciousness—no imprimatur from Mr. Bloom graces this book's dust jacket—but I think he got what he wanted, "a big gritty poem that would just stand / there and spit, accommodating itself to nothing and / too disfigured to be approached, no one / able to imagine what line to take," "something standing recalcitrant in its own nasty massiveness, / bowing to no one, nonpatronizing and ungrateful."[1]

Before *The Snow Poems* is allowed to sink from sight into the Slough of Neglect, and before Ammons's succeeding books of lyrics (such as the much praised *A Coast of Trees*) obscure the curious achievement of this book, let us review it to note some neglected aspects of his work. First, whatever the genius displayed in his concentrated short poems, *The Snow Poems* reminds us that Ammons weaves much of his significant writing into the looser fabric of his longer poems. In fact, he is among the most important practitioners of the long poem in America since Stevens. His output in this form at least equals the volume of all his briefer pieces, and *The Snow Poems* adds another 292 pages to the discursive side of the scale. To classify the book as a long poem at all may seem surprising, since the title is plural and the text is broken into 118 titled parts. But these headings are not titular in any conventional sense, nor even in the manner of Ammons's typical lyrics, which in the *Collected Poems 1951–1971* were usually minimal titles providing the reader with an angle to the poem, e.g., "Guide," "Identity," "Saliences," "Peak." These titles give no such clues. Instead of using diaristic dates (as in the *Tape*) or sectional numbers (as in *Hibernaculum* or *Sphere*) to mark interstices in the long poem, Ammons merely lifts the first line of each passage and places it at the top of the page, much like an editor providing a title for an untitled poem, e.g., "Here I Sit, Fifty in the" (p. 7) or "My Father Used to Tell of an" (p. 229). The continuum of the long poem is not really interrupted: these are simply arbitrary headings for "this long poem's thickets and byways, / flyby's, big timber, high marsh, and / sea lane," as Ammons describes it, in which there is room "for one to turn the wrong way / around this hedge, streamfork / or that, boulder, / pavilion ledge / and take on / unnoticed a different coloring / as if one had come / surprisingly suddenly from / a pure place of belief" (p. 250).

    This is what has attracted Ammons to the long form all along: its spaciousness, its scope, the freedom and possibility of the long job as opposed to the ideal of the fixed, inflexible, gemlike lyric:

> Getting little
> poems off (clusters
> of them) hits
> centers—if lesser centers—
> quicker and
> set-wise like the rocks
> of kaleidoscopes
> makes infinite
> combinations possible, whereas
> the long job's
> demand for consistency
> levels,
> though the one center it
> shoots for
> may be deeper
>   (*Diversifications*, p. 38)

The long poem can be Ammons's omnium-gatherum:

> I've been
> looking for a level
> of language
> that could take in all
> kinds of matter
> & move easily with
>   light or heavy burden:
>   a level
> that could,
> without fracturing, rise
>   & fall
>   with conception &
>   intensity
> (*Tape for the Turn of the Year,* p. 144)

The Snow Poems provide a rough symmetry to the body of Ammons's long poetry, approximately balancing the *Tape* in quantity of pages and in temperament, in multilevel inventiveness and intensity, but it is even more radical than that early experiment. Now there is no roll of adding machine tape for physical continuity and motivation, no automatic order of calendar or colon, no ready parameters: there is simply the lonely poet and the snowy page.

Here is the heart of *The Snow Poems:* Ammons's deep anti-formalism. In the long poems preceding this book, and in many of the lyrics, Ammons had seemed to be talking himself into a formal mode, at least visually. He adopted stanzas and sections against which the flow of the poem had to struggle; and though there often appeared to be no real necessity in the particular form used, no inevitable logic in line break and emphasis, nevertheless he did go to the trouble of employing them. The poems were proficient and they were praised. In *The Snow Poems* Ammons has abandoned all such contrivance of regular measure: poetry resists this "identity certain," he now writes, "yielding to erosion, / horse manure, bird droppings, / pine needles, the wind, moss, / bracket, bract, stone of change, / a troublesome, marvelous garden" (p. 146). He endorses the "hellish paradise" susceptible to shit and wind change, not the artificial order of a stanza:

> this stanza compels
> its way along: a
> break will humble it:
>
> form consumes:
> form eliminates:
> form forms the form

> that extracts of the elixir from
> the passages of change:
> well, we musn't let this
> form reverse itself
> into an opposite
> though parallel
> largely similar insistence:
> must we?
>
> (*The Snow Poems,* p. 169)

This is why *The Snow Poems* is best described as an anti-formal poem, almost a poem-in-progress or -process. It rejects the inflexible structures which drain the elixir vitae of motion, scoffing at all superficially logical metaphors of order, "axioms, postulates, theorems, hypotheses, / hypotenuses, conclusions, paradigms in / neat blue conic sections, curved lines, dots, / lines, and planes, cubes, prisms, cylinders, / spheres, all that good stuff" (p. 186). In the high shimmy uncompletable, it is not a polished mathematical conclusiveness which is essential but energy, range, motion, change. This contentious impulse may have been implicit in earlier Ammons poems, as in the irregular perambulation of "Corsons Inlet,"[2] but it has never been pushed to such drastic practice, to such a resolute extreme.

Finally, *The Snow Poems* reveals more of the man behind the poet than in any previous book. This may seem a trivial point, but it is actually rather significant for Ammons. He has more at stake than the usual exhibitors of self, because he has built a reputation on poems that are lofty, sublime, almost purified of human presence. And though his long poems relax into a more garrulous and comprehensive mode, full of humorous asides and wordplay, they have not sustained any sense of personal anguish and need. *The Snow Poems* shows us the dark side of Ammons's radiant sublimity:

> I no longer go to look about in the world:
> I have become so lonely
> that only the word
> is free enough and large enough to take my
>   mind off
>   the world going day
>   by day over the brink
>   used up but unused:
> how thankful I feel
> bent gutless over
> the vomited void
> to have at least the word
> going anywhere fetching anything:
> pretty soon it may have
> brought me so much
> it will not need to go off again

> and then the word will
> draw me up about it
> (*The Snow Poems,* pp. 191–92)

This may not be the voice of the Romantic Bard or the Peeping Botanist or even the Good Old Boy, but it is that of a person urgently talking to people. *The Snow Poems* is Ammons's most moody and unpredictable work, not eye-catching like the "middle" long poems and not fun to flip through like the chatty and generally extroverted *Tape.* There is no pretention of omniscience: the poet's guard is down, and he is alternately shrewd and unwise, corny and exalted, like most of us. This book can be, like the weather in it, severe and wintry as well as sunny.

So *The Snow Poems* is at once typical and exceptional among Ammons's poems in stubbornly indulging and realizing—at the peril of poet, reader, and critic—his long standing predisposition "to prefer confusion to over-simplified clarity, meaninglessness to neat, precise meaning, uselessness to over-directed usefulness."[3] Accordingly, he does not stage a soaring consummation of the poem, as with *Sphere:* instead, he suspends and scatters us in several directions:

> lunch reservoirs on our rears
> overlook   to set our feet
> look over   on symbolic rock,
>   solid space—
>   *that* is the heave
>
> I am so backward   how many
> in my correspondence   should I
> I have to stand in line   put you
> to hear from myself   down for
>
> we(l)come
> (*The Snow Poems,* p. 292)

"We(l)come": that is the final message, like the bright and poignant "so long" which concludes the *Tape.* In that poem, though, Ammons explains in the last few pages what he has been doing in the whole poem and builds up to his benediction. In *The Snow Poems,* the welcome mat is simply there, another of the clusters of wor(l)ds made and abandoned for us to translate, another element in the poem's mishmash. The form—or more correctly, the lack of it—does not require a polished farewell: the high shimmy remains uncompletable and uncompleted. As with the rest of the poem, its "strands" and its "patches," we must "make something of it: think it over and out" (p. 290).

Notes

1.   From an as-yet uncollected long poem *Summer Place,* written in the summer of 1975, several months before Ammons began *The Snow Poems.* Its 364 rambling tercets, 28 more than *Hibernaculum,* seem a valediction to his stanzaic "middle" long poems. See *Hudson Review* 30 (Summer 1977), 173–209.

2.   Even earlier than "Corsons Inlet," in the "Foreward" to his first book *Ommateum* (Philadelphia: Dorrance, 1955). Ammons wrote: "The poems suggest a many-sided view of reality; an adoption of tentative, provisional attitudes, replacing the partial, unified, prejudicial, and rigid; a belief that forms of thought, like physical forms, are, in so far as they resist it, susceptible to change, increasingly costly and violent. . . . They suggest and imply and rather grow in the reader's mind than exhaust themselves in completed, external form."

3.   From a prose statement, "A Poem Is a Walk," in *Epoch* 18 (Fall 1968), 116.

Veracity Unshaken
[A review of *Sumerian Vistas* by A. R. Ammons]

HELEN VENDLER

There has been nothing like this in American Poetry before Ammons . . .

At a sixtieth-birthday convocation in 1986, the poet A. R. Ammons was asked, "Do poets have a public responsibility?" He replied, without hesitation, "No." But another question—"Is poetry subversive?"—elicited a longer statement:

> Yes, you have no idea *how* subversive—deeply subversive. Consciousness often reaches a deeply intense level at the edges of things, questioning and undermining accepted ways of doing things. The audience resists change to the last moment, and then is grateful for it.

A moment later, he corrected himself:

> It may not be in the long range subversive. We love our conventions, but are afraid of being locked in by them.

It is clear that Ammons believes both that poetry has a public effect and that the effect does not depend on whether poets consciously assume "public responsibility." His wish to draw a distinction between public responsibility (writing with one eye on the topical) and public effect (in the short run, subversion; in the longer run, perhaps, conservation) is only one proof of his careful and anxious intelligence.

Like Ashbery and Merrill, Ammons is a nonideological writer who takes long views. All three have assumed the thankless cultural task of defining how an adult American mind not committed to any single ideological agenda might exist in a self-respecting and veracious way in the later twentieth cen-

Originally published in the *New Yorker*, (15 February 1988): 100–108. Reprinted by permission.

tury. Ammons differs from Ashbery and Merrill in being trained in the sciences. (He graduated from Wake Forest with a B.S.) Perhaps in consequence, he is not afraid to represent the human presence as it has actually occurred in the universe: not at the center but at the edge of its galaxy, which itself is one temporary and random point in a very long historical continuum. He not only sees our existence in that light; he *feels* it to be so. At the same time, he respects the way in which consciousness must be a center unto itself, no matter what its position in the universe.

The title of Ammons' new book, "Sumerian Vistas" (Norton; $15.95), emphasizes his long view of human existence. In his youth, he first turned to Sumer (where writing was invented) as a vantage point. At twenty-nine, he published in his first book, "Ommateum," several lyrics in which he adopted, as a refuge from acute temporal anxiety, the persona of a prophet who had come to ancient Sumer and had perceived the immense distance between besieged life and calm necessity:

> I have grown a marsh dweller
> subject to floods and high winds . . .
>
> rising with a handful of broken
>   shells
> from sifted underwater mud
> I have come to know how high
> the platform is, beyond approach,
> of serenity and blue temple tiles.

The "Sumerian" dweller in catastrophe of that early poem now writes "Sumerian Vistas." Though Ammons' vistas do not deny age (the grave is mentioned fairly often, and a sequence on inscription is entitled "Tombstones"), his tone has not changed; it still has all the spring and backlash and curiosity of his young voice. His titles still show punning casualness ("Working Out," "Abstinence Makes the Heart Grow Fonder") as well as epigrammatic brevity ("Dominant Margins," "Scaling Desire"). As usual, his borrowings from scientific diction—"Information Density," "Negative Symbiosis," "Red Shift"—are used with high freedom; "Red Shift," for instance, is not about stars but about a winter-pale begonia (and its owner) receiving a new infusion of "bright blood" from the spring sun.

Ammons is a poet of determined factual exactness. In poems as neat as laboratory drawings, he tells the truth about biological life—for example, that everything eats something else in order to live. If a jay stops the song of a cicada, and attacks its eyes as if they were just another set of seeds to crack open for food, that is the nature of existence—a matter for even-toned, recognition rather than lament, terror, or indignation. Lament, terror, and indignation nonetheless have their place, as flashes of feeling, in Ammons' poems; but they are components, not determinants, of cognition. Here is "Sight Seed":

> When the jay caught
> the cicada midair, a fluffy,
> rustling beakful, the
> burr-song flooded dull but
> held low: the jay perched and
> holding the prey to the branch
> as if to halt
> indecorous song pecked
> once, a plink that did it,
> but in the noticeable silence
> proceeded at ease
> and expertly to
> take this, then that eye.

When an eye ("I") is consumed, it becomes part of what follows "i," perhaps a "j." It would not be unlike Ammons to intend the pun.

Ammons is so expert in thinking of himself as a corpse, already dissolved into dust and air, that his own dissolution provides an airy poetics of dispersion, reflecting "genetic material's / extravagant loss along the / edging peripheries of accident." The fact of eventual disappearance also suggests an ethics. Given one's end, how should one live? "Backcasting" answers this way:

> I can tell by
> the way
> gravel will spill
> through me some
>
> day it's
> all right to
> mess around: I can
> tell by the way
>
> light will
> find me transparent I
> can't be gross:
> I drift,
>
> slouch about, spoof:
> I true the
> coming-before
> to the consequence.

One can imagine the demands put by Ammons' muse: "Write a poem on dying that will be as light as the dust and transparency you will become. Then deduce from those motes and air a way of living suitable to that ending. From the consequence of eventual dissolution deduce a premise for existence: true the coming-before to the consequence." The deduced premise, for Ammons, is to lessen ponderousness: the poet can mess around, be airy, drift, slouch, spoof. The poem itself must be full of air spaces, loose siftings, casual rhythms, or it will not be the believable messenger of its entropic message.

Ammons was brought up on the Bible (it was the only book in the house, he has said, in his rural North Carolina boyhood), and the earnestness of a Biblical tone has always been part of his repertoire. In the light of that early Biblical impress, his post-Christian (though reverent) position is all the more original. It is still rare to find poetry of serious intellectual premises that can get along without disabling religious or ideological nostalgia.

Ammons shows us what it's like to live with a natural, internalized sense of biological evolution. His imagination takes it for granted. The haphazard evolutionary process—by which the primal soup produced protoplasm, vegetation, vertebrates, amphibians, and, finally, us—is undone, he recognizes, by the equally dubious process by which in return we grind the greenness out of nature. Ammons sums up both in his twenty-two-line poem "Questionable Procedures":

> A bit of the universe's
> business slopped
> over and, strung
> out of the way,
> cooled and lode-slow
> gave rise
> here and there to
> a quickness like
> shade, protoplasm,
> a see-through
> coming and going of
> dots and pulsing veils
> that soon enough filled
> the bit seas:
> the veils and cauls
> toughened, curled
> into rolls, centralized
> backbone: taking to
> the land and coming up
> into us, our agency,
> they milled the
> green continents white.

Why would anyone *want* to sum up all of evolutionary and human history in seventy-odd words? One answer is that lyric poets have always resented the lay notion that their gamut is smaller than that of epic poets, putting certain grand subjects beyond their reach. A second answer is that if evolutionary history lies in the modern secular mind as a myth of becoming, it must have attracted constellations of feeling to itself, and these must be articulated by contemporary poetry. A third answer is that for the appalled observer an evolutionary history that turns destructively on itself deserves comment, the more epigrammatic and memorable the better, "Such a result so soon—and from such a beginning!" said Whitman, stricken by the appearance of his adult face in a hand mirror; but where Whitman supposes an original moral innocence, and glances only at the span of a single life, Ammons supposes an original moral neutrality and deplores human destruction over the whole span of species life. The power of lyric form to clasp even the aeons of the modern evolutionary imagination is as firmly asserted here as in Lowell's "History."

Ammons' work is post-Christian not only in its marginal positioning of man, and in its acceptance of evolution rather than special creation, but also in the way it emphasizes the inevitably aspectual nature of perception and cognition. Like his predecessor Stevens, he denies the univocal positing of a single attainable truth (of the sort conventionally proposed by Christian theology). The title of Ammons' first book, "Ommateum," refers to the compound eye of an insect, and his prose preface to that collection says, "The poems suggest a many-sided view of reality; an adoption of tentative, provisional attitudes, replacing the partial, unified, prejudicial, and rigid."

Tentative and provisional thoughts require discretion and grace in expression. In an interview published in *Pembroke* in 1986 Ammons said:

> To me, the really great poet feels as deeply as anyone these matters, but touches, only and controls them lightly with delicate gestures that just merely register they are there. To me, the second- or third-rate poet . . . begins to bushwhack and hack and cut and try to create an artificial fury because he thinks that will give him the gestures of great poetry, but it gives him just the opposite.

Readers unaccustomed to discretion in gesture prefer loud noises. For them, poetry is a matter of violent statement. But for Ammons a poem is a "disposition . . . rather than an exposition." He has said, "It may be made out of words but it's no longer saying anything. It's just complete." The poem has found a system of relational completeness within itself, and a relational completeness in the company of its fellow-poems; both of these are something silent, and they are more complex than statement, though statement is one of the means to them.

Like most of Ammons' other volumes, "Sumerian Vistas" contains long poems as well as short. ("In short poems, I'm on a tightwire, and in long poems, the plain is wide and the direction uncertain," he has said.) Short poems become riddles in which he often deliberately exploits the ambiguous power of words that can serve as several different parts of speech. In the opening of "Earliest Recollection," for instance, the words "thaws," "snow," "clear," "leaves," "touched," "last," "fall," and "gathering" can each act more than one part in the game of syntax: "thaws" could be a verb or a plural noun; "clear" could be a verb or an adjective. We hesitate, placing them, as we read the lines:

> Thaws snow-clear the fields
> and woods, and leaves
> snow's small weight
>
> touched down last fall
> crinkle to the breezes
> and rise gathering dry.

Ammons' suspension of ambiguous parts of speech in an open field mimics the hovering act of perception itself.

Ammons' shorter poems, like "Earliest Recollection," often recount the vicissitudes of accident or chance, but the longest poem in the new volume, "The Ridge Farm," exemplifies his sense of the sacredness of necessity—that interaction of all universal motions:

> sap, brook, glacier,spirit
> flowing, these are sacred but
> in a more majestic aloofness
> than we can know or reason with.

Ammons acknowledges the deep human wish for the "easy sacredness" of a personal divine providence ("some band or / quality of concern to / recognize us here"), but he calls us to recognize what he sees as a loftier sacredness—"something / high to realize, recalcitrant, / unyielding to makeshift in / its quality." As Ammons, with sternness and accuracy, makes his reports on high impersonal necessity, his country goes on funding television evangelists and papal visits. This standoff would make one despair of the gulf between a poet and his culture were it not that cultures eventually catch up to their poets. "The Ridge Farm," like Ammons' other long poems, offers us a gift we may be reluctant to receive, the privilege of living for a while inside an original and a querying adult intelligence. This intelligence has three chief registers: it notices with joyful precision the Thoreauvian world of natural fact; it spins fine-grained meditations on the mind's ways of being; and it urges an ethics founded on the possibility of cultural illumination and human concern.

Into the hardened hoaxdoms of culture come particles of human veracity and concern, lighting up one partial space. Though he rejects religious superstition, Ammons is still the poet of our Protestant past in his trust in the inner light. That ethical light is intermittent but, he believes, immortal in its recurrence:

> a light catches somewhere, finds
> human
> spirit to burn on, shows its magic's
> glint lines, attracts, grows, rolls
> back space and dark. . . .

> it dwells:
> it dwells and dwells: slowly the
> light,
> its veracity unshaken, dies but
> moves
> to find a place to break out else-
> where:
> this light, tendance, neglect
> is human concern working with
> what is: one thing is hardly better
> or worse than another: the
> split hair of possible betterment
> makes
> dedication reasonable and heroic:
> the frail butterfly, a slightly
> guided piece of trash, the wind takes
> ten thousand miles.

The strictly limited extent of light and concern is not lost on Ammons. "All is in an enormous dark," as Hopkins said:

> Flesh fade, and mortal trash
> Fall to the residuary worm;/world's
> wildfire, leave but ash.

Nonetheless, the Psyche-butterfly ("mortal trash" to Hopkins, a "slightly/guided piece of trash" to Ammons) will travel far in space and time. Properly, Ammons' understated ending has the delicacy of haiku; in fact, it almost rewrites itself into haiku:

> A frail butterfly,
> slightly guided piece of trash,
> wind-borne thousand miles.

Ammons' Oriental quietism and Quaker light stand, in deliberate, if mild, opposition to the murderous ideological intentions of mankind:

I can in beds of flowers hold
my head up, too: whereas,
the forms of intention, the
faces swept chill-firm with
    conviction

can assemble and roll down
streets and declare divisions
that save or kill: I go to
nature because man is scary.

By now, Ammons has amassed a lifetime's worth of wayward, experimental, cursive, volatile verse, ranging from the briefness of "Briefings" (1971) to the long unwinding of "Tape for the Turn of the Year" (1965)—to name two characteristic extremes in his practice. His definitive "Collected Poems," when it appears, will be one of the influential American books of this century, notable for its forgoing of dogmatism in a dogmatic time and for its tender, shrewd, and nonchalant charting of a way to live responsibly within natural fact, scientific imagination, and ethical discovery.

On *Garbage*

DAVID BAKER

Garbage may be one of the central poetic accomplishments of our time.

After disparaging the predominance of the confessional lyric mode over the past several decades, a number of poets and critics have lately turned to the long narrative poem as a popular antidote to the supposed self-absorption of the contemporary lyric. Would that it were so. While the impulse of this loose coterie—I refer mainly to the New Narrative poets, but to others as well—may be laudable in attempting to broaden the scope, subject, and stance of contemporary poetry, too often I find their means to be unimaginative. It is quite true that, like nearly every poetry school, a few fine poets do work in this mode; but in general the work of the New Narrative poets is graceless, formally stiff, rhetorically unremarkable. Too often the formula of their strategies is merely chronological, a sort of proselike clockwork, plodding through plot, arguing that sequence *is* event. But surely, we must know that there are many ways to measure experience and idea. It seems obvious that, after Bors and Jung, after Riceour and Cage, after virtually every theoretical physicist and mathematician, story-telling must reconsider and refigure the notions of time, progression, sequence, narrative, and ultimately idea. . . .

A.R. Ammons's new *Garbage* is a brilliant book. It may very well be a great one, as fine as, or perhaps even superior to, his previous long masterwork *Tape for the Turn of the Year* with its massive, connective inquiries or *Sphere,* that most dense and eloquent longer poem. To be honest, this book has caught me off-guard, following, as it does, fairly closely on the heels of Ammons's *The Really Short Poems of A.R. Ammons. Garbage* is a 121-page poem in eighteen sections, composed in couplets, and nearly composed of a single, winding, astonishing sentence. Ammons is famously capable within the short

"On *Garbage*" first appeared as "The Push of Reading" in *The Kenyon Review* 16:4 (Fall 1994): 161–76, and is reprinted with permission of the author.

lyric mode—distinctive, intelligent, quirky—but the long poem extrapolated from a lyric base is his genius. Sherod Santos's book-length sequence is an intense concentration on a single motif; *Garbage* is about, well, everything—especially since, as Ammons insists, garbage is the primary building-block of the universe. In the wonderful cosmos of this poem, there is nothing that is not "garbage":

> garbage has to be the poem of our time because
> garbage is spiritual, believable enough
>
> to get our attention, getting in the way, piling
> up, stinking, turning brooks brownish and
>
> creamy white: what else deflects us from the
> errors of our illusionary ways. . . .
>
> (18)

Beginning with a description of a trash dump alongside a Florida highway, *Garbage* soon finds itself evolving into a series of connected meditations, each about a different order of refuse, of the wasted, whatever is unused, overgrown, or cast aside. Ammons's speaker discovers that nature everywhere is composed of the decadent and entropic, the aged, the tired—"toxic waste, poison air, beach goo, eroded roads"—and sees in nature, then, enough models to be able to state that "this is a scientific poem // asserting that nature models values" (20). The speaker himself, nearing retirement from his professorship as a writing teacher, feels discarded, decaying, worried about social security and disease:

> a pain in the knee or hipjoint or warps and
> knots in the leg muscles, even strange, binding
>
> twinges in the feet ought to cause you to include
> in the list of possibilities that the high
>
> arch in one of your feet has slipped, shortening
> you shortlegged, your weight misdistributed. . . .
>
> (40)

But Ammons knows his science well; he knows that no amount of material substance ever vanishes, only converts into other matter or energy. And this is the magic of *Garbage*. We become witnesses to something of a generative and evolutionary process—the turning of garbage into utility, decay into new life, an idea into further ideas. A sort of latter day, practical optimist, the speaker transfers his initial observation into aesthetic and pedagogical usage: "I say to my writing students—prize your flaws, / defects, behold your accidents,

engage your // negative criticisms—these are the materials on your ongoing
. . ." and then takes his own advice, instructing our readerly expectations as
well:

> this is just a poem with a job to do: and that
>
> is to declare, however roundabout, sideways,
> or meanderingly (or in those ways) the perfect
>
> scientific and materialistic notion of the
> spindle of energy . . .
>
>   in value systems,
> physical systems, artistic systems, always this
>
> some disposition from the heavy to the light,
> and then the returns from the light downward
>
> to the staid gross: stone to wind, wind to
> stone: there is no need for "outside," hegemonic
>
> derivations of value: nothing need be invented
> or imposed: the aesthetic, scientific, moral
>
> are organized like a muff along this spindle,
> might as well relax: thus, the job done. . . .
>
>   (24–25)

As simply as "thus," a story about aging, about worldly disgust, sharply
converts into an encouragement to see that the world is necessarily composed
of such leavings. An early morning's "senseless" vision of the future with its
"strokes, hip replacements, // insulin shots, sphygmomanometers" brings
with it "a tiny / wriggle of light in the mind that says, 'go on': // that's what it
says: that's all it says" (46). And death's own inevitability becomes an invitation to see, in essence, the entirety of time within the space of a moment:

> [if] death is so persuasive, can't life be: it is
> fashionable now to mean nothing, not to exist,
>
> because meaning doesn't hold, and we do not exist
> forever; this *is* forever, we are now in it; our
>
> eyes see through the round time of nearly all
> of being, our minds reach out and in ten billion
>
> years: we are in so much forever. . . .
>
>   (88)

By the poem's end the speaker has so thoroughly embraced the connected-
ness of things, the cyclic give-and-take of matter, that he sees his own body
now, even in old age, as a kind of garden, a place where life is not lost, but
nourished:

> if you've derived from life
> a going thing called life, life has a right to
>
> derive life from you: ticks, parasites, lice,
> fleas, mites, flukes, crabs, mosquitoes . . .
> (98–99)

Many of the values of *Garbage* seem to have their foreground in the practical, encouraging romanticism of Emerson. Emerson's insistence on the values of utility and frugality precede Ammons's own compulsion to see that
every iota of material substance is used and appreciated, every bit of waste
turned to order and meaning. Emerson spoke of this notion in 1844 in a lecture to the Mercantile Library Association of Boston: "Nature is the noblest
engineer, yet uses a grinding economy, working up all that is wasted today
into tomorrow's creation—not a superfluous grain of sand . . ." (Emerson,
218). There is coherence in such a universe, where a natural order of "work"
performs the tasks of converting matter and energy into more of the same,
and where, for both Emerson and Ammons, these physical transformations
signal similar transformations in understanding, improvements in the spirit.
Even in its more skeptical moments, and even in the ironized language of
postmodern wit and banter, Ammons's *Garbage* enacts an Emersonian cosmology where the wastes of the contemporary soul are converted into consolation, connection, and even hope: "I have a low view of us: but that is why /
I love us or try to move to love us" (106).

Still, this does not begin to characterize the brilliance of the poem itself,
its tremendous variety of tones, its astonishing range of subject matter, its
sheer readability. The voice in *Garbage* is almost disarmingly direct, neither
the mundane voice of an "average" person as in so much contemporary lyric
verse, nor the hyper-dogmatic expression within a scholar's *texte,* nor the epic-
like inflations of a character like Paterson. I almost want to characterize this
voice, again in Emerson's terms, as Man Thinking. He is brilliant, interested
in the political and personal, in hard critique as well as praise, fascinated by
science and philosophy but also by the day's weather and market fluctuations.
He can be very funny but, even so, uses his hilarity for multiple means:

> I just want you to know I'm perfectly
> serious much of the time: when I kid around
>
> I'm trying to get in position to be serious:
> my daffydillies are efforts to excuse the

> presumption of assumption, direct address, my
> self-presentation: I'm trying to mean what I
>
> mean to mean something: best for that is a kind
> of matter-of-fact explicitness about the facts. . . .
>
> (54)

He can wink at us with his self-aware presence; "(check that rhyme)" be nudges at one point. He can let rip the most inventive, spirited catalogues of "stuff":

> The heap of knickknacks (knickknackatery),
> whatnots (whatnotery), doodads, jews-harps,
>
> belt buckles, do-funnies, files, disks, pads,
> pesticide residues, nonprosodic high-tension
>
> lines, whimpering-wimp dolls, epichlorohydrin
> elastomotors, sulfur dioxide emissions, perfume
>
> sprays, radioactive williwaws . . .
>
> (108)

and then minister to our most practical necessities. Here he employs (and mimics) the instructional pragmatism of Franklin's *Autobiography* and of *Walden* in his enumerated "elaboration to prize the essential":

> (1) don't complain—ills are sufficiently
>
> clear without reiterated description: (2) count
> your blessings, spelling them over and over into
>
> sharp contemplation: (3) do what you can—
> take action: (4) move on. . . .
>
> (55)

Ideal and useful, punning and pensive, this voice is a dazzling dance of purposes and speculations, made of whatever material it finds at hand, a patchwork of the cast-off, the trashy, the high-brow, the stern, the inventive, and the true.

This poem's technical style is as sinuous and connective as its subject. Speaking about the cyclic patterns in nature, which "likes a broad spectrum approaching disorder so / as to maintain the potential of change," Ammons also reminds us that such is the method of his writing: "things that go around sometimes go / around so far they come back around: if you // like my form, experience my function" (100). In this way, subjects transmute into others, often recurring, and winding back around to themselves. Where *Sphere* was composed in triplets, *Garbage* is made of couplets, open-ended, highly enjambed, cracked open, making for dramatic momentum. The connection of phrases here illustrates a sort of formal curiosity and encouragement, a push of aesthetic energy. This is not blank verse or syllabic construction (lines here range from seven to twenty-four syllables, most often running between ten and thirteen) nor a reintegration of William's triadic line, though I have heard each of these explanations supposed. Nor is Ammons's lineation accentual, though a five-stress line predominates. In fact, I find the most consistent and remarkable formalization in *Garbage* to be, not the line, but rather the sentence. Indeed, in a poem whose length is nearly 2,500 lines, there are only a handful of sentences. Ammons much prefers the colon to the period, as if to suggest the evolving pattern of his vision. Ammons's colon serves two important purposes: it is connective, extending the imperative relationship of one idea or image to another; and it is explanatory, indicating that each new discourse or narrative is the result or solution of the last, and that each new clause will serve as the forebear of the next. The result is a tumbling, dynamic, resourceful rhetoric and form, able to contain and employ whatever comes its way:

> the rabbit's
> leaps and halts, listenings, are prosody of
>
> a poem floating through the mind's brush: I
> mix my motions in with the mix of motions, all
>
> motions cousins, conveyors, purveyors, surveyors,
> rising from the land, eddying coils of a wash,
>
> bristling with fine-backed black clarity as with
> brookripples over stone, spreading out. . . .
>
> (84)

Garbage may be one of the central poetic accomplishments of our time. With *The Book of Nightmares,* with Rich's achievements, with Merwin's dark lyrics, this poem can tell readers of poetry far into the future what our lives were like at millennium's close, what we thought, what we feared, where we looked for hope. When their archeologists assess our rubble, they will find this simple dignity there: "to pay attention is to behold the / wonder, and the rights, of things. . . ." (94).

INTERVIEWS

An Interview with A. R. Ammons

Cynthia Haythe

In "Grace Abounding," A. R. Ammons remarks, "Ah, what an abundance is in the universe." His work suggests that abundance both in its multiplicity—he has already published fourteen books of poetry and won the National Book Award for the *Collected Poems 1951–1971*—and in its inclusiveness. Refusing to limit himself to any single, static viewpoint, he prefers diversity and motion, seeking to "lean in or with or against the / ongoing so as not to be drowned but to be swept effortlessly / up upon the universal possibilities." In his attempt to explore "everything," Ammons not only experiments with a variety of forms that range from the tiny, circular "Small Poem" to the book-length, linear *Sphere,* but also willingly surrenders perfection to a wholeness that accommodates garbage, weeds, and rust:

> How does the pot pray:
> wash me so I gleam?
>
> prays, crack my enamel:
> let the rust in.
> ("Utensil")

At the same time, Ammons is unmistakably a Southerner—one of the South's finest poets. While his work transcends regionalism and speaks to everyone, it also reflects the stratified and neoclassical outlook of the traditional South. His vision is essentially moral in its advocacy of the classical ideal of moderation and in its recognition of the need for wisdom as well as for knowledge. Exhibiting a sense of degree reminiscent of Alexander Pope, Ammons cautions against excess in *Tape for the Turn of the Year:*

> rely on feeling—
> till it goes too far:
> then

Originally published in *Contemporary Literature* 21 (Spring 1980): 173–90. Reprinted by permission.

> on sweet reason which
> recalls, restores, and
> levels off. . . .

He welcomes new scientific discoveries, but simultaneously sees the importance of reconciling them with timeless ethical and spiritual values. In "Discoverer," he juxtaposes "Kepler's equal areas in / equal times" with "the words of / the golden rule," and he warns all of us not to forget the past as we move toward the future: "feed the / night of your seeking with clusters / of ancient light."

In particular, Ammons remembers his own past. He misses the North Carolina farm which was his home before he married and moved to New Jersey and then to Ithaca, New York, where he has lived and taught at Cornell University since 1964. Ammons, like many Southerners, feels caught between tradition and change. Trying to balance them, he writes poetry "about" the modern South and about the way it might define its future: "too traditional is loss of / change: too changing is / loss of meaning & memory." Most criticism has emphasized his affinity with the romantics, often linking him to Emerson and Whitman, but the following excerpt about North Carolina reveals an awareness of his own limits:

> I stand on the stump
> of a child, whether myself
> or my little brother who died, and
> yell as far as I can, I cannot leave this place, for
> for me it is the dearest and the worst,
> it is life nearest to life which is
> life lost: it is my place where
> I must stand and fail,
> calling attention with tears
> to the branches not lofting
> boughs into space, to the barren
> air that holds the world that was my world. . . .
>
> ("Easter Morning")

My interview with Ammons took place in December 1978 in Ithaca.

Q.   I want to ask you a few questions about your connections to the South because so many reviewers have spoken about you as an Emersonian poet. In your *Diacritics* interview with David Grossvogel you spoke about discrediting the South religiously and intellectually, though you could not emotionally. I wonder if you could say a little more about that: religiously and intellectually you had to break away, but emotionally you feel bound?

A.   My father was a Baptist and belonged to the New Hope Baptist Church, which was about two miles from our house. And my mother was a Methodist since—well, I won't say since—her name was McKee. But there was no Methodist church near us in the country: the nearest church was a fire-baptized Pentecostal Holiness about a mile away. So I was located in at least a Trinitarian disposition with three churches. On Sunday, when no important sermons were to be expected, we would just go to the nearest church. I would always bring a penny, I remember. I never brought—that I can think of—more than a penny to Sunday School. Isn't that amazing? And we were lucky if we had a penny to bring. But anyhow, that religious saturation was very intense for me.

Q. How long would a service last?

A. Well, often we would only go to the Sunday School session, which would last, say, half an hour to forty-five minutes. And then if any of the adults in the family had come, we might stay for the sermon, and that could take anywhere from half an hour to two-and-a-half hours because they often did achieve high physiological levels of involvement and so sometimes would take a long time.

I was sitting on the bow of a destroyer escort in the South Pacific when I was nineteen, and we had anchored near one of the islands. For some reason the level at which the ocean was striking the island—which was a very sharp bank—made me begin to think of that early experience and to think of the details. I could hear roosters crowing ashore and could see little shacks made of fiber—bamboo or whatever. I had an intuition of what life must be like there without the war going on. And then there was the level of the ocean separating the top—the farm and roosters and hens and houses—from the nature of the reality right under the level of the water. I guess that language would be submarine: shells and fish and all that. And it seemed to me that a personal god had not decided exactly what should be above and what below that water line, and that it had fallen out that way as a result of the way the world and the universe were made, and that whatever the nature of God, I would associate him with that, not with the incarnate shell, chicken, hut, coop, or whatever. The experience lasted for a split second but had an intensity that you never would forget if you lived to be a thousand.

Q. It was like Proust eating the madeleine.

A. Yes. You know just like that that something's different. But, you see, then I didn't know it intellectually, how it was to be different. When I went to Wake Forest, I began to read the histories of the individual books of the Bible to get some idea of where that came from—where that word came from—and I began to learn that there were three Isaiahs perhaps, that the style of this was different from that. I learned that Genesis was mainly traceable to Sumerian origins, to the mythologies of another culture and civilization, and that . . .

Q. And the two stories of the Creation.

A. Right. I began to work my way intellectually out of the framework that I had been raised in.

Q. But emotionally?

A. Emotionally, I was still there—and still am. I think there's no getting over the early hell-fire sermons. And terrorizing visions of the consequences of doing this, that, and the other are very deep in me and I'll never be able to get rid of them, unfortunately.

Q.   A sense of sin?

A.   Punishment. Sin and punishment, yes. It leads me to congratulate most of mankind, who must be very thick-skinned if sermons have to be that intense to reach them, because they could have been twenty-five times milder and gotten the message across to me. So I'm only too glad to get out of that particular aspect of the South. I don't live there. I'm not interested in it. And I wish I were freer of it than I am.

Q.   You also said that you come from a rural and defeated South. This sense of a defeated South . . . do you feel it has come into your poetry or into your sense of things?

A.   Oh, yes. It's the Civil War I'm speaking of. I knew that my great-grandfather on my father's side—a man named Joshua Ammons—was killed in the Civil War.

Q.   Do you know which battle?

A.   No, I don't. But I knew that he was educated in Ireland, and consequently was educated, whereas my grandfather, I think, was not, nor did my father go beyond the fourth grade. But there was an educated Ammons somewhere way back there, and he was the one killed in the Civil War. And he wrote home letters that were lost. They were in the bottom of my aunt's trunk, and a young child got in and destroyed them just before I heard of their existence. One never gets over the loss of a great-grandparent like that because he was from Ireland and had no involvement or investment in the things that caused the Civil War one way or the other. But he lost his life. So we were defeated. And I identify very deeply with that defeat, and it seems to me that the South did not become the thing it wished to be.

Q.   Which was?

A.   Which was whatever it wished to be. It wished not to be a part of the rest of the country, and it was not allowed to become what it wished to be. And I think that translates very quickly from national to personal feelings and reverberations. Then later, I discovered that a great-grandfather on my mother's side of the family also was killed, and that merely traumatized me further. So, yes, I identify very deeply with the South emotionally and historically, in some ways. How could I not? I was born in a house on a fifty-acre piece of ground—twenty-five acres of that woods, and twenty-five acres cleared—and lived the first seventeen years of my life there, and didn't leave the county even, except to go on a picnic when I was twelve years old. That was the first time I had ever been out of the county. So, no, I will never be other than that, such as it was.

Q.   How do you feel about living in the North? Do you have a sense of yourself as an exile?

A.   Yes.

Q.   Almost in the sense of a Joycean exile surviving by cunning?

A.   Yes. I was born in 1926, fifty years after the end of that war, but I still feel that the politics of the South went underground with its defeat and that the politics of the rest of the country is another matter. So here I sit in the North, not very much involved with the politics going on around me because it doesn't seem to me to be my country.

Q. Why do you stay in the North?

A. Except for some fairly early acceptances of poems for *The Southern Review* by Guy Owen, the South has never welcomed my poetry particularly, or encouraged it at all. But the North has. And the North has given me a job, has read my poetry, has been very friendly to me—in comparative terms, very friendly. And I live here rather happily, I think, but isolated.

Q. Would you now be just as isolated in the South?

A. I discovered that I was when I went back, after twenty-five years, for a year. It has to do with a twenty-five-year transformation of the self in another location such as the North. And then when you go back, you really can't go home again because *you've* changed, not because the home changed, although it did. I found myself as much a stranger there as here. So I'm now literally homeless.

Q. What enables you to survive in that state?

A. I survive by a kind of ambivalence of hiding and by such an extrusion of creativity.

Q. If you see everything, you see nothing?

A. That's right—everything having been so intricately presented that the revelation blinds out all penetration of sight.

Q. You also spoke in that previous interview of a solitary individual who has a fury in him to go back to his own order and possess it somehow. One might even think of Allen Tate's notion of the Southerner taking hold of his tradition by violence. Don't you suppose that in the future when people teach courses in Southern American literature, you certainly will be on the curriculum?

A. I already am.

Q. You are a Southern writer.

A. Yes, I am.

Q. Do you want to be more recognized as such?

A. When was that interview? That was 1973, wasn't it? Well, I went back and spent the year 1974–75 there.

Q. At Wake Forest. Did you feel you possessed it?

A. I did.

Q. Tell me more about that.

A. They told me that . . . I can't really say this. I possessed it enough and was glad to be re-dispossessed.

Q. You were re-dispossessed?

A. I re-dispossessed myself.

Q. What did you do down there?

A.   I came the hell back to Ithaca. I think if I had remained in the South, I never would have written my poems about the South.

Q.   Do you feel affinities with any of the Southern writers?

A.   Not really. When you speak to me of literature, all regionalism vanishes from my mind. . . . I don't associate regionalism or anything Southern with anything literary. I think they could be associated, but my concerns with literature are almost exclusively literary.

Q.   The sense of looking for a home, for instance, that figures so largely in your work: do you feel affinities with Thomas Wolfe's *Look Homeward, Angel?* I associated the skipper in your poem "Raft" with Huck Finn and his raft. But perhaps those are things you're not aware of, not conscious of when you're writing?

A.   I'm not conscious of them, certainly. But, number two, I'm not doing it because I'm Southern.

Q.   Do you think it could be almost innate?

A.   Oh, yes. I believe in that.

Q.   It seems to me that one could find all sorts of connections in your work with the Fugitive poets. And, looking at some of your very early poems, one might think of Edgar Allan Poe and Gothic affinities.

A.   I think so. And I'm going to show you some of the very early ones that confirm it even more clearly.

Q.   I want to ask you some questions about your readers: do they write you a lot of letters and ask for help and criticism?

A.   Yes, they do. I don't know how many a lot is because I haven't spoken with other poets. But I would say I get an average of three or four letters a week of that kind, which seems to me a lot. I can't answer it all. But the thing I get the most of are booklets and pamphlets of poems that are just sent to me, and I simply have become unable to respond. You know what that would involve: to sit down and actually read a pamphlet of poetry would take hours, and to think about it and try to respond in any way that would actually be useful to the person. . . . It's just out of the question.

Q.   In *Sphere,* you say that you don't understand your readers, that they complain about your abstractions and want you to be more political. Are you referring to some of the letters you receive?

A.   No, to reviewers. Reviewers nearly always say my language is conceptualizing rather than being experiential, and so on. And then I felt all during the sixties, as a Southerner, emotionally unable to make any commitment to what was going on around me. I felt very defensive about my lack of political involvement. When I was a kid, I thought the greatest thing in the world would be to grow up to be rich enough to buy a nice mule. Now I have money to buy a great mule. . . .

Q.   Like Silver?

A.   Silver was an old, boney, worn-out mule and could just barely get along. And so I used to *dream* of having this frisky, wonderful mule. And it seemed to me the greatest thing in the world would be to be able to own one. Now that I could own several, the value is totally irrelevant. So there I was, standing in the middle of the sixties, unable to make any connection between my own past and the events that were going on around me. I felt very defensive and lost. That's what I was complaining about. They want me to be political, but what I do instead of individuating in that direction is to go just the other way toward the deeper layers that we all share. Northerner or Southerner or Easterner or Westerner—what it would take to discover a more generalizable human value rather than a surface, defined, political, issuistic, Movement value.

Q.   Actually, your poems are very political.

A.   That's what I say: All I mean to do is to overturn the Western mind! For that, you don't need a political movement: you need something more radical. That's where I would head—toward the deepest roots of the frameworks by which we dispose ourselves in social and political ways.

Q.   The dedication to *The Snow Poems* reads "for my country." And you showed me an article about you that was published in *People* magazine in 1975. Do you have a sense of wanting to reach everyone in the country? Do you want to be a popular poet?

A.   I do. In the deepest possible way. I would like for the people who are like the people I was raised with, many of whom could barely read or could not read at all, and who were not very well educated . . . those are people I would like to speak to.

Q.   Yet your poems are quite difficult.

A.   Are they really difficult? The corpus, yes. But individual poems can be very accessible, don't you think? I dedicated that book "for my country," which someone has pointed out is a gesture of such size that it's quite ridiculous. But that's not what I meant. Again, it was sub-political. I meant this land—the land I worked as a boy— as being land like other people work everywhere in this country. And I do feel a very deep connection to that soil. And I will say it's for "my country," meaning the United States of America. But if that's taken from me, then "my country" the South. And if that's reduced for me, then "my country" the farm I was raised on. But the nature of the connection is not one to be diminished regardless of the size. So it's for my country. I meant it absolutely. And I still do. My whole theory of poetics has been, as you know, to work out some centralizing means that will not lose contact with the *least* particular, democratically speaking—the coincidental, the single person in the farthest reach. And I have distrusted any centralizing means that is willing to give up whole regions and areas of experience. Yes, I would like to speak to the common man.

Q.   Does this wish to be a democratic or popular poet influence your level of language at all?

A.   I think the way it influences me is that when I have a choice, I choose the word most highly polished in use—that is, the central vocabulary, the monosyllabic often, though I throw in a lot of polysyllabic words. I don't throw them in because they're polysyllabic, but because they happen to be words that point to very particular things. But the main body of my poetry aims toward the use of the central vocabulary, I think. Daily usage. That's what I mean to do, anyhow.

Q. How do you reconcile this wish to be a democratic poet with a wish to climb to the "top" or to go to a specialized and rarefied landscape?

A. I experience a double sense about that. Number one, yes, I want to speak to the common man. Number two, however, is how do you do this? And it seems to me that it works the same way in personal terms as it does in poetic terms. The poem is at once a single poem and representative or symbolic of other poems or experiences. There's no doubt that the ambition in my poetry is unlimited. It's terrifying, in fact. But it seems to me that the way one represents the common man most broadly is to achieve the highest position from which to represent him: that is to say, if you speak to the common man as a common man, nobody's going to listen, right? Which doesn't mean that you aren't still speaking as a common man. You must simply write the best poetry you can so that what you think about the common man will be heard, rather than not. That's the way I feel right now: I would like to speak to the common man, but I would also like to represent him.

Q. A lot of your poems are about mountains. How do you feel now that, in a way, you're a mountain?

A. Astonished!

Q. Do you feel any anxiety about reaching a height and then never again being able to achieve the same height?

A. I think one suffers from that more earlier in one's development when the whole enterprise of your writing seems somewhat fragile. And then you do a really good poem and begin to fear that that was your height and that you'll never revisit that height. That's a terrible self-intimidation and anxiety of the early years. But I think now that I feel myself almost delivered forth, if I may use such language, and that what I do now, positive or negative, pro or con, will only slightly influence all the writing I've done.

Q. Could you say something about the poem that recently appeared in *Epoch,* the one about society liking your unconventional verses best?

A. This brings up a very complex area. First of all, let me speak about the readers again. I mentioned getting pamphlets and booklets from people, but I did not mention the personal letters I get from readers, and I get a good many of them. They are at a very intense level of participation with me and, as I identify them, they are from lonely people—people as lonely as I am in that essential sense in which one knows that one is one person and in one body. I get letters from people that are very deeply moving to me. So I have a very strong attachment to readers.

Now, on the other hand, if you live in a university community, you constantly hear things being explained. It gets to the point where it looks as if the explanation is going to replace the reality. You get articles about the role of the artist in society, and you hear that from so many directions that one day the opposite occurs to you, about the role of society in the artist. That was the title of the poem you speak of. That sets off, though, a prepared chain of reactions, I guess, in that it seemed to me that our society does push us away or keep us away or throw us away from its more rigid structures, wishing not to have them changed in any way, at first. So you feel really intensely alone as a young artist.

Then, however, you start to be accepted and known a little bit here and there, and you find the other side of society showing up. Though it has protected its rigid structure, it is also aware that it is trapped and wants to be changed to some extent. And then it begins to give you honors. This very person, formerly rejected, is now almost humiliated with honors from the society, to the point that he becomes disgusted with the very people whose praise he sought. This infuriates him even more, and he goes off and writes even more unconventional verse, which the society finds that it likes *even* better than it liked the original ones. And, at that point, the nausea is at such a level—and the fire and fury at such a level—that instead of having the society say, "To hell with you (the artist)," the artist says to society, "To hell with you." And that's a scary poem. But it plays through a system of feeling from beginning to end. It certainly doesn't represent all that I feel about society, one way or the other—it's that poem playing its possibility.

Q.   So, in a way, that poem is about success.

A.   Yes.

Q.   Society is almost something that devours you. In a sense, it won't let you fail anymore. Anything you do is all right.

A.   Using no more judgment now in accepting you than it used in rejecting you. That's the unpardonable thing, that society doesn't really expend any time on perceptual accuracy or judgment or exposure to the material either way.

Q.   In *Sphere,* you speak about "this sow century."

A.   Actually, I love sows! But let's face it, they can slouch around sometimes pretty much. It does seem to me that with World War II, the Korean War, the Vietnam War and so on, it's been a very troubled and horrifying century, especially in the middle, which is the middle of my own maturity. In *Sphere* I identified that with the long slouch of a sow belly.

Q.   If you had to pick a time in history in which to live, which time would you pick?

A.   I have no such choice, but I really think maybe it wouldn't be now. It would be about the early nineteenth century in America, or the seventeenth century.

Q.   Why?

A.   I think of America when it was rural . . . the village rural community without cars or that kind of transportation . . . with horses and streams and a nearly pure environment of streams and sky. It must have been very beautiful. Spiritually, I don't know. I think I would suddenly fly way back to something Sumerian or pre-Socratic. I would like to live in a pagan, pre-Christian society.

Q.   Looking back now, how do you feel about your poems in *Ommateum?*

A.   I like them because they seem to me very highly assimilated. That is, without my being very conscious of it at the time, they tell a little story. Each one tells a little story which is like a small myth or a small ritual. And it seems to me that the level of compression and emotional intensity that I was able to achieve by those stories was pretty strong. I certainly think I've written many looser poems since some of those early Ezra poems. I still like some of them very much, to tell you the truth.

Q.   Do you feel any affinity with eighteenth-century England?

A.   I do. I think that century plays out so beautifully some of the formal possibilities, from the high Augustan to the deliberately made ruin. I like that wide range, and I use it myself. I say in one of my poems, "We should all be a shambles." There are times in the world when it wouldn't be appropriate to be in any condition except a shambles. And I like the eighteenth century because it seems to me to support both poles of that extremity of formal value.

Q.   Are there any writers in the eighteenth century that you particularly admire, novelists as well as poets?

A.   I love all the novelists. I know them because I once had a course. The earlier part of the century troubles me more because it carries over from Dryden a little bit in a heavy way for me, although I just read Pope's "The Rape of the Lock" again the other night and enjoyed it a great deal.

Q.   I find that sense of "mock" in your poems a lot. Do you have any notion, like the eighteenth-century writers, of wanting to write epic and of writing mock epic instead, simply because of the times we live in?

A.   Yes, I do. David Ray called *Tape for the Turn of the Year* a mock epic. I think I hadn't been very much aware of that when I wrote it, but then could see the justification for it.

I mentioned that I had this course in the eighteenth century with Bronson at the University of California. He was a very good teacher, and he brought into the classroom a good deal of material not in the text. Street cries of the sellers. And he brought in information about the jails, about the condition of the jails. The eighteenth century had that polarity—real elegance, but just the most incredible lower strata of society.

Q.   I think of Gay's *The Beggar's Opera*.

A.   Right. And you know Johnson's London poem, which shows a pretty rough style of life.

Q.   That discrepancy between high and low certainly does run through your poems. Do you think reviewers have made too much of you as an Emersonian?

A.   I don't think so. I really didn't read Emerson that much or that well before Harold Bloom started speaking of him. When Harold began to speak of my connection to Emerson, I went back myself to try and confirm or renounce this thing, and I found, in nearly every paragraph, a man speaking my central concerns more beautifully than I could say them myself. There's just no doubt about it. I would *love* to renounce it because no one wishes to be that much like or influenced by anyone. But Emerson says the very thoughts that I think I've come up with on my own. I certainly haven't paid much attention to him, but I can open his work at almost any place and see a better thinker and a better writer saying my material for me, for the most part. Thank God he didn't do water colors, as far as I know!

Q. Well, your poems are better than his poems!

A. (laughing) I think my poems may be better than his poems. But I admire them, nevertheless.

Q. How would you reply to those reviewers who accuse you of being a cold poet?

A. I would say they're right. There is an aspect of my work that's defensive. I should appear cold to almost anyone on first contact with my work. But it seems to me that the more of the work they know, the more it returns to them, the more another nature—welcoming and generous, I think—would begin to emerge. Because I don't offer myself quickly or easily to anyone. I'm very defensive and withdrawn.

Q. What were some of the thoughts you had in mind when you dismantled the unity of *Expressions of Sea Level* for the *Collected Poems? Expressions of Sea Level* has its own order, it seems to me, so that the last poem, "Nucleus," looks back at "Raft" and the first poem, "Raft," predicts "Nucleus." One sees "Raft" differently after reaching "Nucleus" and one sees "Nucleus" differently when one remembers "Raft." Why did you dismantle that order when you put those poems in *Collected Poems?*

A. Oh, my. It hurt me to have to do that. I think that *Expressions of Sea Level* is one of my best books. And they produced it beautifully. But I was controlled by that statement of Emerson's—or rather, I was controlled by a sentiment in myself, expressed by Emerson when he said, "In this life that God allows me, let me record from day to day my honest thought without prospect or retrospect." I've forgotten how the rest goes, but it's something like "I have no doubt that my days will appear to have been symmetrical," that some underlying unity will emerge if you remain loyal to the chronology and truthfulness of each day. So when it came time to do the *Collected Poems,* I went for chronology, thinking that I might misjudge the symmetries in making an individual book. I had to decide whether I would be loyal to the symmetry of the book or loyal to some symmetry in myself that I might not even be able to apprehend. I chose the latter because I thought it truer . . . deeper . . . truer to experience than the fabricated book.

Q. Do you think of yourself as a major poet?

A. It depends on the poets you name in that category. I would not put myself among the greatest poets. But if you mean by major poet "one who has found a sufficient means to deal with what he knows," then I think I have found that. Perhaps some great poets have written only short poems, but I think it is still true that our greatest poets have also written long works. Chaucer. Milton. Spenser. Shakespeare. You name them. They're big poets in terms of size and the dimension of the enterprise. In a lyric, you must aim at something essential because you only have time to capture a single thing in its essentiality. You're not multiplying your responses. You're finding the one central response that will find its pure tincture in that single poem. In a philosophical poem, or the larger poem, you're looking for something very different, it seems to me. You're looking for a structure that will satisfy *all* the responses that the human mind and feelings are capable of. You will want vivid images. You will want deep, controlling symbols. You will want a sense of a compressed, mythical narrative at the center. You will want to respond to ideas and statements about the world. You're looking for a controlling system that answers the human spirit in whatever way it shows up. But the lyric doesn't intend to do that. It intends to do something else, just as beautiful but, it seems to me, numerically slighter . . . smaller and purer.

Q. I think of "great" poets as having written large poems that take in a cosmos.

A. Which can have its own structure, hierarchy of value. And that's when tradition begins to be meaningful . . . how that hierarchy finds itself, which value outflanks another.

Q. Could you say a little more about hierarchy?

A. Well, for example, I know of a splendid poet who can write poems of such sensuous intensity that the theme or the object, usually in nature, that he's writing about seems to appear before the mind's eye. It's a beautiful talent and something Keats was so great at, remember? That's a single thing that we need, and he does it beautifully. But we need other things. We need for that sensuous vividness to be placed in another framework until we have a sense of an adequate system that will answer us spiritually and physically in a real way. That's all I mean about hierarchy. The human mind cannot get away from that, as far as I'm concerned . . . the idea that we do stack our values one way or another. And even more fundamental, we cannot handle all the million bits of information that we receive every day except by subgrouping them under controlling suborders and symbols. Otherwise, I think, we would be inundated by the capacity of our body to pick up so much information during the day.

Q. Are the levels rigid or are they moving and changing?

A. Changing. Changing all the time. I see it more clearly when I drop back to something like Sumerian civilization and see the priest there, occupied with—among other things—structuring the pantheon. Who's the top god? That is, what force is primary in their life? What's second? It was sky, air, earth—those very large, general entities. And then there would be more local gods. And finally the household gods, which have a very particular interest for one particular person. And he would have his little god on the shelf, right? I'll never forget that letter of Stevens when he's writing to somebody overseas and says "and get me one of those little wooden Buddhas about six inches high. And every morning when I wake up, it will do me good!"

I don't see how we can get away from amassings of that kind, and valuations. And I say that as a person who would run to the defense of the particular practically as fast as my legs would go. But I'll also begin to group them and say, "Now why don't you go off and do that" and "You go over here and do this."

Q. We could talk about this in relation to your water colors. I had the sense that you're exploring there a landscape that you haven't really explored in your poems; a level you've chosen not to deal with as much as the sky or the air or the earth. You tend to avoid going below the earth or below the ocean. And yet, in the paintings, you seem to be exploring that landscape. Is it a landscape that's too dangerous to explore in the poems, but that somehow can be dealt with in your paintings?

A. I think, at that time, I would not have been able to do it in words. And I can't do it now in words. But I can do it in colors and designs. For example, you know Ashbery's work. John Ashbery is able to write poems in which he has tonalities, surfaces, incoherences, things that I can do in paintings, but I cannot do in words—or I will not. There's something about sense that's communicated with something like the Bible—I think this is where the religion comes back in. I associate word and religion so closely that, to me, you do not have the right. . . . I can't take upon myself the right to disturb the coherence of language. I just can't do it. But I can sit there and start a painting and almost deliberately and willfully do the perverse, the discontinuous, the nonorganic juxtaposition.

Q. It is an unconscious kind of landscape.

A. Yes. They are primordial forms, mainly chucked up: phallic and vaginal, and other deep forms of the energies.

Q. Sometimes, you seem to see that landscape as a fearful place. Other times, however, you see there the very source of the imagination and creativity. You speak both of "subterranean fires" and "refreshing energies of the deeper self." You have to go there to receive energy and force. At the same time, it's a force that could completely overpower you . . . the conscious mind. Do you feel it's a region you have to go to? Do you feel that any poet needs to go periodically to that source?

A. I think I feel just about what you've said. It seems to me if anything is *too* outlined and surface, then it may be drained of any intensity or forming energy. That's bad. The other side of that . . . if you should hit so deep a level of the mind that you have mere energy without structure or any kind of self-declaring means, that would be bad. And so there's some intermediate level that is mixed delight and fright where various levels of formal means announce fresh energies, summon those energies up truly, as much as possible.

I've always been impressed by Ashbery. When he was here, he said that he began his poems often in the most deliberate way. He would just sit down and jostle words around on the side of the page until something would begin to emerge. That doesn't sound like a very deep level of participation. But, on the other hand, it is a kind of conjuration of parts that could get up into a very complicated frame of mind. And it does. And very beautifully. I can't do that in poetry. I never come to a poem a little at a time. I wait until it possesses me. But, with paintings, I'm just like Ashbery. I can sit down and pour a little paint out on the paper, wiggle it around some, push it here, and after a while I begin to see emerge a possibility. And I'm not all that deeply engaged in it—at first, at least—as I think perhaps he may not be at first in his poems. And this may be something I've invented on my own.

But it seems to me incredible that I write poems in such a different manner from my paintings, and that I can't write poems the way I paint, even though I think they speak to the same energies. I just can't do it the same way. I don't want to worry this point to death, but it interests me because I can't understand it. I think I'm onto a little bit of descriptive truth about those two ways of doing things. . . .

"A Place You Can Live":
An Interview with A. R. Ammons

PHILIP FRIED

MR: Did you say that you met William Carlos Williams?

A: I did. I used to be in the sales department of this company in south Jersey. On occasion, I would be up in his area and take him for a ride, because something had happened to Flossie's neck. Is Flossie still alive by the way? (William Carlos Williams' wife, Flossie, died in June of 1976 at the age of 86.) He couldn't drive after one or two of his operations.

MR: The strokes?

A: Yes. I would take him out for drives.

MR: I feel Williams' influence strongly in *Tape for the Turn of the Year.* Don't you mention a Williams event there?

A: Oh yes, the reception for Flossie after he had died, the reception for her in New York.

MR: Right. I feel Williams' spirit running through the *Tape:* a sense of persistence, love of the commonplace, and endurance.

A: I didn't begin by liking him that much. I remember when I came back from Berkeley in the early fifties and settled in south Jersey, some of his poems would come out, one called "The Symphony," I think, came out in *Poetry* magazine, and I really didn't care for that sort of poetry at that time.

MR: What were the qualities that turned you off?

A: It seemed to me somewhat an empty idea, somewhat inane to reproduce the sounds of a symphony. It sounded like writing a poem about a picture, which Williams would also do at times and that contains a distressing element in it. That seemed to me very empty, and also the language seemed to lose tension in the freedom of its flow at times. You know, I have been guilty of that myself subsequently, but in those early days, I was writing the Ezra poems myself, which were very highly assimilated symbolically and allegorically and

Originally published in the *Manhattan Review* 1.2 (Fall 1980): 1–28. Reprinted by permission.

didn't at all lend themselves to that kind of displaying or setting out. I didn't like it.

But Josephine Miles would continue to say to me in a card now and then: why don't you go see Williams. So, finally, ten years later, I did, and by that time, I had come to like his poems. I think it was a kind of political sociological change because I could see people more then than I could in those early days, when I was too transcendental to have any transactions with people!

MR: Was Josephine Miles an important influence on your work?

A: It was personal. I don't think that she and I have ever shared very much in regard to the theory of poetry. But I loved her as a person. She seemed to me so majestic. You know she's crippled and had been from the age of five. She so totally rose above that without denying it that I always had a tremendous respect and love for her.

I never did take any classes with her, but when I was out there (Berkeley) I used to show her my poems, and she would read them and comment on them, and that was a very valuable thing to me. By the way, she continued to do it, and she was the one person I chose out of the world to hassle. So I kept sending her poems, having no idea what a drain this was on her. But I would say on the average of two or three times a year, I would send her one or more poems to read and say something about. And it was a lifesaver to me, because in south Jersey I knew absolutely no one else in poetry.

MR: So you did have a sense of isolation when you were working in the business world?

A: It was total isolation. So much so that in 1956, this would be five years after leaving Berkeley—

MR: And a year after your first book.

A: That's right, which was a vanity publication.

MR: Dorrance.

A: That's right. By the way, they've begun to publish again after all these years.

MR: And it's impossible now to get your book anywhere. But there's a more positive aspect to publishing in such a way now; it is more accepted.

A: Oh, it should be, it is now.

MR: Of course, Whitman was a self-publication.

A: Yes, the trouble with it in those days was that the idea of dignity and credibility was based on this hardbound book. We've moved away from that now, so that a young poet can publish a booklet of his poems and be in just as good company as if Macmillan had done it in gilt-edged leather. That's a wonderful change that's taken place, and so most poetry today is published, if not directly by the person, certainly by the enterprise of the poet himself, working with his friends.

MR: What plan did you have for distribution when you did that?

A: I had no plan whatever. I guess Dorrance must have known that they wouldn't sell, so though they had said they would produce 300 copies, they actually may have printed 300 sheets, but they only bound 100 copies. And I think they eventually threw away the other 200 because they couldn't sell the first 100. In five years, it sold sixteen copies.

Then my father-in-law bought about forty or fifty and sent them to South America, to some of his customers, who couldn't read it.

In south Jersey, though, just to tie off the thread, a year after the publication of this book, I wrote away to the University of Chicago on a home-study thing. As it turned out, John Logan was the reader, and I had seen one or two of his poems which just started to come out in *Poetry* magazine. And so we did one or two lessons, but then dropped that, and I sent him some copies of my book, and he gave them to some people, and so it got one review, in *Poetry* magazine, as a result of that.

MR: When did you start writing? Were you in your teens?

A: Yes, it was nineteen actually. I was in the South Pacific during World War II. I had a little journal. You weren't supposed to keep journals, but I had one anyhow.

MR: Why weren't you supposed to?

A: Because it might be information for the enemy. You know, the war was still on. But I still have that log, telling every place we went and everything we did. Nothing very exciting, but I began to write then and continued through Wake Forest University, which had no writing courses in those days, but I wrote the whole four years.

Meanwhile, I was taking pre-med and science courses, and that's where the combination of poetry and science started. I was never aware that I was writing poetry with scientific terminology. I was just writing from where I was, which was a mixture of science and poetry.

MR: Did science come very naturally to you?

A: I did very well in science, except for embryology, which for some reason I had a terrible time in. I remember the identification of parts through slides was a very difficult thing. But in every other way, I was a very good student in science.

MR: What was it about science that especially appealed to you? Was it the sweep of theory or the precision?

A: I think a combination, and I think that I reacted instinctively then, and that I only now would try to say why. Of course, it would be a reconstruction on my part. I think that I had a strong need at that time to escape certain responsibilities of interpersonal relations and that science gave me a sense of an objective inquiry into an objective subject. And there's a kind of stability in that. It's sort of a pagan way of associating yourself with universals rather than with the coming and going of mortal things.

MR: That's interesting, science as pagan.

A: It seems to me that the pagan tradition is now represented by science. Of course, there have to be modifications, but if you think of the pagan societies as rather carefully paying attention to what the natural forces were around them and then trying to identify with and, as it were, listen to what that force was and appease it, and know something about it, learn its nature, then science does precisely the same thing today.

It puts aside, for the moment, its personal interest in things and tries to know what is the nature of that thing out there. I regard that as a very high value. The humanities often feel opposed to that because that attitude obviously puts human things secondary, whereas the humanities have often claimed that man is the center of everything and has the right to destroy or build or do whatever he wishes. Well, that's an exaggerated statement—just to put it briefly.

There was a very moving article in the *Midwest Quarterly* about what was called archeo-astronomy. It's a combination of archeology and astronomy, and it studies specifically the megaliths and henges like Stonehenge. There are thousands of those places where, through the erection of stone circles and so on, the people were able to bring themselves into correspondence with cosmic order and with the coming—by the way, today is the summer solstice—and that's what those stone circles meant to measure, the winter and summer solstices. But they allied impermanent man with the eternal structure of things.

I came home and told my wife that that article seemed the best review of my work I ever read, but it had nothing to do with it! It's not noticeable from here (referring to the watercolors he has painted and which hang in his house;) but circles and radial points coming from circles are very prominent in all my work, including the painting. Of course, then they talk about something called the sacred center, and once you have a ring of stones, as you approach the center of this, you approach the highest kind of integration you can imagine between the material and the spiritual, between the stone that lasts forever and the starlight which is ephemeral, between man and his time and the larger, apparently eternal.

MR: Poets today seem isolated in their writing; they don't connect with some of these other fields you mention. They seem to just cultivate sensitivity.

A: Do you think anyone who had any sensitivity would ever want to cultivate it? And anyhow we might have to distinguish between sensitivity and sensibility. I've always been worried about people who wanted to be poets, and this distresses me every time a new group shows up for a class. It seems to me if they had ever been hit by the instability and improbability—

MR: They would try to avoid it?

A: Yes. I think true poets are often in flight from their poetry, and it is only when they become fairly heroic that they can stand and look their own poetry and their own self in the face, because most of the big poets we know are monsters.

MR: Monsters in what sense?

A: Well, they're monstrous in their achievement or in their—the size of the pressure is so large and inhuman. It often seems not to be a structure that allows a great range of subtle values. There are those huge, excessive insistences that bring pressure not only on the poor poet himself but on everybody around him. I mean monstrousness of that size, of huge insistence, devouring insistence.

I think it's probably necessary that all people ought to be in flight from such things. It may be absolutely necessary for the vigor of the poetry for that kind of energy to have been invested in it, but it's not the kind of thing you wish to live with, it seems.

A parallel situation is the person who's very boring, let's say, and needs to feel moved, and he goes to the movies, and he finds that the more horrible the movie, the more he's moved by it. Someone who is likely to be a poet would be already overwhelmed by the death of an ant he had stepped on or something else. He wouldn't need to go to the movies to be stirred. He'd already be overstimulated.

Another thing, there are two kinds of poet here. One kind of poet feels very little apparently, or it isn't accessible to him. He has to hack at it. He has to build the poem, and he comes back revision after revision, working his energy up to where he has it. The other kind of poet is doing just the opposite. He has so much anxiety inside, so he's trying to dissolve it away, and instead of making large, hacking gestures to try to build energy into a system, he's being easy and quiet because he knows more is going on than he can handle, and he's trying to dissolve—

MR: Would you say that Lowell was a hacker?

A: Yes, Yeats, Lowell, yeah. I would say that Stevens was a man under great pressure and did beautifully cool things to try to cause it to subside.

MR: You put Stevens in the opposite camp. What about yourself?

A: I am certainly the opposite. Mr. Ashbery is in the opposite. But these two kinds of poet will never understand each other.

MR: So you don't do much revision?

A: You know, one does everything. And in my short poems, I go over them and over them testing them out. Often, I don't change more than a word or two, but sometimes the whole poem is radically changed.

But it is true that for the last ten years in particular, I have practiced over and over, poem by poem, to try to see if I could reach the absolutely crazy point where what is happening in my mind and what is happening on the page seem to be identical. That's the thing I'm working toward. The problem is that once you get there, it no longer seems necessary to write.

MR: Once you feel you can make that connection at will.

A: Once there seems to be a correspondence between the event and the word.

MR: What about the element of communication to a reader? Do you consider that extraneous?

A: It is for me. I'm never aware that I'm speaking to anyone, and I suppose I'm not. I never think of an audience or anyone out there to whom this poem is being addressed.

One thing I do sometimes think of, and that is that if I can get this poem right, then it will represent getting the poem right for other people. That is to say, what happens to me is representative of what can happen in other minds.

MR: So it's a kind of paradigm.

A: Yes, I'm trying to reach a paradigm, and once it's there, the shape is there, then if someone else wanted to test themselves against it . . . but I never have any feeling, direct feeling that there's something I know that I must tell you.

MR: But one of the strongest aspects of your work is the relationship you create with the reader, especially in the longer poems like "Hibernaculum" and *Sphere.* It feels to me like you are reaching out.

A: The thing is, how do you do this? How do you reach that person, and here's the room where I do my work, and obviously I can't shout loud enough to be heard by anyone. So what I have to do is make something, some vehicle that then that person will come in touch with.

That's what I'm listening for, the accuracy of that communication between me and the poem. Certainly I'm interested in communication, but that's not the first thing you have to do. First, you have to build a figure that will make communication possible.

MR: The appearance of your poems on the page seems important. Does this translate into reading out loud, or is it primarily a visual experience?

A: I've done a good many kinds of experiments, right? Some of them look like purposely regular stanzas and some don't. In some, the indentations correspond from stanza to stanza, the same line by line. But in some of them there is the random. I usually feel that I don't have anything to say of my own until I have tripped the regular world, until I have thrown the Western mind itself somehow off, and I think that's what those—if I began to write a sonnet, for example, I think I would be stultified and silenced by that form, because it's my nature to want to trip that form out of existence as a way of making room for myself to speak and act.

I think I feel the same kind of sociological confrontation with things like capital letters and periods, because that belongs to the world I want to dismiss. So I think by the indentation and other devices, I try to throw the expected response out of line and then, it seems to me, I can come through with my own way of saying what I have to say.

By the way, what I've just said is just an attempt at this point to give an explanation for something I did without thinking. It seems to me that the thing a writer must be faithful to is what he feels like doing, though he doesn't yet know why. He feels like doing it, right, and later on perhaps he or someone else, it won't need necessarily be the poet, can find out whether or not he was answering to something accurate within himself or the world around him when he did that.

MR: In "Coon Song" you tell the reader that you won't entertain him but in poems like *Sphere* you do seem to make an effort if not to entertain then to hold. Would you comment on that?

A: A colleague here recently taught that poem in one of his classes and he asked me to come the second day and talk with them. I did, and it's a poem that a reader can have more than one disposition towards (referring to "Coon Song"). But we discovered that once you identify with the coon, the poem clears up. So though it sounds as if there's a speaker in the poem talking against the reader, those things are reconciled if you adopt the point of view of the subject in question, the poor raccoon, who is being hounded by these animals and about to be destroyed by them.

I didn't take time to go through a full exposition of that because it takes a long time. Later on, it's true, I think it's in *Sphere* that I said something about wanting to hold someone's attention. Now, do you know that poem of Frost's about how the more we hide ourselves away, the more necessary it becomes to reveal something about ourselves? ("Revelation," by Robert Frost) Well, there's some such duality going on.

I think I feel that a great deal, that obviously I'm pretty hidden away here, especially with the typewriter at night, writing in a severe state of isolation. And I think I wish to hope that there's someone somewhere to whom I'm speaking and that this poem might bring me closer to. But there has to be a limit on that, because I don't want to be brought too close. But I think I may not be answering your question.

MR: One of the intriguing things about your longer poems is the oratorical voice that goes through so many changes, so many personae. Is it someone orating?

A: All right, I think there's something to that, but the confusion may come from the fact that I'm not always speaking for myself but for others. That's where representativeness comes in. Some of the time I'm speaking my own interest in the matter, and some of the time I'm trying to capture other interests that I have observed. So I try to speak for myself and for others, to the extent they might be able to interest themselves in that particular kind of speaking. At other times, I think the voice is simply a single voice saying, this is me. But not in the long poems. I think in the long poems there's more various kinds of—

MR: There's a drama between the personae. Sometimes it seems there's a medicine man, a circus barker, very showful types of voices, and this relates to your idea of showing forth. What is hidden and what is shown are constant concerns of your poetry.

A: This touches on some of my background, my southern background, and I mention it because I just read a piece by William Harmon on my poems, and he talks about—he said that they were 90% horse sense and 10% goofing around. That is true, in the South there is a great deal of interaction, and people don't tell you simply what they think and feel but they go into all these stories and anecdotes and jokes and they put on a show, and then they mean for the show to take the message through. I think I do that.

Also, the religious thing is very strong in my background, where we had all kinds of preaching and dancing and holy rolling and so on took place, including glossalalia or whatever it is.

MR: Speaking in tongues?

A: Yeah. I've seen people do that for hours.

MR: You do it a little bit in your poems.

A: Just a little. It's incredible to watch a person whose behavior is absolutely regular as if he were buying ham from a delicatessen speaking to you in totally understandable words. Not done in a frenzy. I remember sitting on a bench in church when a person so possessed would come directly and stand in front of you as if telling you how to bake a cake and would go through this rigamarole and be absolutely unintelligible.

MR: You said in an interview once that you felt you repudiated your southern background and yet I've felt this rhetorical thing not as a technique but as the southern background coming through strongly.

A: I think you're right.

MR: As far as spirit of place goes, you have northern landscapes and, of course, the beach and dunes, and yet in this approach we've been discussing you are southern. Why did you decide to leave the South?

A: A lot of things happened. First of all, my father sold the farm that I was raised on, so I knew that route was cut. I couldn't stay there.

MR: But you considered it, though.

A: Yes, I would have been a farmer, I think, but then I went in the navy.

MR: Were you about eighteen or nineteen?

A: Eighteen. But that gave me nearly enough credits to go to college, so when I came out I went. I knew I was relatively smart. I had been valedictorian in grammar school and in high school I had done well, so I figured that—oh, in high school I had been one of six people who had passed the college entrance exam. So I figured I had a chance.

Going to college, I began to inquire into this religious background which was so strong and so severe, and I got it more and more on a rational and historic level, which moved me intellectually from those positions that my family and aunts and uncles would have taken to be natural. See, I was already in exile in that country.

MR: In the sense that you—

A: Was no longer able to accept the doctrine familiar throughout my youth. So moving out of it was a kind of relief, and there at Wake Forest I met Phyllis, who was studying and teaching there a little bit. We got married my first year out of college, when I was principal of the elementary school in Cape Hatteras. And she said, why don't we go to Berkeley, because she had already gone out there a year or two before that.

I did a little graduate work there. Then we came back to south Jersey, which was her home, and I got a job there. And I had felt without interruption the tug to go back to North Carolina. That's my center, that's where my home is.

MR: You have a wonderful poem about going back there underground when you die.

A: But now, this is home, and I feel better here than anywhere in the country. I haven't lived in the South now, believe it or not, for 27 years. I've lived out of it longer than in it. But you know, those first years are crucial. So I guess I'm not at home in either place now, which is sort of terrible, but I'm more nearly at home here now.

MR: You know what southern writer you also remind me of? Faulkner. He wanted to say everything in one sentence. I feel that, too, about your long poems, with the use of the colon. You don't have any periods, and the poem moves; you build speed into it. You want to get everything in.

A: What is the Faulkner story where the giant comes crashing down at the end? It's a perfectly substantial and transsubstantial event at once, a pure illumination in imagination, a pure reality. I'll never be able to write that well. I think that's very beautiful. But you're surely right that it's something one longs to write . . . wedge everything in the world together.

MR: About the colons, was that an instinctive use of punctuation?

A: Yes, it was. I have since heard a great many explanations of the use of them, and they all seem quite reasonable to me. I think they're probably right.

What it feels like to me is a democratization thing, that I won't allow a word to have a capital letter and some other, not. That the world is so interpenetrated that it must be one tissue of size, of letters.

MR: Is that why you tell off Redwood trees?

A: Probably. I come from a pretty deprived background economically, and it was very rough; so it's been hard for me to learn how to deal freely with other people, and I think that language is a way of saying, here's a very complex, interwoven system where we insist that certain kinds of existence be equal for every member.

Also, in retrospect, I think of it as a sort of a geometric or topological surface like terrain, or "landscapes" is a very strong word in my poetry. Yeah, that they are—what is the skin called? Something like that, something that contains. So the colon jump should do that, just connect and connect and connect, until you build not just the assertion you're making but this landscape.

I've never been interested in single discursive statements as such, as explanation, but I'm interested in clusters of those, because then they become, they sort of come to be the thing they represent. They're many-sided.

MR: In your larger poems, you don't have isolated attitudes. Each attitude calls ahead to some future one that will, if not contradict it at least modify it. This creates a sense of emotional speed. The poem gets drawn from the future, pulled out of the present.

A: I may have said somewhere, but I think it's still true, that you don't want the poem to amount to no more than what you already knew when you began to write. Whatever kind of instrument it may be, it must be one capable of churning up what you didn't already know. That's what creativity is, and it is to be surprised by the end of the poem as much as you expect the reader to be surprised. That's why I think Frost is so right to say, you don't have the prepared last line and then try to write a poem that will end there.

MR: Do you write all your long poems in sequence?

A: That's right, I just begin. I do the same for the short poems; they're written the same way. I never—I can show you some drafts—"Corsons Inlet," that poem "Corsons Inlet" was written just like that, from beginning to end, in one sitting. I don't recommend that as being better than anything else. I'm just saying that's the way I did it. I came back to it, of course, and reconsidered it with my best judgment.

If you weren't learning something, what would be the use of doing it. So you can't write out of just what you know. There's no motivation for that. And so I feel always in agreement with that thing that Emerson said in the essay *Nature,* where he says let me record from day to day my honest thought. Today, I say exactly the way things seem to me. Tomorrow, I also say, and it may differ somewhat from what I said the day before, but the difference, while it may be interesting, is not as important as the hope, which he expresses, that if you go on doing this somehow or other you will come to know a deeper thing that unifies all these days. Whereas if you had tried to plunge towards that deeper symmetry directly, there would be no way you could get there.

MR: Which is the whole feeling behind *Tape for the Turn of the Year.*

A: If I go on just speaking, day-to-day, telling it the way I think it is, it may be that the sense of a presence which belongs to that poem will come to be, and will then interpenetrate—

MR: In fact, one day you could even say, as you do, that the prologue I wrote the day before seems phony and forced to me now.

A: Right.

MR: But you don't go back and cross it out.

A: No, it seemed honest then. This is what has seemed to me always so awful about Yeats when he decided to rewrite his youth. He says, it is myself that I remake, but it's himself that he unmakes. The early self was the early self. And he goes back and unmakes that self, and pours his old man into that young man.

MR: What guided you when you assembled your *Collected Poems, 1951–71?* I noticed that you changed the order of poems from the individual books. Were you restoring the original chronological order?

A: Yes.

MR: Then what led you to put them in a different order to start with?

A: That's a good question. I never had much respect for a single book of poems as an entity, although somebody liked the way I did *Expressions of Sea Level* very much and regretted the time when the dismantling of those books returned the poems to chronological order. But I've been interested in the whole work as a single poem and these minor divisions of it into books never seemed to me very interesting. So I'm still . . . my favorite is the *Collected Poems,* and a book like *Diversifications* means hardly anything to me until I get it back in its order. Eventually, if I do another collected poems—

MR: So it's very much in the spirit of *Leaves of Grass,* a single book which grows.

A: Except that I don't revise the early poems.

MR: In the poem "Plunder," you write about the poet as stealing something from reality, or hunting it. Doesn't this somehow lessen the poet's existential status?

A: Well, "Plunder" ends by saying that I'm "indicted." You know, there are two words—indicted to write, it's the old word for to write. But to be indicted by having trampled into those areas—I never understood that poem.

MR: The same thing emerges in a different way in "Motion." Words as music, as motion have as much reality as anything in the world, and yet as a referential system invented by man, words have only a secondary reality, not as important as things. Again, this would seem to put the poet at a disadvantage.

A: I was trying to deal with the difference between words and things. I was trying to insist that somehow, although there was no direct contact between words and things, the motion of mind and thought corresponded to natural motions, meanders, you know, the winds or streams. And that these might be parallel motions and where a level at which the representation was so basic and so close that it was nearly like actuality itself.

MR: There seems to be a little twinge that I hear when you say that. It's as though "nearly like actuality itself" is said with a certain poignance.

A: But you see it's more comforting, finally, to think that you don't touch actuality, because supposing you did? Supposing you could, literally, change something with your imagination, your words.

MR: But you do.

A: I know, but not in the real, not in the absolutely actual.

MR: But where is the absolutely actual? You're just as much the absolutely actual as a stone, and another person, whom you certainly influence and change by your words. Why not give them the full actuality of the stone?

A: Well, it goes like this. I just read, I had never read it before by the way, *The Consolation of Philosophy* by Boethius. He tries to describe the difference between providence and fate. Providence is that source of all things, ultimately God in his terminology, and fate is the action of that against us. We're trapped in that and must suffer the changes of things, but providence itself is this huge, constant, radiant possibility.

Well, you can't change that. And I'm not sure you can change actuality. On the fate side, we may recognize that we have to accept those limitations and the incarnation imposed upon us. So already, the imagination has had to step down a couple of spaces and what we can change, it seems to me, is the structure we make that we think represents things and is our fiction. We can change our fiction and we can change the way we feel about the fiction we make. But we can't really change actuality.

MR: In a Blakean sense—

A: If you're a kind of romantic-consciousness man and said that there is no reality except what I imagine or am conscious of. Emerson went that far. I have never been able. I looked through too many microscopes and drew the pictures of the bugs, so I can't believe that the world is a result of my consciousness.

I think I'm not clear about the place of the imagination in my scheme of things. As a farmer, I guess, I have always believed in the recalcitrance of the external world. You must plant the strawberry plant if you want to get strawberries. You remember that story, someone told me recently a story about Emerson. That one day he was trying to separate the calf from the cow, and he struggled with the calf and as soon as he pulled it away from the cow's udders, it was drinking milk, it would get right back, and this little girl came down the street and saw Emerson in this predicament, and she went over and stuck her finger in the calf's mouth and led it right away. Emerson said, that's what I lack, people who know how to do things!

I've had that yearning in me to know how to do things. But I don't have the freedom, imaginatively, to go out disposing certain kinds of things.

MR: Like Blake with his just obliterating of mountains.

A: Blake is a man I love dearly, because it seems to me he goes all the way, as you're asking us to do. I don't understand that. Isn't it funny how tongue-tied I am about that. I really don't understand the place of imagination in my work. I know that someplace or other I'm stopped, or that I stop myself, or that, through fear or incapacity, I don't know which—

MR: You do seem to be someone who is intoxicated by procedure. I say that in a positive sense. In so many of your poems, you have descriptions of various procedures.

A: How to do things.

MR: Yeah, and as you describe it, the emotion comes through. It seems like a kind of bending of the knee to the world.

A: But also it's like writing a poem, you know, you try to do it well.

MR: Right, and a lot of your poems seem to be concerned with their own procedures as they go along, they reflect back on themselves.

A: Procedure could come to be the essential narrative, you see.

MR: That's a very contemporary value.

A: Then the narrative would take on whatever mystifications and myths that would seem organically proper to it.

MR: Is that because we have no more good stories to tell?

A: Ummmhmmm.

MR: Do you believe that?

A: Well, I believe we don't know how to tell them. We haven't assimilated Freudian psychology, let's say.

MR: As a mythology?

A: Yes. As a symbology, at least, and I think we're puzzled by how to dispose certain materials that we had an accurate level for before, but now if you said a particular word, such as the word "penetrate" . . . I just read Boethius and the woman that he devised to be the representative of philosophy was, he says, sometimes a normal size of woman, but sometimes she was immense and she penetrated the heavens.

But then the word "penetrate" would stop us all, modern readers. I mean we would have to stop there and consider—what is implied by this woman, penetrater, you know, the text has become almost too dense at that point, but that's where we are, and in telling stories now we haven't assimilated the Freudian psychology and post-Freudian psychology well enough that we have returned to a level of innocent speech.

MR: Is that why there is more going on in criticism, with people like Barthes, for instance.

A: Yes.

MR: So you think this period is a stopgap, this dwelling on procedure is a temporary measure?

A: And the emphasis on analysis and criticism is a temporary emphasis. Eventually, we'll get back to the work of art. The imaginative construct is eventually where it is. That's where the energy comes from, and we'll get back there. It's very complicated, but somehow or other we haven't digested all that material and found new ways, a new stance of our own by which we can perceive, without loss of anything that we value, without being inhibited by what we know.

MR: That's a very delicate balance.

A: Very difficult. But if we could get there, we could tell a great story again.

MR: Faulkner told great stories.

A: Yes, but that's sort of pre-Freudian. I'm sure he knew Freud, but he doesn't engage it in his narratives. So in the meantime we have certain contours that compose a kind of narrative. It can be a narrative from one emotional state to another emotional state, if that will describe a figure and that figure, that narrational figure, is the level at which the poem sort of resembles a piece of sculpture. That is, it has found a figure of itself which is not speaking. It was made of speech, but it itself was perceived as silent, like a sculpture.

Many things at that point can be said about that figure, as you can say a great many things, as Barthes and others can say a great many illuminating and wonderful things about a piece of sculpture. But finally the marvelous thing is the figure. And that's what I think is the most we can seek in poetry today, to be accurate about the procedure sufficiently so that a figure comes to appear at the bottom that integrates the whole work.

MR: Do you ever see yourself as telling a story? Can you see yourself in the future—

A: I know that if I tried to write a novel, I would be utterly hopeless and it would be a complete shambles, that I have no fictional ability in the regular way, but I know that my deepest interest is narrative. You see, but I have to do it in poetry, and I have to do it without any resort to the traditional novel.

MR: Robert Penn Warren, for instance, writes narrative poems. In the "Ballad of Billie Potts," though I think he could have cut out the existential comments.

A: I don't know it that well, I have a vague memory. I think I see more than one kind of narrational interest in Warren. There is the surface one, which in his poems seems to have a resemblance to stories and novels and then there may be some deeper narrative, too. That's not true of myself. I have no surface narrational interest, but I am very much controlled by, and interested in, the deeper.

MR: Have you ever tried to write fiction?

A: Yes, I did when I was quite young. It came out sounding a lot like *Tobacco Road*. Glad I got rid of that!

MR: What about short stories?

A: I can't write fiction because I have a lot of problems with interpersonal situations, and I'm very lonely in life, in myself, and deeply afraid that what I feel about things is a minority view and that it would not stand for what other people—so I don't trust my ability to create a figure and then give him true motivation. Because I never believe when I know another person, such as you or anyone else, that I understand where he is coming from, or that I know what's motivating him. You know what I mean? That makes me feel pretty lonely, but it makes me totally certain that I would not be a fiction writer.

MR: But the poems that you write are a tremendous reaching out, in a very strong way.

A: Desperate, almost.

MR: Frost said that what he wrote was out of fear. Is that true for you? Is anxiety one of the motivations?

A: I think that it is definitely one of them, and this goes back to what we were saying towards the beginning, that writing is one way of dissolving the anxiety. You get something else to contemplate there other than the anxiety itself, you get this piece of writing. You may even be lucky enough to find a good line in it, and then that will tend to help things.

MR: I have the sense, too, that you are an epic poet, or a poet with epic ambitions, but also someone who distrusts and undercuts this. I sense this risk and problem in your work. The desire to do it, and the tension of the undercutting.

A: Which forces me to make what I have done provisional. I want to do it, but it must remain provisional, because there is some cinching step that I refuse to take. I don't know what that is, but there is a kind of ultimate commitment that up to now, fifty-four years old, I won't make.

MR: Does that relate to what you said about imagination earlier?

A: It could be, and that would be very interesting to know. There's something in me that wants to experience and say from my own point of view and other points of view, any number of potentially rich and wonderful things, but there is a step which I refuse to take, and I don't even know what it is. It is like believing that what you have just said is really the truth.

MR: I feel that in your long poems you'll have extremely eloquent passages—

A: And then just toss it away.

MR: Yes, then you're horsing around.

A: Yeah, just throw it completely away.

MR: Of course, you never, you don't throw it away.

A: What I mean, tonal.

MR: Sure.

A: Look how easy that was, but it was nothing. That kind of thing.

MR: I'm thinking of the passage in *Sphere* beginning, "there is a faculty or knack . . ."

A: Isn't that a nice passage? I like that.

MR: It's lovely, it's one of my favorites.

A: Me, too. I'm glad you said that.

MR: Especially the line, "a brook in the mind that will eventually glitter away the seas . . ."

A: Isn't that something? I like that. That's what it's all about, it seems to me, to keep trying till you get to some place like that. And then, in a Heideggerian sense, it's a place you can live. You can live in that little passage.

MR: Yes, and others can, too.

A: Well, that's what I mean by trying to be representative. I know that people are there, but I don't know how to speak to them directly, but if I can make something that we can share, then we would be speaking, as you and I are.

Now I feel very close to you since you just said that about that passage. Not because I wrote it and you didn't, but because we share it regardless of who wrote it.

MR: Perhaps to conclude, would you be willing to read that?

A: I'd be glad to.

> there is a faculty or knack, smallish, in the mind that can turn
> as with tooling irons immediacy into bends of concision, shapes
> struck with airs to keep so that one grows unable to believe that
>
> the piling up of figurements and entanglements could proceed from
> the tiny working of the small, if persistent, faculty: as if the
> world could be brought to flow by and take the bent of
>
> that single bend: and immediately flip over into the mirrored world
> of permanence, another place trans-shaped with knackery: a brook in
> the mind that will eventually glitter away the seas: and yet pile
>
> them all up, every drop recollected: a little mill that changes
> everything, not from its shape, but from change: the faculty
> that can be itself, small, but masterful in the face of size and
>
> spectacular ramification into diversity . . .

ESSAYS
◆

A. R. Ammons's Sumerian Songs:
Desert Laments and Eastern Quests

ROBERT KIRSCHTEN

This land where whirlwinds
walking at noon in tall columns of dust
take stately turns about the desert
is a very dry land
—A. R. Ammons, "I Went Out to the Sun"

This landscape is not the portrayal of an impression, it is not the judgment of a man on things at rest; it is nature coming into being, the world coming into existence, unknown to man. . . . It had been necessary to see the landscape in this way, far and strange, remote, without love, as something living a life within itself, if it ever had to be the means and the motive of an independent art; for it had to be far and completely unlike us—to be a redeeming likeliness of our fate. It had to be almost hostile in its exalted indifference, if, with its objects, it was to give new meaning to our existence.
—Rainer Maria Rilke, on the landscape in da Vinci's *Mona Lisa*

Suffering itself is a deception (upadhi); for its core is rapture, which is the attribute (upadhi) of illumination.

—Joseph Campbell

In his early lyrics, especially those collected in his first book, *Ommateum*, in 1955, A. R. Ammons exhibits a complex and mysterious religious attitude.

This essay was written specifically for this volume and is published here for the first time.

This attitude is dramatized in the form of a ritual quest that takes place in a barren, desolate setting, often generalized, like the "dry land" cited above, in Ammons's equally dry understatement. At times, however, this setting is identified as the ancient, Near Eastern country of Sumer, which flourished in the middle of the fourth millenium B.C. in what is now modern Iraq. Written when Ammons first began publishing in the mid-fifties, poems such as "Sumerian," "Coming to Sumer," "Eolith," and "Gilgamesh Was Very Lascivious" each make use of locales that the poet specifies as Sumerian. In addition to these specific locales, generalized Sumerian settings appear in a number of different guises in almost all of Ammons's books. Such settings range "from murky lowlands" and "the desert" in the short poem "Separations" in *Diversifications* (1975) to a Sumerian netherworld in *A Coast of Trees* (1981), where there is a "bleak land of foreverness" (*Trees*, 40) in nothing less than a fast-food restaurant in "Sunday at McDonald's." In *Lake Effect Country* (1983), Ammons's speaker suffers the effects of this "very dry land" when he laments that his "[l]ips [are] twisted with thirst / in the hot country" while observing his own "desert-precious being / swim, wily as snake-water in the sand" (*Lake*, 37). More recently, in 1987, Ammons published an entire collection of poems entitled *Sumerian Vistas*. In this collection, ironically, he does not mention Sumer, yet he indicates its continuing importance for him in the book's title and by using his early desert landscapes (or vistas) to initiate meditations such as that in "Scaling Desire," where "[a] small boulder washed or / rolled down or out / of circumstance lay mid-desert . . ." (*Vistas*, 65).[1]

If Ammons's Sumerian landscapes, whether generalized or specified, initiated his career in the fifties and continued to preoccupy him in the eighties, we ourselves may continue to ask with considerable justification why this poetic locale retains its importance for him. Primarily posed in terms of beginnings, this question may be addressed as follows: although based on historic, geographic, and cultural detail from an ancient civilization, Ammons's postmodern, mythopoeic Sumer is (among other things) a psychological space of personal passage, in which he disengages himself from one mythology while building a new one, and in so doing builds a new, existentially stronger self. The central poetic method in this undertaking is the construction of a ritualized narrative, which is a combination of performance and story, or, to put it another way, the recited reenactment of a personal myth. This ritualized narrative begins realistically in a Sumerian setting and ends up in a mental landscape derived, in part, from Asian systems of thought, which Ammons discovered through his reading of Emerson.[2]

Taken from his richly suggestive article "The Internalization of the Quest-Romance," Harold Bloom's initiating question gives greater focus to this line of inquiry. Bloom's question is based on his own search for a spiritual motive in the varied quests of Wordsworth, Shelley, Blake, Keats, and Coleridge:

. . . [This is] the central problem of Romantic (and post-Romantic) poetry: what, for men without belief and even without credulity, is the spiritual form of romance? How can a poet's (or any man's) life be one of continuous allegory . . . in a reductive universe of death, a separated realm of atomized meanings, each discrete from the next? Though all men are questers, even the least, what is the relevance of quest in a gray world of continuities and homogenized enterprises? Or, in Wordsworth's own terms, which are valid for every major Romantic, what knowledge might yet be purchased except by the loss of power?

In his neo-Freudian mapping of the poetic landscapes of these writers, Bloom answers this question by maintaining that the Romantics do not primarily quest for the things of nature or for unity with nature. Instead, they seek connection with "their Tharmas or id component, Tharmas being the Zoa or Giant Form in Blake's mythology who was unfallen human potential for realizing instinctual desires, and so was the regent of Innocence." According to this view, the libido moves ("falls") outward toward external objects when the inner self is compulsively overfilled. What results is an erotic quest not merely for the surrogate mother or her image but for a similar sustaining power inside oneself. Manifested by "a movement of love" of the ego toward itself, this search, for the Romantics, is actually a fusion of libido and imagination, or, as Bloom says, "desire wholly taken up into the imagination." The "spiritual form" of the Romantics' quests is an allegorical search, symbolically conducted and dramatized through nature, whereby poets seek a kind of internal consciousness, which enables them to overcome any "recalcitrance in the self" that hinders the "mature powers" of the Imagination. The Romantic quest first turns inward to overcome self-defeating ego-passivity, a state in which the libido, working through the ego, endlessly repeats the "cyclic movement from appetite to repression, and then back again." In this state, what the poet must overcome is the erotic force of an ego condemned to "a self-love that never ventures out to others." Romantic transcendence occurs in a second turn of the self outward to the union of the Imagination with its "ongoing creation." This "ongoing creation" is not "redeemed nature" but rather the artistic products of the poet's ongoing process of escaping excessive preoccupation with the self by making anew the externally directed poems of the Imagination.3

Escaping excessive preoccupation with the inner-directed self is also a central topic in Eastern religious thought. In *The Mythic Image,* Joseph Campbell argues that this problem issues not only from a classic model of the Western unconscious but generally from the "field of Waking Consciousness," where "we are separate from each other . . . so long as we hold to this ego-consciousness." Using this observation, we may interpret one of Ammons's preeminent pairs of poetic terms, the One and the Many, not only as metaphysical opposites but also as opposing states of consciousness; for, as

Campbell notes, ". . . what is in the mystical dimension one, is in the temporal-spatial two—and many—the very form of our 'knowledge' (in mystical terms, our 'ignorance') being multiplicity."[4] One way (or "Way") the early Ammons dramatizes the conflict between these states is through the violence of the ordeal or dismemberment, which has mythological and shamanic precedent in the concept of liminal sacrifice. In fact, one of Ammons's basic mythopoeic modes for reconciling the One and the Many—that is, for moving excessive and divisive ego-consciousness (the Many, or many painful earlier selves) outward onto the field of imaginative, unifying, poetic action (the One, or one new self)—is through the purification of the empirical self in the purgatory of his poetic Sumer. The purgatorial identity of land and self is explicit in these lines from the second page of Ammons's *Collected Poems:*

> The sap is gone out of the hollow straws
> and the marrow out of my bones
> > They are
> > brittle and dry
> > and painful in this land (*Poems,* 2)

The sacrificial method of overcoming death and division has considerable precedent in Eastern religions. As Ananda K. Coomaraswamy, scholar of Hindu and Buddhist philosophy, observes: ". . . for this *ignorantia divisiva{,}* an expiation is provided in the Sacrifice, where by the sacrificer's surrender of himself and the building up again of the dismembered deity, whole and complete, the multiples selves are reduced to a single principle."[5] That Ammons's sacrificial action may very well dramatize a philosophic turn toward the East takes further credence from his observation on his methods of indention: "I usually feel that I don't have anything to say of my own until I have tripped the regular world, until I have thrown the Western mind itself somehow off. . . ."[6] Campbell notes that the stage of consciousness following such disengagement is called, variously, in Eastern thought, rapture or illumination or bliss.

If Ammons's Sumer is some kind of purgatory, then one of his major methodological successes, to return to our Romantic vocabulary, is his marriage of heaven and hell. That is, a marriage (or what Bloom calls "an interweaving of purgatory and paradise") in which the poet externalizes the inner-directed self, with its perpetual round of desire and frustration (what Bloom calls the "Promethean libido") in its cyclic, Freudian "hell," onto a lyric model of consciousness in which the questing speaker enables the poet to discover his "mature [poetic] powers" in the ongoing "heaven" of Ammons's work.[7] Like the Romantics, Ammons's quest from purgatory to paradise has at least two major turns: inward into his own mind for the strength and confidence to write, then outward to the objects of his poetic landscape, which free him from excessive self-consciousness while paradoxically reinventing that self with an Eastern, philosophic twist.[8] Insofar as Mircea Eliade claims that *"the symbolic return to chaos is indispensable for any new originating,"* Ammons's barren, often violent, Sumerian deserts become an originary psychic ground for a poetic mythology in which he not only discovers his Blakean Tharmas—in Yeats's words cited by Bloom, "the face I had / Before the world was made"—but also remakes that face and that world over and over again.[9] By continually reinventing this Sumerian, mytho-psychic face and world, Ammons also invents a "way" to solve major artistic problems that confront any writer: namely, the plotting of a rewarding direction for his poetic action and, subsequently, the selection and arrangement of important, technical elements, such as voice, motivation, and kinds of revelation, to name but three. My central claim is that this movement from Sumerian, purgatorial desire to Imaginative Eastern bliss is the major ritualized narrative in Ammons's early work, and, further, that this movement is so important that it plays an essential role throughout his poetry, even as late as his work of the eighties, as manifested in his title for *Sumerian Vistas.*

If Ammons's songs (indeed, his career) begin as laments in Sumerian deserts, how do the routes of his lyric quests take him to Asia, or, more accurately, following Emerson's description of the mystical component in Plato, "the Asia in his mind?"[10] To answer this question, we ourselves may effect a critical marriage by using an Eastern concept of illumination in conjunction with Bloom's romantic, psychic mythology. Thus, we may refine our thesis by summarizing various elements in this discussion:

> Ammons's oppressive, Sumerian, mental landscapes constitute a romantic purgatory that replaces the sacred spaces of his earlier, Christian mythology and enables him to move from fallen nature (excessive self-preoccupation, due in part to the self of his earlier myth) into an internalized nature (a Sumer), which moves him outward to develop new formal and technical poetic powers, whereby he achieves an ongoing creation (the progressive body of his work) in which he continually quests for a new, "heavenly," mythological landscape, i.e., "the Asia in his mind."[11]

In discussing the ritual aspect of Aristotle's conception of catharsis, Joseph Campbell notes that "tragedy transmutes suffering into rapture by altering the focus of the mind." Following Campbell, we may additionally say of Ammons's dark, early poems that, like Aristotle, when he refocuses his mind, his particular "mode of tragedy dissolves and [his] myth begins."[12] Even if Ammons's attempts at rapture seem to be failures—those "visions of . . . losses," as he says in "Prodigal," of a "spent / seer" (*Poems,* 77)—these early lyric rituals are themselves acts of radical refocusing that begin to dissolve his conceptual tragedies and thus begin his new myths.

In this inquiry, my own focus is on the outward-turning element in Bloom's thesis, that is, the movement of Ammons's mind toward those poems that reveal his early, mature powers. Geoffrey Hartman indicates this direction in his article "Romanticism and 'Anti-Self-Consciousness,' " where he claims that one of the English Romantics' central problems was to find a remedy for "the ravage of self-consciousness and the 'strong disease' of self analysis," which is also called "death-in-life." Following Hegel in his *Logic,* Hartman notes that the Romantics found that one remedy for this kind of excessive thought is found, ironically, in further thought, which transcends nature and "its own lesser forms." On this point, Hartman cites the great German idealist:

> The hour that man leaves the path of mere natural being marks the difference between him, a self-conscious agent, and the natural world. The spiritual is distinguished from the natural . . . in that it does not continue a mere stream of tendency, but sunders itself to self-realization. But this position of severed life has in its turn to be overcome, and the spirit must, by its own act, achieve concord once more. . . . The principle of restoration is found in thought only: the hand that inflicts the wound is also the hand that heals it.

Most important for our purposes is Hartman's claim that "the attempt to think mythically is itself part of a crucial defense against the self-conscious intellect"—or, we may say in the case of Ammons, an intellect that self-consciously thinks itself, in Hegel's terms, from a "severed" mythology to a newer one of "concord" and "restoration." Encouraged by poetry and the imagination, this mythic mode of thought moves dialectically between the self and nature in a process of "soul-making," a route that most certainly bears on Ammons's Sumerian strategies, as does Hegel, for later poems such as "Gravelly Run" and "Bridge." For the remainder of this study, therefore, I would like to trace the beginnings of Ammons's route of mythopoeic thought by examining central topics and devices that help to reveal the rich variety of ritualized, formal strategies used by his narrator on his quests.[13]

SUMERIAN LAMENTS

In *Philosophies of India,* Heinrich Zimmer recounts an incident from the legend of Mahayana Bodhisattva Avalokiteshvara, a most distinguished and beloved ambassador of Buddha to this mundane world:

> . . . when, following a series of eminently virtuous incarnations, he was about to enter into the surcease of nirvana, an uproar, like the sound of a general thunder, rose in all the worlds. The great being knew that this was a wail of lament uttered by all created things—the rocks and stones as well as the trees, insects, gods, animals, demons, and human beings of all the spheres of the universe—at the prospect of his imminent departure from the realms of

birth. And so, in his compassion, he renounced for himself the boon of nirvana until all beings without exception should be prepared to enter in before him—like the good shepherd who permits his flock to pass first through the gate and then goes through himself, closing it behind him.

Every pore of the body of Avalokiteshvara contains and pours forth thousands of Buddhas, saints of all kinds, entire worlds. From his fingers flow rivers of ambrosia that cool the hells and feed the hungry ghosts.[14]

Insofar as Ammons's mythopoeic quest moves in its broadest outlines in an actional curvature from "suffering" to "illumination," we may read his early poems analogically along the lines of the legend of Avalokiteshvara. That is, Ammons's speakers dwell in a world that his voice fills with "a wail of lament," which seems to be "uttered by all natural things." This wail issues not from the prospect of Ammons's imminent departure, but from his immersion in realistic, Sumerian vistas of "hells" and "hungry ghosts" that, more often than not, fail to respond to his poetic imagery of comforting "rivers" to "cool" these hells. The point I wish to make is that, like the distinguished Bodhisattva, an "uproar" precedes the attempts of Ammons's speakers at any kind of ritual disengagement. Thus, these hells constitute the inciting condition for his quests and need to be effectively dramatized as states of earthly anguish. If Ammons's myths begin when his pain dissolves (to whatever degree), then this pain must first be established as a formidable force. This initiating condition of a suffering consciousness is most strongly reflected by the lamentational voice that echoes out over Ammons's vast Sumerian terrains.

To my ear, the lamentational voice of the mundane, earthly ego in Ammons's quester consists of at least two aspects, and these need to be distinguished from each other to see what is essentially Sumerian in this voice. The first aspect is biblical. The influence of the Bible on Ammons cannot be underestimated. Recounting how he grew up on a farm in rural North Carolina, he poignantly notes in an interview about his early education that "the only book we had in our house was the Bible."[15] Echoes of the Old Testament can be heard throughout his early work. In a line such as "Dogs ate their masters' hands / and death going wild with joy / hurried about the Sea," his view of the vicious absurdity of life and its attendant mortality has as powerful a resonance as these lines from Ecclesiastes 9:3: "The heart of the sons of men is full of evil, and madness is in their heart while they live, and after that they go to the dead." With regard to spiritual pain expressed in bodily anguish, Ammons's speaker wails in "Song" that "I lost my head first, the cervical meat / clumping off in rot, baring the spinal heart to wind and ice" (*Poems,* 34). Likewise the psalmist cries throughout his own body in Psalms 22:14: "I am poured out like water, and all my bones are out of joint: my heart is like wax; it is melted in the midst of my bowels." And while Ammons's landscapes of "ashen abnegation" (*Poems,* 25) and death bear great likeness to Sumerian deserts and its underworld, they also resemble "the land of darkness" in Job 10: 22: "A land of darkness, as darkness itself; and of the shadow of death, without any order, and where the light is as darkness."

To whatever degree a combination of cultural voices from the ancient Near East, Ammons's speaker differs in several significant ways from those in the Bible. I would like to suggest that these differences may be understood to some degree as "Sumerian" and that they play major roles in the development of the dramatic voice and emotional character of Ammons's early speakers. Discussing the two cultures in *The Sumerians*, C. Leonard Woolley offers a suggestive contrast, which also serves as a strikingly accurate portrayal of the emotional austerity in Ammons:

> Psychologically, the Sumerian was more distant and aloof than the Hebrew—more emotionally restrained, more formal and methodical. He tended to eye his fellow men with some suspicion, misgiving, and even apprehension, which inhibited to no small extent the human warmth, sympathy, and affection so vital to spiritual growth and well-being. And in spite of his high ethical attainments, the Sumerian never reached the lofty conviction that a "pure heart" and "clean hands" were more worthy in the eyes of his god than lengthy prayers, profuse sacrifices, and elaborate ritual.[16]

Woolley's appraisal serves as an accurate psychological description of Ammons's speakers. As befits this poet's austere exterior landscapes, so his interior world is also "distant," "aloof," "emotionally restrained, . . . formal and methodical." His poems—involving narrators such as Ezra the grave robber in "Coming to Sumer" and the speaker in "Eolith," who claims that "the possibility of unloading pity is / not greater than my giving it" (*Poems*, 20)—clearly reveal an attitude toward one's fellowman that is one of "suspicion," "misgiving," and "apprehension." In Ammons's Sumerian vistas, seldom does the speaker evince "human warmth, sympathy, and affection" for others. While these traits make for an unsympathetic coldness in him, they also balance our reaction to him by providing a convincing emotional ground in a hostile cosmos for his overwhelming religious need to offer "lengthy prayers, profuse sacrifices, and elaborate ritual."

Sumerian scholar Samuel Noah Kramer offers evidence for this last point by pushing further the Near Eastern cultural and poetic contrasts we noted earlier. In commenting on a Sumerian poetic essay that predates the Book of Job by a thousand years, Kramer notes that the Sumerian speaker resembles Job but has considerably fewer options: "The main thesis of our poet is that in cases of suffering and adversity, no matter how seemingly unjustified, the victim has but one valid and effective recourse, which is to continually glorify his god and keep wailing and lamenting before him until he turns a favorable ear to his prayers." Like Job, who finds himself in a "land of darkness" and claims that "[m]y soul is weary of my life" (10:1), the Sumerian poet in Kramer's text also cries out that and "for me the day is black" and "[e]vil fate . . . carries off my breath of life." Yet, unlike Job, the Sumerian has not even the slightest hope "to reason with God" (Job 13:3) or that the Lord will answer him "out of the whirlwind" (Job 38:1). Nor is there consolation for him in the fact of a special punishment for the wicked (Job 24). In the cold and heartless Sumerian cosmos, the poet can only enumerate his griefs:

> "I am a man, a discerning one, yet who respects me prospers not,
> my righteous word has been turned into a lie,
> The man of deceit has covered me with the Southwind, I am
>   forced to serve him,
> Who respects me not has shamed me before you.

> "You have doled out to me suffering ever anew,
>   I entered the house, heavy is the spirit,
>   I, the man, went out to the streets, oppressed is the heart,
>   With me, the valiant, my righteous shepherd has become angry,
>   has looked upon me inimically.

> "My herdsman has sought out evil forces against me who am
>   not his enemy,
> My companion says not a true word to me,
> My friend gives the lie to my righteous word,
> The man of deceit has conspired against me,
> And you, my god, do not thwart him. . . .

> "Suffering overwhelms me like one chosen for nothing but tears . . .
> Malignant sickness bathes my body . . . "[17]

Likewise, Ammons's speaker operates under similar situations, in which emotional pain is overwhelming and cannot be removed by appeal to divine intervention. In "A Crippled Angel," the speaker discovers a "crippled angel bent in a scythe of grief" in a temporal world oppressive that "[g]rief sounded like an ocean" (*Poems,* 30). In "I Came in a Dark Woods Upon," the speaker is "dazed with grief" (*Poems,* 28), and in "The Whaleboat Struck," his "body lies south / given over to vultures and flies" (*Poems,* 9). Even in a poem such as "Look for My White Self," about the disengagement of the mundane ego, the speaker is "diffuse, leached colorless, / gray as an inner image with no clothes" and is "wasted by hills" (*Poems,* 37).

GILGAMESH, DEATH, DUST, AND DARKNESS

In its emotional and spiritual darkness, the depth of longing in Ammons's speaker recalls the ancient Babylonian hero Gilgamesh. Dating back approximately to 2600 B.C., *The Epic of Gilgamesh,* or "The Gilgamesh Cycle," consists of tablets containing 12 cantos or songs that describe the exploits of the Sumerian seer and hero Gilgamesh. The son of the goddess Ninsun and a human, a high priest in the city of Uruk or Erech, Gilgamesh was one-third mortal, two-thirds divine, and was known as the god of the netherworld. Fully humanized in the epic tale, he was king and protector of Erech, whose citizens he intimidated by his superior energy and by his formidable sexual appetite. To give peace to the citizens of Erech, the gods sent Gilgamesh a male friend named Enkidu, who was as strong as he and meant to tame him. When Enkidu died prematurely, Gilgamesh was devastated and journeyed far and wide, even to the netherworld, to discover the secret of eternal life. His quest for such knowledge was futile. Even worse, he knew it. In John Gardner's rendering, Gilgamesh says, "I roam the wilderness in quest of a windpuff."[18] When Gilgamesh finally discovered the plant of eternal youth, which he plucked from the ocean floor, a snake stole away with it while he was bathing, and he was left with nothing. As a result of losing the secret of eternal life, Gilgamesh was overwhelmed, like the Sumerian petitioner, with a fate that threatened to annihilate him. Not only did death face him constantly, it pervaded his consciousness like an existential demon:

> The one who followed behind me
>   the rapacious one,
> sits in my bedroom, Death!
> And wherever I may turn my face,
> there he is, Death![19]

Likewise in Ammons's "Consignee," the speaker finds death a constant companion, which restricts his alignment with natural motion: "To death, the diffuse one / going beside me, I said, / You have brought me out of day / and he said / No longer like the fields of earth / may you go in and out" (*Poems,* 8).

After Enkidu's death, Gilgamesh searched for Utnapishtim, an ancestor whom he believed had found everlasting life and who dwelled in the farthest reaches of the earth. To gain Utnapishtim's secret, Gilgamesh traveled westward through dark mountain tunnels and immense deserts, digging wells for water and hunting wild bulls for food and clothing. Though his quest was for immortality, Gilgamesh seemed to roam with little direction, moving whichever way the wind blew. In this translation found in Thorkild Jacobsen's *The Treasures of Darkness: A History of Mesopotamian Religion,* he responds to a sun god, Shamash, who has urged him against his hopeless quest:

Is it (so) much—after wandering and roaming
    around in the desert—
to lie down to rest in the bowels of the
    earth?
I have lain down to sleep full many a time
    all the(se) years!
(No!) let my eyes see the sun
    and let me sate myself with daylight!
Is darkness far off?
    How much daylight is there?
When may a dead man ever see the sun's splendor?[20]

In "Spring Song," although more muted than Gilgamesh, Ammons also cries out for a certain kind of light, "a deep / luminosity" (*Poems,* 49). By rising up from the darkened and deadening ground of elemental "dust," his speaker begins the poem, like Gilgamesh, by driving himself forward through a vast spiritual desert that offers no hope of fulfillment—not the possible renewal of a "phoenix," but merely "no other choice":

I picked myself up from the dust again
and went on
phoenix not with another set of wings but with
no other choice
Oh I said to my soul may a deep
luminosity seize you
and my blanched soul smiled from its need and
dwelt on in the pale country of its bones . . . (*Poems,* 49)

    As pervasive as death, dust is an abiding presence in Ammons's deserts. Dust is not merely a geological detail in this poetic world; it is another form of death, a primal condition of uncontrollable natural force and spiritual depravity, against which, yet in concert with which, Ammons's speakers must act. In "When Rahman Rides," the speaker tells us, "There was the rush of dust and then farther on / a spiral whirlwinding," which leaves him nothing but an "ocotillo" (a spiny desert plant) "in a bloomless month" (*Poems,* 13). In "The Sap Is Gone Out of the Trees," dust pervades both present and past as "the dusting / combine passed over [the wheatfields] . . . long after the dust was gone." At the end of the poem, the speaker sounds as ineffectual as dust, for he tells us that "[t]he wind whipped at my carcass" and he could do little more than utter "Oh" and fall "down in the dust" (*Poems,* 2). Even when dust is not present, Ammons's landscapes are, as Frederick Buell suggests, stifling emotional analogs of "the domain of the Queen of darkness of the Gilgamesh epic" found in Enkidu's surrealistic dream of the netherworld.[21] The word for this land in Sumerian myth is "Kur," which Kramer claims is "cosmically conceived" as "the empty space between the earth's crust and the primeval sea."[22] Kur is a place to which everyone, moral or not, goes at death. As he lay dying, Enkidu told Gilgamesh that he dreamt he saw a man with "paws of a lion" and "talons of an eagle" who "overpowered" and "transformed" him; then,

> He seized me and led me down to the house of darkness . . .
> the house where one who goes in never comes out again,
> the road that, if one takes it, one never comes back,
> the house that, if one lives there, one never sees light,
> the place where they live on dust, their food is mud;
> their clothes are like bird's-clothes, a garment of wings,
> and they see no light, living in blackness:
> on the door and door-bolt, deeply settled dust.[23]

Suffocating and hopeless, dark and dusty, the Sumerian underworld reduces gods and kings to serving mud as they wait on tables. Its residents retain their worldly identities but are frail and wispy, like their birdlike garments "of wings." They are fallen deities, priests, and nobles, personages who once had access to great power or special vision, which they have now utterly lost. In short, like Ammons's "spent / seer" (Poems, 77), they are characters who could easily dwell in the desert cosmos of his early poems.

By driving his narrator through a universe of pervasive dust and darkness, Ammons creates a trancelike state that is not merely hell or purgatory. It is a state for a peculiar kind of transition that takes place, in Eliade's words, *"beyond the realm of the sensorial."* To be sure, Ammons's rituals work their way through the logic of his speaker's body. At times, however, by reducing the clarity of his narrator's physical vision, Ammons provides him an ecstatic, shamanistic view that engages only his "soul" or spirit, not his entire being.[24] One feels, throughout these early poems, that the narrator's consciousness is constantly being separated from his body in a nightmare world of "cleavage" (Poems, 24) where he is losing his head (Poems, 34) or blindly "[d]ropping [his] eyelids among the aerial ash" (Poems, 30). As we have observed, one major aspect of Ammons's early work is his attempt to invent rituals that involve the entire body and thus rescue it from a dismembered or disunified condition. For shamans in many primitive religions, however, such dismemberment is not lethal but initiatory and anticipates the possibility of renewal. As Eliade says, "Every 'trance' is another 'death' " that "reveals the presentiment of re-birth into another mode of being."[25] Consequently, whatever anxiety one feels at death—this feeling, of course, dominates the early Ammons—is transitory and will dissolve upon one's awakening to a higher consciousness. More important, Eliade notes, this awakening is a mythological act of remembering, an *"anamnesis,"* a "re-cognition of the soul's true identity, that is, recognition of its celestial origin." In fact, only after man wakes from sleep, drunkenness, dread, or oblivion will he discover "how to act in this world."[26]

When Gilgamesh came to the island of his ancestor Utnapishtim, he was unable to stay awake for six days and nights, and thus failed in his trial to achieve immortality. In contrast, through his invention of ordeals dramatized in Sumerian settings, Ammons succeeds in ecstatically awakening his narrator to a "true historiographic *anamnesis.*" This kind of remembering aims to recall events that record cultural behavior not in historical but in mythical time, a world of existential, prehistoric experience, which "finds [its] expression in the discovery of our solidarity with . . . vanished or peripheral peoples."[27] Thus, Ammons's poem "Sumerian":

> I have grown a marsh dweller
> subject to floods and high winds,
> drinking brackish water on long hunts,
> brushing gnat smoke
> from clumps of reeds, have known
>
> the vicissitudes of silt, of
> shifting channels flush
> by dark upland rains . . .

By struggling against, then aligning himself with "natural" motions in this Sumerian landscape, Ammons's speaker gains a differentiating knowledge that enables him to gauge various spatial levels. At the somewhat cloudy end of the poem, these depths and heights demarcate a Sumerian space that extends from "underwater mud" to "blue temple tiles." Within this spatial orientation, there comes an ability to judge the existential distance of a certain "serenity," a goal considerably "beyond approach" for this abject "marsh dweller." For he claims that after

> rising with a handful of broken shells
> from sifted underwater mud
> I have come to know how high
> the platform is, beyond approach,
> of serenity and blue temple tiles.

The depth of the speaker's need is thus measured by the geographic space he surveys, which, in turn, produces the questlike development of the poem. From the "dark upland" to "the southern salty banks," the Sumerian's "long hunts" cover considerable external ground while also conveying the equally deep (or "long") internal emptiness of "terror dawn cold across my face." The central movement of "Sumerian" is from dark, oppressive detail ("brackish water" and "gnat smoke") to the idea, if not the reality, of "serenity" (*Poems, 32*).

By taking on the behavior of a Sumerian in a Sumerian setting, Ammons's narrator not only expresses his "solidarity" with a "vanished" people, he awakens through this solidarity from a morass of oppressive sensation to consciousness of the possibility of something higher. This something higher is a "serenity" that is "sacred" insofar as it is associated with the coolness of "blue temple tiles"; and, further, this serenity constitutes a truth about an alternative to human suffering that has been discovered not through historical analysis or time but through the poet's recreation of a vanished culture. Such historiographic awakening has important visionary repercussions in Ammons's dark universe, especially with regard to what he discovers through his myths and rituals. In *Myth and Reality*, Eliade discusses an ancient pair of topics, forgetting and remembering, in Gnostic and Indian philosophy; and in so doing, he sheds considerable light on the value of Ammons's primordial myths:

> . . . the Gnostic learns the myth in order *to dissociate himself from its results.* Once waked from his mortal sleep, the Gnostic (like the disciple of Samkhya-Yoga) understands that he bears no responsibility for the primordial catastrophe the myth narrates for him, and that hence he has no *real* relation with Life, the World, and History.[28]

Ammons's entrance into a primordial past signals an incipient awareness of one of the ancient truths of Eastern thought: Historic reality is not absolute, and insofar as this version of reality is susceptible to change, certain kinds of human suffering associated with historical time will themselves prove mutable—even illusory—and thus subject to disappearance, just as the Sumerians and their culture have disappeared. In Gnostic and Indian thinking, the historical self mired in pain is not the true self. It may be accurate, as Denis Donoghue claims, that one of the social "limitations in [Ammons's] art" is that he "can . . . evade the responsibility of history, circumvent the claims of other people . . . [without] having to bother with the horrors of living in the slums of New York."[29] Even though Donoghue later qualifies the severity of this observation, we may say, in defense of Ammons's early work, that he is all too aware of the massive destruction that history has wrought, and thus has sought a personal, mythico-religious view that enables him emotionally to rise above that destruction. Furthermore, this attitude involves an ancient form of remembering—that is, a discovering and inventing—a truer self than that which is determined by social catastrophe. Again, Eliade:

> Waking, which is at the same time an anamnesis, finds expression in an indifference to History, especially to contemporary History. Only the primordial

myth is important. Only the events that occurred in the past of fable are worth knowing; for, by learning them, one becomes conscious of one's true nature—and awakens.[30]

DIVISION AND RENEWAL

We noted earlier, following Geoffrey Hartman, that a central concern for English Romantic poets was a "fixated" self-consciousness, brought on by excessive analysis that "murders to dissect," as Wordsworth says in "The Tables Turned." This imperious act of the mind to dissect and rationalize results for Wordsworth in a "false" consciousness that negates other aspects of the soul. As he says in *Milton,* Book II:

> The Negation is the Spectre, the Reasoning Power in Man;
> This is a false Body, an Incrustation over my Immortal
> Spirit, a Selfhood which must be put off & annihilated alway . . .[31]

In the early Ammons, there is a similar, fragmenting threat to a kind of holistic consciousness that he greatly values and to which he must awaken from the murderous dissection of division. In fact, many of his later pairs of abstract, philosophic terms—the One and the Many, Order and Motion, Unity and Multiplicity, Center and Periphery—seem derived from his early, mythopoeic preoccupation with the dangers of division. Ammons dramatizes this danger in "Spring Song," where, as we saw, his narrator has a dismembered "soul" that dwells "in the pale country of its bones" (*Poems,* 49). In the second stanza, after a "field"—that is, a new direction or ground of thought—opens on his right, the speaker at first immerses himself in its "arms-high" "golden broom grass." Like a wandering Gilgamesh, he seems to drift aimlessly with the wind as he notes that he "whirled with the wind sizzling there."

In Ammons's case, however, this is a strategic movement that alters the course of the poem by placing the speaker in the hands of nature's (his own mind's) forces. This wind grants Ammons's speaker the power to address vegetation and thus to use the things of nature as dramatic characters to complicate the poem's story line. Ever-worried about what will endure and what will not, especially in the season of growth and renewal, the speaker challenges the grass's "rising shoots" on the matter of change when he says, "Where, if spring will not keep you, / will you go" (*Poems,* 50) When he stoops "to scold the shoots," the narrator nearly falls "in with their green enhancing tips." That is, he nearly falls for or succumbs to a traditional image of growth in spring, which in his desolate world seems to be a sign of separation, for he exits abruptly and "nearly died / getting away from the dividing place." The poem concludes violently with a standard mythological image of darkness and blood, couched in the figures of the sun and moon. As he was at the beginning of the poem, the speaker is left utterly alone in a hostile, surrealistic setting of "sand," which is as empty and bleak as was the unknown desert beyond the gate of sunrise for Gilgamesh:

> At dusk the sun set and it was dark and having
> found no place to leave my loyalty
> I slaughtered it by the road and spilled its
> blood on sand while the red moon rose (*Poems,* 50)

In its response to what will last, Ammons's aggressive answer seems to be: "absolutely nothing"; and his "Spring Song" appears to be the depressing, direct opposite of a traditional seasonal poem, which would celebrate the renewing power of spring by means of fertile natural detail.

However bleak the conclusion to "Spring Song," there is more possibility for renewal than first appears. As Ammons notes in the first stanza, this possibility is not as grandiose as "phoenix . . . with another set of wings," but it nonetheless resides powerfully within the final lines in what Joseph Campbell calls religious "play-logic" or "dream-logic."[32] The key to this dream-logic lies in the considerable natural transformation in the conclusion. The sun sets into darkness; dies; then, when the speaker's "loyalty" is slaughtered ("loyalty" to the traditional promise of renewal in a traditional spring song, as I read the term), its blood is spilled "on sand," and the moon takes on the color of blood, then rises. In archetypal thinking, this is the movement from dawn and rebirth to night, sleep, and death, then to a new birth in the rising of the moon. Most of the speaker's own movement is a passage through darkness, through a dark night of the soul in which all appears to be death and decay. In yet another netherworld of dust and darkness, even the "green enhancing tips" of "golden broom grass" do not offer solace but instead constitute an occasion for fear and suspicion. Without the possiblity of exit, there would be no possibility of passage for this speaker. He would be condemned to a static state of deathless nonmotion. Consequently, in this "pale country," the only possibility for significant change lies in the deathly, yet cyclic, motions of sky gods, namely, the sun and moon. Encountered during the speaker's trials in his desolate landscape, only these archetypal representatives, moving in their eternal continuum from life to death and back to life, animate his world with the possibility of crossing thresholds.

The threshold-promising illumination in this parable about the dangers of division reveals much about Ammons's mythogical methods of unification; for his imagery suggests that his speaker wishes to discover—or, return to—an ancient kind of consciousness in which the meeting of sun and moon signals the life-giving union of other pairs of primitive opposites. These energizing opposites are found, as Campbell notes, "in the Indian Kundalini yoga of the first millenium A.D.," where "lunar and solar channels" are "two spiritual channels on either side of the central channel of the spine, up which the serpent power is supposed to be carried through a control of the mind and breath." In this religious symbolism, there is "the meeting of sun and moon . . . in significant relation to the serpent and the axial staff, tree, or spine." Such symbolism reflects, Campbell goes on to say, that

> a fundamental idea of *all* the pagan religious disciplines . . . was that the inward turning of the mind (symbolized by the sunset) should culminate in a realization of an identity *in esse* of the individual (microcosm) and the universe (macrocosm), which, when achieved would bring together in one order of act and realization the principles of eternity and time, sun and moon, male and female. . . .[33]

This particular "inward turning of the mind," whereby internal and external realities match (and, at times, dramatically mismatch), is one of the central, structural principles in Ammons's poetry, whether in "Spring Song" or in his later major meditations about division and integration, such as "The Arc Inside and Out," "The Unifying Principle," and "Two Motions." In these later poems, several great circular philosophers such as Laotse, Hegel, Plotinus, and Emerson certainly play central roles. However, these later speculative reflections also find a germinating, mythopoeic ground in Ammons's early poetic principle that the division between poetic microcosm and macrocosm reflects a similar inimical division in the human mind.

Whatever its positive (and considerable) analytic powers, the mental act of dividing threatens and obscures access to an ancient state of being that was especially attractive to Sumerian mythmakers. Campbell calls this state the "mystical rapture of non-duality, or mythic identification." He claims that this state of rapture is at the heart of religious imagery and experience throughout the world; it "is symbolized in . . . ancient Egypt's Secret of the two Partners, China's Tao, India's Nirvana, and Japan's development of the Buddhist doctrine of the Flower Wreath." The loss of this state has numerous implications, including the idea of death as an absolute termination, because of the introduction of differentiated, linear time, which begins and ends. In ancient Sumerian myth, this loss was equivalent to Adam and Eve's expulsion from paradise. Here is Campbell's account of such loss, presented in an archetypal narrative of division and unification:

> . . . as we know from an ancient Sumerian myth, heaven *(An)* and earth *(Ki)* were in the beginning a single undivided mountain *(Anki)*, of which the lower part, the earth, was female, and the upper, heaven, male. But the two were separated . . . by their son Enlil . . . whereupon the world of temporality appeared. . . . The ritual marriage and connubium was to be understood as a

reconstruction of the primal undifferentiated state, both in meditation (psychological aspect) for the refreshment of the soul, and in act (magical aspect) for the fertilization and renovation of nature: whereby it was also to be recognized that there is a plane or mode of being where that primal state is ever present, though to the mind and eye of day all seems to be otherwise.[34]

In poem after poem, ranging from "Rack" in *Ommateum* (where "[t]he pieces of my voice have been thrown / away" [*Poems,* 5]) to "Long Sorrowing" in *Sumerian Vistas* (where Ammons's speaker listens for "the voices of / cilates & crustaceans . . . held in a dark unanswerableness / to so much loss" [*Vistas,* 101]), separation or differentiation seems to be the basic human condition for this poet. In its various forms, separation becomes Ammons's Sumerian version of original sin, a mythopoeic occasion of overpowering need for unity or a refreshing, integrating consciousness, which so motivates his speaker that this need generates the basic action in many of his poems.

Undifferentiated Darkness

In addition to its presence in *Sumerian Vistas,* "dark unanswerableness" seems everywhere in the early Ammons. At first, this darkness appears to abrogate all hope of illumination or revelation. Indeed, darkness is often an essential ingredient of the enervating closure in these poems. At the end of "Turning a Moment to Say So Long," the speaker concludes by plunging into a well, then submerging himself in darkness with "night kissing / the last bubbles from my lips" (*Poems,* 10). Likewise, at the end of a poem with a similar title, "Turning," the speaker sounds like a comic Gilgamesh as he falls into another deep hole of water. Instead of ascending on "wings of light," he "fumbled about" in the last two lines "in the darkness for my wings / and the grass looked all around at the evening" (*Poems,* 12). While darkness signals a powerful, deathly alienation in this "unanswerable" universe, it also has a "rich" dimension. This dimension of Ammons's Sumerian darkness is, to some extent, his mystical response to the condition of division in which he finds himself. We may say that Ammons is a contemporary Gilgamesh who seeks his own version of immortality through his continuous quest for a state of nondivision. While he is often frustrated in attaining this state in individual poems, his entire early mythological landscape itself becomes an emotional and spiritual ground in which he reconstructs, as Campbell says, a refreshing and dark "primal undifferentiated state."

Paradoxical and difficult to describe, this mythological realm of undifferentiated darkness is made somewhat intelligible by using mythopoeic iconography to suggest its depth and power. One visual analog may be taken from the terra-cotta plaque of a Moon-Bull and Lion-Bird from ancient Sumer

(c. 2500 B.C.) in the University Museum in Philadelphia. This plaque depicts, as Campbell describes it, "the ever-dying, ever-living lunar bull, consumed through all time by the lion-headed solar eagle." This depiction is not an image merely of predatory victimage. It is a symbolic statement of an eternal, energy-transferring process whereby the bearded bull, with his serene human smile, does not exactly die but instead releases energy in fiery flashes from his legs, which are atop a "cosmic holy mountain" that is said to be "the goddess Earth." While the moon-bull is consumed by the sun's light, he energizes the earth in a round of fertilizing power like that of the Egyptian fertility god Osiris, whose animal was also the bull. In this kind of mythological realm, darkness or blackness does not signal annihilation but a more complex, undifferentiated state of life and death, moments in a cycle of being or eternal flow that can give rise to a "wisdom beyond death, beyond changing time." Campbell claims that this "primal state is ever present" in us, though difficult to visualize, express, or examine. If it is in myths and their provocative images of eternal mysteries that this realm is effectively displayed and experienced, we can see why Campbell concludes that "[t]he state of the ultimate [lunar, mythic] bull . . . is invisible: black, pitch black."[35]

Like Gilgamesh's netherworld, Ammons's Sumerian vistas also serve as thresholds to a nightmare world that is itself a reality that is "ever-dying, ever-living." For Ammons's mental spaces are really dream worlds or dream spaces, often surrealistic, in which familiar directional coordinates and traditional dualisms are dissolved so that the speaker can effect passage from meaningless death. For instance, in "Dying in a Mirthful Place," Ammons's speaker laughs into the face of death by narrating the poem after he has died, even while "buzzards . . . sat over me in mournful conversations / that sounded excellent to my eternal ear" (*Poems,* 13). In this poem, Ammons, like Gilgamesh, searches for a kind of immortality in a barren desert "soil" (on "a hill in Arizona") in which there is "a noiseless / mirth and death" (*Poems,* 13). To some extent, unlike Gilgamesh, he finds immortality; at least, he acquires an "eternal ear." What this eternity is becomes clearer in Ammons's long, three-part poem "Requiem," whose religious title is consistent with its content, namely, another of Ammons's paradigmatic acts of creation. After a middle section of surrealistic "transfigurations" in another Sumerian desert, where there are "trunks of violent trees stalking the vacant land," the opening of the final segment, entitled "Contraction," clearly indicates the poem's paradigmatic promise. "Repenting creation," God claims somewhat defensively that "I do not have to be consistent: what was lawful to my general plan / does not jibe / with my new specific will; what the old law healed / is reopened / in the new" (*Poems,* 46–47). The entire middle section, with its "golden culminations and unfuneraled dead," is a welter of new reopening from old, a series of "primal rhythms" of life and death, part of which sail "into eternity" and part of which, along with "the earth, . . . rolled into time" (*Poems,* 46).

The opposition of time and eternity returns us to Sumer and to the ancient kind of Mesopotamian consciousness that concludes Ammons's poem. Immediately after God claims that he has "drawn up many covenants to eternity," the poet introduces a pseudonarrative that abruptly inserts the mordant finality of the temporal world. This world is represented in Sumerian, historical detail:

> Returning silence unto silence,
> the Sumerian between the rivers lies.
> His skull crushed and moded into rock
>   does not leak or peel.
> The gold earring lies in the powder
> of his silken, perished lobe.
> The incantations, sheep trades, and night-gatherings
>   with central leaping fires,
> roar and glare still in the crow's-foot
> walking of his stylus on clay. . . . (*Poems,* 47)

Like the middle section of the poem, this segment consists of two temporal zones. First, there is an unchanging eternity of the dead, a world of "silence unto silence," in which there is no material change. The "skull" of "the Sumerian between the rivers" (the Tigris and Euphrates, one presumes) "does not leak or peel." On the other hand, there is the active world of "incantations" and "leaping fires" that exist, but do so on an artifact, an ancient clay tablet of cuneiform script, or "crow's-feet." Like Yeats's "artifice of eternity" in "Sailing to Byzantium," the world of these events is also frozen, as is the next image of physical decay in Ammons's poem: a "sick man" in a Sumerian temple who could not be cured by the "anesthetic words of reciting priests." He too is long silenced, for "dust has dried up all his tears," and he "sleeps out the old unending drug of time" (*Poems,* 47). That is, if the priests' words did not end his illness, the "unending drug of time" certainly will, albeit in the form of eternal sleep.

However static and final seem the deathly elements in this section, the poem concludes not on a note of absolute termination but with a round or universal rhythm that conveys an eternity quite opposite that of mordant stasis:

> The rose dies, man dies, the world dies, the god
> grows and fails, the born universe dies
>   into renewal,
> and all endures the change,
> totally lost and totally retained. (*Poems,* 47)

By presenting this paradoxical state of death and "renewal," in which "all," including "the god," is "totally lost and totally retained," Ammons closes his poem with a mystical rapture that assimilates the visible, dualistic world of discrete particulars to a universal realm of archetypal motion. That is, he converts material, historical, and mythological decay—"[t]he rose dies," "the world dies," "the god / grows and fails"—into a reproductive cycle that dissolves the finality of the Sumerian's death in the previous section into something considerably less permanent. Transformed at the close of the poem into a moment on the eternal wheel of Ammons's transfigurations, this Sumerian portrait of pain and suffering seems more like a momentary nightmare than a fully realistic and disturbing termination. Such transformation is even more understandable because the poem's surrealistic atmosphere continually shifts the shapes of objects and laws of creation, until its universe seems to be what is called in Indian thought "deep dreamless sleep," or in Freudian psychology, "the oceanic feeling."[36] To be sure, this is not the world of visual, waking consciousness. Instead, Ammons's mode of poetic motion takes us beyond serial time, with its discrete events and divisions, to a state of "mythic identification," often depicted as a state of darkness, in which life and death dissolve into each other in an eternal round of change that does not change, or, as Ammons says, "dies / into renewal."

Ammons's darkened spaces, as well as his deserts and barren terrains, constitute another way to form mythological base matter or primal chaos, out of which transformation is made possible for the mind. This transformation is really an emotional recreation of the self, which presents its reinvention through a narrative of origins, issuing from unformed natural material. In "Chaos Staggered Up the Hill," the speaker drolly notes that "messy chaos" gets "the daises dirty." Itself a traditional term for unformed cosmic matter, the "chaos" in Ammons's poem engulfs, then dissolves, him, only to offer the possibility of renewal in the poem's final line, where we discover that it has the power "to make us green some other place" (*Poems,* 6). As is the case in so many of his poems, Ammons's setting contains the potential for incipient reversal and thus constitutes, in various forms, the very goal or ground of change that his quester seeks. Ammons's deserts are barren and dry—in a word, chaotic—because they are places for sacred beginnings. They are worlds in need of content, form, and habitation. In this sense, Ammons's Sumerian vistas are anywhere he remakes his universe. Eliade notes that it is through ritual—for example, the raising of the Christian Cross, a variation on the sacred pole or cosmic pillar—that one recreates sacred or habitable space, which is the opposite of "a foreign, chaotic space, peopled by ghosts, demons, 'foreigners' (who are assimilated to demons and the souls of the dead)."[37] In Ammons's early "Sumerian" world, death is constant companion in his land of "great black unwasting silence" (*Poems,* 6), and his constant challenge is—in however rudimentary a form or to whatever small degree—to recenter and resituate himself within a profane, hostile universe. In so doing, his early victories in poetic form are victories in the reforming of his own habitation—in other words, of dwelling in a Sumer that, in Eliade's words, is a "territory" that "can be made ours only by creating it anew, that is, by consecrating it."[38]

Working on the level of ritualized action, Ammons employs this darkness as a spatial coordinate to construct a sacred ground—albeit the ground of his own lyric performance—which results in a revelation that this ground is itself the result and reward of his quester's search. This quester's reward is a new, poetic Sumer so barren and empty that even the speaker's simplest gestures may be read as attempts to reorganize space and time. In reconstituting this world, Ammons's speaker thus performs what Eliade calls "the paradigmatic acts of the gods," namely, the recreation of a time of origin that is itself the making and consecrating of a sacred reality. Ammons's world is no historic Sumer. His primitive settings and scenes are so much "fragments of a shattered universe" that his spatial movements up and down in a poem such as "Choice" not only give direction to his "indirection" but also create direction by giving shape to "mean" or profane "space":[39]

> Idling through the mean space dozing,
> blurred by indirection, I came upon a
> stairwell and steadied a moment to
> think against the stem:
> upward turned golden steps
> and downward dark steps entered the dark:
>
> . . . I
> spurned the airless heights though bright
> and sank
> sliding in a smooth rail whirl and fell
> asleep in the inundating dark . . . (*Poems,* 35)

Like the unformed darkness or primal choas at the beginning of Genesis, the darkness in Ammons's mental allegory is a kind of cosmic base matter or state of somnolence, out of which gods create light. Or, in the case of this poem, out of which the speaker, seeking a kind of sight, emerges enabled to do battle with a god of limited vision, as when, in the conclusion, he "grappled with / the god that / rolls up circles of our linear / sight in crippling disciplines" (*Poems,* 35).

A WISDOM BEYOND DEATH

The Sumerian lunar bull on the terra-cotta plaque described earlier by Campbell is also a mythological variation on one of Ammons's favorite themes, the one and the many. A version of this eternal pair (and process) can also be found in the Indian Śhatapatha Brāhmana, which Campbell cites in *Creative Mythology:* "That One who is the Death on whom our life depends. . . . He is one as he is there, but many as he is in his children there."[40] However ineffable this "pitch black" realm, it is a prominent feature in Sumerian and Asian religions, and there are at least two kinds of wisdom to be derived from it. Both are found in Ammons's early verse, and both kinds give these poems a substance and weight as considerable as anything he has written since. One aspect of this wisdom is its attitude toward death. Perhaps the most striking trait in Ammons's early poems is the contradictory fact that, although his world is filled with death, his speaker finds, as we have noted, a curious solace there. By continuously moving toward a "pitch black" consciousness of undifferentiation, Ammons's speaker not only quests for but simultaneously establishes a mental landscape that philosophically and emotionally subsumes the oppressive world of decay that threatens to overwhelm him. In "Consignee," a circular blackness offers Ammons's speaker a certain consolation, a "wisdom beyond death," which is the opposite of the speaker's daylight vision. After "death, the diffuse one" brings him "out of day," the speaker tells us that he "quarreled and devised a while / but went on / having sensed a nice dominion in the air, / the black so round and deep" (*Poems,* 8).

In its preoccupation with the "black so round and deep," Ammons's stance toward death seems equivalent to an inward, spiritual disengagement found in Chinese mythology, a mythology that, like Ammons, conceives of life and death as evolving from one "featureless, undistinguishable mass." According to an anecdote narrated by Campbell in *Oriental Mythology,* Chuang Tzu (c. 300 B.C.), a Taoist wise man, was criticized for failing to mourn properly the death of his wife. Instead of observing the appropriate rites of lamentation, he was found singing and drumming on a bowl. When reproached, he replied that when his wife died, indeed he first despaired; however, he then began to reflect. In a style as simple and straightforward as Ammons's poem, Chuang Tzu's reflection puts the staggering loss of his wife's death into the larger context of "nature's Sovereign Law":

> . . . pondering on what had happened, I told myself that in death no strange new fate befalls us. In the beginning we lack not life only, but form; not form only, but spirit. We are blent in the one great featureless, undistinguishable mass. Then a time came when the mass evolved spirit, spirit evolved form, form evolved life. And now life in its turn has evolved death. For not nature only, but man's being has its seasons, its sequence of spring and autumn, summer and winter. . . . She whom I have lost has lain down to sleep. . . . To break in upon her rest with the noise of lamentation would but show that I knew nothing of nature's Sovereign Law.[41]

In a comment on this passage, noted Orientalist and translator Arthur Waley offers a gloss that applies equally to Ammons, and may very well be the central emotional focus of *Ommateum:*

> This attitude toward death . . . is but part of a general attitude toward the universal laws of nature, which is one not merely of resignation nor even of

acquiescence, but a lyrical, almost ecstatic acceptance. . . . That we should question nature's right to make and unmake, that we should hanker after some role that nature did not intend us to play is not merely futile, not merely damaging to that tranquility of the "spirit" which is the essence of Taoism, but involves, in view of our utter helplessness, a sort of fatuity at once comic and disgraceful.[42]

A second aspect of Ammons's "wisdom beyond death" centers on a conception of the self in relation to the term "all," a relation that we saw in the conclusion to "Requiem": "and all endures the change, / totally lost and totally retained" (*Poems*, 47). This paradoxical polarity has the status of an ontological assertion in this poem, but it also suggests an ancient Eastern conception of the self. Especially in its "lost" and "retained" aspects, Ammons's conception of the self forms a central element in his response to the overwhelming anguish of personal mortality that attends him in his Sumerian settings and throughout his work. These two opposing aspects of the self—namely, dissolution and reconstitution—point to a continuous, dialectical drama that his voice (or self) undergoes during his quests. One might plausibly argue that the central pilgrimage in his poetry is for the reconstitution of a constantly fragmented self. This drama is so important to him that it is found in the very first poem in *Ommateum*, when his speaker precariously identifies himself: "I am Ezra / As a word too much repeated / falls out of being" (*Poems*, 1) Even in "Muse," published 10 years later in the midsixties, Ammons continues to focus on the "anguish of becoming" when he exclaims, "[H]ow many / times must I be broken and reassembled!" (*Poems*, 99). In Ammons's poetry, this negative disengagement of a culturally dramatized self is positively portrayed by images of death, darkness, and termination: for example, suffocating ("Turning a Moment to Say So Long" [*Poems*, 10]), splintering ("I Came in a Dark Woods Upon" [*Poems*, 28]), killing ("In Strasbourg in 1349" [*Poems*, 3]), wounding ("A Crippled Angel" [*Poems*, 30]), and burying ("A Treeful of Cleavage Flared Branching" [*Poems*, 25]). The impulse toward a disengaged self is positively portrayed by devices that turn substance into a number of disembodied items: color, or its lack ("Succumbing in the still ecstasy / sinuous through white rows of scales / I caved in upon eternity / saying this use is colorless" [*Poems*, 31]); transforming fire ("all miracle hanging fire / on rafters of the sky" [*Poems*, 30]); spirits ("my blue ghost" [*Poems*, 38]), or assimilative motion ("cool thought unpunishable / by bones eternally glides" [*Poems*, 33]).

If Ammons begins in a this-worldly state of real sensory pain, confusion, and death, he transcends these states by questing for a new self, which bears close analogy to the Eastern doctrine of the extinction or emptying of the self. That is, if Ammons seems often to begin at realistic Sumer, he just as often finds himself on the way ("Way") to an Absolute, which is, to a large degree, Oriental. This radical Eastern doctrine of transcendence, so foreign to the

Western mind, may be illustrated by certain species of Buddhism. In *Buddhism: Its Essence and Development,* Edward Conze notes: "The chief purpose of Buddhism is the extinction of separate individuality, which is brought about when we cease to *identify* anything with ourself. From long habit it has become quite natural to us to think of our own experience in the terms of 'I' and 'mine.' " However, Conze goes on to say, this habit can be abolished by thought:

> According to the doctrine of the Old Wisdom School, wisdom alone is able to chase the illusion of individuality from our thoughts where it has persisted from age-old habit. Not action, not trance, but only thought can kill the illusion which resides in thought.
>
> If all our sufferings are attributed to the fact that we identify ourselves with spurious belongings which are not really our own, we imply that we would be really much better off without those belongings. This . . . inference can also be stated in a more metaphysical way by saying that what we really are is identical with the Absolute. It is assumed . . . that there is an ultimate reality, and . . . that there is a point in ourselves at which we touch that ultimate reality. The ultimate reality, also called Dharma by the Buddhists, or Nirvana, is defined as that which stands completely outside the sensory world of illusion and ignorance, a world inextricably interwoven with craving and greed. . . . [This notion] is very much akin to the philosophical notion of the "Absolute," and not easily distinguished from the notion of God among the more mystical theologians, like Dionysius Areopagita and Eckart.[43]

The wisdom to which Ammons aspires does not result in the extinction of his speaking voice, for without that, of course, there would be no poem. Rather, in many of his major meditations, Ammons's speaker effects to some degree and in various forms the "extinction of separate individuality." That is, he severs the connection of the meditating self with the often painful, even monstrous, contents of its thought. This claim at first seems wrongheaded because Ammons's early speakers are so busy differentiating what appear to be fully realistic elements. Their minds are filled to overflowing with complex distinctions, details, and progressions, which are presented in the mode of realistic narratives. However rich and diverse the surface texture of these poems, they often close with a movement—a physical gesture or mental adjustment—that separates the speaker from his antecedent activity and from the dark emotion that attends his act. For instance, after surveying a catalog of historical atrocity in "In Strasbourg in 1349," the speaker waits for the light of morning, then calmly exits not merely Strasbourg, but "[w]hen morning came / I looked down at the ashes / and rose and walked out of the world" (*Poems,* 3). A more severe separation is found in a much gentler poem, "Some Months Ago," which is filled with "bright flakes from . . . mist," when Ammons somewhat surprisingly concludes with "I closed up all the natural throats of earth / and cut my ties with every natural heart / and saying farewell / stepped out into the great open" (*Poems,* 5). He does not tell us what "the great open" is. However, a page later in his *Collected Poems,* we find a similar term with the same adjective, "great," which is designed to resolve conflict between the masculine sun and the feminine moon about the possession of light. At the end of "I Went Out to the Sun," the speaker calls to the sun to resolve the controversy by invoking a comprehensive reality of loss and emptiness that makes the controversy futile: "Why are you angry with the moon / since all at last must be lost / to the great vacuity" (*Poems,* 7).

A Higher Way

These three poems suggest a mysterious, assimilative principle or higher reality lying behind the concrete particulars of Ammons's world. Harold Bloom claims that this reality is "Emerson's 'Nature,' all that is separate from 'the Soul,' " which is identical with the "you" addressed in "Hymn," in which Ammons's speaker asserts, "You are everywhere partial and entire / You are on the inside of everything and on the outside" (*Poems,* 39).[44] While Bloom is surely on the right track, the "you" in "Hymn" also bears a strong resemblance to Laotse's conception of Tao, or The Way. In *Tao Te Ching,* the paradoxical "inside and outside" are predicated of the "formless," "serene," and "empty" Tao:

> There was something formless and perfect
> before the universe was born.
> It is serene. Empty.
> Solitary. Unchanging.
> Infinite. Eternally present.
> It is the mother of the universe.
> For lack of a better name.
> I call it Tao.
>
> It flows through all things,
> inside and outside, and returns
> to the origin of all things.[45]

Like a realm of Platonic archetypes against which the things of this world pale by comparison, this "great open" or "great vacuity" or "Tao" is either inferred or stated abstractly in Ammons's poems. Whereas its concrete function is to offer him solace in an oppressive real world when none is otherwise forthcoming, its own nature appears to be as difficult to grasp as the ineffable pitch-black realm of undifferentiated consciousness discussed earlier. It dwells in the world of "silence unto silence" mentioned in "Requiem," from and to which the dead Sumerian has traveled. Its presence is felt throughout

Ammons's poetry, not only in his early poems but in later lyrics such as "The City Limits" and "A Coast of Trees." This mysterious realm is likely some analog of what Conze calls, as earlier noted, the Buddhist "Absolute . . . which stands completely outside the sensory world of illusion and ignorance." The term "Absolute" is, in fact, explicitly mentioned by Ammons in "Guide":

> You cannot come to unity and remain material:
> in that perception is no perceiver . . .
>
> you cannot
>   turn around in
> the Absolute: there are no entrances or exits
>   no precipitations of forms
> to use like tongs against the formless:
>   no freedom to choose:
>
> to be
>   you have to stop not-being and break
> off from *is* to *flowing* and
>   this is the sin you weep and praise:
> origin is your original sin:
>   the return you long for will ease your guilt
> and you will have your longing:
>
> the wind that is my guide said this . . . (*Poems,* 79)

Insofar as Ralph Waldo Emerson is everywhere in Ammons, Emerson's remarks from "Plato; Or, The Philosopher" on the "Asian" element in the Greek philosopher function well as "our guide[s]" in isolating the Asian Absolute in Ammons:

No man more fully acknowledged the Ineffable. . . . that is, the Asia in his mind . . . the ocean of love and power, before form, before will, before knowledge, the Same, the Good, the One; and now, refreshed and empowered by this worship, the instinct of Europe, namely, culture, returns; and he cries, Yet things are knowable! They are knowable, because, being from one, things correspond. There is a scale: and the correspondence of heaven to earth, of matter to mind, of the part to the whole, is our guide.[46]

If the "perceiver" in "Guide" "cannot come to unity and remain material," then Ammons seems to be saying that the material self somehow disappears when apprehending a wholeness amid a "diversity of sensations"—for instance, the experience of being "glad and sad at once" (*Poems,* 80). In fact, he goes so far as to claim that "origin is your original sin" and "that perception is no perceiver." In other words, he is claiming that the mental act of coming to unity does not necessitate an originating sense of self accompanying the act of knowing. Even worse, such a "Source" of self-consciousness (or "perception") places one "in the mouth of Death." It is, thus, "the Asia in [Ammons's] mind" that leads him to assert several lines later that "to be" truly, you need to find a motionless center in order to "come to unity," for "you cannot / turn around in / the Absolute." You need to "break / off from *is* to *flowing.*" You need not an originating self but a process of consciousness that resembles the Buddhist method of "Concentration." With its emphasis on emptying, this process involves what Conze calls overcoming "vestiges of the object":

> One first sees everything as *boundless space,* then as *unlimited consciousness,* then as *emptiness,* then by giving up even the act which grasped the nothingness, one reaches a station where there is *neither perception nor non-perception.* Consciousness and self-consciousness are here at the very margin of disappearance.[47]

In "Guide," the phrase "wisdom wisdom," repeated twice for emphasis in the poem's conclusion, not only announces the object of Ammons's search for guidance but also sounds like a version of what Conze calls "final salvation" "in the Old Wisdom School." This salvation "requires the complete obliteration of the individual self," such that Conze can conclude emphatically, "Wisdom alone can enter the Great Emptiness."[48] Applied to Ammons, such wisdom does not encompass a determinate personality that "is," but rather, one that is a "flow." This "self" or state is not a place or origin of consciousness but a wind, which is the perfect "guide" (model) for the speaker because it contains nothing of substance but "direction." Perhaps the best way to describe this major aspect of Ammons's poetic self (or lack of self) is through religious poetry. In "The Great Forest Book," or Brihadaranyaka Upanishad, cited by Joseph Campbell in *The Flight of the Wild Gander,* there is an evocative hint as to Ammons's method of concentration, in which the "Self," as a mode of apparently constitutive motion, is really ever-elusive. The "He" mentioned in the next extract is not a transcendental ego that retains its identity while it experiences discrete events in sequences. Beyond categories and self-contradictory while also beyond conventional coordinates of space and time, the "He" is identical with what one worships, namely, what Campbell calls the "rapture" of a consciousness that the gods of "eternal being" (*Poems,* 80) are within us, not without. The subsumptive term for this assimilative mode of "mythic identification" is "the All":

> . . . Him they see not; for as seen, he is incomplete.
> When breathing, He is named breath, when speaking voice, when seeing the eye, when hearing the ear, when thinking mind: these are just the names of His acts. Whoever worships one or another of these, knows not; for He is incomplete in one or another of these. One should worship with the idea that He is just one's self (*ātman*), for therein all these become one.
> That same thing, namely, this Self, is the footprint of this All, for just as one finds cattle by a footprint, so one finds this All by its footprint, the Self.[49]

"Guide" was first published in the *Hudson Review* as "Canto I" in 1960.[50] As late as 1981, Ammons continued to reveal a prominent interest in terms such as emptiness, unity, and an unnameable, ineffable reality that emerges through particulars, which are themselves transcendent signs. In the poem "A Coast of Trees" from his book of the same title, Ammons's speaker conducts quasi-religious meditation that recalls Geoffrey Hartman's observation in *The Fate of Reading* that "we moderns depend on reflective forms that have replaced religious self-consciousness":[51]

> The reality is, though susceptible
> to versions, without denomination:
> when the fences foregather
> the reality they shut in is cast out:
> if the name nearest the name
> names least or names
> only a verge before the void takes naming in,
> how are we to find holiness . . .
>   we know a unity
> approach divided, a composure past
> sight: then, with nothing, we turn
> to the cleared particular, not more
> nor less than itself, and we realize
> that whatever it is it is in the Way and
> the Way in it, as in us, emptied full. (*Trees,* 1)

Ammons's wordplay with Laotse's term "The Way" is especially suggestive here. To achieve a vision of "The reality," the speaker needs to transcend the "cleared particular," which is an obstacle and thus "in the Way." However, as we saw earlier, transcending the particular is an essential part of the meditative process of overcoming "vestiges of the object." The particular that is "cleared," or emptied of self-consciousness, is thus "in the Way" as a necessary step in the process of unifying wisdom. In addition, because inside and outside are categories that no longer apply in this undifferentiated world of mythic identification where space and time dissolve into the One, the "Way" is also "in" the "cleared particular." That is, the Way is both inside and outside the cleared particular, which has been "cleared" of its sensory content. The particular thus becomes an avenue or Way—as do we ourselves—of achieving the "holiness" of "full" union with "The reality" (the All, the One), precisely because we are "emptied" of ourselves and of the contents of the particular.

This verbal play is not simple escapism to a "reality" whose existence is merely problematic. As the mundane self empties of originating thought and motion, it also divests itself of emotion, including the desperate "longing" from which Ammons's early speaker so intensely suffers. This longing is attached to a worldly ego in considerable pain, a state which can be transcended by dissolving empirical opposites such as "elation and dejection" (Conze's words) or "sad and glad" (*Poems,* 80). Such transcendence can be achieved through certain techniques of Buddhist "Concentration," which

> . . . are means for transcending the impact of sensory stimuli and our normal reactions to it. . . . [I]n the fourth Dhyana, one ceases to be conscious of ease and dis-ease, well-fare and ill-fare, elation and dejection, promotion or hindrance as applied to oneself. Personal preferences have become so uninteresting as to be imperceptible. What remains is a condition of limpid, translucent and alert receptiveness *in utter purity of mindfulness and even mindedness.* . . .[52]

This state of "purity" or "even mindedness" beyond "sensory stimuli" corresponds to the "composure past / sight" in "Coast of Trees" and to the "serenity" we saw earlier in "Sumerian." It also corresponds to a moment in "A Crippled Angel" where Ammons's speaker watches the angel "bent in a scythe of grief" emit "[s]moke" from its ears, which centers the angel such that its ears become, surrealistically and realistically, "the axles / of slow handwheels of grief . . ." Yet when the speaker "interposed a harp" (that is, the poem) with its "lyric strings," he watched "the agony diffuse in / shapeless loss" (*Poems,* 29). The transcendence of "disease" and "dejection" through disciplined thought is an ancient commonplace in Asian thought. One form of this meditation is found in Chinese mythology in a Quietist sect (c. 300–400 B.C.) called "the School of Ch'i." Its philosophy is *"hsin shu"* or "The Art of the Mind." The appeal of this discipline or meditation, however, is by no means to the mind alone. Rather, it involves the whole human being in a way that explains that aspect of the human soul capable of attaining what Ammons calls "holiness" (*Trees,* 1). As Arthur Waley notes of *hsin shu:* "By 'mind' is not meant the brain or the heart, but a 'mind within the mind' that bears to the economy of man the same relation as the sun bears to the sky. . . . It must remain serene and immovable like a monarch upon his throne. It is a *shen,* a divinity, that will only take up its abode where all is garnished and swept. The place that man prepares for it is called its temple *(kung)."*[53]

LOSS AND BLISS

It must be noted immediately that, more often than not, Ammons's speaker does *not* attain this divine state. For the most part, he remains mired in the particulars of this world that are not "cleared," or are cleared only to some degree. While he aspires to a meditational "abode where all is garnished and swept," his characteristic stance is that of loss, a loss that turns his speaker into a sympathetic, if not heroic, failure. Ammons's speaker is, after all his questing, "the spent / seer," who in "Prodigal" laments that

> the mind whirls, short of the unifying
> reach, short of the heat
>   to carry that forging:
>   after the visions of these losses, the spent
> seer, delivered to wastage, risen
>   into ribs, consigns knowledge to
>   approximation, order to the vehicle
> of change, and fumbles in blunt innocence
>   toward divine, terrible love. (*Poems,* 77)

By understanding what this speaker aspires to—Ammons's mysterious Asian Absolute—we can better understand where his speaker currently stands. I believe that he stands in a poetic Sumer or lyric condition in which "the spent seer" yearns to disengage himself from "disease" and "dejection" by discovering a certain kind of immortality, yet he never—or seldom—finds it. In "Written Water" from *Lake Effect Country* (1983), Ammons appears doomed to remain this-worldly: "I hope I will go through / the period of hunger / for immortality and be stated— / so that I can rise / / at least from that death into communion with things" (*Lake,* 11). Whatever bliss he attains is as "fragile" as the ability to "look / through" human pain. As he says in "The Bright Side,"

> Bliss is the
> trace of
> existence that
> the idea of
> nothingness—
>
> thinking
> nothingness
> is a presence
> fragile as
> the longing look
> through
>
>   tragedy . . . (*Lake,* 1)

To put Ammons's sense of loss another way, we recall Emerson's remarks on Plato, when he notes a similar opposition between "immortality" and "things" in his Greek master. After acknowledging "the Asia in [Plato's] mind," which is a mystical "ocean of love and power . . . before knowledge," Emerson turns about, as he so often does, toward experience, saying that Plato also cries, "Yet things are knowable!" They are knowable because "[t]here is a scale . . . the correspondence of heaven to earth, of matter to mind, of the part to the whole. . . ."[54] In the final Emersonian analysis, Ammons also knows that there is an existential scale between heaven and earth, that is, between the immortality of the heavenly "Asia in his mind" and the earthly Sumerian deserts where he begins. The reality he ends up with is, precisely, the "scale" he has uncovered in his journey from the vast wastelands of Sumer to the "cool thought" of Eastern mysticism. We may conclude by defining this scale as the tension between the reality he aims for and the reality he must live. The reality he aims for may be expressed in this selection from the sixth chapter of the *Bhagavad Gita:*

> That supernal bliss which
> Is to be grasped by the consciousness and is beyond the senses,
> When he knows this, and not in the least
> Swerves from the truth, abiding fixed (in it);
>
> And which having gained, other gain
> He counts none higher than it;
> In which established, by no misery,
> However grievous, is he moved;
>
> This (state), let him know—from conjunction with misery
> This disjunction,—is known as discipline;
> With determination must be practised this
> Discipline, with heart undismayed.[55]

The reality in which Ammons lives is a middle ground between "supernal bliss" and the existential world of human "misery." This middle ground is really a disciplined refocusing of his mind, which offers a dark, yet serene, meditation that mediates between the extremes of hope and total loss. The knowledge that Ammons finally achieves may not be that of "immortality," but his "determination" within the craft of poetry leaves all of us "with heart undismayed." Ammons's motto may well be this axiom from the School of Ch'i, cited by Arthur Waley: "Throw open the gates, put self aside, bide in silence, and the radiance of the spirit shall come in and make its home."[56] "Radiance," "swerving," and "heart"—all these terms play a central role in these justly famous lines from "The City Limits," where Ammons's radiance results in a harmony of Sumerian darkness and Eastern light, and thus produces a complex serenity in which "fear . . . calmly turns to praise":

>   when you consider
> the radiance, that it will look into the guiltiest
>
> swervings of the weaving heart and bear itself upon them,
> not flinching into disguise or darkening; when you consider
> the abundance of such resource as illuminates the glow-blue

bodies and gold-skeined wings of flies swarming the dumped
guts of a natural slaughter or the coil of shit and in no
way winces from its storms of generosity . . .

                               then
the heart moves roomier, the man stands and looks about, the

leaf does not increase itself above the grass, and the dark
work of the deepest cells is of a tune with May bushes
and fear lit by the breadth of such calmly turns to praise. (*Poems,* 320)

Notes

1.   For this essay, the abbreviations list for Ammons is as follows: *Poems* (*Collected Poems, 1951–1971* [New York: Norton, 1970]); *Diversifications* (*Diversifications: Poems* [New York: Norton, 1975]); *Trees* (*A Coast of Trees: Poems* [New York: Norton, 1981]); *Lake* (*Lake Effect Country: Poems* [New York: Norton, 1983]); *Vistas* (*Sumerian Vistas: Poems.* [New York: Norton, 1987]).

2.   David I. Grossvogel, "Interview / A. R. Ammons," *Diacritics* 3 (Winter 1973): 51.

3.   Harold Bloom, ed., "The Internalization of the Quest-Romance," *Romanticism and Consciousness: Essays in Criticism* (New York: Norton, 1970), 8, 16, 13, 11, 15, 16, 12, 17.

4.   Joseph Campbell, *The Mythic Image* (Princeton: Princeton University Press, 1974), 478.

5.   Ananda K. Coomaraswamy, *Hinduism and Buddhism* (New York, Philosophical Library, 1943), 9.

6.   Philip Fried, " 'A Place You Can Live': An Interview with A. R. Ammons," *Manhattan Review* 1. 2 (Fall 1980): 11.

7.   Harold Bloom, *Romanticism and Consciousness,* 13.

8.   The relevance of such a process for this poet is extremely important, for Ammons has suffered dry spells, extended periods in which he has not been able to write, throughout his career. This may sound unlikely for so prolific and well-known a poet, but he was unhappily in one of these spells when I arrived to teach at Cornell in the late seventies. He turned, during this period, from writing poetry to painting watercolors.

9.   Mircea Eliade, *Myths, Dreams, and Mysteries: The Encounter between Contemporary Faiths and Archaic Realities,* trans. Philip Mairet (New York: Harper, 1975), 79–81.

10.   Ralph Waldo Emerson, "Plato; or, The Philosopher," *Representative Men* in *Ralph Waldo Emerson: Essays & Lectures* (New York: The Library of America, 1983), 645.

11.   In his interview in the *Manhattan Review,* Ammons is explicit about this disengagement from his religious upbringing: ". . . the religious thing is very strong in my background, where we had all kinds of preaching and dancing and holy rolling. . . . Going to college, I began to inquire into this religious background which was so strong and severe, and I got it more and more on a rational and historic level, which moved me intellectually from those positions that my family and aunts and uncles would have taken to be natural. . . . I was already in exile in that country. . . . Was no longer able to accept the doctrine familiar throughout my youth" (14–15). I share this thesis with Frederick Buell ("To Be Quiet in the Hands of the Marvelous," rpt. in *Modern Critical Views: A. R. Ammons,* ed. Harold Bloom [New York: Chelsea House, 1986], 196) and Janet DeRosa ("Occurrences of Promise and Terror: The Poetry of A. R. Ammons." [Ph.D. diss., Brown University, 1978], 64–65); however, my ritualistic line of inquiry differs considerably from theirs.

12. Joseph Campbell, *Primitive Mythology* (New York: Penguin, 1959), 50–51.

13. Geoffrey Hartman, "Romanticism and Anti-Self-Consciousness," *Romanticisim and Consciousness,* 47, 50, 49.

14. Heinrich Zimmer, *Philosophies of India* (Princeton: Princeton University Press, 1951), 534.

15. A. R. Ammons, "Poetry Is a Matter of Survival," interview by Nancy Kober, *Cornell Daily Sun,* 27 April 1973, 12.

16. C. Leonard Woolley, *The Sumerians* (Oxford: Oxford University Press, 1929), 13–14.

17. Samuel Noah Kramer, *History Begins at Sumer* (Philadelphia: University of Pennsylvania Press, 1981), 181, 113–14.

18. John Gardner, *Gilgamesh,* trans. John Gardner and John Maier (New York: Knopf, 1984), 18.

19. Cited by Thorkild Jacobsen in *The Treasures of Darkness: A History of Mesopotamian Religion* (New Haven: Yale University Press, 1976), 207.

20. Ibid., 204.

21. Frederick Buell, 196.

22. Samuel Noah Kramer, *Sumerian Mythology* (Philadelphia: University of Pennsylvania Press, 1944), 76.

23. John Gardner, 178.

24. Mircea Eliade, *Myths, Dreams, and Mysteries,* 95–96.

25. Ibid., 96, 243.

26. Mircea Eliade, *Myth and Reality,* trans. Willard R. Trask (New York: Harper & Row, 1963), 129.

27. Ibid., 136.

28. Ibid., 133.

29. Denis Donoghue, "Ammons and the Lesser Celandine," rpt. in *Modern Critical Views,* ed. Harold Bloom (New York: Chelsea House, 1986), 173–74.

30. Mircea Eliade, *Myth and Reality,* 133–34.

31. William Wordsworth, cited by Geoffrey Hartman in *Romanticism and Consciousness,* 47–48.

32. Joseph Campbell, *Primitive Mythology,* 186.

33. Joseph Campbell, *Occidental Mythology* (New York: Penguin, 1964), 163–64.

34. Ibid., 57–58.

35. Ibid., 54, 57.

36. Ibid., 78.

37. Mircea Eliade, *The Sacred and the Profane: The Nature of Religion* (New York: Harper & Row 1957), 29.

38. Ibid., 32.

39. Ibid., 87, 24.

40. Joseph Campbell, *Creative Mythology* (New York: Penguin, 1968), 216.

41. Chuang Tzu, trans. Arthur Waley, cited by Joseph Campbell in *Oriental Mythology* (New York: 1962), 427.

42. Arthur Waley, cited by Joseph Campbell in *Oriental Mythology,* 427.

43. Edward Conze, *Buddhism: Its Essence and Development* (New York: Harper, 1965), 106, 110–111.

44. Harold Bloom, introduction to *Modern Critical Views,* 7.

45. Laotse, *Tao Te Ching,* trans. Stephen Mitchell (New York: Harper & Row, 1988), 27.

46. Ralph Waldo Emerson, 645.

47. Edward Conze, 101; Janet DeRosa calls this "mirror-consciousness" in Ammons's poetry, 128.

48. Edward Conze, 101.

49.   Joseph Campbell, *The Flight of the Wild Gander: Explorations in the Mythological Dimensions of Fairy Tales, Legends, and Symbols* (New York: Viking, 1951), 195, 198.

50.   A. R. Ammons, "Guide," *Hudson Review* 13 (Autumn 1960), 354.

51.   Geoffrey H. Hartman, *The Fate of Reading and Other Essays* (Chicago: University of Chicago Press, 1975), 118; for a reading of "Guide" similar to mine, see Janet DeRosa, 71–72.

52.   Edward Conze, 101.

53.   Arthur Waley, cited by Joseph Campbell in *Oriental Mythology,* 26.

54.   Ralph Waldo Emerson, 645.

55.   *The Bhagavad Gita,* trans. Franklin Edgerton (New York: Harper, 1944), 34.

56.   Arthur Waley's note, cited by Joseph Campbell in *Oriental Mythology,* 26.

"How Does One Come Home":
A. R. Ammons's *Tape for the Turn of the Year*

WILLIAM HARMON

A. R. Ammons, who was born in 1926 in Columbus County, North Carolina, reached the summit of his career when his big *Collected Poems: 1951–1971* was received with admiration and prizes, including the 1973 National Book Award for Poetry. But one work, *Tape for the Turn of the Year,* which was published in 1965, was presumably too long for inclusion in the *Collected Poems;* and the omission, however understandable, could unjustly draw our attention away from a unique poem that remains one of Ammons's finest and most distinctive achievements. I judge that the *Tape,* possibly Ammons's very best long work so far, belongs among the select group of large poems genuinely American and genuinely great.

A good deal of Ammons's triumph in the *Tape* is a function of his choice of limits: how to start and stop; how much parochial matter to include, and how much ecumenical; how to use a local language in ways that can admit universal subjects without surrendering a personal voice; how to maintain epic pace and scope without sacrificing attention to minute detail. The format—among the silliest-seeming of limits—at first appears to be merely a gimmick, like Jack Kerouac's widely advertised use of long rolls of Teletype paper to facilitate the unbroken delivery of spontaneous prose. And Ammons virtually confesses as much:

> it was natural for
> me (in the House &
>   Garden store one
> night a couple weeks
> ago) to contemplate
>   this roll of
> adding-machine tape, so
> narrow, long,

Originally published in the *Southern Literary Journal* 17 (Spring 1975):3–32. Reprinted by permission.

> unbroken, and to penetrate
>   into some
>   fool use for it: I
> thought of the poem
> then,
> but not seriously:[1]

In time, the reader can calculate that the night in question, a fortnight or so before 6 December 1963, would fall very close to the day—was perhaps the very day (22 November 1963)—of the assassination of President Kennedy, an occasion nowhere distinctly visible and not even present *per se* in Ammons's poem but, all the same, necessary and unavoidable in its extrinsic context of loss and sorrow:

>   now,
>   two weeks
>   have gone by, and
>   the Muse hasn't
>   rejected it,
>   seems caught up in the
>   serious novelty:
>   (*Tape,* p. 3)

In his most recent poem, the book-length *Sphere: The Form of a Motion,* Ammons suggests the general circumstances of the selection of such a tape to help stave off confusion:

> when anxiety rises words too start to stir rising into schools,
>
> moving into sayings (a recourse, though delusional) like winds
> making up before a mild May-evening thunderstorm,
>   the winds
> spilling across the trees, then like surf sucking back in a
>
> growing tug: at such times, I pick up a tape, stick the end
> into my typewriter, and give everything a course, mostly
> because in a storm course is crucial and in proportion to the
>
> storm must be fought for, insisted on.[2]

The tape, evidently about a hundred feet long and three inches wide, becomes the first home of a poem in thirty-three parts in the form of a journal running from 6 December 1963 (a Friday) through 10 January 1964 (another Friday),[3] with entries of various lengths (between 27 and 474 lines, all short) for every day except 24, 25, and 29 December (i.e., Christmas Eve, Christmas, and the following Sunday). The prevailing analogues, I suggest, are a serial-cyclical form like that of *In Memoriam* (a "sad mechanic exercise"[4] to spend time mourning the premature death of an heroic figure) and the general contour of the *Odyssey* (the paradigmatic poem of homecoming):

> my story is how
> a man comes home
> from haunted
> lands and transformations:
> (*Tape*, p. 9)

I hasten to qualify my ascription of a memorial purpose to Ammons's *Tape* by saying again that the specific event and occasion are nowhere explicit. True, the White House is mentioned (*Tape*, p. 28), and certain passages are meditatively elegiac (e.g., pp. 153 and 179); but nothing in this long poem strikes quite the same note of collective sorrow as Ammons's modest "Belief: *for JFK*," written at about the same time as the *Tape* and first published in 1964:

> drums gather and humble us beyond escape,
> propound the single, falling fact:
> time, suspended between memory and present,
> hangs unmeasured, empty
>
> . . . .
> if we could break free
> and run this knowledge out,
> burst this energy of grief
> through a hundred countrysides!
> if bleak through the black night
> we could outrun
> this knowledge into a different morning!
> (*CP*, pp. 180–181)

I maintain that we cannot locate the *Tape* in history without realizing the terror of the public setting, even though the "single, falling fact" itself is never propounded outright. No poem written at that time could ignore the assassination, and any poem that *seems* to must do so as a deliberate strategy of sublimation, reluctance, compensation, or decorum. Ammons copes by controlling his immediate local and temporal materials, connected to a single voice and person, gathered around a hollow core of shock—the gift of emptiness that the poet, at the end of the *Tape*, says he has delivered to the sympathy of the reader:

> I've given
> you my
> emptiness: it may

not be unlike
  your emptiness:
in voyages, there
are wide reaches
of water
with no islands:
    (*Tape*, p. 204)

And, soon after, in language that extends the apocalyptic images of Yeats's "The Second Coming" into a wasteland even blanker than the bestial sphinx's desert, the poet continues his ironic inventory:

I've given you
  the dull days
when turning & turning
revealed nothing:
I've given you the
sky,
uninterrupted by moon,
bird, or cloud:
    I've given
you long
uninteresting walks
so you could experience
vacancy:
    (*Tape*, pp. 204–205)

The public occasion is, then, unspoken but implicit; the private journey is plain as day:

what's the way home?
home?
what's wrong with these
deserts, excitements, shows:
excursions:

home is every minute,
occurring? just like this?
. . . .
    maybe this song
will be about getting
home
and figuring out some
excuse to leave again:
that wd be gd bth cmng &
gng:
    (*Tape*, pp. 28–30)

Here Ammons joins the oldest established permanent floating American symposium, the dialogue—begun on the day the first European explorer left his old home for a new world—about the shapes and uses of nostalgia. The desire and effort to regain a lost past inform a parallel struggle to go home again by somehow moving *back* in time and space. The motif of the lost home and the possibility of return, debated from every angle, animates "The Death of the Hired Man" as well as "East Coker," and Thomas Wolfe embraced it as his chief subject. Ammons's Southern origins may attune him to certain peculiar pitches of the motif as both an inheritance and a habit.

Ammons suggests, in the passage quoted above, that you can go home again, but he adds a note that concerns Wolfe (his fellow Carolinian) less than it concerns Dante and Tennyson who, from antithetical viewpoints, explored the destiny of Ulysses after his long-sought homecoming was done. The *Tape* operates as the parabolic story of such a return and also as an enactment and embodiment of the journey. The beginning on 6 December 1963, I would say, comes about as a project to resist the horrible and potentially numbing dislocation brought about by the assassination. One may recall two widely separated passages in Ammons's other poems: the idea of "time, suspended between memory and present" in "Belief: *for JFK*" alongside the conclusion of the long "Essay on Poetics," which says, "having a project is useful especially during natural suspensions" (*CP*, p. 317). The project during the painful suspension in the *Tape* would seem to be a matter of getting back into time and space by coming home to *something:*

> who are we
> on this globe?
> how & at what cost
> have we survived?
>
> . . . .
>
> maybe one way of
> coming home is
> into silence,
>
> restfulness from words,
> freedom from the mill
> that grinds
> reality into sound:
> (*Tape*, p. 87)

About midway in the *Tape*, near the end of the eighteenth entry (23 December), the poem seems to break down in a fashion that is typical of ambitious modern poems.[5] Ammons approaches his ostensible loss of power by addressing a female spirit, his Muse:

> I admit
> I've shot my load:
> but I can't stop: give
> me a second wind:
>   (*Tape,* p. 101)

And then comes a gap of two days.

In succeeding entries, the poet presents himself as "moorless" in a "firmless" country, but the very admission of such deprivations acts as the source of the "second wind" needed to complete the journey:

> tell me, tell one
> moorless in the drift
>   of broken forms, who is
> the conceiver who
> will pour this
> regurgitated pab
>   into the
>   transfigured
> saucepans, winejars,
> breadbaskets, garages,
> space stations
> of the new time?
>
> . . . . . .
>
> *ecology* is my word: tag
>   me with that: come
>   in there:
>   you will find yourself
> in a firmless country:
>   (*Tape,* pp. 103 and 112)

The centers in motion punctuate the journey, and Yeats again provides the governing geometry: "where is the center / that holds?" The answer is "none," with the exception of the rough circle of lichen representing a mutable, serial ecological equilibrium (*Tape,* pp. 116–121).

The progress of the poem, then, is not according to a known route to a fixed destination. The home is a relative point, an island, floating loose in a moving ocean. At the end of his poem (which turns out to have been, formally, a comedy after all), Ammons admits his lack of plan:

> I wrote about these
> days
> the way life gave them:

> I didn't know
> beforehand what I
> wd write,
> whether I'd meet
> anything new:
> 　　(*Tape,* pp. 203–204)

No authentic modern odyssey can follow, with any hope of success, the tidy rhumbline or great-circle routes of past journeys.[6] In the final extension of relativism, you cannot go home again, to be sure; but the uncertain journey, where motion and mutation are necessary, becomes itself a new home. I suppose many Americans could say today, "Be it ever so mobile. . . ."

As it happens, Ammons's ostensibly random journey repeats in some detail the pattern of earlier homecomings, even to the degree of including, *mutatis mutandis,* a trip to the Underworld. For Gilgamesh, Odysseus, and Aeneas, such excursions provide honor to the dead and prophecy for the quick. In Ammons's re-enactment, the outright ritual, which takes the form of attending a memorial service for William Carlos Williams (who died in March 1963), marks the low point of his journey. Here, in the twenty-second entry (30 December), a dead poet is remembered, a widow honored, and the virtual terminus of the dying year observed with a pessimism that recalls the evacuated landscape of Hardy's "The Darkling Thrush." The service is placed in a setting of loss and descent, with a bus ride akin to dying and a big city akin to hell:

> the dump swarms with
> gulls & smoke:
>
> yesterday I gave
> to the memory of
>
> William Carlos Williams
>
> 　　(reception in NY
> for Mrs. Williams)
> 　　sat in the back of
> 　　the bus up
> & the motor ground my
> head to dust (gray,
> 　　graphitic)
> 　　& a man fell
> in a fit
> in the bus station: three
> men held him till
> he jerked still:
> 　　a crowd circled &
> 　　watched:

> (we're monkeys, scratching
> our heads
> & asses &
> dumb with joy & tragedy)
>
>   so many people
> with bodies only:
>   (*Tape,* p. 129)

Home from this hell—recalling the surprise of Dante in hell and Eliot in hell-ish London that death had undone "so many"—the poet relaxes somewhat ("how good to be back"—*Tape,* p. 130) and, with nowhere to go but up, makes room in his poem for certain pleasures that promise whatever it is that serves as salvation and safety in a floating world. With a clarity of vision and voice, as though with faculties purified and perfected by the experience of an infernal region, the poet-celebrant attends to a comfortable amalgamation of the domestic and the sacred:

> I hear the
> porkchops frying!
> ah,
> there's the sweet, burnt
> smell!
>   sounds in the kitchen,
>   pots lifted
>   with empty
> hushing ring,
> the plunger of the icebox
>   door
>   snapping loose: the
>   sizzling roil of
>   porkchops turned:
>   protest, response:
>
>   flashes of aluminum
> light
>   as the pots work, the
>   glint of tines
>   as the table
>   dresses: the
>   holy
>   slow
>   lifting & turning
> in the spinach pot:
> rituals, hungers,
>
>   motions over
>   fire,

the stance &
tending:
(*Tape,* pp. 132–133)

Suspended astonishingly between these brilliant images of the preparation of
the dinner (smells, sounds, sights) and the actual realization and consumption
of the food (tastes, textures, the kinaesthetic pleasure of being on "the outside
edge of / painfully full"), comes a unique passage that stays in my memory as
the still point of a turning poem. At 6:08 p.m., Monday, 30 December 1963,
the poet hears the voice of his wife, Phyllis:

"You
can
come
sit
down
now
if
you
want
to."
(*Tape,* p. 133)

She speaks nowhere else in the poem; almost nobody, in fact, speaks in the
poem, unless you count the poet himself and various reports of short conversations rendered in indirect discourse. And nowhere else in the poem is a
period used. But here, in a column of ten ordinary monosyllables wholly
faithful to the American idiom (and probably transcribed verbatim) and yet
extraordinarily articulated by subtle rhythmic and harmonic linkages, the lost
poet, fresh from the multiple horrors of hell and death-in-life, hears the welcome words inviting him to share the multiple joys of sitting and sharing a
meal with a woman. "You can come sit down now if you want to": we all have
heard it. But not until Ammons has fixed it on his tape, delicately centered,
shrewdly prepared, have any of us been put quite so close to the radiant comforts of our own immediate routines and our own daily speech.

The ground bass of the (vertical) line is the reverberation of monosyllables, each spaced as though to have democratically equal weight; as the ear
hears them, the syllables gather in tentative patterns.[7] On closer inspection,
the words display an uncommonly high degree of coherence, stability, and
acoustic symmetry. The "down" and "now" at the middle of the line share
consonant as well as vowel sounds. Branching from this center, the halves of
the line seem to be subtle, complex reflections of each other. "Down" and
"now" we have looked at; "sit" and "if" share the same vowel; "come" and
"you" are more faintly linked than "can" and "want," but still linked; and the
two outer syllables, "you" and "to," rhyme perfectly.

Let me try to justify the closeness of my attention to these ten syllables. In the succeeding entry—31 December—Ammons looks ahead:

> after this,
> this long poem, I hope I
> can do short rich hard
> lyrics: lines
> that can incubate
>
> slowly
> then fall into
> symmetrical tangles:
> lines that can be
> gone over (and over)
> till they sing with
> pre-established rightness:
> (*Tape,* p. 143)

Ammons's best short poems satisfy these requirements perfectly—none better, I think, than "Small Song":

> The reeds give
> way to the
>
> wind and give
> the wind away
> (*CP,* p. 222)

In "Reflective"—

> I found a
> weed
> that had a
>
> mirror in it
> and that
> mirror
>
> looked in at
> a mirror
> in
>
> me that
> had a
> weed in it
> (*CP,* p. 170)

—as in "Glass," "Mirrorment," and several other short poems, Ammons may remind us of Heidegger's curious *ereignenden Spiegel-Spiel*, the "coming-to-pass interplay of mirrors" that constitutes our total world.[8] Among the atomic and subatomic particles of language where Ammons loves to dwell, we find the commonest words—"You can come sit down now if you want to"—and those tricky monosyllables *(let, still, fast)* that are so ordinary they often project antithetical meanings that mirror and reverse each other. This is not the place for much more scrutiny of the vitreous aspect of Ammons's poetry, but—having seen the "mirrorment" at work thematically, lexically, and acoustically—we can pause to note two of Ammons's poems that *graphically* demonstrate the reflective nature of poetry. In both, I would say, the medial gap allows the small words to move in two directions—call them priapic and ethical—that the bilateral symmetry suggests and (being yonic) displays:

CHASM

Put	your
self	out
and	you're
not	quite
up	to
it	or
all	in

(*CP,* p. 229)

CLEAVAGE

Soon	as
you	stop
having	trouble
getting	down
to	earth
you	start
having	trouble
getting	off
the	ground

(*CP,* p. 322)

But back to the *Tape.* Beyond the pole of what I have called the still point of the turning poem, a good deal of tape—time and space yet to be taken—remains. The homecoming motif recurs explicitly:

(if you were
sitting on a
distant strand,

> longing for home,
> you'd have to
> conjure up things to
> occupy the time,
> too)
> (*Tape*, p. 136)

and then gives way to a sustained meditation on the occasion of the loss of home, the national catastrophe that may have effected the *dépaysement* in the first place:

> screens
> between us & memories
>   we can't bear:
>   what unmentionables
> of guilt & terror!
> go back & see
> terror as fantasy,
> guilt as innocence?
>
>   but we've
>   purposely lost
>   the road back:
> . . . .
> let's accept this
> provided & open
>   possibility & go
> ahead:
> we may redeem ourselves:
>   (*Tape*, pp. 136–137)

Beyond this point, where a measure of reconciliation and repose is achieved, the pace of the poem slackens and the tone relaxes somewhat, although the presence of the remaining tape to be filled exerts a compulsion and pressure of its own. The twenty-third entry (31 December), one of the longest and most varied, reflects and ruminates:

> last day of the year:
> I've been at this
>   25 days—this
> idle tendance
> of typewriter & Muse—
> nearly a month of Sundays:
>   I'll miss the
>   hovering over time,

> the watchfulness—
>
> . . . .
>
> I anticipate: the
> empty tape is still
>   imposing,
>   frightening:
>   (*Tape*, pp. 144–145)

On the first day of the New Year, the pluralist poet settles into something like acceptance that even promises affirmation:

> beside the terror-ridden
>   homeless man
>   wandering through
>   a universe of horror
> dwells
> the man at ease
>   in a universe
>   of light:
>
>   let's tend our
>   feelings &
>   leave the Lord
>   His problems
>   (if any): He
> got us this far on His own:
> & millions have come
> & gone in joy
>   (predominantly):
>   (*Tape*, p. 155)

The first word of the *Tape*, "today," works as the musical tonic of the whole poem, which I would say is almost all in the key of "today minor"; of the twenty-three December entries, ten begin outright with "today" and four others strike that note very near the beginning. Of the ten January entries, "today" is the first word of eight and the second word of yet another. In this long coda, then, the tonic is asserted most strongly as the note toward which the homecoming must aim. The poet attends to the weather of the day and, from that center, launches casual excursions into ethics and aesthetics. The parenthetical "if any" and "predominantly" in the passage just quoted leave a margin for exploration and questions:

> what of the evil man?
> is he evil because he
> realized himself
> or because he didn't?
>   (*Tape*, p. 158)

see the roads I've
traveled
to come to you:
monsters I've engaged:

have I earned the grace
of your touch?
(*Tape*, pp. 159–160)

Even Odysseus knew (from Tiresias' prophecy) that his return was
impermanent; in any event, however, Penelope would remain the true wife
and, in Ammons's variation, the moving center that generates the complex
series of shifting peripheries:

a man's center is his
woman,
the dark, warm hole
to which he brings
his meaning . . .
you been lookin for a
center to the universe?
's it:
(*Tape*, p. 188)

But, despite the confidence of that colloquial, monosyllabic affirmation of the
certain center, a radiating circumference of salient questions still remains:

reader, we've been thru
a lot together:
who are you?
where will you go
now?
(*Tape*, p. 200)

how do the hopeless
get some fun out of
life?
(*Tape*, p. 201)

have our minds taken us too
far, out of nature, out of
complete acceptance?
(*Tape*, p. 202)

And, in a passage very near the end of the tape, the means of homecoming
are pondered in phrases stated (though not punctuated) as a question:

> coming home:
>   how does one come
>   home:
>
>   self-acceptance
>   reconciliation,
> a way of
> going along with this
> world as it is:
>   (*Tape,* p. 203)

Yet another question toward the end of the poem seems to be in a different key:

>   what
>   must I do
>   to reach
>   the top?
>   (*Tape,* p. 183)

The ordinary journey of return follows the trace of a horizontal homing, and that dimension dominates Ammons's poem; but there is also a vertical impulse, as though upward to the top of the ziggurat of the literary life with its own temptresses, whirlpools, and gigantic one-eyed monsters. In a peculiar way, one goal of this movement is Ithaca: not Odysseus' kingdom but the town in New York (where, in fact, Ammons was to go in September, 1964, to teach at Cornell). The horizontal homing is foolish in a most serious way; the ambition to climb the poetic-academic mountain, spoken honestly by an honestly idiosyncratic poet, reaches beyond earnest folly into burlesque. The first adumbration of the politics of avarice is "straight":

>   I know you,
> man:
>   am grateful to the
> order, however imperfect,
> that restrains you,
>   fierce, avaricious: the
> Top: Olympus,
> the White House, the Register:
>   (*Tape,* p. 28)

But, before a page is turned, Odysseus is analyzed and the spirit of Avarice animates two further incarnations, one vulgar and one most tender:

> Odysseus screwed a lot but
> never got screwed: or

> if he did, he screwed back
> harder, first
> chance he got: he never

"took nothing lying down":

And the quasi-Odyssean poet considers himself in Homeric singing robes:

> my song's now
> long enough to screw a
> right good-sized article
> with:
> flexible to vault me
> to the Top:
> I hope it will lift me into
> your affections:

> that's what I need:
> the top I've chosen,
> the mt I wd climb:
> (*Tape,* p. 29)

Through six thousand or so line-feed and carriage-return operations, the progress of the tape represents a homecoming in one dimension and a mountain-climbing in another.

In yet a third dimension, the poem moves toward its own language, a mother tongue clearly analogous to a mother country. "Language," says Heidegger, "is the house of being"; and Gary Snyder, slightly less metaphysical and resonant, says, "My language is home."[9] Any such house or home can come to mean the "place" one starts from and also the unaccountable origin to which he tries to return. The search for a lost or missing language has preoccupied American poets from the beginning, and none has found a thoroughly accommodating idiom without some sacrifice. The vernacular excludes certain necessary ranges of dignity, but the high style precludes certain necessary ranges of practical detail.

Not too far along the midway of his circus, the modest Ammons, having just called his growing tape "accomplished florescence," favors his own spacious idiom:

> empty places
> make room
> for
> silence to
> gather:
> high-falutin
> language does not

> rest on the
> cold water
> all night
> by
> the luminous
> birches:
>   (*Tape*, p. 131)

> poetry has
> one subject, impermanence,
> which it presents
> with as much permanence as
> possible:

> .   .   .   .

> only the lively use of
>   language lives:
>   can live
>   on dead words
>   & falsehood: the
> truths poetry creates
>   die with
>   their language:
>   stir any old
> language up,
> feel the fire in it &
> its truths come true
>   again:
>   the resource, the
> creation, and the end of
>   poetry is
>   language:

> .   .   .   .

> poetry is art & is
>   artificial: but it
> realizes reality's
> potentials:
>   (*Tape*, pp. 145, 176–177)

"I've been looking," he says later, "for a level of language—

>   that could take in all
>   kinds of matter
>   & move easily with
>   light or heavy burden:
>   (*Tape*, pp. 143–144)

The reader who has been confronted with unambiguous examples of such a level of language should not really need assurance of this sort, but very few poets seem willing to surrender the occasion for putting in their two cents' worth. It is not simply unnecessary; it is often inconsistent or even contradictory. Ammons assembles a series of examples of the most assured use of the widest range of American idioms, and throughout the poem he adds asides, which are not really needed, to justify his practices:

> I've hated at times the
> self-conscious POEM:
>   I've wanted to bend
>   more, burrowing
> with flexible path
> into the common life
>   & commonplace:
>
> .   .   .   .
>
> poetry has no use, except
> this entertaining play:
>   passion is
>   vulgar when not swept up
> into the cool control
> of syllables:
>
> .   .   .   .
>
> unity & diversity: how
> to have both: must:
>   it's Coleridge's
>   definition of a poem:
> (*Tape,* pp. 144, 178–179, and 185)

Well. Maybe; maybe not. The last thing a shrewd critic wants to do is go too far in applying a poet's critical *dicta,* delivered in a didactic mode, to the same poet's actual performance in a mimetic mode.

Such mundane aesthetic meditations do serve one good purpose in the *Tape.* They furnish a range of territory somewhat in the middle distance, a "mesocosm," if I may invent a word, between the terminal extremes of epic macrocosm and lyric microcosm. In Ammons, these poles are as extreme as in any poet since Tennyson. We have come to assume lately that the traditional cosmological dimension of epic is no longer available to poets because of the great and specialized complexity of the natural sciences, which have moved, in education and in daily life, to a zone far removed from the arts. Ammons, however, at one time or another a major in "pre-med, biology, chemistry, general science," a Bachelor of Science from Wake Forest College, and a regular reader of *Scientific American,*[10] can manage the hard words and long numbers with a graceful authority unmatched by any contemporary. The details of the immediate day—weather, meals, stray memories—would shrivel into unredeemable triviality without a macrocosmic perspective, just as the general cosmology would vaporize into unredeemable gaseousness without the mundane, pedestrian, diurnal detail:

10,000 yrs

> Troy
> burned since then:
> but the earth's been
> "resting"—entering
> a warm
> cycle: the Sumerians
> had not, that long ago,
> compiled
> their
> holy bundle of
> the elements of civil-
>   ization, nor
> had one city-state stolen
> it from another:
>   (*Tape,* pp. 6–7)[11]

> the 200-inch glass
> shows a
> billion-billion galaxies:
> what is God
>   to this grain of sand:
>   (*Tape,* p. 201)

Toward the end of the *Tape,* in the thirty-first and thirty-second entries (8 and 9 January), the poem, momentarily threatened with a stale flattening of imagination, takes two surprising turns that introduce further dimensions of experience and language. Having committed himself, early on, to work on the "crusty/hard-clear surface" (*Tape,* p. 6), the poet stays away from things deep and dark; even his own childhood memories deal with sensations of surfaces, ordinarily cold and austere. Against the "black night" of "Belief: *for JFK,*" the poet early in the *Tape* proposes a morning that is not a mourning:

> may this song be plain as
> day, exact and bright!
> no moonlight to loosen
>   shrubs into
> shapes that
> never were: no dark
>   nights to dissolve
>   woods into one black
>   depthless dimension:
> may this song leave
> darkness alone, deal

> with what
> light can win into clarity:
> (*Tape,* p. 4)

But, as the poem nears its completion, the determination to avoid the dark depths is weakened:

> deep down inside are
> fireworks
> & a whole mess of rivers:
> (*Tape,* p. 186)

And what follows is a large vista, recalling panoramic symbolic paintings by Bosch or Chagall, of human figures acting out a range of activities and attitudes: solicitude, anger, song, lechery, suffering, squabbling, disappointment, love; but, after a sketch of this "very interesting/country," the poet stops:

> I'm afraid to visit:
>   wd take another tape to
> get there:
>   (*Tape,* pp. 186–187)

And, returning to affairs of his own place and moment, he tells about a visit to a refuge for wild birds. Here, with images of Canada geese slipping and skidding on a melting edge of a lake, the poet's language similarly begins to slip and slide:

> two bald iggles
>   been sighted out
>   there:
>   tell me:
>   can you beat that?
>   I looked for any but
> couldn't find some:
>   (*Tape,* pp. 188–189)

The thirty-second entry (9 January), which follows immediately after this passage of lexical dissolution, presents the images of a rainy day in a synthetic comic language that "Katzenjammerish" describes with as much precision as I can muster:

> today ben
>   der clouds
> downwashen
>   die rainingdroppes

                    und
                tickleticklen
                der puddlepoolens
                    (*Tape,* p. 189)

In this penultimate entry of the *Tape,* the orbits of idiom and reference both reach their greatest scope. At the beginning and end, English dissolves into a funny, mud-luscious effigy of language, as though the poet were digging into the very bottom of his bin of old verbal resources. At the same time, between these Germanic boundaries, he seems to lift his idiom to its most sublime height. In virtually the only episode in the poem that qualifies as "mysterious," the poet addresses a familiar compound Other whose characteristics demand a range of imagery that calls up, all at once, the elemental universes of Buddhism, Christianity, and pre-Socratic atomism:

                the tenderspoken
                assurer: the gentle
                    enlightener &,
                till enlightened,
                        protector: arrive:
                        say you're
                        going on a journey
                & need one to teach:
                teach me,
                father:
                        behold one whose
                        fears
                        are the harnessed
                        mares of his going!
                fiery delights,
                        pounding hoof
                        & crystal eye:
                        where before
                        dread
                        & plug-mule
                            plodded:
                clod:
                mere earth:

                . . . .
                unto a clod, how unlike:
                dance!
                    throw in:
                    throw yourself
                        into the river
                        of going:
                where the banks also flow:
                        (*Tape,* pp. 190–191)

Since universal flux works here as both subject and context, it is as good a place as any to comment briefly on the predominant punctuation of the *Tape,* which is the colon. As we have seen, there is only one period in the whole work—at the speech of Wisdom-Penelope-Phyllis that I have called the still point (pun intended) of the turning poem: even the last word of the poem is followed by a colon. For a while, I thought this device both gimmicky and derivative; MacLeish, I judged, had worn out the colon by overusing it for a didactic effect that I experienced as a rather sanctimonious inconclusiveness. As time went on, however, I changed my mind, and now I believe that Ammons's choice is a most effective strategy. It is not simply a question of preference or taste (Ammons has said, "I like the action of the colon"[12]); the suggestion of flowing seems necessary in long works. They must move. One may recall Pound's Canto I, which begins "And" and ends "So that:" and also C. S. Lewis's argument in favor of the style of *Paradise Lost:* "Continuity is an essential of the epic style. If the mere printed page is to affect us like the voice of a bard chanting in a hall, then the chant must *go on.* . . . We must not be allowed to settle down at the end of each sentence." Lewis then persuasively demonstrates how "Milton avoids discontinuity by an avoidance of what grammarians call the simple sentence."[13] In Ammons's case, a certain readjustment is necessary, but it need not be radical or large. In his diminished epic, he does avoid discontinuity; he does so by an avoidance of what grammarians call the period.

In the final entry (the thirty-third, 10 January), with the end of the tape of the *Tape* in sight, the Odyssean poet achieves a satisfying, if not final and terminal, consummation of his complex voyage. The model homecoming finds accomplishment in an economical summary of the odyssey, a bright salute to the world, and a courteous *nunc dimittis:*

> old castles, carnivals,
> ditchbanks,
> > bridges, ponds,
> > > steel mills,
> > > > cities: so many
> interesting tours:
>
> the roll has lifted
> from the floor &
> our journey is done:
> thank you
> for coming: thank
> you for coming along:
>
> the sun's bright:
> the wind rocks the
> > naked trees:

so long:
(*Tape,* p. 205)

"So Long!"—a lovely, enigmatic expression that gives the title to the valedictory poem of *Leaves of Grass*—adds Ammons to the roll of American poets who have attempted the highest flights. Whitman used *So long!* as a striking refrain, novel but durable. "A salutation of departure, greatly used among sailors, sports, and prostitutes," runs the definition Whitman gave William Sloane Kennedy. "The sense of it is 'Til we meet again,'—conveying an inference that somehow they will doubtless so meet, sooner or later."[14] In the poem itself, Whitman could be describing Ammons's enterprise. "Enough O deed impromptu and secret," he says; "Enough O gliding present—enough O summ'd-up past. . . ." Compared to Ammons's conclusion, Whitman's may sound melodramatic:

> Remember my words, I may again return,
> I love you, I depart from materials,
> I am as one disembodied, triumphant, dead.

But I think we have room for both poets. One, in 1860, found affectionate words for his blessing on the reader. The other, as 1963 turned into 1964, found, by a miracle of fortune and genius, the unrepeatable conjunction of occasion and voice to add another grand long poem to our national treasury.

Notes

1. *Tape for the Turn of the Year* (Ithaca, N.Y.: Cornell Univ. Press, 1965), pp. 2–3; hereafter cited in the text as *Tape.*
2. *Sphere: The Form of a Motion* (New York: Norton, 1974), p. 52.
3. Nothing internal specifies the years, but the dustjacket gives 1963–1964. In the poem, 13 December is a Friday, as was the case in 1963. Richard Howard is wrong in locating the setting as December-January 1964–1965. Having misconstrued the date, Howard then mistakes the prevailing attitudes: "Mooning around the house and waiting for *Expressions of Sea Level* to come off the press in December of 1964, the poet produced, in a two month period, and with a determination to reach an end that became more than obsessive, became self-destructive, 'a long thin poem' written on a huge roll of adding-machine tape run through the typewriter to its conclusion. . . ." *Alone with America: Essays on the Art of Poetry in the United States Since 1950* (New York: Atheneum, 1971), p. 9. A similar dismissal marks Helen Vendler's complaint about the "merely fussy" in Ammons's work: "There is a fair amount of this sort of thing, especially in the rather willed long poem *Tape for the Turn of the Year* (you buy a roll of adding-machine tape and type on it for a couple of weeks until the tape is all typed and then you have finished your poem)." "New Books in Review," *Yale Review,* LXII (1972–1973), 421. Even Harold Bloom, one of Ammons's earliest and most vocal champions, concludes that the *Tape* is "a heroic failure that is Ammons's most original and surprising invention"; not even faint praise could be so damning. *The Ringers in the Tower: Studies in Romantic Tradition* (Chicago: Univ. of Chicago Press, 1971), p. 280.

4.   *In Memoriam,* V. "A use in measured language lies," Tennyson says in this stanza. I suggest that the edges of the tape serve Ammons as such a measure. He discusses margins and indentations in "The Limit," *Collected Poems: 1951–1971* (New York: Norton, 1972), pp. 266–267; hereafter cited in the text as *CP.*

5.   Such breakdowns occur in Hopkins' "The Wreck of the Deutschland" (Stanza 28), Pound's *Cantos* (particularly LXXIV), Williams' *Paterson* (Book III), and Eliot's "East Coker."

6.   Pound's Canto LXXIV suggests the progress of the modern *commedia:* "By no means an orderly Dantescan rising / but as the winds veer."

7.   No pronounced rhythm forces the words into one pattern or another. Trochees prevail, but so unobtrusively that "trochaic pentameter" suggests a regularity that the line does not obey.

8.   See Thomas Langan, *The Meaning of Heidegger: A Critical Study of an Existentialist Phenomenology* (New York: Columbia Univ. Press, 1959), p. 121.

9.   See Langan, pp. 108–112, and Gary Snyder, *Regarding Wave* (New York: New Directions, 1970), p. 42.

10.   See autobiographical statement, *Diacritics III* (Winter 1973), 2, and *CP,* pp. 314–317.

11.   Typically and consistently the sophisticated primitivist, Ammons works on peripheries, surfaces, margins, edges, beaches, and origins. In the eighth entry (13 December, *Tape,* p. 56) the poet buys the complete plays of Aristophanes, some of the oldest jokes on record. Subsequently, Ammons refers to *The Thesmophoriazusae* (*Tape,* p. 57) and *The Ecclesiazusae* (*Tape,* p. 90). But, while these references are witty and incidental, Ammons's preoccupation with Sumer—perhaps the earliest civilization of which we know—is steadfast. "The holy / bundle of elements" appears in "Discoverer" (*CP,* p. 137): somewhat later, the "Essay on Poetics" includes the passage, "the holy bundle of / the elements of civilization, the Sumerians said" (*CP,* p. 300). Many of Ammons's earliest poems refer to Sumer, and his latest poem, *Sphere: The Form of a Motion,* mentions the Sumerian divinity Enlil (p. 71). It is interesting to note that among the *me*'s, the scores of elements of Sumerian civilization, of which about sixty have survived in myths, we find the usual institutions (godship, kingship, lordship, crafts) and some not so usual: sexual intercourse and prostitution, descent into the nether world and ascent from it, fear and outcry, weariness, and the troubled heart. See S. N. Kramer, *Sumerian Mythology* (New York: Harper, 1961), p. 66.

12.   In conversation, July 1973.

13.   C. S. Lewis, *A Preface to Paradise Lost* (1942; reprinted New York: Oxford Univ. Press, 1961), p. 45. Cf. Coleridge: "The reader should be carried forward, not merely or chiefly by the mechanical impulse of curiosity, or by a restless desire to arrive at the final solution; but by the pleasurable activity of mind excited by the attractions of the journey itself. Like the motion of a serpent, which the Egyptians made the emblem of intellectual power; or like the path of sound through the air; at every step he pauses and half recedes, and from the retrogressive movement collects the force which again carries him onward." *Biographia Literaria,* xiv.

14.   See *Leaves of Grass,* ed. Harold W. Blodgett and Sculley Bradley (New York: Norton, 1965), pp. 503–506.

One: Many

ALAN HOLDER

After passages on the movement of cows, the nature of language, the physics of snow-laden trees, Ammons' *Essay on Poetics* announces that its subject is "one: many" (p. 300). A great number of Ammons' poems could properly make such an announcement. Indeed, the relationship of One to Many, or of unity to multiplicity, has claim to being his single largest subject. Apprehending a world full of diverse entities, the poet muses on the possible connections among them, ponders the making of a coherent whole or wholes out of reality's variegated, abundant discreteness.

I *The One and the Many as a Traditional Problem*

In giving as much importance to the One and the Many as he does, Ammons brings to mind Emerson, who in his essay "Plato; or, The Philosopher" saw two "cardinal facts" lying forever "at the base" of the world: "1. Unity, or Identity; and 2. Variety. . . . It is impossible to speak or to think without embracing both." Apart from Emerson, consideration of the relationship of the One to the Many has engaged a number of minds, and in one form or another this question may be said to go back to the beginnings of Western philosophy. Early Greek philosophers, such as Thales and Anaximenes, asserted the coherence of things by positing an elemental substance out of which all the world's beings and objects had been made. Anaximander, a pupil of Thales, found the basis of all things in an indefinable substance he designated as the Infinite or Boundless. The Pythagoreans appeared to believe in a divine Unity or One.[1] All these theories accepted a One, or Unity, and a Many that came out of it. Parmenides, however, posited his One as the only true being. The Many, associated with motion and change, was unreal, an illusion. Parmenides' thought was taken up in Plato's *Parmenides,* a work

Originally published in *A. R. Ammons* (Boston: Twayne Publishers, 1978), 52–73.

that served, through a misreading, as an important source for the theories of Plotinus. He posited a formless, ineffable One, which he regarded as synonymous with absolute good. Through an emanation or overflow of the One, there had emerged, in a series of stages, all things that were. With increasing distance from the One had come increasing division and multiplicity. The further anything was removed from the One, the further it was from goodness. The One and the Many were totally opposed. Existing at the greatest distance from the One was the material universe. Man was to strive to return to the One through mystical union, putting away multiplicity. The One was formless, and a soul had to make itself formless to approach it.[2]

In his magisterial study of romanticism, *Natural Supernaturalism,* M. H. Abrams devotes a good many pages to showing how Plotinus' treatment of the One and the Many, together with other Neoplatonic thought, became intertwined with Christianity, and shaped the theories of various philosophers, particularly Fichte, Schelling, and Hegel, as well as Marx. In differing ways, human history was conceived by them as a fall from unity and goodness into multiplicity and evil. This fall was seen as a necessary prelude to a circuitous journey having as its goal a return to unity, though a higher one than that which was lost (this conception, like the next, constitutes an important difference from Plotinus' thought). Romantic theory typically held that in such unity "all individuation and diversity survive. . . ." Such an ideal can be found in Coleridge, Schiller, and Hegel. Coleridge called it "multeity in unity," and "it served him, as it did Schiller, as the norm both for life and for beauty. . . ."[3] Coleridge saw the history of the race as well as of the individual as moving in a circle from the One back to the One by way of the Many. The return to Unity in romantic thought "is often signalized by a loving union with [a] feminine other, upon which man finds himself thoroughly at home with himself, his milieu, and his family of fellow men."[4] Abrams shows how such notions of a fall from and return to unity are reflected in the poetry not only of Coleridge, but also of Blake, Wordsworth, and Shelley, as well as in the works of Eliot and Lawrence in our own century.

Had Abrams extended his attention to modern philosophers, he might well have cited Alfred North Whitehead. In *Process and Reality,* Whitehead describes the relation of God to the world in terms of the One and the Many.[5] (Whitehead is of particular interest here because Ammons seems to have studied him at one time.)[6] Though Whitehead gave short shrift to Coleridge in *Science and the Modern World,* his remarks on the One and the Many seem related to Coleridge's notion of "multeity in unity."

As even this miniscule outline indicates, Ammons' concern with the One and the Many can be seen as linking up with a long line of Western thought, and he has unquestionably been aware of at least some of the thinkers involved.[7] But whatever his acquaintance with the treatment of the One and the Many in Western writings, his interest in that subject must almost certainly have been quickened by his one-time exploration of Eastern philosophy. In an interview, as already indicated, he singled out Lao Tse as one of the Chinese thinkers that he had read. Lao Tse expounded the doctrine of Tao or The Way, which refers both to the manner in which the whole world operates, and to the original or undifferentiated Reality from which the universe has evolved. A synonym for The Way is One. Thus, the concept of Tao intersects with the philosophy of Plotinus, the two furnishing part of the background of Ammons' interest in the One and the Many.

But lest I fall into the critical sin of aggrandizing my subject by simple association, I hasten to say that the One and the Many as treated in Ammons' poetry does not have the scope or grandeur that it has in Plotinus or Coleridge, or quite the conceptual complexity of Whitehead. Unlike its formulation in Hegel, say, it is not related to history (which Ammons has, by and large, not cared to bring within his poetic purview—he attempts to dispose of it in the poem "History"). Nor is it related, except in a few instances, to society, as it is by Lao Tse. No large fables or dramas are constructed by Ammons, as they are by Shelley and Blake, in his handling of the theme. Comparatively modest in his approach, he deals with the One and the Many in short poems or briefly in longer ones. Its interest for him tends to be epistemological rather than moral or spiritual, and to be focused on the world of physical things and processes. Placed beside the writings of Coleridge and Emerson, or of other romantic figures whom he undoubtedly has read, his treatment of the theme seems comparatively narrow, specialized. But that theme has an undeniable hold on him, surfacing in poem after poem, and it takes on weight and urgency as he wrestles with it.

II   *The One and the Many as an American Problem*

Before investigating Ammons' treatment of the One and the Many, I would like to suggest that there is something in the situation of an American that may impart special force to this particular subject (and that we see reflected in Emerson and Whitman, and, perhaps less obviously, in Stevens). Our national ideals include the celebration of the individual, of his uniqueness and right to freedom. But we also espouse brotherhood and the notion of a shared American-ness, the things that bind us together. Our country encompasses great physical as well as human diversity, and yet purports to be a single nation, the *United* States of America. That is to say, our geographic and social characteristics, as well as our political principles, necessarily involve a tension, if not a contradiction, between, on the one hand, the idea of variety and individualism, and, on the other, the idea of unity. Thus, apart from the intrinsic appeal of the question of the One and the Many for the human mind, the cultural conditions of being an American may operate to give it special interest.[8]

That such is the case with Ammons is indicated in the very poem whose title points up his preoccupation with unity and multiplicity, "One: Many." The lines of this piece jump from California's features to Maine's, thereby spanning the variety of the American continent. Considering other places in America, and reminding one of Whitman, Ammons talks of "the homes . . . the citizens and their histories, / inventions, longings." He is struck by the diversity of the country, believes it to be "enriching, though unassimilable as a whole / into art" (even as he incorporates it into his verse). He finds in America "out of many, one; / from variety an over-riding unity, the expression of / variety."

In *Sphere,* Ammons again connects the One and the Many with America, saying:

> . . . I can't understand my readers:
> they complain of my abstractions as if the United States of America
> were a form of vanity: they ask why I'm so big on the

> one: many problem they never saw one: my readers: what do they
> expect from a man born and raised in a country whose motto is *E
> plurisbus* [sic] *unum.* . . . (S, 65).

Still, if being an American has heightened Ammons' interest in the One and the Many, in unity and multiplicity, it has done so indirectly. For this interest rarely takes the form it does in the passages just quoted. Rather, it is typically manifested in solitary musing stripped of social or cultural content.

III *Unity*

In at least two places in *Collected Poems,* unity exerts an unqualified appeal for Ammons, though the nature of that unity is not the same in both cases. "Sphere"[9] posits the fetus in the womb as enjoying a utopian existence. It is in a state of perfect equilibrium, of "warm unity," in which the self possesses a universe. Being born is a fall into multiplicity. Here, unity is a physical-psychological condition. In "Image" it is a religious concept, one that the poem represents as being in disrepute. Men have attempted to embody the divine through different images, whose disappearance has rendered the very assumption of its existence suspect, but only for "the ignorant and stupid," who "promote the / precision of the visibly defined." The speaker wishes that "the notion of unity could get around," a notion that apparently involves eschewing any attempt at constructing an image of it. For unity is indefinable and invisible (this is reminiscent of Plotinus' One).

But it is precisely this kind of unity that Ammons rejects in "Guide." The first two stanzas present parallel assertions: (1) "You cannot come to unity and remain material"; and (2) "you cannot / turn around in / the Absolute." Connecting unity with death, the poem tells us sardonically that there we will have our longing to go back to our origins satisfied. (Just such longing manifests itself in "Sphere," which speaks of "the dark original water.") It is the discrete entity, fallen out of unity, removed from origins, that is joined to life: "a peachblossom blooms on a particular / tree on a particular day: / unity cannot do anything in particular."

For Ammons, the paradox is that what should be an ultimate fullness, a joining together of the Many into the One, is typically characterized by deprivation, attrition. In *Tape* he says ". . . we can approach / unity only by the loss of things" (*T,* 23). In "Looking Over the Acreage" the conception that "all-is-one" is dismissed by saying it is a state "where nothing is anything." *Hibernaculum* may be said to carry this to its logical extreme, totally depriving totality of content: "the sum of everything's nothing" (p. 379).

In these examples we find a revulsion from or dismissal of the idea of unity being expressed through a series of explicit statements. In other poems the attitude is not simply stated but poetically embodied. "Early Morning in Early April" ponders the scene before it, where mist has produced an effect of glass, hanging glittering drops in the *trees:*

> what to make of a mist whose characteristic
>
> is a fine manyness coming dull in a wide
> oneness: what to make of the glass
> erasures, glass: the yew's partly lost.

We have here a shift from the brilliance of the individual drops to their luster-less accumulation as mist. This is reinforced by the sound shift from the high pitch and definition of "*fine* ma*ny*ness" to the low pitch and blur of "co*m*ing d*u*ll . . . / *o*neness." The scene contains shining and obscurity, as the many are transformed into the one (unity). A philosophical problem has been con-cretized as a visual puzzle (and aural pattern), with the poem obviously favoring the brilliant appearance of the many.

In "Staking Claim" the speaker excitedly praises the power of the mind, its ability to attain unity: "it can go up up to the ultimate / node" where opposites merge. It can go

> all the way to the final vacant core
> that brings
> things together and turns them away
>
> all the way away
> to stirless bliss!

But the celebrating voice here subverts itself. Notice, first, that the core attained is vacant. (Ammons may have had in mind The Way or Tao of Lao Tse, often designated as Nothing, in which case the first and fourth lines are punning.) Second, the recurrence and jarring juxtaposition of "way" and "away" make for strain and even ludicrousness, heightened by *"stirless bliss."* The attempt at climax through internal rhyme produces, in my ear anyway, an effect of anticlimax, which I regard as intentional. Also, the poem's example of opposites merging is "ascent and descent a common blip." The last word makes the joining of the two movements trivial or nonsensical. Moreover, the poem ends in a manner that further undermines its ostensible commitment to unity:

> . . . the leaves
> breaking into flocks around me taking
> my voice away
> to the far side of the hill
> and way beyond gusting down the long changes

"Way" and "away" here are operating explicitly in a direction opposite to the poem's original thrust, becoming the path to the world of change rather than to the stirless bliss of unity.

A rejection of unity may be found as well in "Mean," assuming I am right in my interpretation of this remarkable poem's use of "singular":

> Some drippage and spillage in
> active situations:
> efficiency's detritus,
> fall-out from happenstance:
> a, probably calculable,
> instrank of frabigity:
> people accustomed to the wide terrain
> know, with little alarm, some
> clumps are dissolving:
> singular's the terrible view
> from which the classy gods
> take up glassy lives.

The piece begins with a laconic notation of mechanical imperfection in "active situations," which I take to be nothing less than the ways in which the world works, operations which are "efficient," but that involve certain losses. These the poem seems initially to regard with matter-of-fact acceptance. However, as in "Staking Claim," the voice here subverts itself. Pretending to a dry, detached tone, the poem produces a parody of detachment through the

measured phrasing and seemingly technical vocabulary of "a, probably calcu-
lable, / instrank of frabigity." "Instrank" and "frabigity" indeed! These, meant
to sound like engineering terms, are but nonce words amounting to nonsense
(see the diction of "Even"). The poem gives its true feelings away when it
refers to the "terrible view" of the gods. What Ammons is speaking of here, I
believe, is the gods' perception of the totality of things as constituting a
unity—this accounts for the use of "singular" (which I also take to have a sardonic connotation, namely, "remarkable"). This privileged perception of unity
(shared by "people accustomed to the wide terrain"—see the "wide oneness"
of "Early Morning in Early April"), is the view from afar. The gods presumably think in terms of the "mean," or average, of the totality. Close up, there
is the fate of the parts that go to make up the whole, parts regarded simply as
dissolving clumps. The discrepancy between the status of such clumps and
that of the gods is immense, and bitterly rendered by the jarring cross-rhyme
of "classy" and "glassy" (the latter term probably meant to suggest "hard,
removed"—see "Glass"). In "Mean" the sense of how the universe operates is
comparable to that in Epistle I of *Essay on Man,* but without the essential element of Pope's acceptance. The poem is much closer to Emily Dickinson bitterly watching a flower "beheaded" at play through the ordering operations
of a nature watched over by an approving God. Unity, in "Mean," is associated with divine meanness or heartlessness.

If "Staking Claim" and "Mean" see the apprehension of unity as available to at least some people, other Ammons poems look upon such a state of
mind as unattainable. In "Corsons Inlet" Ammons finds that he is capable of
discerning local coherences "but Overall is beyond me." In this poem he is
made glad by his limitation. But in the opening stanzas of *Essay on Poetics*
(p. 296) he seems at least somewhat rueful that the wholeness he can achieve
in lyric poems encompasses only limited materials. Both here and in "Corsons
Inlet" there is a fatalism about the limits of mind in bringing the world's
diversity into unity. The opening of "Russet Gold" might also be read in this
way. Ammons seems to be saying there that he does not expect to receive a
vision of the coming together of things. Satisfaction must be found in contemplating humble, individual items, such as drops on a piece of cellophane,
bark loosening "on a soggy stick."

IV   *Multiplicity*

Drops and bark are in the domain of multiplicity and discreteness. This need
not be regarded merely as something that has to be settled for when the
approach to unity fails. Rather, multiplicity is often seen as precious in
Ammons (a corollary of his attitude toward form, for the realm of the multiple and the realm of forms are identical).

A poem in *Ommateum* may be regarded as foreshadowing this prizing of multiplicity. Looked at in such a way, "In the Wind My Rescue Is" falls into place in the Ammons canon, whereas in the context of that first volume alone, it is something of an anomaly. How could the wind, so dangerous in early Ammons, function as a rescuing agent?[10] It operates as such by providing "the seed safety / of multiple origins." In so doing, it works against the speaker's self-appointed task of constructing an edifice out of stones of the earth, gathering them "into *one* place" (my italics). That is, an impulse toward building an imposing unified structure, a static entity, is happily checked by a force connected with looseness, movement, and multiplicity.[11]

The wind may be said to function in a related way in "Saliences," where it is a "variable" making for changes in the dunes setting of the poem. The resulting multiplicity is linked to freedom of the imagination. Freedom and multiplicity are also joined in "One: Many," though here it is the "freedom of each event to occur as itself." That is to say, multiplicity is related to, if not equated with, an open-ended universe capable of generating unique occurrences, unconstrained by an *a priori* pattern (see the ending of Stevens' "Sunday Morning"). While "One:Many" talks of keeping both one and many in operation (as do Coleridge and Whitehead), it seems primarily concerned with avoiding formulations that impose unity by destroying diversity. Such formulations lack richness and constitute thin abstractions.

A similar view shows up in *Tape,* which speaks of "the inexhaustible / multiplicity & possibility / of the surface," as opposed to the "depths," which are conceived of as a "few / soluble drives, / interesting, but to be / returned from" (p. 13). Here there is not a single unity in question, but a series of unities (including, say, the notion of the unconscious). Nevertheless, the enchantment with the variegatedness of phenomena, rather than with the abstract formulations that attempt to organize or fuse them, is obviously close to the slant of "One:Many." In "Celestial" the multiplicity of the mundane calls forth Ammons' affection. Beautiful dusk scenes are regarded as partly composed of the "mean and manyful," and the poem ends with praise of the multitudinous and ordinary, the "millions whose / creation was superb, if not special."

V   *Ascents and Descents*

The attraction to unity and the counterpull of multiplicity are related to and sometimes directly dramatized by Ammons' use of ascents to and descents from allegorical or symbolic heights. While occurring mostly in the volumes after *Corsons Inlet* and *Tape,* this device came to him early in his career, judging by the placement of "Choice" in *Collected Poems.* Confronting the speaker in that work is a stairwell with golden steps leading upward and dark steps going down. The upward path is linked (like unity) to the immaterial. Such a connection, that is, between ascent or height and the immaterial, appears repeatedly in the poems. (The complementary connection joins descent and the material.) The speaker of "Look for My White Self," a purged, cleansed being, a ghost, associates himself with a mountain, a "height of snow." The spirit in "Bridge" climbs "higher and higher / toward the peak no one reaches live." A poem that speaks of "the world beyond," which "burns dimension out of shape," is called "Peak." In "Loft" the title refers to a level of perception akin to "abstractions's gilded loft" occupied by the speaker in "Levitation," who is investigating "the / coming together of things" (an explicit linking of height and the quest for unity). "The Unmirroring Peak" speaks of "the highest heights" achieved by mind, where all is "immaterial."

We might say that the decision in "Choice," to descend the dark steps rather than ascend the golden ones, prefigures several rejections in Ammons of the climb to height. "Peak," for example, seems to reject "the world beyond," and chooses, though somewhat ambiguously, "the apple," symbolic of this world. Two other rejections of height occur in poems which employ a device used throughout Ammons' works, namely, a verbal exchange between a human speaker and inanimate object. In one, "Mountain Talk," when asked by the mountain whether he really wants to share its "unalterable view," the speaker goes on counting his "numberless fingers," a not very felicitous image that seems to amount to an endorsement of multiplicity, as opposed to the oneness of the mountain's prospect (see "Height"). In "Kind," mocked by a giant redwood glorying in its "height and distant view," the speaker defends his preference for weeds and "stooping" (the poem may owe something to Emerson's poem "Fable"). This is similar to the use of height and weeds in "High and Low," where the speaker, dissatisfied with his ascent to a mountain risen within him

> rubbled
> down the slopes to
> small rock
> and scattered weed.

The conversion of "rubble" to a verb nicely initiates the descent to modest and nondescript multiplicity, to disorder ("*scattered* weed"). "Convergence," which follows immediately on "High and Low" in *Collected Poems*, also deals with climbing a symbolic height, this one representing a "joining" of the speaker's sorrows (so suggesting, like the title, a kind of unity). But the position gained is made dubious, being described as "the peak of / illusion's pyramid," which suggests something other than a peak in Darien. In "Reward" the title refers to what is earned by a hard climb to a peak, namely, that "the / major portion of the view was / descent."

Moreover, the "gain" through ascent that we find in "Offset," a poem which carries no suggestion of a subsequent descent, causes us to question it.

That gain is described as "extreme & invisible"; "the eye / seeing nothing / lost its / separation," and "self-song / . . . became continuum." The self, or its song, has become indistinguishable from its surroundings. It may be said to have achieved unity. In this reworking of the theme of the self's dissolution, Ammons reminds us of Emerson in his famous "eyeball" passage in *Nature.* There Emerson says that in the woods he feels "uplifted into infinite space,— all mean egotism vanishes. I become a transparent eyeball; I am nothing; I see all; the currents of the Universal Being circulate through me; I am part or parcel of God." Emerson's seeing all while Ammons sees nothing may not be an absolute difference; remember Ammons saying that "the sum of everything's nothing." But where Emerson regards his experience as a supremely privileged moment, Ammons, it seems to me, is troubled by the loss of self in its experience of height and unity. Notice the striking fate of the quester in "Separations"; ascending a white mountain, he perishes, "swilling purity."

"One More Time"—the title might well be acknowledging Ammons' fondness for employing symbolic heights—talks of going to "high" places where there is a reduction "to rock, the single substance." That this is related to the perception of unity is clear when the one choice open at the heights, namely, going down, results in a coming upon "deepening multiplicity, / trifling, discrete abundance, / bottomless diversity." The poem obviously values the variety attendant upon descent, endowing it with the paradoxical quality of being at once trifling and bottomless.

But of course the recurrence of heights in Ammons suggests an ongoing urge to scale them, or, we can say, ascend to unity. The purified speaker of "Look for My White Self" pictures himself as "singing" at a height of snow. Experiencing a seizure of height, the man in "Moment" feels he is undergoing a destruction that is "blessed." The "bodiless loft" in "Loft" places the speaker "above the level of most / perception," and in "Levitation" the investigator of the "coming together of things" may be cramped, even endangered, by his abstractions, but enjoys his triumph over the ground's downward pull, its persistent, would-be reductiveness, emphasized by the poem's rhymes. The sojourner among the elemental presences of height in "Cougar" does not want to forego them. Attaching an heroic air to his enterprise, the poem is similar to Stevens' "How to Live. What to Do," with its two climbers who come upon an "heroic height." *Tape* identifies poets with peaks, albeit "peaks of need," who release "cold / majesties," and are "cut off / from the common / stabilizing ground of their / admirers" (p. 130). "The Unmirroring Peak," describing the constantly changing world by what might be called disrespectful syntax, plainly celebrates the height above change achievable by the mind.

Height, while sometimes representing an undesirable remove from the material and multiple, cannot be refused or retreated from without some misgivings. The point is made through Ammons' nice appropriation of two clichés in "Cleavage":

Soon	as
you	stop
having	trouble
getting	down
to	earth
you	start
having	trouble
getting	off
the	ground

The cleavage here is not just present in the typography, but in Ammons' attitude toward heights and low places, unity and multiplicity. (His ambivalence was dramatized relatively early in his career in "Hymn," which spoke at once of leaving earth to go up "into the . . . undifferentiated empty stark" [unity] and staying on earth "with the separate leaves" [multiplicity].)[12]

VI   *High and Low*

In perhaps a dozen of the poems, height, or at least some form of upward movement, *combines* with lowness or descent to figure in an important way different from those we have been considering. The simultaneous presence of the two placements or movements signals experiences or conditions or moments of particular felicity for Ammons. In "Choice," having selected the *descending* steps of the staircase, the speaker achieves "high purity." "Bridge," which symbolizes an ideal combination of body and spirit through a bridge arching over a pond, renders reflections in the water by saying "people / rising on the bridge / descend into the pond." "Open," celebrating sexual pleasure, presents the human body in terms of "magnified territories of going down / and rising." These examples all involve human activity. Other combinations of ascent and descent, highness and lowness, are seen in nature. In "Locus," a tree with winter-burnished leaves that has been transfigured from a "ruin . . . to / stillest shining," is introduced in this way: "the small oak / *down* in the / hollow is / lit *up*" (my italics). "Admission," coming immediately after "Locus" in *Collected Poems,* and intimating the possibility of some sort of transcendence, begins: "The wind high along the headland, / mosquitoes keep low." Celebrating light, "The City Limits" notes that "birds' bones make no awful noise against the light but / lie low in the light as in a high testimony." (For a poem that echoes the language here but *splits* high and low, see "Tussock.") The human and the natural combine to form a high-low pattern in "Ground Tide," where Ammons, experiencing euphoria while riding over a series of ascents and descents, talks of easing out "into the open / failing slopes, led by the spiritual, risen stream." In "Definitions," telling us "The weed bends /

down and / becomes a bird," Ammons says "I / have got my / interest up in / leaf / transparencies," going on to see an attractive dispersal of himself in nature. Such fusions of high and low, or ascent and descent, are obviously of great significance to Ammons, self-contained entities not subject to the ongoing dialectic that characterizes consideration of the One and the Many in his poetry (though there is one poem, *Pray Without Ceasing,* in which Ammons questions his attraction to high-low fusions).

VII   *Center and Periphery*

The figures of "center" and "periphery" are as prominent in the poems as those of ascent (height) and descent (lowness). The two sets of figures can be shown to be related if we keep in mind that Ammons associates unity with order, multiplicity with disorder. (In a few poems—"Kind," "Meteorology," "One More Time," and *Essay on Poetics*—the height and periphery figures actually intersect.)[13] "Identity," using a spider web as its starting point, clearly identifies the center of the web with order, its periphery with disorder. "The Misfit," celebrating the fact unassimilable into theory, places such a fact at "the edge" or boundaries, which the "nucleus," or center, "fails to control." A passage in *Tape,* after linking order and center, joins multiplicity to periphery and, implicitly, to disorder (p. 113).[14] This connection of multiplicity and periphery is effected again in the poem entitled "Periphery," and complementing it is the joining of center and unity. The quest for essential truth in "The Arc Inside and Out" is rendered in terms of stripping away peripheries and coming to a center of "oneness."

Just as unity sometimes figures as something difficult, perhaps even impossible to reach, so does center. The sea in "Expressions of Sea Level" speaks to us "far from its center." Only its edges are articulate and visible— the first word of the poem, noting the action at those edges, is "Peripherally."[15] "Meteorology" advises us to confine the self to " 'extremities & superfices' / the unenterable core's rusty / lode shut up." *Hibernaculum* tells us that the poet's hope that he can find in a "central / core's center the primordial egg of truth" is an illusion (p. 372). The setting sun of "Left" is treated as the center of the dome of the sky, which is "inscrutable by clarity / & undifferentiation." This phrase, somewhat inscrutable in itself, may be said to receive amplification and explication by the next (and final) poem of *Collected Poems.* "The Arc Inside and Out." This work indicates that one possible way to unity would involve the elimination of reality's superficial data, possibly producing a "distilled / form." This I take to correspond to the "clarity" in "Left." The second path to unity, "Arc" suggests, would be through inclusiveness, a conceptual shoveling together of the world's abundance, "plenitude / brought to center. . . ." This may be said to correspond to "undifferentiation" in "Left." "Arc" sees neither method as working, for, as in *Hibernaculum,* the hope of reaching center is an illusion.[16] The very poem entitled "Center" points up the elusiveness of that entity:

> A bird fills up the
> streamside bush
> with wasteful song,
> capsizes waterfall,
> mill run, and
> superhighway
> to
> song's improvident
> center
> lost in the green
> bush green
> answering bush:
> wind varies:
> the noon sun casts
> mesh refractions
> on the stream's amber
> bottom
> and nothing at all gets,
> nothing gets
> caught at all.

Note that the effect of the song is at first disordering ("capsizes") and then organizing, with the objects named in lines 4–6 approaching the song's center. But that center is lost in a bush oddly separated from its color, that coming apart countering the preceding centrifugal movement (indeed the lines about the bush are so written as to require, as is often the case with Ammons, an act of taking apart by the reader). Moreover, instead of a clear, unifying center, we get a sense of multiplicity, through the varying action of the wind (see "Saliences"). There is a further effect of what might be called uncentering in the construction of the last three lines. Coming up against a surprising comma (one would expect no break after "gets"), the reader is momentarily tempted to regard "noon sun" as the subject of "gets," with that verb operating as parallel to "casts." That is, the sun casts but gets nothing at all. As it turns out, "gets" is actually functioning as an auxiliary verb, taking "nothing" as its subject. But the essential meaning is not changed by the corrected reading. For when we get the lines straightened out, we are still left with "nothing." A center may be said to exist but cannot be grasped.

Baffled in the quest for center, we are left with periphery. But as with multiplicity, Ammons does not necessarily regard location there simply as a matter of deprivation. In "Square" he claims "The formulation that / saves damns"[17] and declares himself a "periphery riffler." The gayly ostentatious play of sounds in this last phrase would appear to indicate that Ammons takes satisfaction in being away from a clarifying center, the saving-damning formulation (though he cagily does not get too far away). He is content to root about in that which cannot be formulated, the "riddling underbrush."[18] In the piece entitled "Periphery," he begins by complaining about such terrain, difficult "thickets." Periphery is linked to multiplicity here, the latter regarded as a host of precise, discrete phenomena but leading only to crude conclusions. Deciding to penetrate toward the center (that is, presumably, toward a more satisfying form of truth), he hesitates, and is rewarded:

> . . . I came on a spruce
>
> thicket full of elk, gushy snow-weed,
> nine species of lichen, four pure white
>   rocks and
> several swatches of verbena near bloom.

The reward is precisely the multiplicity (nine species!) he originally found unsatisfactory. The strong *k, sh* and *ch* sounds here add to the effect of the thicket's richness.

But periphery cannot always content. It is associated in "Locus" with an oppressive sense of time's passage, and, in *Essay on Poetics,* with the dangerous possibilities of chance and "entropy" (p. 316) that at other times engage Ammons. Periphery can also mean the superficial for him (see *Essay on Poetics,* p. 312), and in "Object" he berates himself for being too ready to accept it:

> X out the rondure of
> the totally satisfying
> and all other sizable areas
> near the central scope:
> that degree, that circumference,
> put aside: the leftovers,
> though, pips & squeaks,
> think to pick up, shovel
> up, if possible: that is what
> is left: stuffing the central
> experience into the peripheral
> bit overinvests though &
> creates aura,
> wistfulness and small floating.

Starting here with the self-admonition to eliminate the center, he ends up by regarding the subsequent absorption with the peripheral as an overvaluation leading only to minor apprehensions.[19]

VIII   *Polar Clusters*

Drawing together the elements discussed in this chapter, it is possible to set up two groups or clusters that may be said to constitute the poles between which Ammons' sensibility oscillates:

One (Unity)	Many (Multiplicity)
formlessness	form
order	disorder (entropy)
stasis	motion
height	ground level
center	periphery[20]

The respective conjunctions of formlessness and order, form and disorder, may seem peculiar, but I believe the basis for these joinings has already been furnished. To summarize this point, formlessness is the quality of the overall order, of the One, while form is the quality of each of the discrete entities making up the Many, entities whose separate beings are not gathered up into an order, but exist in disorder.

   While the above bipolar scheme is, I believe, valid as far as it goes, there is something within the body of Ammons' poems which makes necessary a supplement to that scheme. He is concerned not only with the form, say, of a raindrop, but also with form in a more abstract sense, for example, that of a physical law which governs the behavior of individual entities. There is in him the impulse to find or contemplate such forms, which may figure as ascents to a height, or penetrations to a center, *without* going all the way to total Unity. There are, then, two ways of regarding the relationship of the One to the Many in Ammons, which can be illustrated as follows:[21]

I   the world as
        a totality

II   a particular aspect
        of the world

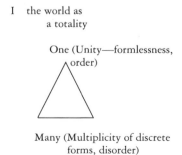

One (Unity—formlessness, order)

Many (Multiplicity of discrete forms, disorder)

One (Form—a specific pattern governing a selection from the Many)

Many (Multiplicity of discrete forms, disorder)

But even within the limits of the second scheme, Ammons exhibits the oscillation, the dialectical movement present between the One and Many clusters originally designated. He is attracted now to disorder or discrete entities, now to pattern. "Saliences," which, as already noted, moves from an emphasis on multiplicity to one on order, uses its title word to designate approvingly both the individual features of landscape *and* the forms that those features assume. In *Tape* the attraction both to the individual entities and to the forms arising from them shows itself plainly. The poem notes that "facts get lost" in an hypothesis, "while one fact/ or two, / . . . can't make a meaning" (*T,* 176). In *Essay on Poetics* Ammons tells us "I proceed a little way into similarity and / withdraw a bit into differentiae" (p. 302), which is another way of saying he alternates between a quest for pattern or form and a regress into unordered discreteness. In the same poem he talks of celebrating both unity and multiplicity (p. 304), and states, in an unabashedly prosy passage:

> . . . the mere massive pile-up of information
>
> is recalcitrant to higher assimilations without great loss of
> concretion, without wide application of averaging: things are
> reduced into knowledge: and truth, as some kind of lofty reification,
>
> is so great a reduction it is vanished through by spirit only. . . .

When this happens, "The mind searches its culture clutch for meaningful / or recurrent objects" (p. 308). We might note the use of the words "higher" and "lofty," an example of the association in Ammons of height and the search for form, in the sense represented by the second triangle above. The traditionally honorific content of these terms is here undermined by Ammons' unease with the abstraction involved, the remove from the particular. At the same time, he feels the need for at least limited forms—"recurrent objects." But in the same poem he seems to point to the possible dangers even of these. Speaking of oneness in connection with both social organization and poems, he says "oneness is / not useful when easily derived . . . manyness is not truthful when / thinly selective" (p. 315). At first appearing to be set in balanced antithesis, these statements are actually complementary, both coming down on the side of a large, rich multiplicity. Yet in *Extremes and Moderations* Ammons finds that diversity "is not ever-pleasing," and cites an example of his interest being commanded by the form an aggregate of fine particulars took, rather than by the particulars themselves. The poem strongly rejects those who cannot rise above the concrete (p. 329).

IX   *Search for Synthesis*

Drawn now to the One, now to the Many, Ammons repeatedly seeks (especially in *Tape* and *Essay on Poetics*) for a mode of synthesis, a vantage point that will take adequate account of both. In "One: Many" he explicitly sets up such a goal: "To maintain balance / between one and many by / keeping in operation both one and many" (p. 138). This poem seems primarily interested in cautioning against a unity that is achieved through destruction of diversity. But at the end of the poem, he says, rather too easily, that events (the operation of multiplicity) take on "inevitable balances." What started out as a presumably difficult task for consciousness—"To maintain balance etc."—has been displaced by something that is done for us, something that simply happens. A solution, then, to the problem of the One and the Many is merely to assume that the two are reconciled or synthesized in the course of events. Similarly, *Tape* asserts that "high entropy / is not loss of pattern" (p. 123), and that unity may "afford the / individual / more comfortably than / division could" (p. 186). But these statements of reconciliation or synthesis are simply assertions, unearned. In the same vein, *Tape* also says that reality can go in many ways at many levels and still display "discernible unity" (p. 165). For a moment the poem seems to question what it has said, as an arbitrary imposition of order, but then focuses on a reconciliation of the One and the Many.

Not given to easy or sweeping solutions, but offering partial, limited reconciliations, are those passages in Ammons which suggest synthesis through what might be called many onenesses, or a multiplicity of unities. These are related to, and overlap with, the limited forms spoken of earlier. Ammons, in such passages, is in effect admitting, like Stevens, that he cannot bring a world quite round. Thus, despite its apparently pretentious title, "The Unifying Principle" turns out to be troubled and modest. Untypically concerned with welding a social unity out of diverse individuals, it offers us not *the* principle, but a series of possible principles, or rather, objects, for example, "a / phrase shared, an old cedar long known." *Essay on Poetics,* after announcing that its subject is "one: many," speaks of the

> mechanisms physical, physiological, epistemological, electrical,
>
> chemical, esthetic, social, religious by which many, kept
> discrete as many, expresses itself into the
> manageable rafters of salience, lofts to comprehension, breaks
>
> out in hard, highly informed suasions, the "gathering
> in the sky" so to speak, the trove of mind, tested
> experience, the only place there is to stay, where the saints
>
> are known to share accord and wine, and magical humor floats
> upon the ambient sorrow: much is nearly stable there,
> residencies perpetual, more than less. . . . (p. 300)

The initial profusion of adjectives itself creates a sense of the many that the passage wants to preserve, even as it talks of climbing the heights to understanding ("rafters," "lofts," "highly informed"), the discovery of unities or patterns. Also, in the country of the mind made up of such patterns, we notice that "stable" and "perpetual" are both qualified. Moreover, on the page before this passage, Ammons has converted "center," usually synonymous with unity or the One, into a term eliminating the notion that there exists *the* center: "reality is abob with centers: indeed, there is / nothing but centers" ([p. 299]; this is reminiscent of Whitman's statement in *Song of Myself* that "there is no object so soft but it makes a hub for the wheel'd universe"). *Tape,* which can talk too easily of unity, also contains lines that emphasize a plurality of centers, calling for their proliferation (*T,* 116).[22]

That poem connects such centers to motion, and *we* can connect what I have called the multiplicity of unities in Ammons to [certain] patterns [of] motion. Any such pattern may be said to constitute *a* unity for Ammons, so long as its rootedness in motion and its limited nature are kept in view. Such would seem to be what he is suggesting in the opening of *Hibernaculum,* with its linking of motion, form, center, and periphery:

> A cud's a locus in time, a staying change, moving
> but holding through motions timeless relations,
> as of center to periphery, core-thought to consideration,
>
> not especially, I'd say, goal-directed, more
> a slime-and sublime-filled coasting, a repeating of
> gently repeating motions, blissful slobber-spun webs. . . . (p. 351)

The offering of the chewing of a cud as an example of "timeless relations" is a deliberate and wonderful indulgence in the outrageous. This yoking together of slime and the sublime is a piece of play, Ammons treating his philosophical preoccupations humorously, to produce what is primarily a charming *tour de force,* but one that points up the interrelationship of some of his key concepts.

At one point in *Hibernaculum,* Ammons appears to grow impatient with two of those concepts. After tracing movement back and forth between center and periphery, the poem dismisses them as "two nothings" (p. 373). The passage in question speaks of "tangles," and is itself somewhat tangled and inconsistent, but despite its narrow focus (it is discussing the poet's activity versus the critic's activity), it distinctly appears to move toward what seems a general nihilism, this stance displacing the question of reconciling center and periphery.

That passage can be thought of as a precursor of the final poem of *Collected Poems,* "The Arc Inside and Out." For *Hibernaculum* associates center and periphery, its "two nothings," with "impoverishment" and "abundance," respectively. These are echoed in the characterization in "Arc" of the two possible ways, noted earlier, of handling the problem of the One and the Many. The first, the casting off of peripheries, would result in an "impoverished diamond," while the second, the piling up of the world's diversity, would constitute a "heterogeneous abundance / starved into oneness." Either approach is seen as a passage to nothing. What "Arc" does is to forego the problem of reconciling the One and the Many, of penetrating to center or strenuously investigating periphery. It takes on a nihilistic view but not a dismal one, settling for an arc, that is, existence in a physical world, gratifying to our senses. Within or without the arc there is only nothing.[23] It is as though Ammons has become fatigued by the rigors of wrestling with unity and multiplicity, and is throwing off wearying consciousness, willing himself into simplicity and enjoyment. He does not wish to leave the arc, to go inside it or outside it:

> . . . neither way to go's to stay, stay
> here, the apple an apple with its own hue
> or streak, the drink of water, the drink,
>
> the falling into sleep, restfully ever the
> falling into sleep, dream, dream, and
> every morning the sun comes, the sun.

The domain depicted is like the one we get in Stevens' "Sunday Morning," without the central awareness of death. While we may resist this retreat into the sensory, it is rendered in a striking way, the repetitions making for cadences untypically passionate and seductively lovely.

In *Diversifications,* in the third of "Three Travelogues," which describes a walk along a woods' edge, Ammons again takes up the quest for the One, in the form of center. This time, in a magical moment, involving the kind of ideal high-low fusion spoken of earlier, but which is now related to the question of the One and the Many rather than transcending it, Ammons comes to center after meandering through "margins" (periphery) and multiplicity. He does so not through the effort he expends, but by hearing from flawed and broken elements, "a branch-trickle whose small music / . . . brought the world / whole and full again and to itself."

Notes

1. See Francis M. Cornford, *Plato and Parmenides* (New York, 1951), pp. 4ff.
2. See R. T. Wallis, *Neoplatonism* (London, 1972), pp. 61, 88.
3. M. H. Abrams, *Natural Supernaturalism* (New York, 1973), pp. 185, 186.
4. Ibid., p. 255.
5. Alfred North Whitehead, *Process and Reality* (New York, 1936), pp. 529–30.

6. Ammons indicated this in a letter to me (October 9, 1973), replying to certain queries I had made about his work.

7. That awareness includes at least some knowledge of Plotinus. In reading him, Ammons says in *Hibernaculum,* he found his mind "increased" (p. 370).

8. See Michael Kammen, *People of Paradox* (New York, 1973), passim.

9. This poem is not to be confused with Ammons' long poem *Sphere: The Form of a Motion.*

10. Was Ammons struck by this paradox in making his choices for *Selected Poems?* In the version of "In the Wind My Rescue Is" printed in that volume (p. 22), he eliminated the first stanza, which explicitly names the wind as a rescuing agent, and gave the piece the title "I Set It My Task."

11. For a poem that might be regarded as a counterstatement to "In the Wind My Rescue Is," see "Apologia Pro Vita Sua."

12. His ambivalence can also be illustrated by juxtaposing "High and Low," which regards descent and weeds favorably, with "The Wind Coming Down," which speaks of "terraces of mind" that "weedroots of my low-feeding [cannot] shiver."

13. In *Sphere* (p. 12), Ammons, somewhat playfully, indicates that the two sets of figures are indeed related.

14. Notice the use of "edge" in this passage, and see *Essay on Poetics,* which joins "edge" and "accident" (p. 306).

15. The poem finds the whole expressed in the part, but the means of that expression remain at the periphery.

16. Center may be unattainable because, as is sometimes the case with unity, there is nothing there. See *Essay on Poetics,* p. 299.

17. See *Tape's* statement "when we solve, we're / saved by deeper problems" (p. 171).

18. This last phrase echoes "riddling through the underbrush" in "Thaw," which is an action ascribed to the wind. Putting the two poems together, we see another association in Ammons' mind between the wind and multiplicity.

19. "Object" is one of several poems where Ammons is self-critical because he has shirked strenuous enterprise, presumably of the imagination. See "Lion: Mouse" (whose closing lines echo "Object") and "Banking" (which strongly calls to mind Emerson's "Days"). In "Cut the Grass," the directive of the title is a comically trivial self-command.

20. It may be of interest to take note at this point of the Pythagoreans' Table of Opposites as it appears in Cornford's *Plato and Parmenides,* p. 6. One grouping of related terms includes the following: Limit (a quality associated with the One), Unity, Resting; the second set includes Unlimited (associated with multiplicity), Plurality, Moving. Emerson, in his essay on Plato, identifies unity with rest, diversity with motion.

21. I constructed this diagram shortly before coming upon the excerpt from *Sphere* printed in *Diacritics* 3 (Winter, 1973), 57–[59]. There Ammons says: "for me . . . the one-many problem figures / out as an equilateral triangle (base: diversity and peak: unity)."

22. "Turning" may be read as endorsing any given form ("glass bead") as a center.

23. Contrast the use of "inside" and "outside" in this poem with their use in "Hymn." The notion of arduous quest, present in "Hymn," is rejected in "Arc."

A. R. Ammons:
Dwelling in the Flow of Shapes

HELEN VENDLER

In the mid-nineteenth century, William Dean Howells came east from Ohio for the first time and visited the birthplace of one of his literary heroes, Nathaniel Hawthorne, only to find that the citizens of Salem took a dim view of the writer who had indicted their civic past. With characteristic irony, Howells remarked in his literary reminiscences:

> The advantages to any place of having a great genius born and reared in its midst are so doubtful that it might be well for localities designing to become the birthplaces of distinguished authors to think twice about it. Perhaps only the largest capitals, like London and Paris, and New York and Chicago, ought to risk it. But the authors have an unaccountable perversity, and will seldom come into the world in the large cities.

A. R. Ammons exhibited just that unaccountable perversity of genius in contriving to come into the world in the rural hiddenness of Whiteville, North Carolina. Because of his coming, the literary map has changed, and as we have the New York of Whitman, and the Pennsylvania of Stevens, and the Massachusetts of Lowell, we now have the North Carolina of Ammons. There are states, many of them, still without a genius of the place. In celebrating the sixtieth birthday of A. R. Ammons, one celebrates as well the birth of North Carolina in his poems. But although Ammons is a poet of his place of birth, he is also a migrating nomadic spirit. The finding of self through place is his most characteristic invention, and it has not stopped with North Carolina. He possesses in Ithaca, as someone said, the most famous back yard in the world, tirelessly examined and freshly loved.

Like most writers, Ammons could not remain where he was born. Almost all artists find it necessary to migrate to capital cities or university

Originally published in *The Music of What Happens: Poems, Poets, Critics* (Cambridge: Harvard University Press, 1988), 310–42. Reprinted by permission.

towns—places with books, reviews, presses, students, fellow writers. And yet the universe remains measured outward from home. We all remember that the young Stephen Dedalus inscribes in his book an outward-looking series of locations going from Clongowes Wood to the universe. Ammons will inscribe, in his "Essay on Poetics," a modern version of such a series:

> subatomic particle
> atom
> molecule
> cell
> tissue
> organ
> organ system
> organism
> species
> community
> living world

Ammons can locate himself, imaginatively, at all these levels of at-home-ness, from the invisible world of the quarks to the ecosphere of the cosmos.

We might see North Carolina, then, not as the beginning of an Odyssean journey that has ended in another Ithaca, but as the central shape in a series of concentric circles, forming that sphere reaching out to an infinite circumference. And we would be justified in preferring the figure of concentric circles to the linear figure of a journey because of Ammons's own frequent return to the material of his boyhood as something always within himself, never something he has left behind. The sublime poem "Easter Morning," Ammons's "Elegy in a Country Churchyard," tells us as much:

> I have a life that did not become,
> that turned aside and stopped,
> astonished:
> I hold it in me like a pregnancy or
> as on my lap a child
> not to grow or grow old but dwell on
> it is to his grave I most
> frequently return and return
> to ask what is wrong, what was
> wrong, to see it all by
> the light of a different necessity
> but the grave will not heal
> and the child,
> stirring, must share my grave
> with me, an old man having
> gotten by on what was left.

These lines, I am certain, will be as familiar in a hundred years as Wordsworth's "There was a time when meadow, grove, and stream, / The earth, and every common sight, / To me did seem / Apparelled in celestial light / The glory and the freshness of a dream." The arrested, blocked sadness of Ammons's lines makes us share a death—the death of those possibilities in himself that were brutalized and stunted by events of his youth.

To write of home has never been simple for Ammons—home was too mixed, too harsh, and too painful to be the subject of simple nostalgia. Even the early poems of home face squarely the savagery of country life. No one can easily forget "Hardweed Path Going," the poem of the butchering of the boy's pet hog. The objects of affection in the country are few—a bird, a hog. The pet bird is set free before the hard weather sets in. Only Sparkle, the pet hog, is left. The iron routines of country life continue:

> don't forget to slop the hogs,
> feed the chickens,
> water the mule,
> cut the kindling,
> build the fire,
> call up the cow.

In the midst of dreary chores, there brightens the moment of affection: "Sparkle . . . / You hungry? / Hungry, girly?" Then the hog is killed. The parent senses the son's distress—"She's nothing but a hog, boy"—but the poem ends with no happy ending:

> Bleed out, Sparkle, the moon-chilled bleaches of your body
>   hanging upside-down,
> hardening through the mind and night of the first freeze.

Ammons, like the other poets of the Sixties, was engaged in revising his predecessors. Sparkle the hog could not have appeared, I think, in a poem by Frost, nor could the words, "Hungry, girly?"—Frost's classicism would not have permitted it. In fact, it is when we read Ammons that we see how distant Frost is from his rural characters, even when they are adapted from his own experience. We recognize, by the contrast with Ammons, how much Frost becomes the narrator, rather than the sufferer, of his poetry. Ammons's poem on Nelly Myers is suffered rather than narrated:

> I think of her
>   but cannot remember how I thought of her
> as I grew up: she was not a member of the family:
> I knew she was not my mother,
>   nor an aunt, there was nothing

visiting about her: she had her room,
    she kept her bag of money. . . .
    she never went away, she was Nelly Myers, we
    called her Nel,
small, thin, her legs wrapped from knees to ankles
in homespun bandages: she always had the soreleg . . .
mother, not my mother, grandmother, not my grandmother,
slave to our farm's work, no slave I would not stoop
to:
I will not end my grief, earth will not end my grief,
I move on, we move on, some scraps of us together,
      my broken soul, leaning toward her to be touched,
listening to be healed.

These early poems of Ammons's are obstinate commemorations of reality, tributes determined in their obligation of exactness to hog-killing, soreleg, and hardship. Whitman gives them some of their courage, but they are homelier and more domestic than Whitman's work tends to be. They embody, in fact, a new style declaring itself. They are written perhaps in revolt against the more allegorical pieces that Ammons had been writing in his twenties, and to which he would return. Even as he writes these early realist pieces, something in him knows that the historical specificity of home is not the only truth about home. The rest of Ammons's work is a struggle between the trawling net which gathers in every detail of home (down to the latest car-repair bill) and the planetary telescope that takes a galactic view of, among other things, home.

    Writing of home raises the question of language. Frost had brought the sentence-sounds of his own speech so powerfully to the fore that no subsequent American poet could afford to neglect his comparable cadences. The language of home appears early in Ammons, in the "First Carolina Said-Song" and the "Second Carolina Said-Song," both of them apparently "found art," one spoken by an aunt, the other by a patient in a veterans' hospital in Fayetteville. The aunt's begins:

    In them days
      they won't hardly no way to know if
        somebody way off
          died
            till they'd be
            dead and buried

        and Uncle Jim

    hitched up a team of mules to the wagon
    and he cracked the whip over them
      and run them their dead-level best

> the whole thirty miles to your great grandma's funeral
> down there in
> Green Sea County . . .

And it ends, after a comic anecdote,

> we got there just in time to see her buried
> in an oak grove up
> back of the field:

> it's growed over with soapbushes and huckleberries now.

If there was, for Ammons, a music of home, it lay in this sort of language, and the truest image of home in Ammons's poetry remains, I would say, in the ongoing voice—musical, humorously paced, rhythmic, inexhaustible—that we associate especially with his long poems. These are poems without periods, halted only by the suspensions of colons: they resemble the melting spring water, flowing down into river and sea, to which Ammons compares lyric itself. In the long poems, Ammons abstracts the music of the tireless southern voice from the dialectical and lexical forms visible in the Carolina said-songs, but the voice is no less, however, a product of that dialect. Something else in Ammons may also be a product of southern talk—a willingness to digress and to expatiate, rather than to conclude and to straighten. In "Corsons Inlet," Ammons discovers that openness, not closure—whether of thought or of form—is the necessary condition of his poetic:

> no arranged terror: no forcing of image, plan,
> or thought:
> no propaganda, no humbling of reality to precept:

> terror pervades but it is not arranged, all possibilities
> of escape open: no route shut, except in
> the sudden loss of all routes:

> I see narrow orders, limited tightness, but will
> not run to that easy victory:
> still around the looser, wider forces work:
> I will try
> to fasten into order enlarging grasps of disorder,
> widening
> scope, but enjoying the freedom that
> Scope eludes my grasp, that there is no finality of vision,
> that I have perceived nothing competely,
> that tomorrow a new walk is a new walk.

The new walks that Ammons has been taking ever since he made this joyous claim on existence have led to many homes, from the smallest parcel of back yard to the whole United States, a country whose motto, *E pluribus unum,* enunciates one of Ammons's basic paradoxes, the relation of the many and the one (as he says in "Sphere"). Beyond the continent, home extends out to the planet, to the galaxy, and even to the universe. Because poetry must express through form what it says in content, each of the shapes delineated as a dwelling place bestows on the self and on language a different contour. "Dwell[ing] in the flow of shapes"—a phrase from "Sphere"—might be thought of as a variation on the Wordsworthian dwelling in spots of time. But where Wordsworth stabilizes time as a spot in space, Ammons propels space into temporal flow. The temporality, and temporariness, of any dwelling makes it alive, quick with possibility; destination would, for Ammons as for Wordsworth, be death.

The mind tends to wall itself in with a home; therefore, says Ammons in "Sphere," contradict that tendency, force mind out into the universe: "force mind from boxes to radiality." If American poetry, to Ammons's anxious eye, is becoming a poetry of boxes, it too should be forced into a different sort of home:

> most of our writers live in New York City
> densely: there in the abstractions of squares and glassy
> floors they cut up and parcel out the nothingness they
>
> think America is: I wish they would venture the rural and
> see that the woods are undisturbed by their bothering
> reputations and that the brooks have taken to flowing
>
> the way they always have and that the redwing pauses
> to consider his perch before he lights in a cedar.

Ammons does not say explicitly what he expects New York poets to learn from the flowing of the brooks and the pauses of the redwing, but we deduce that it has something to do with a poetry that would not be cut up and parceled out. The unpredictability of natural movement, which is always "uncapturable and vanishing" like a brook, is the rural and organic intuition, brought from home, that governs the motion of Ammons's lines. "While a leaf," he says, "may not answer one's questions, it waves, a / nice language, expressive and complete" ("Hibernaculum"). Though there is a whimsicality in such a salute, Ammons is serious in his claim that the natural brotherhood of gesture unites the poet and the moving world, roots the poet kinesthetically in the cosmos. "My brotherhood's immense," the poet continues, "and if the gods / have vanished that were never here I do not miss them."

At the other extreme from the back yard, as I have said, is the planet; and Ammons, in one of his less successful moments of didacticism, addresses it (in "Extremes and Moderations") as a home already polluted, about to die choked with waste:

                                              the
          artificial has taken on the complication of the natural and
              where
          to take hold, how to let go, perplexes individual action: ruin
          and gloom are falling off the shoulders of progress: blue-
              green

          globe, we have tripped your balance and gone into
              exaggerated possession:
          this seems to me the last poem written to the world
          before its freshness capsizes and sinks into the slush.

This passage comes from the later Ammons, a poet who, increasingly turning
from the domestic to the cosmological, makes his home everywhere.

But I want to return for a moment to the famous dwelling in the shape
of North Carolina. I have said that Ammons turned to home events and characters—the hog-killing, the memory of Nelly Myers—and to home language, its music and its lexicon, heard in the said-songs. These, however, are
largely mimetic efforts—a transcription of what is in some sense already
"there." But in every poet's life there comes a moment in which the poet
must forsake mimesis, must decide to impose inner motions on outer material. At this moment, Ammons begins to compose an idiosyncratic and masterful score which his thematic and lexical material will obey. This important
moment comes for Ammons in his early composition "Four Motions for the
Pea Vines." The musical intent is clearest in the last of these four musical
movements, which compose a rural suite. I want to quote the whole of this
fourth movement to give an idea of the rhythms Ammons has here made the
masters of his subject-matter:

          slow as the pale low-arcing sun, the women move
              down windy rows of the autumn field;
          the peavines are dead:
          cornstalks and peapods rattle in the dry bleach
              of cold:

          the women glean remnant peas
              (too old to snap or shell) that
          got past being green; shatter from skeletal vines
              handfuls of peapods, tan, light:

          bent the slow women drag towsacks huge
              with peas, bulk but little
          weight: a boy carries a sack on his
              shoulders to the end of the rows:
          he stoops: the sack goes over his head

> to the ground: he flails it with a tobacco stick,
>   opens the sack, removes the husks, and
> from sack to tub winnows
>   dry, hard crackling peas: rhythms reaching through
> seasons, motions weaving in and out!

The Keatsian gleaning and winnowing, the Hopkinsian boy, the Williamsesque exclamations are signs of early influences on Ammons. But beyond and above these we see the musical composition of a North Carolinian genre scene. The present-tense rhythm moves from the dead pea vines and the slow stopping women to the active boy, with an arousal into energy characteristic of Ammons, who summons here a network of sounds bringing to life the shattering handfuls, the sack on the shoulders, the flailing stick, the husks and the tub, the crackling peas. In these sounds and motions of home, home lives again in an aesthetic world, one shaped to Ammons's rhythmic measure. One of Ammons's earliest poems had prayed for such a firm personal possession of the real: the title, "This Black Rich Country," refers at once to the soil of home and the earth of mortality, and though the poem enunciates a refusal of "symbolic forms," its own verse rhythms are such a form:

> Dispossess me of belief:
> between life and me obtrude
> no symbolic forms:
> . . . . .
> leave me this black rich country,
> uncertainty, labor, fear: do not
> steal the rewards of my mortality.

Through his mimetic stubbornness, his musical exactness as he varies from stops to quavers, his scientific metaphysics, and his syntactic amplitudes, Ammons constructs a rich poetic universe to serve as home, a universe at once mimetic and allegorical.

Sometimes Ammons's vertiginous sense of the many-leveled world (at once cosmically enormous and minutely particular) dismays even his own imagination. In his famous poem-of-the-whole, "Cascadilla Falls," he tells us that he once picked up a stone and "thought all its motions into it":

> the 800 mph earth spin,
> the 190-million-mile yearly
> displacement around the sun,
> the overriding
> grand
> haul

> of the galaxy with the
> 30,000 mph of where
> the sun's going;
> thought all the interweaving
> motions
> into myself.

The poem ends with the dismay of consciousness at its own limits:

> Oh
> I do
> not know where I am going
> that I can live my life
> by this single creek.

Ammons's wish to think with the mind of the universe, to comprehend reality not simply with anthropocentric vanity but truly from within, to put the motion of mind among all other physical motions, to become not a single vector but the resultant of all vectors, is his most ambitious aim. He is, I think, the first poet to have the conceptual equipment (gained in his own early scientific training) to think this way. Wordsworth, who had, like Ammons, a sense of the large motions of the universe, foresaw the day when a poet to whom scientific concepts were not foreign or unnatural would write a new sort of poetry:

> If the labours of Men of science should ever create any material revolution, direct or indirect, in our condition, and in the impressions which we habitually receive, the Poet will sleep no more than at present; he will be ready to follow the steps of the Man of science . . . If the time should ever come when what is now called science, thus familiarized to men, shall be ready to put on, as it were, a form of flesh and blood, the Poet will lend his divine spirit to aid the transformation, and will welcome the Being thus produced, as a dear and genuine inmate of the Household of man. (Second Preface to *Lyrical Ballads*, 1850)

The Household of man, thus defined, is, to Ammons, "home" in the widest sense. "Our being's heart and home," said Wordsworth in *The Prelude* (VI), "is with infinity, and only there": the sense of that infinity is strong in "Cascadilla Falls" and in many of Ammons's long poems, which by their very ebb and flow give us the motions of oceans, of winds, of the drift of continents and the sedimentary accretions of time.

Ammons does not deny the perils of magnitude: the self can get lost in infinity. In a short wry poem called "Concerning the Exclusions of the Object," he wonders whether he has not lost his own small self in his galactic concerns (both physical and metaphysical): "head full of stars, / cosmic / dust in my teeth," "how," he asks, "can I expel these roomy stars?" The journeying up and down between two elements—earth and sky, the particular and the general—animates so many of Ammons's poems that it could be said to be their *modus vivendi,* and in some it is. But I sense in others where this vertical journey might seem to be at issue, an odd twist or spin put on the poem which in itself denies that the vertical polarities of small self and cosmic dust, particular and general, ground and air, can really be separated. The poem does not begin at A and go to B, or begin at A, go to B, and then go back to A. Rather, its structure is cunningly confused. It will consider its own *process* in either direction, and a process is neither A nor B; next it will poise itself on a *hypothesis* which, neither A nor B, resolves itself into a question about the *value* of journeying from A to the furthest B; that will be succeeded by a *hypothesis* of journeying from A to a place less than maximum B; in the end, the poem will praise the "interval designed, / apparently, for design." I want to quote the poem I have been describing, "Two Possibilities," to exemplify this twist, because to describe Ammons's theme of "home" without showing, if only briefly, the paradoxical and perplexing structures of "home" would be to simplify his labyrinths.

> Coming out of the earth and going
> into the earth compose
> an interval or arc where
> what to do's
>
> difficult to fix: if it's
> the coming
> out that answers, should one with all
> thrust come out and
>
> rise to imagination's limit, leaving
> earthiness, maximally
> to mark the change, much below:
> if it's
>
> going in, should one flatten out on
> coming, lie low
> among bush
> and rock; and keep the residence
>
> near the palm of the hand, the
> gross engrossed and palpable:
> Well, there is an interval designed,
> apparently, for design.

"We have an interval," says Pater in the conclusion to *The Renaissance,* "and only an interval,"—but he does not tell us whether our gem-like flame is to burn at a great altitude or close to earth with the gross engrossed and palpable. Ammons's use of the Paterian word may not be an allusion, but it does ask where our being's heart and home is, where we should, in this world, keep our residence. By teasing and twisting our conflicting impulses toward transcendence and immanence, Ammons suggests that in the twist itself, and in its manifestation as design, lies the human home least distorted by transcendence.

I have spoken of Ammons's home of origin, rural North Carolina; and I have spoken of the home of consciousness, the maximal universe of human physical, geological, and organic knowledge; but one must also, in speaking of Ammons, look to the metaphysical home of the ideal and of the affections, which he calls, in one of his most famous poems, "The Eternal City," borrowing Saint Augustine's notion of the City of God. The poem could not perhaps have been written before the annihilation of the world became an imaginative fact. Ammons envisages here the destruction of everything we know as civilization, and the efforts of those who must begin to construct their home anew. It is a poem that suggests many interpretations; it could be about the ruin of a love, or a family, or a home, or an ideal—anything in which one could have placed one's faith and one's affection. What interests Ammons is the human determination to build home afresh, even in the wake of ruin. To that end he places us in a consciousness that moves ingeniously even in cataclysm; it remembers the past as a model, it acknowledges the devastated present, and it envisages a restored perfection in the future:

> After the explosion or cataclysm, that big
> display that does its work but then fails
> out with destructions, one is left with the
>
> pieces: at first, they don't look very valuable,
> but nothing sizable remnant around for
> gathering the senses on, one begins to take
>
> an interest, to sort out, to consider closely
> what will do and won't, matters having become
> not only small but critical: bulbs may have been
>
> uprooted: they should be eaten, if edible, or
> got back into the ground: what used to be garages,
> even the splinters, should be collected for
>
> fires: some unusually deep holes or cleared
> woods may be turned to water supplies or
> sudden fields: ruinage is hardly ever a
>
> pretty sight but it must when splendor goes
> accept into itself piece by piece all the old
> perfect human visions, all the old perfect loves.

Ammons's home is composed, as this poem suggests, of the minutely practical and the sublimely ideal; his actions range from taking an interest in splinters to the reconstruction, with Wordsworthian resolution and veneration, of a former splendor.

It is not surprising that the final home, for Ammons, claims a theological, or (if I may coin a word) theopoetic dimension. As the human will reaches out, like Whitman's spider, for a first frail belief, and then for the first word articulating the first belief, a web of faith and language is constructed across the void:

> to lean belief the lean word comes,
> each scope adjusted to the plausible: to the heart
> emptied of, by elimination, the world, comes the small
>
> 17
>
> cry domesticating the night: if the night is to be
> habitable, if the dawn is to come out of it, if day is ever
> to grow brilliant on delivered populations, the word
>
> must have its way by the brook, lie out cold all night
> along the snow limb, spell by yearning's wilted weed till
> the wilted weed rises, know the patience and smallness
>
> of stones: I address the empty place where the god
> that has been deposed lived: it is the godhead: the
> yearnings that have been addressed to it bear antiquity's
>
> 18
>
> sanction: for the god is ever re-created as
> emptiness, till force and ritual fill up and strangle
> his life, and then he must be born empty again.
>
> ("Hibernaculum")

The resurrection of joy in the face of emptiness and death, of which Ammons has been speaking in this poem, can be seen in the end of "Easter Morning," to which I shall return.

In Ammons's most paradoxical moments of faith, he declares that our home is nowhere but in motion itself. It is not in our place of birth, because we leave that place of origin; it is not in our affections, because we can forsake them and they us; it is not in knowledge, because knowledge evolves always by its own perpetual self-destruction; it is not in a god, because the god is forever becoming emptied of significance. "Can we make a home of motion?" he asks in "Sphere," and answers, "Motion is our place":

> If
> nothing shaped stays and shapelessness is dwellingless, where

> can we dwell: as shapes (bodies) we dwell only in the flow
> of shapes, turning the arcs of mortality: but the imagination,
> though bodiless, is shaped (being the memory or imagined
> memory of shapes) and so can dwell in nothingness: the
>   human
> being is as inscrutable and unformulable as a poem, or, if
>   possible, more so.

In the flow of shapes, real or imagined, our body and spirit, it would seem, can find an unformulable home. But recently, in a more reckless moment, Ammons has thrown shape itself aside as "hateful exactitude" rather than "shapely assertion," claiming rebelliously that only "nothingness's / wide amplitude / makes his place" ("On Being"). If the human condition is one of motion into continual approximation, then home is one of our delusional systems, and we live forever not at a center, but on an expanding periphery. Foxes have holes, and the birds of the air their nests, the gospel tells us; ships have their stopping points, and so even do tigers, says a recent Ammons poem, but the creatures of consciousness do not. "I run on," says the poet in "Coming Round" (a poem of 1983),

> ruffling the periphery,
> the treadmill's outwheel,
>
> declining center
> or any loss of it
>
> and no longer
> crying help.

The creation of a centerless periphery in form has been Ammons's most original formal invention, seen in a spectacular way in the long poems, in a fiercely experimental way in *The Snow Poems,* written in his fiftieth year. But what I would like to notice particularly here is how little these various forms of home form a hierarchy in Ammons's mind. They are, rather, points of orientation through which he circles again and again: the home of origin, the home conceived by scientific knowledge, the home of metaphysical value, the home of the reconstituting of the sacred, the home found in motion, the home in nothingness, the decentered home on the treadmill's outwheel. If, in the early moments of the long poem "Hibernaculum" (quoted earlier), it is the home of the sacred at which Ammons pauses, he will circle back, later in the poem, to the home of origin, as he decides that he does not want to be buried in New York State, but rather in North Carolina:

> I don't think I want to be buried here in these rocky
> hills: once underground, how could I ever get my arms
> free of the silk and steel, how could I ever with those

feet travel through the earth to my sweet home country
where all the flesh that bore me, back through grandfathers
and grandmothers, lies, and my little

brothers and my little sister I never saw, born before
me and dying small.

In thinking of these matters in the work of A. R. Ammons, we recall his line
of self-definition in "Sphere": "Grief is all I know and joy all I understand."
For Ammons, the thought of his own burial underlies "Easter Morning." The
first part of the poem says, "Grief is all I know of home," as the ravages of a
harsh childhood are retold—not only the life that did not become, but the
shocks encountered and withstood without help to mitigate their terror:

> The child in me that could not become
> . . . stands there by the road
> where the mishap occurred, crying out for
> help, come and fix this or we
> can't get by, but the great ones who
> were to return, they could not or did
> not hear and went on in a flurry and
> now, I say in the graveyard, here
> lies the flurry, now it can't come
> back with help or helpful asides, now
> we all buy the bitter
> incompletions, pick up the knots of
> horror, silently raving, and go on
> crashing into empty ends not
> completions, not rondures the fullness
> has come into and spent itself from.

But the poem, after saying, "Grief is all I know" in its first part, says in its latter moments, "Joy is all I understand," as the inscrutable but beautiful communications and motions of migrating birds convey "a sight of bountiful
majesty and integrity." The dance of nature's motions, at the end of "Easter
Morning," is said to be "permanent in its descriptions / as the ripples round
the brook's / ripplestone," the beautiful Emersonian type of the joy which, in
the Heraclitean conflagration of all things, balances the terrors and incomple-
tions of life. The flood of extinction sweeps over all forms of home, but for
Ammons, as for Wordsworth, there is nonetheless something that remains:

> the
> seventeen-year-old self is gone and with it the well and

84

> wellsweep, chinaberry tree, the mother and father, the two

sisters, living but lost back there, and Silver, Doll, all
the jonquils, the smokehouse, mulberry tree, but when I was

last by, the pecan tree's still standing, the same one, big,
the lean growths and lean shades vanished: more death done
than to do, except that memory grows, accumulating strata
    of

change, and the eyes close on a plenitude, suddenly, directly
into nothingness.

Plenitude and nothingness—as two words for home—coexist in every adult mind. Ammons conceives of plenitude and nothingness in a single word, adding to the American canon a poetry of home at once North Carolinian, American, and universal. We find in this poetry of tenderness and rueful humor the intimate structures of home—the house, the people, the landscape, the graveyard; the feelings of home—the yearnings, the affections, the failures, the fears; and the speculative metaphysical extensions of home—shapes, centers, identities, memories, gods. To imagine for a moment the disappearance of all the poems I have been quoting is to realize that in addition to describing home, these poems are themselves a home that sixty years ago had neither been conceived not constructed. But now the poems are here, through the genius of the poet who, choosing North Carolina to be born in, has become the genius of that place and of many others. Some of us have found, in these poems, a home for our own spirits, words for intimations we were unable to articulate alone. In this way, language becomes a habitable place, and place finds a home in language; American poetry enlarges its canon, and a new universe—the *Collected Poems* of A. R. Ammons—becomes, to use Elizabeth Bishop's phrase, "a mirror in which to dwell."

II

A classic poem, when it appears, comes not as a surprise but as a confirmation:

I have a life that did not become,
that turned aside and stopped,
astonished:
I hold it in me like a pregnancy or
as on my lap a child
not to grow or grow old but dwell on

it is to his grave I most
frequently return and return

> to ask what is wrong, what was
> wrong, to see it all by
> the light of a different necessity
> but the grave will not heal
> and the child,
> stirring, must share my grave
> with me, an old man having
> gotten by on what was left.

This is the beginning of A. R. Ammons's revelatory poem "Easter Morning." The central sentiment is not altogether unprecedented—Robert Lowell said, "Always inside me is the child who died"—but Lowell was speaking of a younger self continuous in some way with his adult self ("Always inside me is his wish to die"). Ammons is talking about a self that stopped, that never became, that is buried in a grave that does not heal. And yet that self is not dead; it is a "child, stirring." Robert Frost talked, more distantly, of a road not taken in the past; Ammons's metaphor of the child—buried, or in a womb, or on a lap—is alive with pain and quick with dismay. Ammons's lines rivet us where we stand and we find ourselves uttering them as though our own life had suddenly found its outlet-speech: "I have a life that did not become . . . the grave will not heal." Ammons's arrow strikes straight to the heart, and to the unhealed grave in it. "How did you know," we ask Ammons, "when we didn't know, ourselves, till you told us?" This is a poetry of eerie power, dependent not so much on the particular circumstances of Ammons's life as on his unsettling skill as an allegorist. Anything he tells us about his life ("I have a life that did not become") turns out to be true of everyone: he is a poet of the universal human condition, not of particular idiosyncrasy. This great poem, "Easter Morning," turns out to be about the damage which every child undergoes as members of his family—a sibling, an aunt, a grandparent—die. It is an elegy in a family churchyard. When Ammons now goes back to North Carolina, the relatives he knew are dead:

> when I go back to my home country in these
> fresh far-away days, it's convenient to visit
> everybody, aunts and uncles, those who used to say,
> look how he's shooting up, and the
> trinket aunts who always had a little
> something in their pocketbooks . . .

The catalog goes on to include uncles and teachers and Ammons's mother and father—all in the churchyard, dead, their world gone. And Ammons remembers himself as a child, shocked and blighted and deflected out of ordinary growth by these deaths:

> the child in me that could not become
> was not ready for others to go,
> to go on into change, blessings and
> horrors, but stands there by the road
> where the mishap occurred, crying out for
> help, come and fix this or we
> can't get by, but the great ones who
> were to return, they could not or did
> not hear and went on in a flurry and
> now, I say in the graveyard, here
> lies the flurry, now it can't come
> back with help or helpful asides, now
> we all but the bitter
> incompletions . . .

In the desolate market of experience where none come to buy (as Blake said) Ammons stands, with his uncanny plainness of speech, the lines running on like an explanation and an apology at once, heedless and pell-mell, every so often stopped by a pulling-up-short, a bewilderment, an obstacle, an arrest in emotion:

> I stand on the stump
> of a child, whether myself
> or my little brother who died, and
> yell as far as I can, I cannot leave this place, for
> for me it is the dearest and the worst
> it is life nearest to life which is
> life lost: it is my place where
> I must stand and fail.

I am not sure whether the strange and complex resolution of the poem (in which Ammons watches the flight of eagles, and is grateful for perennial natural patterns and fresh insights alike) serves to resurrect the dead on this "picture-book, letter-perfect / Easter morning." And I wonder whether the long anguish of the poem can be excerpted at all. But to write about Ammons's volume *A Coast of Trees* (1981) is first of all to give notice of the existence of "Easter Morning" as a new treasure in American poetry, combining the blankest of losses with the fullest of visions. It is a poem which should be published all alone, in a three-page book by itself; it is so complete it repels company.

Nevertheless, it has company, and distinguished company, in this collection of short poems. Ammons always oscillates interestingly between the briefest of brief lyrics ("Briefings," "Uplands") and the longest of long poems ("Sphere," "Tape for the Turn of the Year"). Ammons's bedrock is his conviction of the absolute interconnectedness of all phenomena. The atmosphere (so to speak) over his bedrock is formed by his quick, almost birdlike, noticing of all epiphenomena constantly occurring in the universe—a flight of moths here, a rill of snow-melt there. The short poems record the noticings; the long poems offer the metaphysics of multiple connection. Yet even this description is too divisive. Even in the short poems, Ammons's metaphysics of multiple connection is present in an abbreviated form, represented sometimes by syntax, sometimes by rhetorical figure (notably repetition of a word or a word-root in syntactically significant positions). For instance, Ammons writes about the difficulty of putting a name, or names, to reality—and about the attendant paradox that the closer the approximation of the name to the event the more acutely one feels the frustrating gap between what has been achieved and what absolute fidelity to reality would be. Using his favorite dense repetition, he grieves, "the name nearest the name / names least or names / only a verge before the void takes naming in."

The sound of the writing verges on riddle, and hovers near theological paradox, but the sentiment is neither a riddle nor a mystification. It is a precise denomination in a series of self-joining words: "the name nearest the name names least or names only . . ." This statement of a divergence takes on itself semantically the form of an obsessive connection. And though the creation of the formal barrier of art excludes "reality," it is surely a wonderful mutual relation that makes the terrain of the excluded ("cast out") exactly equal, as a two-piece verb, the terrain of the included ("shut in"): "when the fences foregather / the reality they shut in is cast out." Almost every statement of fear or loss in Ammons occurs in a line that paradoxically consolidates a strict, practical linguistic gain—often as simple a gain as a word humming in resonance with another word, or a triumphant conclusion to a long syntactical suspension. The suspended syntax arises from Ammons's inexhaustible wish to explain; he is the poet par excellence of the bifurcating line of argument, a line that is interspersed with "I suspect" or "well, maybe" or "in fact" or "after all" or "that is" or "probably" or a sequence of "but's." To that extent his poetry is the utterance of that endless rhetoric he calls "reason":

> Reason can't end:
> it is discourse, motion
> to find motion, reason to
> find reason to abandon
> reason.

But against the straight "thruway" of reason Ammons sets another formal motive, which he calls "shape": shape wants to wind discourse up, to give it a rondure, a closure. The shapeliness—almost spherical—of so many of Ammons's short lyrics asserts that a moment or a mood has its own being to proclaim in a determinate form. If that form is violated, something else is produced—even another poem perhaps, but not the original one, which, in being amended, is forever gone. The shape of a poem is inviolate:

> it is as
> it is: it can't be cast
> aside except to cast
> shape aside, no part in it
> free to cast free any
> part.

The rigidity of this verse defies us to shift a single word, to misplace a single "it" or "cast." The verse rejoices in its imperviousness to tinkering: it braces its "no" against its "any," its "free" against its "cast free," its "part" against "part," creating a wind-proof, storm-proof shelter against the inversions of chance. Ammons's loquacity of "reason" so plays against his geometry of "shape" that the exhilaration of the combat of the two motives equals in interest the plangent tales he tells of the life of the spirit.

These are twice-told tales; Ammons moves easily in the line of our poets. Like Traherne, he calls a poem "Poverty"; like Herbert, he sees a silk twist (in Ammons, "silk lines") coming down in radiance from heaven; like Keats, he stands (in the majestic poem called "Swells") on the shore of the wide world till love and fame sink to nothingness. Like Yeats, he feels the pull of the balloon of the mind (Yeats tried to tether it; Ammons says, "I have let all my balloons aloose"); like Emily Dickinson, he feels an affinity for that "neglected son of genius," the spider, working like the poet "airy with radiality"; like Oliver Wendell Holmes, he writes "An Improvisation for the Stately Dwelling"; like Williams and Hopkins, he offers perpetual praise of the world of sight. In Ammons these earlier poets have found the ideal reader—the reader who himself writes a new poem as a variation on the older one.

Ammons's own newness—it bears repeating—lies in his finely calibrated sense of the actual, nontranscendent motions of the natural world. He is not in a hurry, as most of his predecessors (Emerson, Whitman, Dickinson, Hopkins, Moore) have been, to move from natural fact to patriotic or religious or philosophical enthusiasm. Ammons is true to himself in ending "Easter Morning" with the natural fact of bird-instinct, seen in a new configuration, rather than with the transcendent resurrection of the body in spirit. The natural universe is so real to Ammons's imagination that his poem about the earth rolling in space is spoken with an ease foreign to most efforts to "imagine" a cosmic perspective. Only Wordsworth had a comparable iron sense of fact:

> We go around, distanced,
> yearly in a star's
>
> atmosphere, turning
> daily into and out of
> direct light and

> slanting through the
> quadrant seasons: deep
> space begins at our
>
> heels, nearly rousing
> us loose: we look up
> or out so high, sight's
>
> silk almost draws us away.

(Frost, who yearned for vision, said we can look "Neither out far nor in deep"; Ammons, in his love of sight, is silently corrective.) Ammons is tugged between sentiment and stoicism, and the play between those two motives is as entrancing as the play between the flow of discourse and the shape of poetry. He is as tender as Keats and as harsh as Keats, reaping some of the same benefits. He does not rise to Wordsworth's full bleakness, but he has more humor and more waywardness than Wordsworth.

"Swells" gives full range to Ammons's sentiment and stoicism alike, to his precise sense of physical motion (in this case, wave-motion), and to his firm momentum-rounding-into-shape. When hundreds of conflicting motions are assimilated into one wave, a paradoxical calm results:

> The very longest swell in the ocean, I suspect,
> carries the deepest memory, the information of actions
> summarized . . .
>   so that the longest swell swells least.

Ocean floor and mountain are alike places where gigantic motions have been summarized into a near stillness:

> I like to go
> to old places where the effect dwells, summits or seas
> so hard to summon into mind, even with the natural
>
> ones hard to climb or weigh; I go there in my mind
> (which is, after all, where these things negotiably are)
> and tune in to the wave nearly beyond rise or fall in its
>
> staying and hum the constant, universal, assimilation.

To climb the summit or find that summary so hard to summon to mind, and there to hear the hum (as Stevens called it) of the universal pantomime, might be in another poet a forgetful sublimity. But Ammons, like Keats, cannot forget the world where men sit and hear each other groan; he ends his poem by saying he has sought out the summit for "rest from the ragged and rapid pulse, the immediate threat / shot up in a disintegrating spray, the many thoughts and / sights unmanageable, the deaths of so many, hungry or mad." Mortality swells so agitatingly into presence at the end of the poem that the hoped-for-contemplative calm is shaken and bruised. The ills of the body and of the spirit are all there are; we die hungry or mad, our pulse ragged or rapid. In nature, of course, there is nothing "unmanageable"; the word is meaningless in the cosmos, and takes on meaning only through human will, afflicted by thoughts and sights too painful to be borne. If only, like the geologic strata or the ocean floor, we could manage "the constant, universal assimilation: the / information, so packed, nearly silenced with majesty." But we do not, and cannot, for long. The possibility, and the impossibility, of psychic assimilation are held in equilibrium in the long oceanic swell of this Stevensian poem—which should be read with Stevens's "Somnambulisma" and "Chocorua" as its predecessors.

It is a mark of Ammons's variety that it is very hard to generalize about his practice in *Coast of Trees*. Almost every poem has a distinctive shape and a set of new strategies, imitating the variety of nature:

> a dance sacred as the sap in
> the trees, permanent in its descriptions
>
> as the ripples round the brook's
> ripplestone: fresh as this particular
> flood of burn breaking across us now
> from the sun.

Ammons matches his loneliness and his freshness to the solitary, permanent, and renewed acts of nature; and in his "central attention" he keeps the universe alone. The poems enable us to watch this poet going about the business of the universe, both its "lost idyllic" and its present broken radiance. He has been about this business for years now, but I notice in reading this collection how much more secure his language has become. Once, he was likely to err both in amassing scientific words too lavishly and in affecting too folksy a tone. Now the scientific world in Ammons is beautifully in balance with the perceptual one, and the tone is believably, and almost perfectly, colloquial. The lines are as near as we could wish to the ripples round the ripplestone.

III

Ever since Schiller distinguished naive from sentimental poetry, we have been worried by the pathetic fallacy (as Ruskin named it). It is the aesthetic version of the tree falling in the woods; does it make a sound if nobody is there to hear it? Is nature hospitable of itself to meaning (by its rhythms and its orders, its catastrophes and its variety), or are our symbolic uses of it truly abuses, a foisting of our sentiments onto an inert and indifferent scenery? This question has become one that no modern "nature poet" from Wordsworth on can avoid addressing in a perfectly conscious way.

Hopkins, because he was a religious poet, at first assumed an authenticating God transmitting symbols through the book of the creatures:

> These things, these things were here and but the beholder
> Wanting; which two when they once meet,
> The heart rears wings bold and bolder
> And hurls for him, O half hurls earth for him off under his
>   feet.

This rapturous confidence in the Keatsian "greeting of the spirit" could not persevere in Hopkins's ultimately dualistic moral world, where ethics took a necessarily higher position than the aesthetic. At the end, all the diversity of the world (and with it, all its symbolic potential) had, for Hopkins, to be wound onto two spools, parted into two flocks, the elect and the damned:

> Lét life, wáned, ah lét life wind
> Off hér once skéined stained véined varíety / upon, áll on
>   twó spools; párt, pen, páck
> Now her áll in twó flocks, twó folds—black, white; / right,
>   wrong; reckon but, reck but, mind
> But these two; wáre of a wórld where bút these / twó tell.

Stevens's great explorations into the question of the pathetic fallacy (beginning with "The Snow Man," itself a variant on Keats's "In drear-nighted December") occupy him throughout his life, as he meditates the plain sense of things, the bare particular of the natural rock, and the fictive leaves that cover the rock and are a "cure" of it. Ashbery's poems (to cite a contemporary example) are full of jokes on the pathetic fallacy: but jokes are a way of using the convention, even if in a climate of gentle irony. In all these cases, the coincidence of nature with feeling or insight is the problem: is it a trick we play on ourselves, or a means of understanding—even a secular equivalent of grace?

I have written before on Wordsworth's magisterial (and in certain ways conclusive) meditations on this subject in the Immortality Ode: Wordsworth decided that our ability to use transferred epithets bestowing human adjectives on natural scenes ("the *innocent* brightness of a *new-born* day") was a way of objectifying our own feelings about innocence and birth, an activity necessary if we were to think about innocence and birth at all. ("We thought in images," says Lowell of poets.) The intercourse between soul and nature, in Wordsworth's view, clarifies the soul to itself and also endears natural sights (previously merely visual) as they become repositories of a moral and personal gestalt:

> The clouds that gather round the setting sun
> Do take a sober coloring from an eye
> That hath kept watch o'er man's mortality.

Once the habit of reciprocal looking and feeling is formed, looking taps feeling just as feeling transfigures looking: nature then appears to be an originating lamp rather than a reflecting mirror.

In the poetry of A. R. Ammons, the question of the pathetic fallacy is raised again and again, most luminously and painfully in his great poem "Grace Abounding," where the title makes explicit his claim that in states of inchoate feeling he finds a relief so great in the clarification offered by a visual image chanced upon in nature that the feeling corresponds to that which Bunyan named "grace abounding." We recall that in the biblical formulation, where sin abounds, grace will the more abound: in Ammons's frame of things, the emphasis changes from sin to misery. In the poem, where he is trapped in a vise of misery, the sight of a hedge completely encased and bound down by ice so strikes him that he realizes that it is an image, perfectly correspondent, of his inner anguish, the more anguishing because his misery had as yet remained unimaged, unconceptualized, and therefore indescribable. The relief felt when the hedge strikes his eye, and his state is at last nameable, is grace—not offered by Ammons as an "equivalent" to Bunyan's grace, but as *the same thing,* a saving gift from an external source. A poet who has felt that unexpected solace will seek it again.

Ammons looks literally for sermons in stones, books in the running brooks. He has been reproached for the minuteness of his detail, for scrutinizing every letter of the natural alphabet, even every syllable in the genetic code, seeking to extract from each item its assuaging human clarification. If a hedge of ice can explain him to himself, why so can a pebble (and it has) or a wave (and it has). "Grace Abounding" is a critical poem in Ammons's canon because it tells us his habitual state—one of a mute congestion of burdened feeling that must go abroad, baffled, letting the eye roam aimlessly, if minutely, until it feels the click that tells it, when it sees the hedge of ice, that that visual form is the mirror of its present feeling. Of course, while the eye is performing its apparently aimless scrutiny, before the connection can be made, before the appropriate image catches the eye, the work seems dull, even servile. This tedious phase of ruminative watching occupies the first part of Ammons's "Meeting Place," published in *Poetry* (October 1982). The creek water (says Ammons in "Meeting Place") has motions, yes; the wind contributes its motions, yes; the falls also does. These are, Ammons grants, "indifferent" actions. So much for the truths of modernity. After that, the poem turns atavistic, suggesting that all matter shares deep affinities of behavior. From subatomic particles to forms determined by physical law (the sphere of a waterdrop, the body's extensional limits in dance) our human motions obey the same tendencies as nature's motions. Ammons both affirms and questions this axiom of "ancestral" actions in the second part of his poem: "is my / address attribution's burden and abuse? . . . have I / fouled their real nature for myself / by wrenching their meaning, if any, to destinations of my own / forming?"

No poem becomes significant solely by asking questions about *poiesis* and the pathetic fallacy. But when we follow the course of "Meeting Place" we see that it enacts the meeting itself. The apparently random and tediously prolonged inquiry into the most fugitive motions of the creek is Ammons's becoming "multiple and dull in the mists' dreams," his version of Keatsian "indolence." By the time Ammons reaches the end he is claiming the powers of the magus: "when I call out to them . . . / an answering is calling me." The second surprising word in the poem, after "dull," is "howling": the spirits that arise in "Meeting Place" arise from a place like hell ("A minist'ring angel shall my sister be / When thou liest howling!"). These spirits would remain fettered and imprisoned forever without the releasing spell of "figures visible." In making the imprisoned figures ancestral ones, Ammons is being not only Freudian but Christian: Adam and Eve were the first figures released in the harrowing of hell.

The utter congruence between Christian grace and *poiesis* in Ammons is nowhere clearer than in the other new poem printed in the same issue of *Poetry*, "Singling and Doubling Together," a colloquy with God (or with a divine immanence in all things, after the Buddhist model). The simplest way, perhaps, to think about Ammons's central assertion in this poem is in terms of the Christian doctrine of the Incarnation—that God "risked all the way into the taking on of shape / and time." I have here made the verb into an active one ("God risked"), but Ammons has written it as a participial adjective, skirting the problem of voluntariness in God's circumscription of himself; Ammons's "you," risked into time, "fail and fail with me, as me" (Hopkins: "I am all at once what Christ is, since he was what I am"). But Ammons's ecstatic Hopkinsian ode to a presence in leafspeech and bush-snappings and pheasant-flight is deliberately undoctrinal and intimate, reminding us of Whitman's equally lyrical, but entirely sensuous, doublings of self. Ammons originally thought to call this poem (as the typescript shows) by a religious title, "Communion": it defines *poiesis* as Herbert defined it: "It is that which while I use / I am with thee." Ammons's single long sentence composing the ode contains no surprises like "dull" or "howling" in "Meeting Place": cast in the form of a love poem (Stevens: "And for what, if not for you, do I feel love?"), "Singling and Doubling Together" requires the decorum of unclouded praise. The poem deliberately takes the form of spherical perfection, as its first line—"My nature singing in me is your nature singing"— engenders, having come full circle, its close—"changed into your / singing nature, when I need sing my nature nevermore." By ending with its poet's death rather than with the transcendent persistence of an immanent singing, the poem is true to its earthly origins rather than to its religious antecedents;

but in fact the beauty of the poem lies in its intertangled breaths of hymn and observation, of grace and birds and bushes. Its incantatory tonality is utterly different from the tones of the sedulous naturalist at the opening of "Meeting Place" (the poems meet, of course, in their endings).

It is odd to turn from these high lyrics to the epigrams of Ammons's 1982 collection, *Worldly Hopes;* the contrast reminds us that Ammons is always oscillating between his expatiations and his "briefings" (as between, from another angle, his hymnody and his nihilism). The short poems here are more of Ammons's experiments in the minimal. The question is, how few words can make a poem, and how densely can a few words be made to resonate. Here is "Providence":

> To stay
> bright as
> if just
> thought of
> earth requires
> only that
> nothing stay

"To stay bright as if just thought of / Earth requires only that nothing stay"— Ammons's art in brevity forbids this sort of rewriting (which all bad poems can sustain). The couplet that I have turned the poem into robs the poem of the doomed *rime riche* of its first and last lines, its form of measure (two words per line), and the wit of the line-breaks ("bright as—" turns out not to be "bright as day" but "bright as if," a curl of thought). My couplet (which of course will not scan, either) also loses Ammons's philosophic emphasis on the "trivial" words "as," "if," "just," "of," and "only"—the sort of words whose insidiousness interested Wittgenstein, too.

"Providence" trembles, with the lightest of touches, toward some reminiscences (Frost: "Nothing gold can stay"; Stevens: "Required, as a necessity requires"). And like many of Ammons's short poems, it burdens itself with a title of overwhelming philosophical or religious significance (others in this volume include "Righting Wrongs," "Subsumption," "Epistemology," "Oblivion's Bloom," "Immortality," and "Volitions"). "Providence"—the word is religiously defined as God's loving care for us—represents Ammons's grafting of an American Protestant mentality onto Keats's discovery of the ambiguous mercy of mortality. In its seven lines (formal "perfection" would demand eight), the poem recalls various early poems of Yeats in which the eighth line is designedly dropped to symbolize loss.

Even Ammons's simplest lyrics have points to make of the sort I have mentioned in "Providence." An ingenious and eccentric angle of vision or play of metaphor in them catches the eye; but something also catches the breath:

I went back
to my old home
and the furrow
of each year
plowed like
surf across
the place had
not washed
memory away.

The backdrop of this poem ("I Went Back") is essentially Shakespearean (the furrow of time, the obliterating sea, the memory of the poet). But rewritten, the poem takes on another cast:

I went back to my old home,
And the furrow of each year,
(Plowed like surf across the place),
Had not washed memory away.

There is something Blakean about the poem-as-quatrain ("I was angry with my friend . . . : / And it grew both day and night. / Till it bore an apple bright"). (This may be an irrelevant comparison; but we grasp at straws in trying to describe poetic effects.) Once again, here, Ammons departs from the eight-line "norm" to suggest, by adding a ninth line, the persistence of memory beyond the "natural" term of its physical moment. The energizing phrase of the poem is clearly "plowed like surf across the place," said of the furrow: the other phrases are far more conventional. In a complex image the furrow (singular) of each year (of an aggregate many), plowed (as of earth) like surf (as of ocean) across the place, is said to have failed to obliterate memory. This image is like a triple exposure in photography: first, there is the physical family farm (home); second, there is its spiritual form plowed as far as the eye can see by the furrows of Time; third, the plowed form is washed over by a new form of deluge, a surf of inner oblivion that has an intent to drown and erase the past. A fourth form, memory, then comes to replace the first, at least in the poem; but the memory being identical to the physical farm revisited, they join and merge.

If these brief forms seem constricting at times, it is because we know Ammons's discursive amplitudes. I have not found any poem in *Worldly Hopes* to equal the sublime "Easter Morning," which appeared in *Coast of Trees*. There are new versions here of themes Ammons has touched before: they range from the artist's defense of his life (a fairly savage and sardonic version called "The Role of Society in the Artist") to exercises in pure verbality ("Shit List"). Science, as always, provides apt metaphors ("Precious Weak Fields,"

"Reaction Rates," "Working Differentials") and the antagonisms of writing are made ever more cunning.

In Ammons, the compulsion to form lurks as a danger. When he says that a poem "begins in contingency and ends in necessity" he is of course right, but necessity need not always wear a necessitarian aspect; it can assume an openhanded stance too, as it sometimes does in Williams or Stevens: "rooted they / grip down and begin to awaken"; "It was like a new knowledge of reality." As Ammons packs words ever more densely and punningly, perhaps necessity begins to usurp some of the place of contingency.

If we step back, after reading Ammons's account of the alternate burgeoning and collapse of "worldly hopes" (as religion would call them) as well as his hymns of thanksgiving for "grace" with which we began, we can see in him a representative figure for the persistence of the Protestant vein in American poetry. He uses the strategy of religious language with much of Dickinson's attachment to it, but he preserves, as Dickinson did not, the tonality of genuine prayer (resembling in this Stevens above all). If this were all he offered—religious language, religious tonality—Ammons would be simply a poet of religious nostalgia, a whited sepulcher. That he is not, we must attribute to two virtues of style which coexist with the religious elements and counterbalance them. One is the grounding of reality in the seen (like Williams, he finds his ideas in things). And the other is his stubborn inclusion of the recalcitrant detail, the hard ragged edge resisting the spherical sheerness of ultimate religious vision. In his naturalist speech, in his untroubled admitting of the psychic origins of the pathetic fallacy, Ammons is modern; in his willingness to substitute the word "grace" for the poetic experience of nature in lieu of the words "pathetic fallacy," he argues, like all poets, for the primacy of feeling in the naming of inner response. If the clarification conferred by the natural world—there is one in almost every poem by Ammons—feels like what Bunyan named "grace," then it *is* grace. What does not feel like a fallacy cannot be truthfully called one. Ammons is sure that the number of fluid inner states is infinite, and that the only matrix of possibility ample enough to correspond with the inner world is the massively various outer world, and the only mediating instrument between the liquid currents of mind and the mountains and deserts of matter is language, that elusive joiner of rivers to rock:

> I tangled with
> the world to
> let it go
> but couldn't free
>
> it: so I made
> words
> to wrestle in my
> stead and went

off silent to
the quick flow
of brooks, the
slow flow of stone

Words are the scapegoat in the fiction that Ammons here names "Extrication": they wrestle with the angel of matter for us.

The Poetry of Ammons

NATHAN A. SCOTT JR.

It was, however high the phrases, the common thing from which Dante always started, as it was certainly the greatest and most common to which he came. His images were the natural inevitable images—a girl in the street, the people he knew, the language he learned as a child. In them the great diagrams are perceived; from them the great myths open; by them he understands the final end.
—Charles Williams, *The Figure of Beatrice*

Shall we call this the Poetic Way? It is at any rate the way of the poet, who has got to do his work with the body of this world, whatever that body may look like to him, in his time and place.
—Allen Tate, "The Symbolic Imagination," in *The Forlorn Demon*

It has been a privilege over the past twenty-five years to watch the steadiness with which A. R. Ammons has gradually consolidated his position as one of the major poets of our period—such a privilege, indeed, as one takes the people of an earlier generation to have enjoyed as they watched the progress of a Frost or an Eliot or a Stevens or an Auden. There may be those, however, who feel their present sense of Ammons's distinction to be somewhat remarkable in the light of the various mannerisms and idiosyncrasies wherewith he can so much try the patience of even his most lenient readers. At a certain point in his book-length poem of 1965, *Tape for the Turn of the Year*, he says, offhandedly, "Maybe I write / too much," and so he does: the logorrhea can be released by his glancing at a weed or by his being touched by the merest

We are grateful to W. W. Norton and Company, Inc., for permission to quote from Ammons's poems and to reprint in their entirety "Triphammer Bridge," "Hymn," and "Meeting Place" from the following volumes: *Collected Poems, 1951–1971* by A. R. Ammons. Copyright © 1972 by A. R. Ammons. *Lake Effect Country* by A. R. Ammons. Copyright © 1983 by A. R. Ammons.
Originally published in The *Southern Review* 24 (Autumn 1988): 717–43. Reprinted by permission.

breath of wind. Very little is required for his loquaciousness to be set going: as he says in the long poem "Summer Session 1968,"

> in my yard's more wordage than I
> can read:
> the jaybird gives a shit:
> the earthworm hoe-split bleeds
> against a damp black clump:
>
> the problem is
> how
> to keep shape and flow.

And sometimes, as his talk profusely and aimlessly maunders along, the shape and flow not being kept, he cannot resist self-mockery—as when, for example, at a certain point in "Summer Session" he jocularly tosses off the admission "I scribble, baby, I mean/I breeze on."

Or, again, one is frequently brought close to utter exasperation by his penchant for clogging his discourse with the scientific jargon of the autodidact who is devoted to *Scientific American,* as in the poem called "Mechanism" which bids us to

> honor the chemistries, platelets, hemoglobin kinetics,
>   the light-sensitive iris, the enzymic intricacies
>   of control
>
> the gastric transformations, seed
>   dissolved to acrid liquors, synthesized into
>   chirp, vitreous humor, knowledge,
>
> blood compulsion, instinct: honor the
>   unique genes,
>   molecules that reproduce themselves.

Though he makes large room in his meditations for "the / violence, grief, guilt, / despair, absurdity" of the world, Ammons seems regularly to be a cheerful, happy poet—one for whom it is not at all out of character at the end of a poem to sign off by saying "toodleoo" (as in "Cold Didn't Keep the Stuff"). So it strikes us as a little odd when he permits himself such a querulousness as he expresses when he remarks in Canto 122 of his long poem *Sphere:* "I can't understand my readers: / they complain of my abstractions." But even odder than the uncharacteristic petulance is the unconsciousness it conveys of what is so much a part of his own distinctive signature, for, if there is anything for which his readers must indeed make generous allowance, it is precisely his frequent recourse to a strange kind of rough, windy rhetoric of high (too high) generality that thins out and diminishes the experimental force of his witness—as when, again and again, his tone is that of the following passage from his "Essay on Poetics":

> I am seeking the
> mechanisms physical, physiological, epistemological, electrical,
>
> chemical, esthetic, social, religious by which many, kept
> discrete as many, expresses itself into the
> manageable rafters of salience, lofts to comprehension, breaks
>
> out in hard, highly informed suasions, the "gathering
> in the sky" so to speak, the trove of mind, tested
> experience, the only place there is to stay, where the saints
>
> are known to share accord and wine, and magical humor floats
> upon the ambient sorrow: much is nearly stable there,
> residencies perpetual.

Indeed, so infixed in his bias toward abstractions that on some he confers a recondite kind of tenor and prestige—such terms as "nucleation," "periphery," "curvature," "surround" (used as a noun), "salience," "node," "molecule," "suasion"—and they pop up on page after page, forming a language that simply will not linger in the mind.

Nor does one find particularly engaging his special sort of heartiness—about, say, how nice it is to "eat a pig dinner sometimes and sit / down in a deep chair that rightangles/your uplumping belly out/[and] cuts off the avenues of circulation," so that "boluses of air/form promoting gastric/distress." And the ribaldry—of which there is a good deal—never seems unforced and is never invigorating, being regularly marked by the grossness of the locker room, as in the following anecdote tacked on at the end of a poem called "Poetry Is the Smallest" (in *The Snow Poems*):

> poet friend of mine's
> dick's so short
> he can't pull it long enough   still his fat wife's
> to pee straight with: radiant every morning:
> not to pee on   he humps well, probably,
> anybody by surprise   stringing her out far and
> sideways, he hunkers   loose on the frail hook:
> into the urinal so far   and, too, I notice she
> he looks like, to achieve,   follows his words
> relief: closely like one who
>   knows what a tongue can do.

So, in approaching the massive body of work which Ammons has now produced, captiousness has much to batten on. But our great good fortune is the man's fluency, for, despite all the dross, there are, literally, dozens and dozens of poems whose splendor will make one want to shout, breathlessly (in something like the terms with which the late Delmore Schwartz greeted Ralph Ellison's *Invisible Man* in 1952): Reality (hear! hear!) is not mocked as long as such poems can be written. And I begin by offering but one poem in evidence, the poem he calls "Triphammer Bridge":

> I wonder what to mean by *sanctuary,* if a real or
> apprehended place, as of a bell rung in a gold
> surround, or as of silver roads along the beaches
>
> of clouds seas don't break or black.mountains
> overspill; jail: ice here's shapelier than anything,
> on the eaves massive, jawed along gorge ledges, solid
>
> in the plastic blue boat fall left water in: if I
> think the bitterest thing I can think of that seems like
> reality, slickened back, hard, shocked by rip-high wind:
>
> *sanctuary, sanctuary,* I say it over and over and the
> word's sound is the one place to dwell: that's it, just
> the sound, and the imagination of the sound—a place.

So it is that Ammons rejoices in and savors the very word "sanctuary" and finds the meaning of the word in "the/word's sound," in "just/the sound, and the imagination of the sound"—a kind of "jail," yes, for it shuts out and shelters us against the bitterer shocks of rain and "rip-high wind," but yet a place like "a bell rung in a gold/surround," indeed "the one place to dwell," this place that we are granted by the munificence of nothing other than the imagination itself. Before such a poem as this which talks not about itself but about its subject and which refuses to say all that it means, yet presenting an absolutely perfect transparency—before such a poem criticism must simply be struck dumb, for it can do nothing but admire the mastery with which the parts of the whole have been selected and so joined together that the whole seems not to have any parts at all. And it is with this kind of mastery that we are confronted throughout large tracts of Ammons's poetry.

Harold Bloom and various others have insisted on the necessity of our regarding him as standing in a line of descent that leads directly back to the great original avatars of American Romanticism, Emerson and Whitman—and so he does. Which is perhaps to say that, beyond all else, Ammons is a poet of the Sublime. For the most fundamental premise of all his principal meditations is that the sheer ontological weight and depth of the world are such as to invest all the finite things of earth with an incalculable complexity and inexhaustibility, so much so indeed that really to savor the full-fledged otherness of the immediate givens of experience is to find them testifying to their own finitude by their silent allusions to a transfinite dimension within themselves.

The English philosopher G. E. Moore was greatly charmed by the old saying of Bishop Butler's to the effect that "everything is what it is and not another thing"—so charmed indeed that Moore found in this proposition the central motto of his own philosophy. But for Ammons—for the poet who says that "if a squash blossom dies, I feel withered as a stained/zucchini and blame my nature"—such a proposition must seem only a kind of stupid claptrap, since he knows (like Theodore Roethke) that to perform an act of true attention before a worm or a vine or a blade of grass is in turn to know that not even the humblest creature of earth can be platitudinized into being merely what it is rather than another thing. Indeed, he is a poet who convinces us that he believes that, through indolence of spirit, to refuse to be radically amazed by that surplusage of meaning that may be found in a garden slug or a spider weaving its web is to reduce the world to a sort of lackluster slum.

The seventeenth-century Chinese treatise on the art of painting, *The Mustard Seed Garden Manual,* suggests that a painter, if picturing a man in the presence of a mountain, should render the man as slightly bent in an attitude of reverent homage to the majesty of the mountain, just as the mountain should be made to appear as if it, too, is saluting its visitor; or, if a lutist is being pictured beneath the moon, he, as he plucks his instrument, should seem to be listening to the moon, and the moon should appear to be listening to his music. And, Emersonian that he is, Ammons would, I suspect, be quick to approve of such instructions, for, like the sage of Concord, he, too, considers the world to be an affair of reciprocities and affinities and profound "correspondences" between matter and spirit. Which is to say that, in his sense of things, we dwell in a universe that requires us to be in commerce with that which transcends the human, with that which Longinus called the Sublime. True, given the evidence presented by his poetry, it would appear that, at least for Ammons *qua* poet, the traditional apparatus of the Sublime, the apparatus of the Christian mythos, represents a structure of thought to which he is generally disinclined to have recourse. Yet the whole drift of his poetic arguments clearly reveals his intention to make such a testimony as Wordsworth voices in "Tintern Abbey":

> I have felt
> A presence that disturbs me with the joy
> Of elevated thoughts; a sense sublime
> Of something far more deeply interfused,
> Whose dwelling is the light of setting suns,
> And the round ocean and the living air,
> And the blue sky, and in the mind of man:
> A motion and a spirit, that impels
> All thinking things, all objects of all thought,
> And rolls through all things.

Here, for example, in the great poem entitled "The City Limits," is one of Ammons's purest and most beautiful accounts of the Glory that indwells the world:

> When you consider the radiance, that it does not withhold
> itself but pours its abundance without selection into every
> nook and cranny not overhung or hidden; when you consider
>
> that birds' bones make no awful noise against the light but
> lie low in the light as in a high testimony; when you consider
> the radiance, that it will look into the guiltiest
>
> swervings of the weaving heart and bear itself upon them,
> not flinching into disguise or darkening; when you consider
> the abundance of such resource as illuminates the glow-blue
>
> bodies and gold-skeined wings of flies swarming the dumped
> guts of a natural slaughter or the coil of shit and in no
> way winces from its storms of generosity; when you consider
>
> that air or vacuum, snow or shale, squid or wolf, rose or lichen
> each is accepted into as much light as it will take, then
> the heart moves roomier, the man stands and looks about, the
>
> leaf does not increase itself above the grass, and the dark
> work of the deepest cells is of a tune with May bushes
> and fear lit by the breadth of such calmly turns to praise.

This light, this radiance, that "does not withhold/itself" is what Wallace Stevens (in "Notes Toward a Supreme Fiction") calls the "candor" in things, that munificence which leads them to unveil themselves, so that they may be shown forth as what they most essentially are. Or, another equivalent is what Hopkins (in "God's Grandeur") speaks of as "the dearest freshness deep down things"—which is that informing *élan* or power that enables all things to be what their inner entelechies intend them to be. This freshness, this candor, this radiance is something temperate and gentle: though it "pours its abundance" everywhere, it does not by force invade that which is "overhung or hidden" or which chooses to refuse it. Nor can one see it as one sees a rose or a gazelle: it is not *here* or *there,* since it is, as Stevens says, the "insolid billowing of the solid" ("Reality Is an Activity of the Most August Imagination," *Opus Posthumous*), that ontological energy wherewith "the glow-blue/bodies and gold-skeined wings of flies" are given their special kind of presence. "When you consider the radiance," when it is truly considered—*then,* "then/the heart moves roomier," and fear is turned to praise. So if, when you look at violets, you consider the radiance, you don't then dismiss them with a shrug, saying that they are simply what they are and not another thing: instead, you exclaim (with Walter Savage Landor): "Good God, the violets!" Which is a response elicited by some obscure recognition that the violets are an outward and visible sign of an inward and spiritual grace.

True, the radiance is *within* the violets, or they are "accepted into" it. But, then, as Emerson, Ammons's great master, says in the third volume of his *Journals,* "Blessed is the day when the youth discovers that Within and Above are synonyms." And, indeed, Ammons's poetry is frequently to be found envisaging the numinous and the sublime as Above. Yet he is constantly expressing his discomfort with and his mistrust of great heights. The Emerson of *Nature* is convinced that, when one is high and lifted up, "all mean egotism vanishes": in the loftiest and most exalted regions, he says, "I become a transparent eyeball; I am nothing; I see all; the currents of the Universal Being circulate through me." But the quite different testimony being made by Ammons's fine early poem "Hymn" strikes a note that one hears again and again in "The Unmirroring Peak," in "Choice" and "Kind" and "High and Low" and "Convergence" and "Offset" and countless other poems. He says in "Hymn":

> I know if I find you I will have to leave the earth
> and go on out
>   over the sea marshes and the brant in bays
> and over the hills of tall hickory
> and over the crater lakes and canyons
> and on up through the spheres of diminishing air
> past the blackset noctilucent clouds
>   where one wants to stop and look
> way past all the light diffusions and bombardments
> up farther than the loss of sight
>   into the unseasonal undifferentiated empty stark
>
> And I know if I find you I will have to stay with the earth
> inspecting with thin tools and ground eyes
> trusting the microvilli sporangia and simplest
>   coelenterates
> and praying for a nerve cell
> with all the soul of my chemical reactions
> and going right on down where the eye sees only traces
>
> You are everywhere partial and entire
> You are on the inside of everything and on the outside
>
> I walk down the path down the hill where the sweetgum
> has begun to ooze spring sap at the cut
> and I see how the bark cracks and winds like no other bark
> chasmal to my ant-soul running up and down

> and if I find you I must go out deep into your
>   far resolutions
> and if I find you I must stay here with the separate leaves.

The "you" being addressed in the "Hymn" is the ultimate source of all the plenitude with which the world is furnished: it is Being itself, the aboriginal reality from which everything else springs, what Stevens speaks of in "Notes Toward a Supreme Fiction" as "the whole,/The Complicate, the amassing harmony." And Ammons's choice of an anthropomorphic idiom for his salute to this aboriginal reality is merely a conceit. He knows, of course, that a conventional wisdom says that, in order to find it, one "will have to leave the earth/and go on out" beyond the earth. Yet he finds himself most deeply nourished by the natural order of common things, by "the sea marshes" and "the hills of tall hickory" and the sweetgum when it begins "to ooze spring sap at the cut." He does not want to be any sort of aviator or angel, flying off into the "diminishing air" of the world beyond, for, amidst that "unseasonal undifferentiated empty stark," he fears that there is nothing to be beheld but a kind of blind glitter of nothingness. He does not, in other words, propose to take the Absolute by direct assault, believing as he does that, as a poet, he (as Allen Tate puts it) "has got to do his work with the body of this world." As he says, "I know if I find you I will have to stay with the earth," and he has no intention of searching after the eternity of Platonic heavens, since he suspects that such heavens will be found to be merely what he speaks of in the poem called "Convergence" as "the peak of/illusion's pyramid." So his is the vigilance of a man on whom the things of this world are pressing all the time, and he believes that it is in them that (as Charles Williams says) "the great diagrams are [to be] perceived; [that] from them the great myths open." Which is to say that, whether he knows it or not, Ammons's patron saint is not Dionysius the Areopagite but St. Athanasius, for, in his dealings with the things of earth, his Way is not the Way of Rejection but rather the Way of Affirmation.

In its reflections on the relation of the Sublime to the mundane order Ammons's poetry resorts, however, far more frequently to the polarity between the one and the many or between unity and multiplicity than it does to the polarity between the heights and the lowlands of the world; but his mistrust of any sort of mystical angelism is in no way altered by the change in figure. The poem entitled "Early Morning in Early April" in his book of 1971, *Briefings,* pictures, for example, a landscape overhung with a rainy mist that has "hung baubles" on the trees, underlacing the maple branches "with glaring beadwork," and the poem says:

> what to make of it:
> what to make of a mist whose characteristic
> is a fine manyness coming dull in a wide

> oneness: what to make of the glass
> erasure, glass: the yew's partly lost.

The unstated assumption is that the diversity, the variety, the multifarious-
ness, belonging to all the concrete particularities with which our world is
furnished, offers the human spirit an essential kind of delight and nourishment—whereas the staircase leading to unity takes us (as the poem "Staking
Claim" says)

> all the way to the final vacant core
> that brings
> things together and turns them away
>
> all the way away
> to stirless bliss!

And *Tape for the Turn of the Year* registers an even more emphatic reprobation
of unity: it says (in the entry for 9 Dec.) that

> we can approach
> unity only by the loss
> of things—
> a loss we're unwilling
> to take—
> since the gain of unity
> would be a vision
> of something in the
> continuum of nothingness:
> we already have things:
> why fool around:
> beer, milk,
> mushroom cream sauce,
> eggs, books, bags,
> telephones & rugs:
> pleasure to perceive
> correspondences, facts
> that experience is
> holding together, that
> what mind grew out of
> is also holding together:
> otherwise? how could we
> perceive similarities?
> but all
> the way to unity is
> too far off

Sometimes (as in "Left," the penultimate piece in the *Collected Poems*) the
image of the "center" connotes the same range of meaning over which the

notion of "unity" presides, as the image of "periphery" replaces that of "multiplicity." And this lexicon of height and unity and center makes a strangely cryptic language, but one which, for all its enigmaticalness, intends to warn us away from that black mysticism or magical gnosis which seeks some kind of unmediated contact with the Sublime. We are not angels, and, as Ammons often wants in effect to remind us, the path, the narrow and direct path, that we must take into felicity and wisdom is one that leads *through* the immediate, concrete, finite things of this world in which the Sublime is incarnate. As he says in the eighty-sixth canto of his extraordinary long poem "Hibernaculum,"

> the sum of everything's nothing: very nice: that
> turns the world back in on itself: such as right
> when you possess everything, you'd give everything
>
> up for a sickle pear: I hope my philosophy will turn
> out all right and turn out to be a philosophy so as
> to free people (any who are trapped, as I have been)
>
> from seeking any image in the absolute or seeking
> any absolute whatsoever.

In short, what we confront is (as Jean Cocteau once phrased it) *le mystère laic,* the "lay mystery" or the secular mystery of transcendence within immanence.

Ammons's profound reverence for this secular mystery is expressed in a vast number of his poems, and it forms one of the principal strands of his work. Here, for example, is the testimony he makes in the opening part of the beautiful poem entitled simply "Still":

> I said I will find what is lowly
>   and put the roots of my identity
>   down there:
> each day I'll wake up
> and find the lowly nearby,
>   a handy focus and reminder,
> a ready measure of my significance,
> the voice by which I would be heard,
> the wills, the kinds of selfishness
>   I could
> freely adopt as my own:
>
> but though I have looked everywhere,
>   I can find nothing
>   to give myself to:
>   everything is
>
> magnificent with existence, is in
> surfeit of glory:

nothing is diminished,
nothing has been diminished for me.

This devotion to what is "lowly," to the "lovely diminutives" of the world (as Roethke called them—snails and weeds and cockroaches), this sense of "everything" as "in surfeit of glory," as "magnificent with existence"—it is precisely this which attests to Ammons's fidelity to a vision such as Blake's that wants to declare that there is nothing so paltry, so inglorious, as not to be indwelt by holiness and capable of being a means of grace—not even wind-swept grasses and "dry-burnt moss": "nothing is diminished,/nothing has been diminished for me."

So it is (as the poet and critic Richard Howard has suggested) a "littoral" range through which Ammons's poetry moves: which is to say that he gives his allegiance to the coastal regions of the world. The sea, as Melville's *Moby Dick* reminds us, is "the region of the strange Untried": it is "the immense Remote, the Wild, the Watery, the Unshored." And he who seeks a complete and final vision of reality, who desires a direct and unmediated encounter with the Sublime, will risk what Melville calls "ocean-perishing," amidst "the heartless voids and immensities" of the Unshored. But, regarding as mis-guided all schemes for scorning or smashing the quotidian in the illusory quest of some immediate contact with the *Mysterium Tremendum* (since they yield only "the unseasonal undifferentiated empty stark"), and with his sharp sense—as he says in the long poem "Extremes and Moderations"—that "the/lofted's precarious," Ammons conceives the only possibility for com-merce with the transcendent to be by way of its incarnateness within imma-nence. So he elects not "the region of the strange Untried" but, as he indicates in his relatively early (1965) and most famous deliverance, "Corsons Inlet," the shore line, an inlet into "the immense Remote." As he says in this remark-able poem, "Overall is beyond me: is the sum of these events/I cannot draw, the ledger I cannot keep, the accounting beyond the account."

What needs, then, to be recognized, if Ammons's poetry is to be deeply taken hold of, is that the metaphysical vision constantly at work in this poetry is one whose controlling idea is that of analogy. The classical exponents of the analogical method of predication—whereby notions derived from what is already known are made applicable to that which is relatively unknown in virtue of some similarity between the two otherwise dissimilar "analogues"—are, of course, such figures as Albertus Magnus and Aquinas and Cajetan and Suarez. But, without plunging into the thickets of their speculations, we may simply say that the metaphysical principle of analogy asserts a kind of co-inherence between *essentia* and *esse:* it asserts, as it were, that reality is *in* things and yet also *beyond* them, that God is at once like and unlike His cre-ation. Between Him and His creatures there is, in other words, an analogy of *being (analogia entis)*: which is to say that the transient existence belonging to the creature may be a significant image or reflection of the being of God. Yet the doctrine of the *analogia entis* also posits a certain *via negationis,* since, by reason of the incommensurability between God and all things belonging to the creaturely order, it intends to "negate" in the divine Cause all the finite and imperfect properties that belong to the effect. In short, though we may behold God not in His naked glory but only in and through the world of His creation, the *ordo creationis* does itself afford but a limited kind of vision: we only "know in part," for, as St. Paul says, "now we see through a glass, darkly." But, even if seeing darkly, what we see may not be dismissed as merely illusory, given the *analogia entis ad Deum et creaturam.*

Now it is such a structure of thought that is over and again to be found shaping Ammons's poetic utterance, and nowhere more emphatically than in one of the central poems of his career, the extraordinary title poem of his book of 1963, *Expressions of Sea Level.* The place at which the meditation it records occurs is a littoral place: it is the shore line, the land's edge, from which he looks out toward the ocean, the region of the Wholly Other, of the Numinous, of the *Mysterium Tremendum*—toward that which "is hard to name." And since "there is no way to know/the ocean's speech," the poem fixes its attention on the way "the ocean/marks itself/against the gauging land/it erodes and/builds." Since "the sea speaks far from its core,/far from its center," Ammons turns for "expressions" and "hints" of what is purported by the deep to "broken, surf things," and he notices the evidence they give to "keen watchers on the shore" of how they have been touched by the sea and of how high its tides have risen. He says:

> how do you know the moon
> is moving: see the dry
> casting of the beach worm
>   dissolve at the
> delicate rising touch:

> that is the
>   expression of sea level.
> the talk of giants,
> of ocean, moon, sun, of everything,
> spoken in a dampened grain of sand.

Since the ocean's speech is "speech without words," since it is "only in the meeting of rock and sea . . . [that]/hard relevance [is] shattered into light," for "a/statement perfect in its speech" one must turn to the things of earth, to littoral things, for signs or "expressions of sea level": one must turn to the "tide-held slant of grasses," to "the/skin of back, bay-eddy reeds." As he says in "Identity," another of the poems in *Expressions of Sea Level,*

> I will show you
> the underlying that takes no image to itself,

> cannot be shown or said,
> but weaves in and out of moons and bladderweeds,
> is all and
> beyond destruction
> because created fully in no
> particular form.

So, given the radical otherness of that which is most truly foundational or ultimate and given the necessity of its being caught, as it were, on the wing, it is not surprising that Ammons should be obsessively preoccupied with "saliences." The term has something like a talismanic status in his lexicon, and the frequency of its recurrence belongs to his distinctive stylistic signature. He is always searching for whatever may be described as protuberant, conspicuous, noteworthy instances of "statement" that disclose something of ultimacy. "Consistencies," he says in the poem which he calls "Saliences,"

> rise;
> and ride
> the mind down
> hard routes
> walled
> with no outlet and so
> to open a variable geography
> proliferate
> possibility.

And he is on the lookout for

> fields of order in disorder,
> where choice
> can make beginnings,
> turns,
> reversals.

It is the saliences, he says, that "spread firmingly across my sight" and that give him "summations of permanence."

In many of the remarkable books which Martin Heidegger was issuing in the 1940s and 50s—in *Erläuterungen zu Hölderlins Dichtung,* in *Über den Humanismus,* in *Holzwege,* and in various others—he brooded deeply on how "withdrawn" and "distant" and "hidden" Being is, distant because it is never to be encountered nakedly and in itself but only in and through the things of earth which it "assembles" and supports. Yet at the same time, with an equal intensity, Heidegger was also meditating on how Being, as he liked to say, "hails" us, this hailing an affair of nothing other than the generosity with which Being permits the things of earth to "come-to-presence." And, were Ammons familiar with Heidegger's late phase, one would expect him to feel prompted to salute this difficult German thinker as one offering a powerful confirmation of his own basic sense of reality, for it is precisely such a dialectic as Heidegger's between absence and presence that most centrally organizes much of Ammons's poetry. For him, too, "the underlying that takes no image to itself,/cannot be shown or said"; for him, too, it is hidden and distant. Nevertheless, his poetry is frequently breaking into the language of doxology (as in the poem "Cut the Grass" which gratefully marvels at "the wonderful workings of the world"), for, after all, there are saliences: there are epiphanies, there are revelations *enough* to make us feel bidden to "consider the radiance." So the poet of "This Bright Day" is, indeed, a happy poet:

> Earth, earth!
> day, this bright day
> again—once more
> showers of dry spruce gold,
> the poppy flopped broad open and delicate
> from its pod—once more,
> all this again: I've had many
> days here with these stones and leaves:
> like the sky, I've taken on a color
> and am still:
> the grief of leaves,
> summer worms, huge blackant
> queens bulging
> from weatherboarding, all that
> will pass
> away from me that I will pass into,
> none of the grief
> cuts less now than ever—only I
> have learned the
> sky, the day sky, the blue
> obliteration of radiance.

The disclosures that come by way of "saliences" never carry such finality, though, as to permit us in any rigid way to schematize the world at hand, and nothing is for Ammons more iniquitous than the mind's arrogant reification of its own designs of reality. In the strange language he employs it is the term "line" that stands for the abstraction which wants to bring the world to heel by substantializing itself, and the passionate rejection of any and all forms of hypostasis that "Corsons Inlet" expresses strikes a note that is to be heard over and again throughout Ammons's poetry:

> I went for a walk over the dunes again this morning . . .
>
> the walk liberating, I was released from forms,
> from the perpendiculars,

> straight lines, blocks, boxes, binds
> of thought
> into the hues, shadings, rises, flowing bends and blends
>   of sight:
>
>   I allow myself eddies of meaning:
> yield to a direction of significance
> running
> like a stream through the geography of my work:
>   you can find
> in my sayings
>   swerves of action
>   like the inlet's cutting edge . . .
>
> in nature there are few sharp lines: there are areas of
> primrose
>   more or less dispersed;
> disorderly orders of bayberry; between the rows
> of dunes,
> irregular swamps of reeds,
> though not reeds alone, but grass, bayberry, yarrow, all . . .
> predominantly reeds:
>
> I have reached no conclusions, have erected no boundaries,
> shutting out and shutting in, separating inside
>   from outside: I have
>   drawn no lines:

Ammons wants us, in short, as he says in *Tape for the Turn of the Year* (the entry for 7 Jan.), to "get out of boxes, hard/forms of mind:/go deep:/penetrate/to the true spring."

Indeed, so fearful is he of intoxication with false closures and reified postulations that in one of his early poems, "This Black Rich Country," he prays: "Dispossess me of belief:/between life and me obtrude/no symbolic forms." His assumption is that the world with which we must reckon is so mobile, so dynamic, so restless, that in the degree to which we are overly charmed by the Idea, by the mind's fabulations, we may well be to that extent rendered incompetent at coping "with this/world as it is." So he wonders in the *Tape* (in the entry for 10 Jan.) if "our minds [have] taken us too/far, out of nature, out of/complete acceptance," and he suggests (in the entry for 9 Dec.) that

> those who rely on any shore
> foolishly haven't faced
> it that
> only the stream is reliable:

It is in fact his sense of the restless transiency in things that prompts him to think of the wind as his "guide," his tutor, and that leads him in scores and scores of his poems to make gales and tempests the prime mover in the drama of life: in no other body of lyric poetry in the English language is the landscape so abidingly windswept: sometimes the winds are hard and steady, and sometimes they are soft and gentle, but the air is constantly astir—and Ammons keeps it so, because the wind overruns and brushes aside "lines" and fences and boundaries, taking everything (as he says in "Saliences") "out of calculation's reach." The wind reminds us (says the poem "Guide") that "you have to . . . break/off from *is* to *flowing*": as it scuds across the terrains we occupy, sweeping in its wake whatever it comes upon, it makes us know how utterly provisional every moment is and how specious therefore all our reified concepts and intellections are. Indeed, Ammons as poet finds himself required to acknowledge that not even language may be reified: as he says in the poem "Motion,"

> The word is
> not the thing:
> is
> a construction of,
> a tag for,
> the thing: the
> word in
> no way
> resembles
> the thing, except
> as sound
> resembles,
> as in *whirr,*
> sound:
> the relation
> between what this
> as words
> is
> and what is
> is tenous: we
> agree upon
> this as the net to
> cast on what
> is: the finger
> to
> point with: the
> method of
> distinguishing,
> defining, limiting.

And thus poems themselves

> are fingers, methods,
> nets,
> not what is or was:
> but the music
> in poems
> is different,
> points to nothing,
> traps no
> realities, takes
> no game, but
> by the motion of
> its motion
> resembles
> what, moving, is—
> the wind
> underleaf white against
> the tree.

The fine simplicity of this statement about the kind of simulacrum of reality that the poem may proffer wants to be completed only by the great passage in "Hibernaculum" which speaks of that wherein the poetic word finds its best nourishment:

> if the night is to be
> habitable, if dawn is to come out of it, if day is ever
> to grow brilliant on delivered populations, the word
>
> must have its way by the brook, lie out cold all night
> along the snow limb, spell by yearning's wilted reed till
> the wilted reed rises, know the patience and smallness
>
> of stones.

Now it is just his great success in *Tape for the Turn of the Year* in getting "out of boxes, hard/forms of mind," in breaking "off from *is* to *flowing*," that makes this poem of more than two hundred pages so exemplary a case of Ammons's art and one of his more impressive accomplishments in the medium of the long poem. It originated during the closing weeks of 1963 in a curious kind of stunt. Eight years earlier his first book, *Ommateum,* had been published by an obscure vanity press in Philadelphia and had been generally ignored—but the brilliant second book, *Expressions of Sea Level,* was to be published by the Ohio State University Press in 1964. He is, of course, today the Goldwin Smith Professor of Poetry at Cornell University, but at the end of '63 he was without academic honors or preferments of any other sort. True, he had at that point recently appeared at Cornell to present a reading of his poems—the result of which, as it seemed, might be the offer of some kind of tenuous teaching appointment. And, as the year drew to a close and as he (in the rural flatlands of New Jersey near Philadelphia) awaited at once the delivery of his copies of the new book and some word about his prospect at Cornell, it occurred to him one day to purchase a roll of adding-machine tape and to run the entire tape through his typewriter by way of producing "a long/thin/poem," a skinny poem "plain as/day, exact and bright!"

The poem took the form of a diary, with entries extending from the sixth day of December, 1963, through the tenth day of the following January. And it is a great bucket that catches everything his days bring: the smells of his wife's cooking, what "the checker at/the A & P said," weather forecasts heard on his radio, shopping in Philadelphia at Wanamaker's, the dismantling of the Christmas tree, his attempts at throwing off a bad cold, what he and his wife have for dinner of a certain evening over at "Sompers Point/at Mac's" (fried shrimp for himself and crab for her)—all this being accompanied by such asides as "just went to take a leak" and "(I had/lunch after/'who cannot love')." And he offers frequent interstitial reports on the progress of his writing, as the tape slowly winds down from his typewriter into the wastebasket over the five weeks that this "serious novelty" is being composed. The poem is simply drenched in the reality of the quotidian: its language is that of one who has given himself up to the world and who has no regrets about his surrender. Yet, for all the commitment to "the ordinary universe," Ammons in no way relinquishes here his contemplative vocation, and, as day follows day, he is constantly engaged in a labor of reflection on how all the good things each day brings may "be managed,/received and loved/in their passing." Indeed, in his grateful acceptance of the *claritas,* the radiance, that belongs to the quiddities and haecceities of the world, he puts us in mind of the Williams of *Paterson,* especially when he (in the entry for 23 Dec.) recites his Morning Office:

> release us from mental
> prisons into the actual
> fact, the mere
> occurrence—the touched,
> tasted, heard, seen:
> in the simple event is
> the scope of life:
> let's not make up
> categories to toss ourselves
> around with:
> look: it's snowing:
> without theory
> & beyond help:

> I accept:
> I can react with
>   restlessness & quiet
>   terror, or with
>   fascination &
>   delight: I choose the
> side of possibility:

In the entry in the *Tape* for 31 Dec. Ammons says: "after this,/this long poem, I hope I/can do short rich hard/lyrics: lines/that can incubate slowly/then fall into/symmetrical tangles." And, indeed, the books that followed—*Northfield Poems* (1966), the *Selected Poems* (1968), *Uplands* (1970), and *Briefings: Poems Small and Easy* (1971)—presented a large and brilliant achievement in this mode: one will think of "Reflective," "One:Many," "Saliences," "Peak," "Sphere," "Upland," "Periphery," "Cascadilla Falls," "This Black Rich Country," "This Bright Day," "He Held Radical Light," "Early Morning in Early April," and a vast number of other poems as exemplifying the kind of mastery that Ammons was regularly demonstrating in his work of the late 60s and early 70s. But already in the *Tape* and in "Summer Session 1968" (in *Uplands*) he had shown that, despite his respect for the short, hard lyric, he had the sort of sensibility that liked the chance for expatiation, for the leisurely exploration of a large theme; and this penchant he submitted to again and again in the mid- and late 70s, for it was during this period that he issued a major series of long poems—the book-length poem *Sphere: The Form of a Motion* (1974), the cycle of *The Snow Poems* (1977), and those which were collected in the *Selected Longer Poems* of 1980 ("Pray Without Ceasing," "Essay on Poetics," "Extremes and Moderations," "Hibernaculum," and, again, "Summer Session").

These big poems disclose, of course, the extraordinary *ambitiousness* by which Ammons's career has been driven, and there are those, on the one hand, who have a great enthusiasm for them and those, on the other, who regard them as merely facile and as evidencing no capacity for the kind of systematic "argument" that the long poem needs to sustain. Toward the end of "Hibernaculum" he says of his own poetic procedures:

>   if there is to be
> no principle of inclusion, then, at least, there ought
>
> to be a principle of exclusion, for to go with a maw at
> the world as if to chew it up and spit
> it out again as one's own is to trifle with terrible
>
> affairs.

But, if there is any principle of exclusion operative in the long poems that followed the *Tape,* it has the effect only of shutting *people* out, the whole realm of transaction with the neighbor, with (as it might be said in Ammons's slang) "the human surround." Everywhere we hear only of I, I, I—"I went to the summit and stood in the high nakedness"; "I find I am able to say / only what is in my head"; "I really do not want to convince anyone of anything"; "still I am not high on the bestseller lists, the Wonderful / Award is gradually being given to someone else." Hardly at all do these poems admit into themselves the concrete, palpable circumstantiality of our human togetherness: indeed, "Hibernaculum" breezily acknowledges (in Canto 109) that, "if the population of the earth is four billion people, / then [it has excluded] nearly four billion people." But the poems are open to whatever else happens to cross Ammons's mind. "I don't want shape," he says in *Sphere;* and he speaks there also of being "sick of good poems, all those little rondures / splendidly brought off, painted gourds on a shelf." Which is an aversion that most assuredly appears to be controlling such poems as the "Essay on Poetics" and "Extremes and Moderations" and "Pray Without Ceasing," and they have not, therefore, despite their numerous local felicities, succeeded in claiming the sympathy of many readers who have found their shapelessness to be alienating.

Ammons is, of course, clearly committed to a radically open kind of form in these long poems. Already by the mid-60s the colon had become a special hallmark of his compositional method, for he had chosen consistently to use it instead of the period for a full stop. And, when it is separating two independent clauses, the function of the colon is nowhere more exactly defined than in Fowler's *Dictionary of Modern English Usage,* where it is said to be "that of delivering [in the clause that follows the colon] the goods that have been invoiced in the preceding words." Which is to say that the grammatical function of the colon is that of propelling us forward, of inducing advance, of generating movement, *motion.* Indeed, in poem after poem ("What This Mode of Motion Said," "Motion for Motion," "Four Motions for the Pea Vines," "Two Motions") Ammons is meditating on motion, and we have in fact already noticed his saying in the poem entitled "Motion" that "by the motion of / its motion / [the music / in poems] resembles / what, moving, is." In other words, in his sense of things reality is not primarily an affair of neatly contoured forms: on the contrary, it *is* effluence, something flexuous and cursive. And thus the poem (as he says in "The Swan Ritual") needs to be "a going concern . . . beyond all binds and terminals," not something neatly shaped like a painted gourd on a shelf but something (as "Corsons Inlet" puts it) that is "willing to go along, to accept / the becoming / thought, to stake off no beginnings or ends, establish / no walls." So he aims in his long poems at such an inclusiveness and such a variety as will in some measure be commensurate with the breadth and heterogeneousness of a world without circumference.

Yet, despite the indeterminate, inorganic kind of form that these poems embrace, a certain consistency is observable in the relentlessness with which he holds fast to a few governing preoccupations. He is, for example, in the "Essay on Poetics" and in "Extremes and Moderations" brooding as always on the nature of the poetic enterprise. Or, again, for all its *disjecta membra,* "Pray Without Ceasing" appears to be an uncharacteristically melancholy rumination on "terror, pity, grief, death," on the "falling back and away / of time-sunk persons and places." "Hibernaculum," on the other hand, is quintessentially an Ammons poem, in its beautiful reiterations of the kind of reverence for the vast alterity and magnificence of the created universe that so much of the poetry expresses. And *Sphere* brilliantly and movingly rehearses another theme that is deeply a part of Ammons's thought, that "the categorizing mind" must so "come to know / the works of the Most High as to assent to them" and to "celebrate Him and offer Him not our / flight but our cordiality and gratitude":

> if we are small
> can we be great by going away from the Most High into our own
> makings, thus despising what He has given: or can we, accepting
>
> our smallness, bend to cherish the greatness that rolls through
> our sharp days, that spends us on its measureless currents: and
> so, for a moment, if only for a moment, participate in those means
>
> that provide the brief bloom in the eternal presence: is this
> our saving: is this our perishable thought that imperishably
> bears us through the final loss: then sufficient thanks for that:

True, these long poems of Ammons's middle period are, in their prolixity and diffuseness, sometimes flawed, and some of his readers have, therefore, accorded them a very imperfect sympathy. But they are all filled with his special kind of eloquence, and they all belong to what he speaks of in *Sphere* (in the sixteenth canto) as that "anthology [which] is the moving, changing definition of the / imaginative life of the people" of our time.

In his work of recent years, however—in the poems collected in *A Coast of Trees* (1981), *Worldly Hopes* (1982), *Lake Effect Country* (1983), and *Sumerian Vistas* (1987)—he has returned to the short, hard lyric, and the song is simply stunning in its purity and grace. In the "Essay on Poetics" at a certain point he playfully turns inside-out and upside-down William Carlos Williams's notion that there are "no ideas but in things," inviting us to consider various alternatives—" 'no things but in ideas,' / 'no ideas but in ideas,' and 'no things but in things.' " Yet in the same poem he avows, very much in the accent of Williams: "I think what I see." And, indeed, in his late work he wants to put aside all "engines of declaration" and to do nothing other than present what he beholds: he wants to "turn / to the cleared particular" and to elicit in us the realization (as he says in the title poem in *A Coast of Trees*) "that whatever it is it is in the Way and / the Way in it, as in us, emptied full."

Nor can one fail to be reminded by the drift of Ammons's testimony in the poems of the 80s of how deeply religious his basic sensibility is. Midway through the "Essay on Poetics" he says: "I am just going to take it for granted / that the tree is in the backyard: / it's necessary to be quiet in the hands of the marvelous." And it is in an attitude of such admiring gratitude and veneration that he faces the manifold things of this world—which, as he says in the poem "Vehicle," "praise themselves seen in / my praising sight." Moreover, when he suggests that a spruce bough in winter and a running brook and a squirrel bunching branches "praise themselves seen in / my praising sight," he intends to be taken not as merely turning a phrase but as speaking in full seriousness—which is surely made evident in the great poem "Singling & Doubling Together" from *Lake Effect Country:*

> My nature singing in me is your nature singing:
> you have means to veer down, filter through,
> and, coming in,
> harden into vines that break back with leaves,
> so that when the wind stirs
> I know you are there and I hear you in leafspeech,
>
> though of course back into your heightenings I
> can never follow: you are there beyond
> tracings flesh can take,
> and farther away surrounding and informing the systems,
> you are as if nothing, and
> where you are least knowable I celebrate you most
>
> or here most when near dusk the pheasant squawks and
> lofts at a sharp angle to the roost cedar,
> I catch in the angle of that ascent,
> in the justness of that event your pheasant nature,
> and when dusk settles, the bushes creak and
> snap in their natures with your creaking
>
> and snapping nature . . .
>
> even you risked all the way into the taking on of shape
> and time.

The poem wants to say that the coruscations of glory borne by leafspeech and pheasant flight and bush-snappings are nothing other than the blaze of the Sublime that, to be sure, is "beyond / tracings flesh can take" but that, by virtue of its immanence within all the things of earth, yet permits them to *come-to-presence,* finding its tongue in the poet's song (which becomes *our* song in those moments when we are most truly human). In short, the "you" being addressed in "Singing & Doubling Together" is simply the Wholly Other, the Incomparable, "the dearest freshness deep down things": it is none other than Being itself, " 'that / which is to be praised' " and invested "with / our store of verve." And this aboriginal reality is addressed as "you," not because Ammons conceives it to be *a* being with personal attributes but rather, presumably, because he feels it to present itself with the same sort of graciousness that one encounters in the love of another person. He chooses not, in other words, to talk about "God" but, rather, to speak of that which approximates what Teilhard de Chardin called *le milieu divin.* Or, we might say that Ammons is a poet of what Stevens in a late poem, "Of Mere Being," in *Opus Posthumous,* called "mere Being": we might say that he is a poet of that which, though not coextensive with all things, yet interpenetrates all things with the radiance of its diaphanous presence.

Though Harold Bloom's exuberant enthusiasm for Ammons's poetry, in its various expressions over many years, has no doubt been insufficiently modulated, he was surely right when, in his book of 1971, *The Ringers in the Tower,* he declared him to be "the central poet" of our generation, for this indeed is what he is. And he holds such a position in part because his special *pietas* speaks so deeply and so reassuringly to a malaise by which few reflective people of our period are untouched. It might be said to be simply an ennui of the human, a weariness of looking out upon a world that seems everywhere to be besmudged by ourselves, to have been shaped by some form of human intentionality—which leads in turn to a profound yearning to descry some "otherness" in reality which cannot be made subservient to the engines of our planning and our manipulation. But it will not suffice, of course, to find this otherness to be nothing more than the inert blankness of what Coleridge called "fixities and definites," for we seek (in Stevens's phrase) "a kind of total grandeur at the end," not a grandeur, as it were, overhead but *in* "the vulgate of experience," in "the actual landscape with its actual horns / Of baker and butcher blowing." And it is of just this that Ammons's poetry offers a presentment—as in the great final poem in *Lake Effect Country,* "Meeting Place":

> The water nearing the ledge leans down with
> grooved speed at the spill then,
> quickly groundless in air, bends
>
> its flat bottom plates up for the circular
> but crashes into irregularities of lower
> ledge, then breaks into the white
>
> bluffs of warped lace in free fall that
> breaking with acceleration against air
> unweave billowing string-maze

floats: then the splintery regathering
on the surface below where imbalances
form new currents to wind the water

away: the wind acts in these shapes, too,
and in many more, as the falls also does in
many more, some actions haphazardly

unfolding, some central and accountably
essential: are they, those actions,
indifferent, nevertheless

ancestral: when I call out to them
as to flowing bones in my naked self, is my
address attribution's burden and abuse: of course

not, they're unchanged, unaffected: but have I
fouled their real nature for myself
by wrenching their

meaning, if any, to destinations of my own
forming: by the gladness in the recognition
as I lean into the swerves and become

multiple and dull in the mists' dreams, I know
instruction is underway, an
answering is calling me, bidding me rise, or is

giving me figures visible to summon
the deep-lying fathers from myself,
the spirits, feelings howling, appearing there.

A. R. Ammons and John Ashbery: The Walk as Thinking

Roger Gilbert

If the fifties and sixties are in part marked by a reaction against various modes of abstraction, and a turn to a purified form of representation that claims for itself the status of sample rather than metaphor, the past twenty years have seen a pronounced shift back to what Robert Pinsky calls "the discursive aspect of poetry," an aspect that encompasses all the ways in which poems deal directly with ideas.[1] But where poets like Frost, Warren, and Roethke tend to represent wisdom as originating beyond the poet's own consciousness, more recent poets, most notably A. R. Ammons and John Ashbery, have insisted on the coextensiveness of consciousness and insight. For them understanding occurs not as a revelation of truth but as an ongoing process of thinking, a process not to be dissociated from experience as a whole. Their poems follow in the mode of Stevens' "An Ordinary Evening in New Haven," charting the incessant shifting and gliding movements of the poet's meditation as it comes into fitful contact with a reality beyond itself.

Ammons and Ashbery are thus poets of thinking, rather than poets of truth or wisdom. They are more concerned with rendering the *experience* of reflection, its rhythms and contours, than with delivering completed thoughts that can claim the status of truth. Discussing the "complex forms of contemporary discursiveness," Charles Altieri usefully analyzes "the opposition between thinking and thought," and traces the valorization of thinking as a central Romantic enterprise descending from Wordsworth and Shelley to Stevens. Altieri's prejudice against what he calls "the scenic imagination," however, leads him to dismiss the empirical situation of the poet-thinker: "instead of a self positioned in the world, the poetics of thinking explores a transpersonal self virtually coextensive with the world's existence *as* an object of concern."[2] By "object of concern," I take Altieri to mean an object of

Originally published in *Walks in the World: Representation and Experience in Modern American Poetry* (Princeton: Princeton University Press, 1991), 225–50. Reprinted by permission.

thought rather than perception; the "transpersonal self" of the poem is coextensive with the world in this sense because both are abstractions that exist solely in the language and "thinking" of the poem. I want to emphasize the *persistence* of the world as an empirical reality that informs poetic meditation at its most profound. The walk, I would suggest, appeals to poets of thinking precisely because it enables them to anchor thought in the world, to provide the mind with a continuous yet ever-changing point of reference that can keep it from becoming sealed in its own discourse.

. . . . .

The names of Ammons and Ashbery are commonly linked both on the basis of their shared penchant for a sophisticated form of meditative poetry and through Harold Bloom's impassioned advocacy of the two as contemporary figures of comparable "strength."[3] It hardly needs to be pointed out, however, that beyond their deployment of the meditative mode, they are in fact profoundly different poets. Indeed it might be said that they constitute in their very *difference* from each other discursive counterparts to the pair of poets Gary Snyder and Frank O'Hara. Like Snyder, Ammons is a poet of nature, in the sense that his poems center on natural phenomena, however strenuously they seek to translate those phenomena into the realm of the spirit.[4] Conversely, Ashbery is overwhelmingly preoccupied with the same ambience of cultural density, geographically epitomized by New York City, that provides the subject matter of his close friend Frank O'Hara. But where Snyder and O'Hara approach their respective realms primarily by means of mimesis or transcription, each setting down as directly as possible the phenomena that interest him, Ammons and Ashbery confront these same realms reflectively, taking them primarily as grounds against which to measure the workings of their own consciousnesses. They thus repeat the difference between nature and culture that separates Snyder and O'Hara, but in a far more introspective key. The external conditions they behold—for Ammons, unity in diversity, the struggle for survival, ineluctable causality; for Ashbery, ephemerality, disjunctiveness, flatness of surface—provide each with potent correlatives for the way consciousness opens onto reality.

Walking is a central motif in both men's work, in part because it offers a bodily analogue both to the movement of thinking and articulating in language, and to the larger flux of reality as it enters the senses.[5] It thus represents a meeting place of the discursive and the phenomenal, two elements whose coordination is a central project in their poetry. The analogy between discursiveness and walking has been most clearly stated by Robert Pinsky, whom I have already cited:

> Definitions of the term "discursive" tend to divide into two apparently contradictory senses. On the one hand, the word describes speech or writing which

is wandering and disorganized; on the other, it can also mean "explanatory"—pointed, organized around a setting forth of material.

These opposites are reconciled by the radical sense of motion over terrain; the word signifies going through or going over one's subject. Whether digressively or directly, at a walk or at a run, the motion is on ground and by foot, putting its weight part by part onto the terrain to be covered.[6]

Similarly, the poet David Antin has written, "I can imagine my impulse to speak, to move through language to some formulation, to some new place as being like a kind of walk."[7] These statements show how pervasive the identification of discursive language and walking has been among recent poets. Both Ammons and Ashbery exploit this figurative identification by representing themselves as literally walking, thus giving a kind of experiential body to the discursive motions of their poems.

As I have suggested, however, the motion of the walk also functions for them as analogue to the motion of reality itself. Like Stevens, Ammons and Ashbery share a Heraclitean sense of reality and experience as incessantly flowing and becoming. This theme takes on a different inflection in each poet's work; Ammons tends to emphasize change, the ongoing transformation of spatial entities, whereas Ashbery represents process as a purely temporal succession of moments, in which no fixed object can be grasped. Thus where Ammons is generally able to find some principle of stability underlying the world's shifting appearances, Ashbery is more frustratingly trapped in the slipperiness of temporality. For both poets, however, motion is the dominant feature of the world, and both find a wide array of images for this motion: Ammons ends his long poem *Sphere* with a virtual litany of such images—gliding, sailing, riding a roller coaster—while Ashbery speaks in one poem of the "vehicular madness" of experience.[8] Unlike these images, however, which suggest an essentially passive relationship to the motion of time and world, the walk offers a measure of control, illusory perhaps but nonetheless important for the act of shaping the flux of experience into a poem. For both Ammons and Ashbery the walk becomes a vehicle for exploring the swifter, more evanescent motions each seeks to embody in his poetry.

A. R. Ammons occupies a privileged place in this study, since he is the poet who has reflected most explicitly on the symbiotic relation of poem and walk. I want here to focus on the ways in which his own poetic representations of the walk enable him to unite discursive thought and concrete perception, permitting them to flow almost imperceptibly into one another. The centrality of the walk to Ammons's formal and imaginative methods has been noted by several critics. Richard Howard, for example, writes that Ammons "is the poet of walking, and his is the topography of what one pair of legs can stride over, studies in *enjambment* indeed." Similarly, David Lehman calls him "one of poetry's great walkers, who composes while walking and whose poems keep to a peripatetic pace"; while John Hollander writes, "As a poet of nature he walks in the country accompanied by the moving shadow cast by the light of his own consciousness."[9] The fullest treatment of this motif in Ammons's poetry is by John Elder, who writes that "like Wordsworth, Ammons is a walker," and who recognizes the special role of the walk in his creation of "a balanced field of vision and reflection": "He is always conscious of walking through his own mind, and of the way the mental and terrestrial spheres express each other's particulars, as they spiral together through the unifying processes of poetry."[10] The insistence of this metaphor indicates how essential it is to Ammons's own conception of his poetry, which he has repeatedly described as having "the form of a motion."[11]

Yet the walk functions as more than metaphor in many of Ammons's poems, most notably his two masterpieces "Corsons Inlet" and "Saliences." Both these poems present themselves as meditations unfolding in the course of actual walks; and both seek to integrate the phenomenal data of the walk with its accompanying stream of thought. They use the walk to lend a formal unity to the formless flux of consciousness, to stake out beginning and ending points, and to establish a spatial ground for the poem's temporal wanderings. The physical walk thus plays an indispensable role in firming up and shaping the analogical, discursive "walking" that the poem enacts, enabling the poet to coordinate his inner processes with the real time of experience, and so to be simultaneously faithful to the limitations of particular circumstance and to the expansive possibilities of pure thought.

"Corsons Inlet" is a volatile balancing of these two conditions, alternating between tight contractions to perceived particulars and broadly general assertions. Ammons originally titled the poem "A Nature Walk," but while this certainly lays greater emphasis on the formal coincidence of poem and walk, it also tips the balance too far in the direction of a universal "Nature," and away from the restrictions of the local. In naming the poem after the place in which it is set, Ammons implicitly announces his fidelity to the particulars of his walk, his refusal to synthesize them into some larger conception that would replace or dissolve them. Indeed this refusal constitutes the central discursive gesture of the poem, a fact that accounts for a peculiar discordance between its style and theme. Over and over Ammons tells us that he has "reached no conclusions," committed no "humbling of reality to precept," "perceived nothing completely"; yet he does so in a tone of calm authority and certitude that seems radically at odds with his meaning.[12] One might say that the grammar of statement in the poem clashes with the more fluid kind of syntax associated with the walk itself, so that we are being given both a representation of consciousness in flux and a series of firm claims retrospectively imposed on that flux. The poem's strength lies in its ability to balance this didactic mode of assertion with evocations of a more genuinely open consciousness caught up in the becoming of experience.

The poem opens with a straightforward narration of the walk in its purely external aspect:

> I went for a walk over the dunes again this morning
> to the sea,
> then turned right along
>   the surf
>
>   rounded a naked headland
>   and returned
>   along the inlet shore:
>
>   it was muggy sunny, the wind from the sea steady and high,
>   crisp in the running sand,
>   some breakthroughs of sun
>   but after a bit
>
> continuous overcast:[13]

Ammons's language here is at its most mimetic, reminiscent of Williams and Snyder in its alignment of topography and typography. The shape and rhythm of the poem both work to capture the experiential contours of the walk; as David Lehman writes: "Such poems as the frequently anthologized 'Corsons Inlet' feature a more rambling gait, uneven lines with jagged edges that suggest a grammar of space; the poet constantly shifts his margins in an effort to set up antiphonal patterns apposite for 'a walk over the dunes' beside 'the inlet's cutting edge.' "[14] Ammons makes subtle use of spacing here and throughout the poem to convey not only spatial forms, like that of the headland, but also temporal rhythms, as in the contrast between "some breakthroughs of sun," slightly indented to suggest its intermittent character, and "continuous overcast," which is set off on the page in a way that seems to mime the condition of linear stasis it describes. This kind of mimesis, however, is somewhat foreign to Ammons, who does not share Snyder's willingness to let his experience embody its own meaning. These opening lines must therefore be seen as a deliberately restrained prologue, in which the merely physical aspect of the walk is laid out so as to establish the ground of the poem's discursive utterances. It is essential to the poem's procedure that it *begin* with the physical experience, since this provides the necessary frame for its assertions, locating them temporally and spatially and so reminding us of their provisional, circumstantial character.

Unlike O'Hara, Ammons sets his walk in the past tense, thus acknowledging the inevitable gap that intervenes between occasion and composition. This gap becomes palpable in the course of the poem, since its discursive assertions are all cast in the present tense, and so are sharply differentiated from its mimesis of the walk as an event in the past. This grammatical difference creates a problem for the reader, however; are we to interpret the poem's thought-content as taking shape *after* the walk, during the act of composition? Or does the poet's thought unfold in the course of the walk itself? At first Ammons maintains the temporal separation between walk and thought, as if meditating on an experience that had already taken place; but as the poem continues this division is slowly blurred, until walk and reflection become virtually indistinguishable.

The structure of the poem as a whole may thus be described as a gradual convergence of seeing and thinking, perception and reflection, two modes of consciousness that are at first kept rigorously distinct:

> the walk liberating, I was released from forms,
> from the perpendiculars,
>   straight lines, blocks, boxes, binds
> of thought
> into the hues, shadings, rises, flowing bends and blends
>   of sight:

Here Ammons insists that his walk is *not* contaminated by the rigid forms of thought, but is given over entirely to the subtle continuities of perception. A firm opposition is thus established between thought, with its sharp, angular schemata (imitated in the very sound of the words "blocks, boxes"), and sight, with its "flowing bends and blends," its apprehension of curve and gradation. Yet while Ammons is clearly valorizing the flowing contours of perception, his compartmentalizing of thought and sight in fact *exemplifies* the "blocks and boxes" of thought, a contradiction that the poem must wrestle to overcome.

While persuasive at first, the opposition between thought and sight turns out to be dangerously constricting as the poem proceeds, since it presents as mutually exclusive aspects of experience that the poet ultimately hopes to unite. While the passage ends with a colon, suggesting that it will be followed by some illustration of the "flowing bends and blends of sight," it in fact gives way to a more blatant instance of "thought," that is, abstract statement, though now framed in terms taken directly from the landscape of the walk:

> I allow myself eddies of meaning:
> yield to a direction of significance
> running
> like a stream through the geography of my work:
>   you can find
> in my sayings
>   swerves of action
>   like the inlet's cutting edge:
>   there are dunes of motion,

> organizations of grass, white sandy paths of remembrance
> in the overall wandering of mirroring mind:
>
> but Overall is beyond me: is the sum of these events
> I cannot draw, the ledger I cannot keep, the accounting
> beyond the account:

This conversion of the landscape into a metaphor for the poem represents an overly facile solution to the problem of mediating between sense experience and thought; the notion of "mirroring mind," which recurs throughout Ammons's work (see his poem "Reflective") is here given too literal a realization. Note especially the use of the familiar allegorical "of" construction ("white sandy paths of remembrance"), which has the effect of denying the empirical reality of its first term.[15] This allegorizing of the landscape is, I think, an inevitable outcome of Ammons's overly rigid distinction between perception and thought at the outset of the poem. Like Stevens in "An Ordinary Evening in New Haven," Ammons begins with a static polarity that forces him to commit crude reductions in his effort to bridge the poles. This passage is thus the equivalent of canto II of "An Ordinary Evening," in which Stevens internalizes New Haven too fully, rendering it "an impalpable town." Like Stevens, Ammons must blur his initial polarity if he is to arrive at a subtle and nuanced account of experience. Accordingly, as the poem proceeds, a more fluid relationship between the literal details of the landscape and the poet's meditation on his own consciousness begins to emerge, in which the landscape does not act as a mere emblem of mind, but rather provides the means by which mind measures its own uncertainties and fluctuations.

The poem's central assertion, as I have said, is its denial of totalization, of the possibility of achieving an "Overall" understanding. All that the poet can do is to enumerate or record, one by one, the separate "events" of both mind and nature as they occur, without seeking to amass them into a larger configuration. Yet the very denial of such a synthesis itself constitutes an act of synthetic thought, an attempt to generalize at the most all-encompassing level. Throughout his work Ammons weds this insatiable penchant for generality with a nominalist distrust of all general concepts; as a result his poetry must keep in constant motion, oscillating between provisional efforts to theorize about the cosmos and adamant returns to the hard data of experience.

Such a return to the immediate circumstances of the walk takes place in the next lines:

> in nature there are few sharp lines: there are areas of
> primrose
>   more or less dispersed;
> disorderly orders of bayberry; between the rows
> of dunes,
> irregular swamps of reeds,

> though not reeds alone, but grass, bayberry, yarrow, all . . .
> predominantly reeds:

The passage begins with another general assertion, but thereafter shifts to an account of particulars—somewhat disorientingly, since we are abruptly brought from the level of "nature" as a whole to the localized landscape of the poem without any evident transition. In cataloging the different forms of vegetation he sees, Ammons now adopts in his own language the kind of self-modifying looseness that he didactically invokes in the discursive portions of the poem. At first calling attention to the "irregular swamps of reeds," he at once feels compelled to point out that these contain "not reeds alone, but grass, bayberry, yarrow, all. . . ." He trails off because he knows he can never adequately account for the multifarious particulars of the scene, that he will always be guilty of some degree of oversimplification. The "all" thus stands as a gesture toward the many organisms he has had to omit from his catalog; and it is followed by a new formulation that returns to his initial reduction, but this time acknowledges its inadequacy: "*predominantly* reeds" (italics mine). The three lines nicely illustrate the essential trajectory of Ammons's thought, as he moves from a too singular account of the world ("reeds") to a futile effort to represent its full complexity and multiplicity ("though not reeds alone"), finally coming back to his first account with a new awareness of its partial nature ("predominantly reeds"). They thus begin to offer an antidote to the stark mind/world dualism that led Ammons to allegorize the landscape in the previous passage. Now the poet is able to represent mind and world simultaneously, not by subordinating one as vehicle to the other as tenor, but by depicting mind in the process of grasping world in all its complexity. Seeing and thinking have begun to coalesce.

In the next lines Ammons returns to the assertive mode that runs throughout the poem, alternating with more tentative, exploratory passages:

> I have reached no conclusions, have erected no boundaries,
> shutting out and shutting in, separating inside
>
>> from outside: I have
>> drawn no lines:
>> as
>
> manifold events of sand
> change the dune's shape that will not be the same shape
> tomorrow,
>
> so I am willing to go along, to accept
> the becoming
> thought, to stake off no beginnings or ends, establish
>> no walls:

Ammons's claim that he has not separated "inside / from outside" stands in direct contradiction to the various dualisms we have already observed in the poem. Yet if Ammons's poem never quite behaves the way he keeps insisting it does, it nonetheless manifests a genuine tendency toward "the becoming / thought," in its less assertive passages at least. The ever-shifting shapes of dunes are his central emblem of mind in motion, an image that will be stunningly developed in "Saliences." A more relevant image of mental process for our purposes comes in his claim to be "willing to go along," in which the literal and analogical dimensions of the walk merge, as they have been implicitly merging throughout the poem. In Ammons's own words (from "A Poem is a Walk"), the walk is "an externalization of an interior seeking," representing with physical immediacy the restless wanderings of a mind that is rarely content to stand still. The problem with the poem up to this point is that Ammons has spent too much time striking a pose, and not enough time "going along," an imbalance that he will shortly begin to remedy.

The notion of transition as "soft," impossible to fix at a given place or moment, is elaborated in another descriptive passage:

> by transitions the land falls from grassy dunes to creek
> to undercreek: but there are no lines, though
>   change in that transition is clear
>   as any sharpness: but "sharpness" spread out,
> allowed to occur over a wider range
> than mental lines can keep:

This again conveys the poet's vision of change as minutely incremental, too gradual to be assimilated to "mental lines." The landscape is no longer merely a metaphor for the poet's consciousness; although this image of natural transition clearly has relevance to what Ammons calls "the becoming thought," it also retains its integrity as a view of the landscape. Indeed this passage itself serves as a transition to the poem's central exploration of the place and its inhabitants, as Ammons leaves behind his posturing and gives us an extended representation of mind caught up in the becoming of world:

> the moon was full last night: today, low tide was low:
> black shoals of mussels exposed to the risk
> of air
> and, earlier, of sun,
> waved in and out with the waterline, waterline inexact,
> caught always in the event of change:
>   a young mottled gull stood free on the shoals
>   and ate
> to vomiting: another gull, squawking possession, cracked a crab,
> picked out the entrails, swallowed the soft-shelled legs, a ruddy
> turnstone running in to snatch leftover bits:

> risk is full: every living thing in
> siege: the demand is life, to keep life: the small
> white blacklegged egret, how beautiful, quietly stalks and spears
>   the shallows, darts to shore
>   to stab—what? I couldn't
> see against the black mudflats—a frightened
> fiddler crab?

In this brilliant passage, sight and thought are at last fully united. We are no longer conscious of any gap between the experience of the walk and the meditation that it prompts; the verb tenses waver between past ("a young mottled gull stood free") and present ("white blacklegged egret . . . quietly stalks"), suggesting that Ammons is no longer intent on separating occasion and composition. Most importantly, the poem is no longer alternating, as in its opening passages, between two extremes of discourse, one a detached, flat reportage of external phenomena, the other a rather strident assertion of the poet's own nominalism. Now exactly rendered perceptions are blended with a flexible meditation that always maintains contact with the world through which the poet walks. As in the central sections of "An Ordinary Evening in New Haven," where Stevens carefully measures the mutual impingements of mind and reality, Ammons here succeeds in representing the fluid interminglings of thought and perception, now seen as interdependent rather than mutually exclusive. Like Stevens, then, Ammons moves toward the notion of "a visibility of thought," a state in which seeing and thinking can no longer be differentiated, as they had been in the poem's opening lines.

Much of the power of this passage lies in its adoption of what Linda Orr calls "an imitative language," one that stands in sharp contrast to the language of assertion that has previously dominated the poem. As Orr points out, "Sentences in poems-of-process must be doubling back all the time, qualifying, contradicting. . . . The poet must be alert to any tendencies for rest and sweep the words up again."[16] In this respect the language of this passage most resembles that of Bishop's "The End of March," with its incessant qualifications and questionings of its own perceptions. But Ammons is more intent on interpreting what he sees than Bishop; hence he is constantly broadening out from particular phenomena to larger ideas of order. Unlike its earlier assertions of a general stance, however, the poem's conceptual language now remains firmly tied to the minute particulars of the walk, representing the poet's moment-to-moment effort at making sense of the landscape before him.

The most prominent feature of this landscape is expressed by the recurrent term "risk," which evokes both the terror and the exhilaration of natural freedom. Throughout the passage Ammons expresses a simultaneous awareness of the aesthetic dimension of the scene and the savage struggle for life that underlies it. This doubleness is epitomized in the first line: "the moon was full last night: today, low tide was low." Full moon and low tide can both be seen as aesthetic phenomena, each permitting a human spectator to *see* more than is normally visible. But in the next line this aesthetic bonus is revealed as a terrible danger to the creatures who inhabit the shore: "black shoals of mussels exposed to the risk / of air / and, earlier, of sun." Suddenly we are made aware of the helplessness of creatures for whom air and sun are not pleasures but threats.

Yet having acknowledged this darker aspect of the scene, Ammons cannot help continuing to dwell on its beauty, as in the lovely line "waved in and out with the waterline, waterline inexact," which seems to embody, in its undulating rhythm and evocative use of repetition, the motions it describes, like the line in which Bishop describes the wet string rising and falling in the water. But the next line again underscores the predicament of the mussels, while translating it into an existential condition: "caught always in the event of change." Change itself is the source of both beauty and terror here, combining freedom and risk in one violent spectacle. The brilliant description of the feeding birds does not seek to pass judgment on the predators, but sees their activity as deeply natural, if also deeply frightening. Responding to the sight, the poet again takes refuge in generalization: "risk is full: every living thing in / siege: the demand is life, to keep life." The key word here is "full," which takes us back to the full moon, and implies that what seems destructive is in fact a form of plenitude, the fullness of life desperately holding on to itself, even if it be at the expense of other life.[17]

The next lines offer a particularly fine rendering of the concurrent beauty and savagery of nature. Ammons has to interrupt his description of the "small white black-legged egret" to exclaim "how beautiful," then goes on to tell of how it "quietly stalks and spears / the shallows." What follows is a striking instance of the way Ammons cues the poem's syntax to the phenomenological time of the walk: the egret "darts to shore / to stab—what? I couldn't / see against the black mudflats—a frightened / fiddler crab?" The torsions of the sentence create the effect that it is unfolding simultaneously with the perceptions it describes, a device we have seen in Williams, Bishop, and Snyder as well. This temporalizing of syntax is an important element in Ammons's style, since it permits him to give a verbal form not only to the flux of phenomena but to "the becoming thought." Just as important here is the poet's acknowledgment of his own limited perspective; he does not have a godlike vantage on the scene—"Overall is beyond me"—but can only see according to his position at any given moment. He is willing to speculate about what he cannot see, however, and his surmise is in no way less harsh than the realities he has witnessed: he is careful to specify that his hypothetical fiddler crab is "frightened."

From the terror of "every living thing in siege," the poet has but to turn his head to observe a different spectacle, one with less baleful implications:

> the news to my left over the dunes and
> reeds and bayberry clumps was
> > fall: thousands of tree swallows
> > gathering for flight:
> > an order held
> > in constant change: a congregation
> rich with entropy: nevertheless, separable, noticeable
> > as one event,
> > > not chaos: preparations for
> flight from winter,
> cheet, cheet, cheet, cheet, wings rifling the green clumps,
> beaks
> at the bayberries
> > a perception full of wind, flight, curve,
> > sound:
> > the possibility of rule as the sum of rulelessness:
> the "field" of action
> with moving, incalculable center:

Here again perception modulates into thought all but imperceptibly, in part with the aid of Ammons's beloved colon, which helps to enforce the sense of continual forward motion that all his poems try to embody. Now rather than the vision of nature as an ongoing struggle for life in which every creature must work for itself, he beholds a more delicately balanced picture of "order held / in constant change." For all its multiplicity, the gathering of swallows coheres into a single phenomenon, "a congregation / rich with entropy." That last phrase resembles the earlier "risk is full" in its insistence on the plenitude made possible by change and disorder. The syntax of this passage consists not of a shifting hypotaxis imitating the temporality of particular events, as in the previous passage, but of a looser paratactic sequence of clauses held together only by colons. It thus approximates the state of order in multiplicity embodied by the swallows, in which individual entities form a larger whole not by virtue of any specific transactions among them, like the predatorial transactions of egret and fiddler crab, but simply through their contiguity, their co-presence in a shared space.

Still describing the swallows, Ammons gives us a vivid series of close-ups that emphasize the restlessness of this pseudo-organism: "wings rifling the green clumps, / beaks / at the bayberries." The word "full" returns once more in the phrase "a perception full of wind, flight, curve, / sound," again evoking a condition of maximal activity, in which too many things are occurring at once to be perceived completely. Clearly this condition is an exhilarating one for Ammons, suggesting "the possibility of rule as the sum of rulelessness: / the 'field' of action / with moving, incalculable center."[18] It could be said that the poem's own "moving, incalculable center" lies somewhere between these two alternative visions of natural process and change, the predatorial, Darwinian vision of "every living thing in siege" and the more harmonious "congregation / rich with entropy" of the swallows. That moving center is in fact simply the poet's own body, as his use of the coordinate "to my left" suggests. Rather than locating the phenomena he describes in objective spatial terms, he acknowledges the central place of the body and the perceiving self in balancing different aspects of the environment. His walk thus becomes a vehicle for achieving a kind of equilibrium between the news to the right and "the news to [the] left," the harsh and the harmonious possibilities of life. Ultimately Ammons's Thoreauvian temperament inclines him to see order rather than struggle as the dominant principle in nature; thus it may be significant that he turns *from* the predators *to* the swallows. Spatially the two are symmetrically balanced, but temporally the second replaces the first, allowing the poet to move toward a final affirmative vision of an order that transcends individual struggle.

From the swallows, with their evocation of a "soft" order, shapeless but unified, the poet's gaze narrows to discrete objects with definite forms:

> in the smaller view, order tight with shape:
> blue tiny flowers on a leafless weed: carapace of crab:
> snail shell:
> > pulsations of order
> > in the bellies of minnows: orders swallowed,
> broken down, transferred through membranes
> to strengthen larger orders: but in the large view, no
> lines or changeless shapes: the working in and out, together
> > and against, of millions of events: this.
> > > so that I make
> > > no form of
> > > formlessness:

Ammons here acknowledges that nature offers countless instances of hard-edged form—flowers, shells, organisms—but insists that phenomenologically these represent details in a larger picture that contains no "lines or changeless shapes." The very act of turning his gaze to small, formally perfect items may relieve the poet of the burden of comprehending the "millions of events" constantly working together; but that relief can only be momentary, since his primary commitment remains with "the large view," the difficult vision of process and multiplicity microcosmically represented by the swallows.

Reflecting further on the large view, Ammons now chooses to characterize it with a rather surprising word, "serenity":

> orders as summaries, as outcomes of actions override
> > or in some way result, not predictably (seeing me gain
> > the top of a dune,

                the swallows
        could take flight—some other fields of bayberry
                could enter fall
                berryless) and there is serenity:

            no arranged terror: no forcing of image, plan,
        or thought:
        no propaganda, no humbling of reality to precept:

        terror pervades but is not arranged, all possibilities
        of escape open: no route shut, except in
            the sudden loss of all routes:

The very absence of a controlling will, the poet argues, creates a sense of
peace, despite the ongoing struggle he had earlier depicted. Terror *is* a pervasive force here, he concedes, but it "is not arranged," and hence not evil. He
takes comfort in the knowledge that "all possibilities / of escape [are] open"
(what possibilities of escape for the hapless mussels, we might ask), that "no
route [is] shut, except / in the sudden loss of all routes." The last phrase, evidently a reference to death, seems a fairly drastic qualification of the sense of
freedom and serenity being evoked here; yet after all it is a mark of
Ammons's willingness to "accept the becoming thought," even if it leads him
back to the darker vision of "every living thing in siege" that he has been
working to overturn.

    The poem's closing lines shift back into the rhetoric of assertion that had
been abandoned in the middle section:

            I see narrow orders, limited tightness, but will
        not run to that easy victory:
            still around the looser, wider forces work:
            I will try
            to fasten into order enlarging grasps of disorder, widening
        scope, but enjoying the freedom that
        Scope eludes my grasp, that there is no finality of vision,
            that I have perceived nothing completely,
                that tomorrow a new walk is a new walk.

Once again the poet gives us a statement of policy, though now oriented
toward the future rather than the past, and so less self-congratulatory in tone.
Ammons's use of capitalization to distinguish between vision in process
("scope") and a totalizing perspective ("Scope") is perhaps overly subtle, but
the contrast is clear nonetheless. If the preceding lines are a little too comfortably abstract, however, the final line beautifully returns us to the poem's generative occasion, and gives us a formulation at once concise and concrete:
"tomorrow a new walk is a new walk." This is I think deeply satisfying both
in its air of cadential firmness and in its implicit denial of closure. For once the

poem's paradoxical conjunction of authority and provisionality does not seem contradictory, perhaps because the line refers beyond itself to experience. In reminding us that the poem's meditation has been framed by a particular walk, Ammons locates its categorical claims in time and space, and so softens their authority. These are my thoughts today, he tells us; tomorrow I will change my mind. We should recall at this point that the poem's first line announced, "I went for a walk over the dunes *again* this morning" (italics mine), implying that this walk is already one of a potentially open-ended series, and should not be taken as in any way definitive or unique. Ammons does not claim that this particular walk, like Frost's walk in "The Wood-Pile," for example, deserves to be singled out from the poet's experience because it has yielded a special insight; tomorrow's walk will be equally valuable in the thoughts that it occasions.

Taken by itself, this closing line may seem a striking but ultimately empty declaration, paying lip service to a principle it cannot truly observe. After all, "Corsons Inlet" is a poem fully conscious of its centrality to the poet's oeuvre; it is not by accident that it has become the most anthologized of Ammons's poems, for its rhetoric aims at the very "finality of vision" whose possibility it denies. Remarkably enough, however, Ammons chose to take his last line literally: the next day he went for another walk, and wrote another poem about it.[19] He thus confronted, more squarely and explicitly than any other poet, a problem central to the mode of representation that the walk poem exemplifies, the problem of repetition. If "tomorrow a new walk is a new walk," that is, if all experience is equally valuable, equally fresh, can one simply go on writing poem after poem based on walk after walk? Surely at a certain point sameness will overcome newness, and monotony will set in. Frank O'Hara wrestled with this danger, ultimately destroying the very grounds on which his walk poems are based out of a restless urge to move on. But Ammons is not as restlessly innovative as O'Hara, although in a subtle way he may be the more daring of the two. For he takes up the challenge of repetition with unprecedented directness, writing a second poem the day after his great manifesto was composed, and taking as his occasion another walk in precisely the same setting.

That poem, "Saliences," while less immediately accessible, is for a number of reasons a better poem than "Corsons Inlet." It does not contain the manifesto-like rhetoric that to my mind mars certain portions of the earlier poem ("I have drawn / no lines"); instead it feels its way more tentatively towards insight. In a sense, then, "Corsons Inlet" can be described as the prescription of which "Saliences" is the enactment. Rather than obsessively *telling* us that it will "accept the becoming thought," it simply does so. In its narrower, more linear format, the poem seems to embody pure mental process, a sharply focused flow of consciousness directing itself at an outer scene, while retaining a strong sense of its own interiority. Its language, as David Kalstone has demonstrated, is a remarkable effort to embody "a whirl of motion, self merging with the outer world. . . . The rhythm, the short lines and relentless alternation of noun and participle practically blot out differences between actions of mind and nature."[20] Where the language of "Corsons Inlet" is leisurely, taking its time to look the landscape over and draw out all its implications, "Saliences" is rapid and concentrated; as Harold Bloom puts it, the poem "punches itself along with an overwhelming vigor, showing its exuberance by ramming through every blocking particular."[21]

All these characterizations of the poem's language, however, must be qualified by a recognition that "Saliences" is structurally divided into two very different parts, the division being explicitly marked by an asterisk. These two parts correspond to two separate writing occasions, both occurring on the same day.[22] Stylistically, the first part is far more tumultuous, tracing the poet's rapt contemplation of the dunes in their constant metamorphoses, both festive and fearful:

> Consistencies rise
> and ride
> the mind down
> hard routes
>   walled
> with no outlet and so
> to open a variable geography,
>   proliferate
> possibility, here
> is this dune fest
>   releasing mind feeding out,
> gathering clusters,
> fields of order in disorder,
> where choice
> can make beginnings,
>   turns,
>   reversals,
> where straight line
> and air-hard thought
> can meet
> unarranged disorder,
>   dissolve
> before the one event that
> creates present time
> in the multi-variable
>   scope:[23]

As in "Corsons Inlet," Ammons here celebrates the power of natural process to counteract "consistencies," to "open a variable geography" and allow the mind to "make beginnings, / turns, / reversals." Once again the landscape offers an image of the mind in motion, although now, as Kalstone points out, the two can hardly be distinguished grammatically; hence neither is subordinated as vehicle to the other's tenor. What is most striking about this section of the poem is its insistence on *presence,* both spatial and temporal. This is reflected in its barrage of present participles and gerundives, which continues to the end of the section, and in its evocation of "the one event that / creates present time," a phrase reminiscent of the phrase "caught always in the event of change" in "Corsons Inlet." An equally strong sense of spatial presence is created by the use of such demonstrative pronouns as "here" and "this": "here / is this dune fest." Indeed if one did not know that these lines, like all Ammons's poems, were composed at the typewriter, one might easily assume that they had been scribbled in a notebook as the poet stood amidst the dunes. In any case, the poem's fictional presentation of its own utterance is more important than the literal circumstances of its composition; and in this first section of "Saliences," Ammons appears eager to bring himself and his poem as close to the flurrying events of dune and wind as he possibly can through the resources of language.

Another feature that distinguishes "Saliences" from "Corsons Inlet" is the relative lack of prominence of the first-person pronoun, which only enters in the second part of the poem. As Kalstone notes, "an elaborate syntax keeps the 'I' from making assertions in any ordinary way."[24] Thus the poem suppresses the kind of self-aggrandizing claims that are scattered throughout "Corsons Inlet" ("I have reached no conclusions," "I make / no form of / formlessness"), instead preferring to articulate its themes through a more difficult process of meditative discovery. The abstract "mind" substitutes in the opening lines for "I," perhaps because it is better suited to illustrate the movements of "feeding out" and "gathering" on which the poem centers. But it is important to note that the lack of an "I" here does not constitute an effort to transcend or escape the self; as in "An Ordinary Evening in New Haven," the absence of the first person in fact signals a more radical subjectivity, in which the self becomes the very ground of discourse rather than a mere grammatical element.

The next part of the first section explores one variable in "the multivariable / scope":

> a variable of wind
> among the dunes,
> making variables
> of position and direction and sound
> of every reed leaf
> and bloom,
> running streams of sand,
> winding, rising, at a depression
> falling out into deltas,
> weathering shells with blast,
> striking hiss into clumps of grass,

```
against bayberry leaves,
    lifting
the spider from footing to footing
hard across the dry even crust
toward the surf:
wind, a variable, soft wind, hard
steady wind, wind
shaped and kept in the
bent of trees,
the prevailing dipping seaward
of reeds,
the kept and erased sandcrab trails:
wind, the variable to the gull's flight,
how and where he drops the clam
and the way he heads in, running to loft:
wind, from the sea, high surf
and cool weather;
from the land, a lessened breakage
and the land's heat:
wind alone as a variable,
as a factor in millions of events,
leaves no two moments
    on the dunes the same:
```

As in canto XII of "An Ordinary Evening," the wind here acts as an emblem of pure process, a "force that traverses a shade," sweeping together all the particulars of the scene in its violent motion. The passage brilliantly conveys the wind's restlessness and power in its insistent repetitions and drum-like sequence of present participles; the phrase "striking hiss into clumps of grass" is a particularly felicitous example of Ammons's gift for onomatopoeia. Although the wind thrusts itself on the poet's attention through its pervasive influence, it enables him to catalog all the other elements of the scene as well: reeds, dunes, trees, gulls. It thus epitomizes what Ammons means by "salience," namely any element or feature in the field of perception that obtrudes itself, allowing it to be grasped as an entity. On this point I must take issue with Bloom, who tells us that "Saliences etymologically are outleapings, 'mind feeding out,' not taking in perceptions but turning its violent energies out into the field of action."[25] Whatever the word's etymology may be, it is Ammons's usage that matters; and while Bloom quotes the phrase "mind feeding out," he does not cite the next words, "gathering clusters." These perceptual clusters, it seems to me, are what Ammons means by saliences, not the "violent energies" of pure mind.

Indeed it is the role of these saliences precisely to *defeat* the autonomous energies of mind, to force mind to change in accordance with external forces, as the next lines make clear:

```
          keep
      free to these events,
      bend to these
      changing weathers:

      multiple as sand, events of sense
      alter old dunes
      of mind,
      release new channels of flow,
      free materials
      to new forms:
      wind alone as a variable
      takes this neck of dunes
      out of calculation's reach:
      come out of the hard
      routes and ruts,
      pour over the walls
      of previous assessments: turn to
      the open,
      the unexpected, to new saliences of feature.
```

Shifting into the imperative mode, Ammons now adopts a more didactic manner, although again the absence of the first-person pronoun keeps these lines from taking on the assertive tone of "Corsons Inlet." Indeed we do not know whether the imperatives are directed to the reader or the poet himself; both seem equally likely. What sets this passage apart from similar passages in the previous poem is precisely the notion of salience, a notion that gives the poet a firmer means of relating external and internal change than the metaphorical "of" (which nonetheless briefly reappears in the phrase "old dunes of mind"). Saliences are phenomena that one cannot help noticing; they thus force the mind to admit new objects, to break out of the "hard / routes and ruts" of its "previous assessments." By staying open to the world, the mind will always find stimuli for change; it is only when the mind remains trapped in itself, "walled / with no outlet," that it stagnates.

The first section of the poem features change raised to an almost apocalyptic pitch, in which "no two moments [are] the same." The sense of dizzying proximity to the "dune fest," of being fully caught up in the interplay of wind and landscape, keeps the poet from apprehending any principle of constancy other than change itself. While this vision has its liberating aspect, "free[ing] materials / to new forms," it is ultimately too thoroughgoing an abandonment of identity and wholeness for Ammons. In the second section, written after some time had passed, he attempts to redress the balance, laying emphasis on the larger constancy that underlies the frenetic change of the first section:

> The reassurance is
> that through change
> continuities sinuously work,
> cause and effect
>   without alarm,
> gradual shadings out or in,
> motions that full
>   with time
> do not surprise, no
> abrupt leap or burst: possibility,
> with meaningful development
> of circumstance:

The word "reassurance" indicates how disturbing the violent change depicted in the first section really is to Ammons, however much he may have seemed to welcome it. A new calm prevails, one that seems to bespeak a greater distance from the events being described.

Recollection in tranquility is the dominant tone of this second section, which next moves into the past tense and a more conventionally narrative grammar:

> when I went back to the dunes today,
>   saliences,
> congruent to memory,
> spread firmingly across my sight:
> the narrow white path
> rose and dropped over
> grassy rises toward the sea:
> sheets of reeds,
> tasseling now near fall,
> filled the hollows
> with shapes of ponds or lakes:
> bayberry, darker, made wandering
> chains of clumps, sometimes pouring
> into heads, like stopped water:

The poet no longer depicts himself as present in the scene; his spatial and temporal separation from it now permits him to perceive it in a calmer, larger view. For the first time the "I" enters the poem, suggesting that self and world are no longer caught up and blurred together by the wind as actual and grammatical agent, but have regained their sharp-edged autonomy. Particular objects stand out with a clarity they lacked in the previous passage, where they entered only as indexes of the wind's power. The volatile flux of the first section gives way to a sense of solidity and permanence: "saliences, / congruent to memory, / spread firmingly across my sight." A crucial change has taken place in the notion of saliences; where in the previous section they represented the obtrusion of new phenomena, here they are "congruent to memory"; that is, they are phenomena that give a firmness to sight precisely through their *familiarity*. Fortunately we share the poet's memory, that is if we have read "Corsons Inlet," since the sights he remembers from his previous walk in this landscape are all recorded in his previous poem. Thus we too feel a pleasant sense of recognition as we encounter the reeds and bayberry once more; for us as for Ammons they are reassuringly solid and familiar, signs that we know where we are.

Ammons's reprising of the cast of characters from "Corsons Inlet" continues in the next passage, as constancy is again emphasized:

> much seemed
> constant, to be looked
> forward to, expected:
> from the top of a dune rise,
> look of ocean salience: in
>   the hollow,
> where a runlet
>   makes in
> at full tide and fills a bowl,
> extravagance of pink periwinkle
> along the grassy edge,
> and a blue, bunchy weed, deep blue,
> deep into the mind the dark blue
>   constant:
> minnows left high in the tide-deserted pocket,
>   fiddler crabs
> bringing up gray pellets of drying sand,
> disappearing from air's faster events
> at any close approach:
> certain things and habits
>   recognizable as
> having lasted through the night:

The beauty of this passage lies in the ease with which it integrates a purely aesthetic appreciation of phenomena with a more reflective awareness of what it means for these things to have "lasted through the night." Rather than focusing sharply on each object and observing its particular functions, as he had in "Corsons Inlet," the poet's gaze flits about the scene more lightly, touching each thing once as if to confirm its presence and then moving on. There are occasional pauses to savor details, as in the lovely lines on the "blue, bunchy weed": "deep into the mind the dark blue / constant." Evidently these are the "blue tiny flowers on a leafless weed" of "Corsons Inlet"; but now they have taken on a deep, penetrating blueness that can only be the result of their constancy, as they rouse an answering memory in the mind. Once more I must differ with Bloom, whose more visionary bent leads him, I think, to distort Ammons's phenomenal acuity; he says of the lines on the blue flower: "[Ammons] finds himself now in an astonishing equilibrium with the particulars, containing them in his own mind by reimagining them there."[26] But it is memory rather than imagination that gives these flowers their resonance for Ammons; because he had seen them the day before, he perceives them now not merely as being but as *continuing.*

Not everything continues, however, as we learn in the next lines:

> though what change in
> a day's doing!
> desertions of swallows
>   that yesterday
> ravaged air, bush, reed, attention
> in gatherings wide as this neck of dunes:
> now, not a sound
> or shadow, no trace of memory, no remnant
>   explanation:
> summations of permanence!

The swallows, so prominent a part of "Corsons Inlet," have flown away. This single departure, although it is one the poet himself had anticipated when he wrote of their "preparations for flight," rends a hole in the fabric of constancy that the previous lines have woven. In effect the very *absence* of the swallows becomes a salience more obtrusive than the familiar "look of ocean salience" in the previous lines. The poet's effort to counter the changes wrought by the wind in the first half of the poem by focusing instead on continuities is thus brought up short, as he is forced to acknowledge that loss or departure has decisively altered the face of the landscape, however much still remains intact.

This recognition precipitates the poem's magnificent close, in which a still larger vision of constancy is achieved:

> where not a single single thing endures,
> the overall reassures,
> deaths and flights,
> shifts and sudden assaults claiming
> limited orders,
> the separate particles:
> earth brings to grief
> much in an hour that sang, leaped, swirled,
> yet keeps a round
>   quiet turning,
> beyond loss or gain,
> beyond concern for the separate reach.

Ammons's scope has widened now to include the earth as a whole, the "Over-all" that he had insisted was beyond him in "Corsons Inlet." From this per-spective, all "shifts and sudden assaults" are incidental to the "round, / quiet turning" that encloses them. At this farthest remove, in which the poet assumes the vantage of an astronaut, the "separate particles" no longer show up as anything more than motes. This sense of reassuring quietude and con-stancy has thus been purchased at the price of the intimate, phenomenal involvement with the landscape evidenced in the poem's previous lines. The poet cannot simultaneously maintain contact with the particulars of the scene and with the greater whole that includes them; he can only oscillate between these mutually exclusive perspectives.

The poem as a whole executes a gradual tracking movement from close-up to long shot. In the first half, the poet is so near to the landscape that all separation is lost, and he becomes another dune at the mercy of the wind. In the second half, he keeps enough distance to make out the separate forms clearly, to let the salient features of the landscape emerge and be recognized. But the absence of the swallows impels him to back away still farther, until all particular losses are dissolved in a "summation of permanence." The mobility of perspective that is a central feature of the walk is thus converted by Ammons into a structural and thematic principle: "Saliences" dramatizes an effort to find the proper distance from which to view the world. Ultimately, of course, the poem underwrites the necessity of movement itself, since each perspective must sacrifice one "salience" or aspect of reality in favor of another. Only by remaining in continual motion can the observer perceive the world's minute, flurrying changes in appearances, its solid but transitory objects, and the permanent whole that encompasses them by turns.

The poem thus *incorporates* motion or mobility far more fully than does "Corsons Inlet," which invokes motion as a didactic concept without wholly giving itself over to motion as a poetic principle. Between them the two poems display the full range of possible relationships between thinking and seeing: "Corsons Inlet" is more leisurely, allowing individual thoughts to emerge natu-rally from particular phenomena, and binding them into a whole by means of a programmatic rhetoric that insists on the impossibility of wholeness; while "Saliences" announces its theme from the outset, pursuing it in a more sus-tained way as it finds various embodiments in the landscape. Both poems, however, insist on the interdependence of thinking and perceiving; the virtue of particulars for Ammons lies precisely in their ability to become saliences, impingements that alter the mind's direction, insuring that thought, like the world, remains constantly changing, constantly moving. The two poems are vivid illustrations of the worldliness of thinking, of the mind's inability to sep-arate itself from external events and phenomena. That two such utterly differ-ent yet masterful poems could be written on successive days, about walks in the same landscape, is the ultimate testimony to Ammons's faith in change, his knowledge that "tomorrow a new walk is a new walk."

Notes

1. Robert Pinsky, *The Situation of Poetry* (Princeton: Princeton University Press, 1976), p. 134.

2. Charles Altieri, *Self and Sensibility in Contemporary American Poetry* (Cambridge: Cambridge University Press, 1984), p. 104.

3. David Perkins, for example, in his *A History of Modern Poetry: Modernism and After* (Cambridge, Mass.: Harvard University Press, 1987), titles one chapter "Meditations of the Solitary Mind: John Ashbery and A. R. Ammons." Harold Bloom's most extended commentary on the two poets is to be found in his *Figures of Capable Imagination* (New York: Seabury, 1976), along with an important earlier essay on Ammons in *The Ringers in the Tower* (Chicago: University of Chicago Press, 1971).

4. Ammons is apparently aware of, and probably admires, Snyder's work, as evidenced by a passing reference in section 24 of his long poem *Sphere* to the title of his fellow poet's volume *Regarding Wave*.

5. Denis Donoghue compares the two poets as walkers, first evoking a tradition of Romantic walks beside the sea of which Ammons is an heir, then noting Ashbery's urban variation on it: "Ashbery's poems belong to this Romantic or post-Romantic tradition, even though his walks are not as marine as Ammons's. His beaches are more often city streets" (*Reading America* [Berkeley: University of California Press, 1987], p. 303).

6. Pinsky, *The Situation of Poetry*, p. 134.

7. Quoted in Sherman Paul, *In Search of the Primitive* (Baton Rouge: Louisiana State University Press, 1986), p. 53.

8. A. R. Ammons, *Sphere* (New York: Norton, 1974), p. 79; "No Way of Knowing," in John Ashbery, *Self-Portrait in a Convex Mirror* (New York: Viking Penguin, 1975), p. 56.

9. The three quotes all appear in the collection of essays *A. R. Ammons,* ed. Harold Bloom (New York: Chelsea House, 1986), pp. 54, 256, and 258.

10. John Elder, *Imagining the Earth* (Urbana: University of Illinois Press, 1985), p. 137.

11. The phrase "the form of a motion," which is taken from William Carlos Williams's short poem "The Wind Increases," is the subtitle of Ammons's long poem *Sphere.* See also Ammons's poem "Untelling," quoted by Richard Howard in his *Alone with America,* enlarged ed. (New York: Atheneum, 1980), p. 56.

12. Robert Pinsky notes the tension between the poem's "tentative, doubting quality" and its "assertive, proscriptive tone" (*The Situation of Poetry,* p. 151). Pinsky uses this conflict as the basis for a relatively negative assessment of the entire poem; but I think he misses the way the poem itself struggles to resolve the conflict, succeeding beautifully in its middle section.

13. A. R. Ammons, *Selected Poems,* expanded ed. (New York: Norton, 1986), p. 43.

14. Bloom, *A. R. Ammons,* p. 245.

15. Linda Orr also expresses uneasiness with the poem's "repeated use of metaphor created by the *of* prepositional phrase" (ibid., p. 141).

16. Ibid., p. 245.

17. This passage may owe something to the chapter on "Spring" in *Walden:* "I love to see that Nature is so rife with life that myriads can afford to be sacrificed and suffered to prey on one another; that tender organizations can be so serenely squashed out of existence like pulp,—tadpoles which herons gobble up, and tortoises and toads run over in the road; and that sometimes it has rained flesh and blood! With the liability to accident, we must see how little account is to be made of it" (*Walden* [New York: Norton, 1966], p. 210).

18. The phrase "field' of action" is almost certainly a conscious allusion to Charles Olson's notion of composition by field, a method Ammons could be said to enlist in the service of more mimetic aims. William Carlos Williams, under Olson's influence, entitled a late essay "The Poem as Field of Action."

19.   I am assuming that the clear indications given in the course of "Saliences" that it is composed on the day following the walk of "Corsons Inlet" are accurate; Ammons tells us, for example, that the swallows which had been so much in evidence the previous day have now departed.

20.   *A. R. Ammons,* ed. Bloom, p. 110.

21.   Ibid., p. 20. This is from Harold Bloom's first essay on Ammons, "When You Consider the Radiance," which he reprints as the "Introduction" to his volume of essays on the poet. It is characteristic of Bloom's reading both of this poem and of Ammons's work as a whole (indeed of all Romantic and post-Romantic poetry) that he views the particulars as obstacles rather than aids to the poet's imagination; his insistence on Ammons's effort to transcend the given substance of the natural world leads him to misread the poem rather seriously, as I will go on to show.

22.   The poet was kind enough to show me the original typescript of the poem, which clearly reveals that it was composed in two sections (they were originally numbered I and II), and at separate times, although both are dated on the same day.

23.   Ammons, *Selected Poems,* p. 47.

24.   Bloom, *A. R. Ammons,* p. 110.

25.   Ibid., p. 20.

26.   Ibid. p. 22.

A. R. Ammons, or the Rigid Lines
of the Free and Easy

STEPHEN CUSHMAN

For Bishop the *ars poetica* is a way of escaping apologies and essays; for Ammons it is a characteristic mode. In his long poem "The Ridge Farm," first published in 1983, he turns once again to the idea of form:

> don't think we don't
> know one breaks
> form open because he fears
> its bearing in on him
> (of what, the accusation,
> the shape of his eros, error,
> his guilt he must buy
> costing himself)
> and one hugs form because
> he fears dissolution, openness,
> we know, we know:
> one needs stanzas to take
> sharp interest in and
> one interests the stanza
> down the road to the wilderness:[1]

Nearly thirty years after his claim that the poems of his first volume, *Ommateum* (1955), "suggest and imply and rather grow in the reader's mind than exhaust themselves in completed, external form,"[2] Ammons continues his extensive meditation on poetic shapes and structures.

That thirty-year meditation is neither continuous nor consistent, emerging more prominently, for example, in the early triad of *Expressions of Sea Level* (1964), *Corsons Inlet* (1965), and *Northfield Poems* (1966) than in the later one of *A Coast of Trees* (1981), *Worldly Hopes* (1982), and *Lake Effect Country* (1983). In one book, *Uplands* (1970), the word "form" does not appear at all,

Originally published in *Fictions of Form in American Poetry* (Princeton: Princeton University Press, 1993), 150–86. Reprinted by permission.

although we do find "order," "structure," "shape," and, in the poem "Summer Session 1968," the cognate "formality" ("formality they can define themselves against").[3] Conversely, in the long poems *Tape for the Turn of the Year* (1965), "Essay on Poetics" and "Hibernaculum" (both in *CP*), *Sphere: The Form of a Motion* (1974), *The Snow Poems* (1977), and *Sumerian Vistas* (1987) comments and observations on poetic form abound. That most, if not all, of Ammons's significant statements about form appear in poems rather than in critical prose is no accident. In his work, the abstraction "form" connotes more than it denotes, charged as it is with Ammons's best fiction-making powers. "The Ridge Farm," "Corsons Inlet," *Sphere*, "Essay on Poetics," and *The Snow Poems* most clearly reveal these powers at work.

The passage from "The Ridge Farm" uses "form" in suggestive ways. Unlike the "completed, external form" Ammons renounces in the foreword to *Ommateum*, where "external" suggests nonorganic rigidity and "completed" implies the kind of autotelic closure Olson, among others, was lobbying against when Ammons wrote his first poems, "form" in the later poem both repels and attracts. In a familiar gesture, the passage opens with Ammons's version of epanalepsis, an enjambed line that begins and ends with the same word: "don't think we don't." Here this self-enclosing pattern, one Ammons uses in different ways throughout his work, is revealed by the conventions of Ammons's lineation rather than by the unaided contours of his syntax. Usually, epanalepsis ("a taking up again") involves a sentence that ends with its opening word or words or a figure in which the same word or clause is repeated after intervening matter.[4] In this opening line, Ammons breaks his syntax against a line to discover a buried repetition, one to which the syntactic pattern alone would not normally call attention. If "one breaks / form open because he fears" it, one also breaks form, such as the form of a syntactic pattern, to reveal other hidden structures.

The humor implicit in this passage arises from its deliberate self-betrayal. Ostensibly, someone speaking on behalf of a group, perhaps of poets, readers of poetry, amateur psychologists, or homespun metaphysicians, claims that "we know, we know" all about form. The tone of mock-weariness may also signal Ammons's acknowledgment that his readers have already heard more than enough about his ambivalence towards form: when form repeats itself without variation, he fears its preempting power, as it becomes a figure of compulsion or obsession, "the accusation, / the shape of his eros, error, / his guilt." The nonetymological, purely auditory association of "eros" with "error" suggests that when human drives lead into patterns repeated for the sake of pattern alone, they necessarily mislead. But when form is all that prevents Ammons from the complete dissolution of self into the alien world of nature ("the wilderness") or poetic autism, or both, as in many of the poems of *Ommateum*, then form is something to be hugged. We know, we know all this, as we know that "one needs stanzas," as instances of poetic form, when one strolls down the road into wilderness. Likewise, we know that because life "is / all one it must be divided / and because it is / divided it must be all one" (*SV* 28); Ammons has been telling us so in poem after poem about "the one-many problem" (*Sphere*) or "the one:many / mechanism" ("The Fairly High Assimilation Rag").[5]

But while the passage extols the stanza, it builds no stanzas, although other parts of "The Ridge Farm" do. In fact, the passage neither breaks nor hugs form in any remarkable way. Ammons casts this passage in the familiar shape of a left-justified stichic column, the lines of which fall mostly between the lengths of traditional trimeters and tetrameters. In his *Collected Poems,* this shape appears only twice among poems written between 1951 and 1955 ("Chaos Staggered" and "Bees Stopped"), but with the poems written between 1966 and 1971, grouped mostly in *Uplands* and *Briefings* (1971), it becomes, along with the tercet, one of his dominant visual patterns. At least once in the passage, the faint trace of an iambic sequence becomes audible:

$$\text{because he fears / its bearing in on him}$$
/ / / / /

Because Ammons is a self-proclaimed "free-versite,"[6] an occasional iambic string may seem like a simple accident of language, inhering in the structure of English. But to argue this is a bit naive, since iambic forms can be broken, and usually are by Ammons, as easily as they can be constructed. Furthermore, this particular iambic eddy corresponds neatly to an expression of formal claustrophobia, one that the next section of "The Ridge Farm" echoes:

> wherever mortality sets up a net
> or responsibility's strictures harden
> I mount into a whirlwind and
> buzz off, clearing a streak
> I spend the night in sonnets but the
> next morning pack my bag with free verse
> the road is my winding song sheet
> the rivers, branches, brooks purl
> my uneasy pleasures.
>
> (*SV* 28–29)

Here the net of mortality and the hardened strictures of responsibility are both associated with sonnets, in which Ammons spends his nights, presumably confronted by, among other things, "the shape of his eros, error, / his guilt," images of which surface from the unconscious in dreams. But with morning he escapes into free verse, traveling down Whitman's open road, singing himself toward death ("winding song sheet"). Whereas many would associate night with liberation from the conscious mind into dreaming, and so with liberation from sonnets into free verse, Ammons associates night with limitation, as the unconscious mind dominates him until he is released by waking.

At its best, the breaking of form establishes a principle of "uneasy pleasures." The poet breaks to remake to break again. The flight from form is
constant, and the refuge in form temporary. Behind the ironic humor of
Ammons's know-it-all voice and his stanzaless advertisement for the stanza
lies a deep confusion, confusion that vexes not only this passage but also the
entire poem "The Ridge Farm" and much of the thirty-year work that precedes it. The confusion is about the relationship of polarities, specifically the
polarity of form and formlessness. But confusion has its structures, too, and
one structure of confusion is the chiasmus.[7] Significantly, chiasmus structures
the second half of the passage from "The Ridge Farm," the first having relied
on the parallelism of "one breaks . . . and one hugs." First, Ammons sketches
a chiasmus with the sequence "one . . . stanzas . . . interest . . . and / one
interests . . . stanza." But then he gives the fully realized, exact inversion in
the final four lines:

> life, life: because it is
> all one it must be divided
> and because it is
> divided it must be all one

Parallelism and chiasmus are both rhetorical schemes, and Ammons uses both
often. They indicate an acute rhetorical self-consciousness, which despite his
apparent nonchalance reveals that even if meter and stanza vanish, language
and thought have not collapsed into formlessness. In this particular passage,
parallelism yields to chiasmus, so that its overall structure is one of inversion,
since chiasmus is the opposite of parallelism. The truth of the passage, then, is
that while we say "we know, we know" about the parallel aspects of form (it
both threatens and comforts), "we," an imagined group collected around
Ammons's speaker, remain deeply confused and uneasy about the polarity of
form and formlessness.

One way Ammons manages confusion is with paradox:

> recalcitrance, fluency: these:
> too far with one and the density
> darkens, the mix slows, and bound
> up with hindrance, unyielding, stops:
> too far with the other and the bright
> spiel of light spins substanceless
> descriptions of motion—
>
> always to be held free this way,
> staggering, jouncing, testing the
> middle mix,
> the rigid line of the free and easy.
>
> (SV 5)

In the phrase "the rigid line of the free and easy," confusing opposites have been reconciled felicitously. By "testing the / middle mix," Ammons moderates extremes, avoiding both darkened density and substanceless spiel. But still one wonders what the rigid line of the free and easy, with its pun on "line" as both verse line and outline, would look like. Predictably, as in most of Ammons's work, the line looks like a line in nature:

> but I like the ridge: it was a line
> in the minds of hundreds of generations
> of cold Indians: and it was there
> approximately then what it is now.
> five hundred years ago when the white
> man was a whisper on the continent:
> it is what I come up against:
> it regularizes my mind though it has
> nothing to do with me intentionally:
> the shows that arise in and afflict
> nature and man seem papery and
> wrong when wind or time tears
> through them, they seem not only
> unrealistic but unreal: the ridge,
> showless, summary beyond the trappings
> of coming and going, provides a
> measure, almost too much measure,
> that nearly blinds away the present's
> fragile joys from more durable woes.
>
> (SV 10)

The ridge line combines recalcitrance with fluency, as a few lines earlier Ammons calls "its rolls my fixed ocean." In pairing the ridge line, a natural form, with the rigid line of the free and easy, a poetic form, Ammons continues the tradition of Whitman, who reads Emerson's organic analogies in "The Poet" as prescriptions for substituting natural for textual forms.[8] Such substitutions appear everywhere in Ammons's work. Winds, waves, brooks, waterfalls, snowfalls, mountains, dunes, elm trees—again and again these natural forms suggest texts to be read in poems attempting to become their figurative analogues.

But, most important for Ammons, the ridge line gives him a limit to "come up against": "it regularizes my mind." Etymologically, *regularize* is related to *rule* and suggests a straight stick or pattern. Psychologically, it suggests a form to hug when the mind, irregular, fears its own dissolution. Still, although the ridge comforts, it also threatens to overwhelm, and confusion hovers:

> the ridge,
> showless, summary beyond the trappings

> of coming and going, provides a
> measure, almost too much measure.

At least two echoes of earlier poems from the volume *Corsons Inlet* sound here. The phrase "the trappings / of coming and going" grafts the opening of "Gravelly Run" ("I don't know somehow it seems sufficient / to see and hear whatever coming and going is") onto the description in "Dunes" of a mound of sand as "a trapping / into shape" (*CP* 55, 158). In "The Ridge Farm" the power of the ridge leads the mind beyond the trappings (both adornments and entrapments) of the coming and going of temporal phenomena. As a geological feature, it transcends human history, specifically the history of the European settlement of North America. As a relatively fixed feature outside that history, it also "provides a / measure, almost too much measure." Once again epanalepsis signals a local rhetorical intensification, as consciousness registers both aspects of the "measure" the ridge provides. The relatively fixed ridge becomes a measure "that nearly blinds away the present's / fragile joys" (again iambic), since those joys depend on the trappings of coming and going. What stands fixed outside human time necessarily denies human joys, as well as human woes. A line that begins and ends with the word "measure" suggests an emblem for the ridge itself: although a part of the continuum, it seals itself off, self-contained and isolated.

Behind this section of "The Ridge Farm," as behind many of Ammons's meditations on form, hovers Williams. Certainly, the influence of Williams is complicated and can be too easily overstated, but Bloom, in what is otherwise a fine essay, surely confesses to deafness when he declares: "I cannot detect in [*Ommateum*] the voice of William Carlos Williams, which indeed I do not hear anywhere in Ammons's work, despite the judgments of several reviewers."9 Bloom judges rightly when he discounts Williams's voice from *Ommateum*. Its strange, mythic "chants," as Bloom calls them, do not have much in common with Williams's more literal, concrete investigations, nor do the poems of *Ommateum*, with their long, irregularly indented clusters of lines, sometimes stichic, sometimes strophic, suggest the shapes of Williams's art. But from the late fifties or early sixties on, Ammons's work demonstrates an awareness of Williams, whether in its use of the rigorously enjambed, short-line stanza, which is one of Williams's trademarks, or in its deepening commitment to the minimally noted fact—what Bloom calls "Ammonsian literalness"—or in direct quotation and allusion, as in this passage from "Corsons Inlet":

> the possibility of rule as the sum of rulelessness:
> the "field" of action
> with moving, incalculable center:
>
> in the smaller view, order tight with shape:
> blue tiny flowers on a leafless weed: carapace of crab:
> snail shell:

pulsations of order
in the bellies of minnows: orders swallowed,
broken down, transferred through membranes
to strengthen larger orders: but in the large view, no
lines or changeless shapes: the working in and out, together
and against, of millions of events: this,
so that I make
no form of
formlessness.[10]

(*CP* 150)

Commenting that "in a difficult transitional passage, the poet associates the phrasal fields of his metric with the 'field' of action on every side of him," Bloom either ignores or does not recognize Ammons's direct reference, signaled by his use of quotation marks, to the title of Williams's important essay "The Poem as a Field of Action" (1948). Among other relevant remarks, that essay argues that "our prosodic values should rightly be seen as only relatively true."[11] Furthermore, if in doubt about the presence of Williams in "Corsons Inlet" and in the period of Ammons's life from which it comes, one has only to look to the piece that precedes it in the chronologically arranged *Collected Poems.* Titled "WCW," this short poem exults: "What a / way to read / Williams!" Even the most skeptical antagonist of influence theory, let alone its chief formulator, would have a difficult time ignoring these signs.[12]

The transitional passage from "Corsons Inlet" is difficult, but it bears directly on "The Ridge Farm" and on a larger discussion of form. In the lines "this, / so that I make / no form of / formlessness," the antecedent of "this" appears to be "the working in and out," recalling "the coming and going," "of millions of events," each reflecting some degree of order. This working in and out, then, reveals itself to the "I" of the poem, informing and instructing his poetic procedure ("so that I make"). The question is, What do these lines mean? Do they mean that having been instructed by the events of Corsons Inlet, the "I" will not attempt to impose a form on an overall, subsuming formlessness, a kind of undifferentiated plenitude that transcends the polarities of form and no form?[13]

At least one statement from *Sphere* could be enlisted in support of this reading: "The shapes nearest shapelessness awe us most, suggest / the god."[14] Formlessness, then, is an attribute of what is too large and remote to be trapped into shape, call it the god, the Most High, the One, or Unity. But although this reading may persuade locally, it presents two problems for "Corsons Inlet." First, Ammons admits quite explicitly, in terms that suggest his differences with Emerson, that "Overall is beyond me," and "Scope eludes my grasp." In other words, the working in and out of millions of events does not lead Ammons toward the apprehension of transcendent formlessness, even though forms nearest an ideal formlessness may awe him most. Instead, they reveal to him the contours of form in a natural landscape where "terror pervades" because a controlling form appears to be missing. But he refuses to fasten himself to the limited forms he can recognize ("I . . . will / not run to that easy victory"), vowing instead to extrapolate from limited forms to larger, more inclusive ones. Meanwhile, he knows and celebrates the knowledge that no form he discovers can be all-inclusive.

Second, if it is true that for Ammons formlessness is an attribute of overall Unity, then there must be two kinds of formlessness with which he concerns himself. Like Stevens's two versions of nothing in "The Snow Man," Ammons's versions of formlessness imply both a condition to be aspired to and a condition to be escaped from. When he explains in "The Ridge Farm" that "one hugs form because / he fears dissolution, openness," he cannot mean that formlessness offers him order or stasis, which some would consider attributes of Unity. He means that form defends him against extreme randomness, chaos, and disintegration. The declaration of mental independence in "Corsons Inlet," "I was released from forms," is deceptive. It does not mean that the speaker now enjoys an Emersonian transparency, as he becomes one with formless Unity. It means that having shed preemptive, a priori forms of thought, he must discover or invent new forms to ward off the terror of dissolution. The search for new form is every bit as urgent as the flight from old, and it is this urgency, and the preoccupation with form it engenders, that links Ammons so closely with Williams.

"Measure" is Williams's word. In "The Poem as a Field of Action," he announces, "The only reality that we can know is MEASURE" (SE 283). To Williams the all-inclusive reality of measure meant many things, including both prosodic form and the mental processes prosodic form can signify. When Ammons admits that the ridge line "provides a / measure, almost too much measure," we cannot help but hear Williams's voice, as in the passage from Paterson, book 2, in which Williams answers Pound's canto 45:

> Without invention nothing is well spaced,
> unless the mind change, unless
> the stars are new measured, according
> to their relative positions, the
> line will not change, the necessity
> will not matriculate: unless there is
> a new mind there cannot be a new
> line, the old will go on
> repeating itself with recurring
> deadliness.[15]

In addition to the word "measured" and Williams's own use of epanalepsis ("unless the mind change, unless"), this passage has in common with Ammons's "The Ridge Farm," as with "Corsons Inlet," a preoccupation with lines: lines of verse, the outlines of shape, and the conceptual lines of mental connection.

Ammons's most important sustained consideration of lines, measure, and form occurs in *Sphere: The Form of a Motion*. A question in the earlier "Hibernaculum" anticipates this title: "Are there any concepts to circulate: can / anyone form a motion:" (*CP* 366–67). Can anyone take the working in and out of millions of events, the continual change of coming and going, and give it conceptual and poetic form that will not destroy it? In the language of the foreword to *Ommateum*, published nineteen years before *Sphere*, can one make poems that do not exhaust themselves in completed, external form? In "Summer Session," Ammons formulates his dilemma succinctly: "The problem is / how / to keep shape and flow" (*CP* 248). The ambiguity of whether *flow* is part of the direct object or part of the infinitive exemplifies the kind of shifting play of significance, the continual metamorphosis of meaning, that Ammons cultivates and wants to protect against overdetermining forms. But "the form of a motion" may also have another meaning for him. Williams's poem "The Wind Increases," first collected in the "Della Primavera Trasportata" sequence (1930) and later included in his *An Early Martyr* (1935), poses the question "Good Christ what is / a poet—if any / exists?" then answers:

> a man
> whose words will
> bite
> their way
> home—being actual
> having the form
> of motion[16]

Here Williams experiments with typographic simulations of motion, as Ammons does most adventurously in "Corsons Inlet." Both poets attempt to bring their printed words and lines as close to forms of motion as they can in the frozen world of the typesetter.

In *Sphere*, however, words and lines do not simulate motion. In fact, they do the opposite, simulating the completed, external forms of tercets, four to a numbered section, of lines the length of Blake's fourteeners. One reader has even suggested that *Sphere* is metrical, its lines organized by a seven-stress accentual norm.[17] But the norm is actually typographic, the five, six, seven, or more major stresses merely reflecting the accentual nature of English in long lines; and yet other consciously manipulated structures give the verse of *Sphere* a dense auditory texture:

> this measure, maw, can grind
> up cancers and flourish scarfs of dandelions, manage the
> pulp of hung ticks and be the log the stream flows against
>
> for a whole year: its mesh can widen to let everything

> breeze through except the invisible: it can float the
> heaviest-blooded scalding dream and sail it into the high
>
> blue loops of possibility: it can comprise the dull
> continuum of the omnium-gatherum, wait and wait, without
> the alarm of waiting, getting as much being out of motion
>
> as motion out of being: multiple and embracing, sweet
> ingestion, the world bloat, extension pushed to the popped
> blossoming of space, the taking of due proportion's scope.
>
> (S 28–29)

The engine of this verse is repetition. In *Sphere* Ammons does not say only once something he can say several times, running it instead through permutations of extended qualification, variation, and apposition. This richly self-reflexive passage both describes and exemplifies Ammons's measure. Auditory repetitions bind words and associate meanings. Alliteration, a recurrent device in *Sphere,* links "measure," "maw," "manage," and "mesh," all words that suggest the control and enclosure of form. In other phrases, a thick intertwining of consonants and vowels gives Ammons's language a tautness that belies his casual tone. Examples here are the various incarnations of the phonemes /k/, /ʌ/ ("short" *u*), /ə/, and /m/ in "it can comprise the dull / continuum of the omnium-gatherum" or of /p/, /s/, /bl/ and assorted shadings of sounds represented by the letter *o* in "the world bloat, extension pushed to the popped / blossoming of space, the taking of due proportion's scope."

Parallelism shapes the passage syntactically, as all its finite verbs ("can grind . . . manage," "can widen," "can float," "can comprise") establish the rhythm of anaphora. Unlike Whitman, however, Ammons does not align the beginnings of parallel clauses at the left margin, choosing instead to coil them irregularly around lines and stanzas. Among his short lyrics, "The City Limits," the closing poem of *Briefings* (1971), uses the same technique. Grouped in the same section of *Collected Poems* as "Essay on Poetics" and "Hibernaculum," which also use long-line tercets, "The City Limits," more than any other short poem, foreshadows the technique of *Sphere.* Next, as in "The Ridge Farm," the parallel movement ends in chiasmus, a figure that recurs throughout *Sphere:* "Getting as much being out of motion / as motion out of being." Once again, it cannot be simple coincidence that this figure of confusion appears in a passage about poetic form. One might argue that the neat verbal flourish of chiasmus reflects anything but confusion, since it deftly snaps contraries into a satisfying balance. But this deftness is precisely the point. Chiasmus, as Ammons uses it here, is a trick of language, one that allows him to tie off a rapidly extending, open-ended line of thought, imposing an apparent aphoristic certainty where none can exist. Being and motion, like shape and flow, stasis and change, form and formlessness are remote, conceptually difficult abstractions. They resist reductive formulation, and yet reductive formulation is what chiasmus offers. Chiasmus, in its extreme over-statement, banishes shadings and overlappings. Significantly in this passage, the lines following the chiasmus are about extension and overextension "pushed to the popped / blossoming of space," an image of the formlessness, dissolution, and openness that chiasmus defends against.

Still, what is most remarkable about this passage is not the compulsive gathering of auditory and syntactic patterns into its "maw," but rather its sudden closure. End-stopped sections are rare in *Sphere.* There are only 32 out of 155. Enjambment dominates Ammons's poem. One way to describe *Sphere,* and by extension all those poems, short and long, in which Ammons uses regular stanzas as purely graphic groupings divorced from their auditory origins, is to say that the three-line stanzas and the four-stanza sections are Ammons's tropes of form, shape, and fixity, while enjambment is his trope of motion, flow, flux. The real measure of *Sphere* lies in neither the mere stanza nor the perpetual enjambment but in Ammons's manipulation of the align-ment between the two. With only thirty-two of its sections closed, *Sphere* works broadly across intervals of openness and closure.

Through the first eighteen sections, intervals between closed sections are minimal. If a numbered section does not end with a closing colon, then the next one will. Alignment between section and conceptual movement is rela-tively high. But with section 19 and its gestures toward Emersonianism ("oh, it's spring, and I'm more transparent than ever: / . . . my idealism's as thin as the sprinkled / sky and nearly as expansive:"), the intervals between closed sections grow, and conceptual movements begin to expand. For the rest of the poem, Ammons's measure grows out of the rhythm of expansion and contrac-tion, as intervals between closed sections increase and diminish. Most striking and significant is the longest interval in *Sphere,* which falls between the end of section 122 and section 150. In its expansiveness, this interval corresponds to the longest section of "Song of Myself," number 33 in Whitman's death-bed edition. In this section, with its long catalogues, Whitman is afoot with his vision, "speeding through space. . . . speeding through heaven and the stars" (*CP* 63). His expansion includes not only a cosmic vision of our universe but also an empathetic vision of human suffering, which Whitman associates with "walking the old hills of Judea with the beautiful gentle god by my side" (*CP* 62). Not surprisingly, Ammons's interval of expansion also culminates in a view of earth under the aspect of eternity:

> from other planets,
> as with other planets from here, we rise and set, our presence,
> reduced to light, noticeable in the dark when the sun is
>
> away: reduced and distanced into light, our brotherhood
> constituted into shining, our landforms, seas, colors
> subsumed to bright announcement: we are alone in a sea that

150

shows itself nowhere in a falling surf but if it does not
go on forever folds back into a further motion of itself:
the plenitude of nothingness! planets seeds in a coronal

weaving so scant the fabric is the cloth of nakedness:
Pluto our very distant friend skims a gulf so fine and far
millions and thousands of millions of years mean little to—

how far lost we are, if saving is anywhere else: but light,
from any distance or point we've met it, shines with a similar
summation, margin affirmational, so we can see edges to the

black roils in central radiances, galaxies colliding in
million-year meetings, others sprung loose into spiral
unwindings: fire, cold space, black concentration.

(S 77)

This grand passage with its crucial realization, "how far lost we are, if saving
is anywhere else," closes a movement that begins twenty-eight sections earlier
with the introduction of—not coincidentally—Whitman: "I'm just, like
Whitman, trying to keep things / half straight about my country" (S 65).

In the course of *Sphere's* greatest expansive movement, after which its
intervals contract to one of four sections and then the final, self-contained section, Ammons meditates again on measure:

seek the whole measure that is ease
and ramble around without constriction or distortion
(debilitating exclusion) until the big sky opens the freedom

between design and designed airiness.

(S 71)

The phrase "the whole measure that is ease" recalls "the rigid line of the free
and easy." Another paradox, it is most fully illuminated by Ammons's earlier
ars poetica, "Corsons Inlet." There he asserts that he recognizes only "transitions":

by transitions the land falls from grassy dunes to creek
to undercreek: but there are no lines, though
    change in that transition is clear
    as any sharpness: but "sharpness" spread out,
allowed to occur over a wider range
than mental lines can keep.

(CP 149)

This description of the natural continuities of an inlet also describes
Ammons's own poetic practice, as in *Sphere* in which form realizes itself "over

a wider range than mental lines can keep," if mental lines are drawn according to local line-to-line, stanza-to-stanza readings. Because the important patterns in *Sphere* take place across 155 sections, it is easy to miss them. Only when one reads the poem trying "to fasten into order enlarging grasps of disorder, widening / scope" (*CP* 151) does the operation of its form emerge.

2

Although Ammons shares with Williams both the word "measure" and the preoccupation with breaking and making form it signifies, there is also something important the two poets do not share. Whereas one generated reams of critical and theoretical writing intended to explain what he thought he was doing, the other has produced almost none. With the exceptions of the two-page "Note on Prosody" (1963) and the two-page "Inside Out" (1983),[18] Ammons's comments on poetic form outside his poems remain limited to occasional brief notes and remarks in various interviews:

> I've done a good many kinds of experiments, right? Some of them look like purposely regular stanzas and some don't. In some, the indentations correspond from stanza to stanza, the same line by line. But in some of them there is the random. I usually feel that I don't have anything to say of my own until I have tripped the regular world, until I have thrown the Western mind itself somehow off, and I think that's what those—if I began to write a sonnet, for example, I think I would be stultified and silenced by that form, because it's my nature to want to trip that form out of existence as a way of making room for myself to speak and act.[19]

Here Ammons shares with Williams a distrust of the sonnet, although he finds it merely stultifying, whereas Williams, in a characteristic overstatement, calls it "fascistic" (*SE* 236).[20] But while these remarks gesture toward an aesthetic ideology and interest any devoted reader of Ammons, they add relatively little to discussions of form found in his poems. Passages in "Corsons Inlet," *Sphere,* and "The Ridge Farm" do not necessarily deepen or unfold just because one knows Ammons has read Lao-tse and wants to unsettle the Western mind.

More complex are his comments in "A Note on Prosody." First quoting the fourth through eleventh lines of "Close-Up," a poem placed in the 1956–60 section of *Collected Poems* and included in *Expressions of Sea Level* (1964), Ammons explains: "Here the box-like structure of rhymed, measured verse is pretty well shot. The emphasis has shifted from the ends of the lines (see German sentence structure, see the concluding emphasis that rhyme itself imposes) toward the lefthand margin" (202). The shifting of "emphasis" toward the left margin corresponds to enjambment, although Ammons does not use that term. Instead, he turns to figurative elaboration: "What I think is illustrated by so tiny a fragment of verse is that both ends are being played against a middle. The center of gravity is an imaginary point existing between the two points of beginning and end, so that a downward pull is created that gives a certain downward rush to the movement, something like a waterfall glancing in turn off opposite sides of the canyon, something like the right and left turns of a river" (202–3). Finally, having identified "a downward pull" and considered the use of the caesura in traditional couplets, he concludes: "I think the quoted fragment and these thoughts suggest that a non-linear movement is possible which uses both the beginning and the end of the line as glancing-off points, so that the movement is not across the page but actually, centrally down the page" (203).

Several points are significant here. First, the conclusion that "a nonlinear movement is possible . . . centrally down the page" is true, as "Close-Up" shows, but that downward movement owes more to the extreme brevity of most of the lines than it does to enjambment. Second, the modesty of wondering whether or not "a few things" in his verse "reflect important little real things that are happening to poetry" (202) is attractive but also misleading. The things he notices in his verse do indeed reflect important little real things that are happening in poetry, since they reflect the technique Williams developed over fifty years and left to contemporary poets as his legacy. Although Bloom is right in arguing that Williams's voice contributes little to Ammons's many mountain fables, he would be wrong if he tried to maintain that Ammons could have given this poem its downward pull without the example of Williams.

But third, and most important, Ammons's discussion of poetic form turns here, as it does throughout his poems, on the figurative use of a natural image, the waterfall. In turning to nature for his emblem, Ammons not only confirms his affinity with Whitman and the post-Emersonian habit of interchanging the natural and the textual, but he also reveals the habit of his poetic imagination that makes the writing of critical pieces like "A Note on Prosody" unnecessary. For Ammons the natural and the textual remain inseparable. Each figures the other completely. One of his poems about a detail in nature is also about itself, not in a crudely allegorical way, in which natural phenomena are reduced to mere signs for poetic processes, but in a richly figurative one that demonstrates how the operations of nature instruct and replicate themselves in the operations of poetic imagination, which in turn informs the perception of nature. In this way, Ammons differs greatly from Williams. Unlike his modernist predecessor, he does not interest himself in trying to argue that the breaking and making of poetic form reflects a shift in scientific paradigms toward Einsteinian relativity, that it demonstrates the linguistic realities of an American idiom, or that it represents a new way of counting and keeping time in verse. Each of these arguments literalizes poetic form in a way that Ammons seeks to avoid. His preoccupation with form derives from an unswerving attention to the way his own mind works, confronting itself and nature. How are perceptions received? How do perceptions inform concepts? How do concepts knit themselves into patterns that influence perception?

For Ammons, then, the word "form" often signifies poetic form and leads him to some image from nature: a log against a stream, the line of a ridge, a waterfall, an inlet. But the word "form" also signifies the abstract structures of cognition. The poem about nature, then, is both about poetic style and about mind. In *Tape for the Turn of the Year* (1965), Ammons describes these interrelating forms:

> I feel ideas—as forms of
> beauty: I describe
>   the form as
> you describe a pear's
> shape:
>   not idea as ideal—
> ideas are human products,
>   temporal & full of
>   process:
>   but
> idea as perception of form,
> outside form that
>   corresponds
> to inner form, & inner to
> outer.[21]

The statement "I feel ideas—as forms of beauty" would seem to point to the Platonic abstraction of form as essence; yet Ammons moves quickly to dissociate himself from Platonism: "not idea as ideal" because "ideas are human products, / temporal & full of / process." Instead, by "idea" he means the recognition and registration by the mind of an external shape or structure in the world ("outside form"), not as an earthly copy of a Platonic essence, but as the natural analogue of mental shape and structure. The chiastic pattern of "outside form that / corresponds / to inner form, & inner to / outer" only relates structures in nature to structures in the mind. A statement of philosophy rather than aesthetics, it tells nothing about the poem. But the self-description emerges earlier with "I describe / the form as / you describe a pear's / shape." In other words, once the correspondence between inner and outer structures registers, the poet attempts to describe that correspondence with the same immediacy and specificity one might use to describe a pear or other concrete physical object.

For Ammons, then, poetic form mediates between abstract mental forms and concrete physical ones. Most of his poems ground themselves in natural physicality to authenticate his abstractions. A good example comes from the first section of "Four Motions for the Pea Vines," the ninth poem in the 1961–65 section of *Collected Poems* and included in *Corsons Inlet:*

> the rhythm is
> diffusion and concentration:
> in and out:
> expansion and
> contraction: the unfolding,
> furling: . . .
> the rhythm is
> out and
> in,
> diffusion and concentration:
>
> the dry pea from the
> ground
> expands to vines and leaves,
> harvests sun and water
> into
> baby-white new peas:
>
> the forms that exist
> in this rhythm! the whirling
> forms!
> grief and glory of
> this rhythm:
> the rhythm is.
>
> (*CP* 130–31)

The question prompted by the thrice-repeated line "the rhythm is" is "What rhythm?" The rhythm of the pea vines? The poem? The mind? The answer is all three. On one level, the poem sets out to describe the physical motions of pea vines growing: "expansion and / contraction: the unfolding, / furling." But with the word "rhythm," the poem abstracts the repeated motions of the pea vines into figurative status: the rhythm of the pea vines also corresponds to the rhythm of the mind, or at least Ammons's mind. The phrase "diffusion and concentration" accurately describes the way the shapes of his poems represent that mind, as they alternate loose, easy chat with hard compressed formulation. Also, the rhythm "in and out / . . . out and / in" corresponds to Ammons's habit of alternating mental with natural realities. But then there is also the very real way in which the rhythm of the pea vines corresponds not only to the overall poetic shape Ammons gives his meditative pattern but also to the prosodic structure of the verse itself: "the lines of winding-up, / loosening, depositing, / dissolving: / the vehicles!" The clearest example of self-description comes when Ammons reverses "in and out" to "out and / in":

> the rhythm is
> out and
> in,
> diffusion and concentration.

Here the word "in," isolated at an indented left margin, becomes an image of inwardness and concentration, as it roughly centers itself on the page.[22] This moment of local self-description corresponds to another a few lines earlier: "light, the vehicle of itself, light / surrounding." An example of epanalepsis, the longer line becomes an emblem of its own surroundedness, bounded on either end by the word "light" as we are surrounded by the natural phenomena of light, "the vehicle of itself." In a larger way, the first section of "Four Motions for the Pea Vines" is likewise surrounded by the refrain "the rhythm is." The poem considers, among other things, the "grief and glory" of a rhythm that, no matter how far it diffuses, expands, and unfolds, is inevitably compelled to circle back on itself, effecting its own confinement.

The three-way identity of natural form, mental form, and poetic form (meaning both imaginative shape and prosodic structure) cannot help but suggest the Romantic myth of organicism, particularly the boldly hyperbolic American versions initiated by Whitman. As Hollander comments on the fulfillment of Emersonian prophecy in "The Poet" by *Leaves of Grass,* "Organic form is to be the emblem, then, of the authenticity of the text, although the precise nature of the form is not made clear." In fact, the imprecise nature of what poetic form has to do to be considered "organic" harasses many discussions. Is organicism a condition the poem aspires to in its imaginative movement but not necessarily in its prosody? In its prosody only? In both? Wesling's definition of organic form is helpfully clear and usefully concise: "This, or the illusion of it, is what the successful poem has when it justifies the arbitrariness of its technique; and what the failed poem lacks, when its technique seems obtrusively imposed. . . . I would define organic form as convention in its innovative guise."[23] Although Wesling singles out rhyme to stand for technique and convention, other techniques and conventions also work with this definition.

In Ammons's case, the myth of organicism embodies itself in subtle and complex ways, although Waggoner is not alone in taking Ammons's organicism at face value: "Ammons, like most of his best contemporaries, has moved all the way toward practicing the theory announced in 'The Poet' and elaborated in 'Poetry and Imagination.' "[24] But for someone who "has moved all the way" toward practicing Emersonian theory, Ammons has much to say on the subject of artifice and artificiality in poetry, and in his poetry in particular. In *Tape,* for example, he states baldly: "poetry is art & is / artificial: but it / realizes reality's / potentials" (*T* 177–78). In "Extremes and Moderations," he adds:

> everything, they say, is artificial: nature's the
> artwork of the Lord: but your work, city, is aimed unnaturally
> against time: your artifice confronts the Artifice.
>
> (*CP* 335)

And in "Hibernaculum," he ponders artifice in the context of the promotion of art over nature Oscar Wilde preaches, for example, in his essay "The Decay of Lying" (CP 381–82).

Predictably, Ammons's only explicit commentary on organicism comes in the course of a poem, the long "Essay on Poetics," originally published in 1970. The earliest of the longer poems that use the long-line tercet ("Hibernaculum," *Sphere,* and "Summer Place" are the others), "Essay on Poetics" maintains a relentless loyalty to its own stanzaic regularity, even as it interpolates into the midsts of various stanzas three shorter poems, three long quotations from scientific texts, and one column of words. After each of these interruptions, the respective stanzas pick up where they left off, often in the middles of lines. Ostensibly a meditation on the nature of the lyric versus its own longer "linear mode," Ammons's "Essay" at one point reads Williams's dictum "no ideas but in things" into various alternatives: " 'No things but in ideas,' / 'no ideas but in ideas,' and 'no things but in things' " (CP 308). These revisions of the famous refrain of *Paterson* lead to an extended figuring of different poetic modes in terms of the stages of water flowing, as it goes from snow-melt to brook-rapids, to slow river, and finally to sea:

genius, and

the greatest poetry, is the sea, settled, contained before the first
current stirs but implying in its every motion adjustments
throughout the measure.

(CP 309)

Both the word "measure" and the image of a river running to the sea suggest that the dialogue with Williams and *Paterson* continues throughout this section. Holder contends that here Ammons is pointing up "the inadequacy of William Carlos Williams' famous prescription for the poet."[25] Certainly, Ammons is examining that prescription critically ("one thing / always to keep in mind is that there are a number of possibilities"); yet in the adoption of Williams's image of the river running to the sea, an image that despite his own brooks and falls he does not use often, Ammons may also be making his pact with Williams, who in his own way challenges the organicist label applied to him.

As Henry Sayre has argued convincingly, Williams's "notoriously inadequate explanations of the so-called variable foot are most usefully seen as efforts to defend as organic what through the 1940s and 1950s is more and more evidently a formally mechanical and arbitrary practice."[26] Like Williams, Ammons invents a three-line stanza that is mechanical (in Schlegel's sense of the word), arbitrary, and artificial. But unlike Williams, Ammons does not try to defend that artificiality with a rhetoric of traditional organicism. Instead, the exact opposite is true. He challenges the rhetoric of traditional organicism and flaunts the artificiality of his form. The challenge to organicism, or more precisely, literary organicism, comes near the end of "Essay on Poetics" in a long passage that begins

> the point of change, though,
> brings me to a consideration of the adequacy of the transcendental
> vegetative analogy: the analogy is so appealing, so swept with
>
> conviction, that I hardly ever have the strength to question it.
>
> (CP 315)

In his "consideration of the adequacy of the transcendental / vegetative analogy," Ammons subverts the literary rhetoric of organicism by confronting it with scientific literalism. As this passage argues, it is naive to think that a particular tree realizes itself according to innate individual laws. In fact, what is innate in a particular tree is not its own uniqueness, but quite the opposite, its preordained genetic code, which nature protects against "haphazard change." The uniqueness of a given tree, then, results when its genetic "printout" is modified from outside by "the bleak periphery of possibility," which includes "variables of weather, soil, etc." [CP 316].

Ammons's revised organicism has important implications for his poetics. If a tree develops according to a code that is genetically preordained and a given tree varies only according to local external modifications, then a truly organic poem is one that figuratively does the same. A truly organic poem reflects both the predetermination of structures it cannot change and the local variation of those structures where other conditions modify them. In Wesling's terms, Ammons's poem justifies the arbitrariness of its stanzaic regularity by letting that arbitrariness stand for predetermination, the poetic analogue of a locked-in genetic code. Each stanza is a printout of the predetermined pattern; and yet, like a given tree, a given stanza varies according to local effects—effects, in its case, of syntax, diction, rhythm, enjambment, and typography. Ammons multiplies organic analogies by quoting passages of prose, as Williams does in *Paterson*. One passage celebrates "a good worm" that has "developed segmentation or reduplication of parts, permitting increase in size with completely coordinated function," an apt self-description of "Essay on Poetics." Another passage describes "the molecular bricks out of which living matter is made," adding that "a mere random pile of such bricks does not make a living structure, any more than a mere pile of real bricks makes a house" (CP 314). By analogy, this statement also describes Ammons's own poem, as its stanzas are the brick-shaped blocks that attempt to build a living structure instead of a mere pile.

"Essay on Poetics" provides a key to Ammons's formal intentions, especially in those poems that seem at first to organize themselves arbitrarily around regular typographic patterns, such as stanzas or indentations. In those poems, short and long, arbitrary regularity is the artifice by means of which Ammons, as he explains in *Tape*, "realizes reality's / potentials." Although what nature predetermines for a white oak evolves through a series of favorable mutations, and so is not arbitrary in the way the selection of a stanza shape may be arbitrary, the stanza shape nevertheless represents the given, whether it be the organic given of a genetic pattern, the mental given of binary concepts, the linguistic given of modern American English, or the literary given of poetic tradition. One does not invent these; one inherits them. When Ammons closes "Hibernaculum" with the outrageously flippant stanza

> I'm reading Xenophon's *Oeconomicus* "with
> considerable pleasure and enlightenment" and with
> appreciation that saying so fills this stanza nicely.
> (*CP* 388)

he tweaks the noses of both the traditional formalist for whom the stanza is necessarily a metrical and auditory reality, never merely a typographic one, and the naive organicist who believes that a poem should never compromise content to fulfill the demands of a predetermined form. But beneath the humor lies more serious meaning. Disciple of Socrates, military leader, and historian, Xenophon presides over the close of "Hibernaculum" as a representative of the accumulated weight of a philosophical, historical, and literary past. His *Oeconomicus*, undoubtedly a model for the chapter "Economy" in Thoreau's *Walden*, casts Socrates in a dialogue on household management and married life, two subjects the domestically hibernating Ammons contemplates in "Hibernaculum" and elsewhere. In its casual way, Ammons's final stanza is about demands and expectations generated by the past, demands and expectations he did not create but still must meet. These exert a pressure on him that shapes his utterances.

"Extremes and Moderations," which falls between "Essay on Poetics" and "Hibernaculum" in the 1966–71 section of *Collected Poems*, opens and closes with remarks on its own four-line stanza, unique among Ammons's longer poems. The introduction of the stanza again recalls Wesling's formulation that successful organicism involves the justification of arbitrary technique:

> constructing the stanza is not in my case exceedingly
> difficult, variably invariable, permitting maximum change
> within maximum stability, the flow-breaking four-liner, lattice
>
> of the satisfactory fall, grid seepage, currents distracted
> to side flow, multiple laterals that at some extreme spill
> a shelf, ease back, hit the jolt of the central impulse.
> (*CP* 329)

The admission that the construction of stanzas "is not in my case exceedingly difficult" anticipates the end of "Hibernaculum" in its unabashed acknowledgment of an artificiality that neither the traditional formalist nor the naive organicist could justify. Meanwhile, the description of the stanza as "variably invariable" continues the argument from "Essay on Poetics," abstracting it from the realm of white oaks and genetic printouts, yet preserving the conjunction of general predetermination with specific modification. Although "variably invariable" takes the rhetorical shape of oxymoron, Ammons's version of organicism demonstrates the necessary congruity of the variable and invariable. Images of water flowing through the stanza, "the flowbreaking four-liner, lattice / of the satisfactory fall, grid seepage, currents distracted / to side flow," prefigure images of form in *Sphere*. In both poems, Ammons's images of flowing water recall the etymological meaning of *rhythm* (Greek *rhein:* to flow), while his images of the stanza as "lattice," "grid," "log the stream flows against," and "mesh" describe the phenomenology of verse structure in new terms. Etymologically, a *stanza* is a stopping place, a place to stand. The word suggests a phenomenology of writing and reading that involves a series of stops between which one crosses white space or silence to get to the next stop. More recently in poetic tradition, occasional enjambment between stanzas may vary the stop-and-go pattern; yet such enjambment remains exceptional in most verse and should remain exceptional, according to those, such as Paul Fussell, who place high value on stanzaic integrity.[27] The stanzaic repetition of stops and starts reflects the origin of stanzas in the strophic divisions of song, divisions that allow a singer to sing new verses to a recycled tune.[28] As verse becomes more removed from its historical origins in song, structures that originated as auditory modes become increasingly visual. In Ammons's stanzas the removal from auditory origins is complete, his various images of the stanza implying a different model for writing and reading. Instead of a phenomenology of stopping and going, his stanzas generate one of speeding and slowing. If going ever stops, it stops only partially with a colon, and even then, as *Sphere* demonstrates, it stops much less than it continues.

The speeding and slowing of perpetual going, the presentation of some resistance or channel that flow must overcome or follow, revises another Romantic metaphor, that of the Aeolian harp. Although that image runs on wind and Ammons's on water, they share the fiction of an essential passivity. For Shelley in "Ode to the West Wind," the desire for inspiration leads to the petition "make me thy lyre," while for Coleridge in "The Eolian Harp," the image leads him to ask whether "all of animated nature," himself included, "be but organic Harps diversely fram'd" over which "sweeps / Plastic and vast, one intellectual breeze, / At once the Soul of each, and God of all?"

At the close of "Extremes and Moderations," written about the time that, as Bloom points out, "the motions of water . . . replaced the earlier guiding movements of wind" in Ammons's poetry,[29] the Romantic metaphor surfaces in final remarks on the stanza:

it's Sunday

morning accounts for such preachments, exhortations, and
solemnities: the cumulative vent of our primal energies is now and
always has been sufficient to blow us up: I have my ventilator
here, my interminable stanza, my lattice work that lets the world

breeze unobstructed through: we could use more such harmless
devices.

(CP 340–41)

Punning on the Latin for wind (*ventus*), Ammons describes his ventilating
stanza as both a device for passively letting the world breeze through and for
venting his prophetic anger over human uses and abuses of nature. Whether
he describes the stanza in terms of wind or water, it remains his typographic
version of the Romantic harp. In each case, the image of sweeping over or
breezing through functions to naturalize poetic artifice. If the poetic imagination simply presents itself in the form of a harp or stanza to be acted upon by
a wind or a stream, then that imagination cannot be held responsible for what
results. The burden of structuring the poem shifts away from the poet, so
that, at least in Ammons's case, he escapes having to account fully for his
form. Whereas Ammons's revision of organicism allows him to justify arbitrariness by redefining "organic" in terms of scientific literalism, his version of
the Aeolian harp allows him to do so by trivializing his own role as maker of
"harmless / devices."

Nowhere in Ammons's work have issues of form and formlessness, arbitrariness and organicism, poet as artificer and poet as innocent bystander
caused more disagreement and more misunderstanding than in *The Snow
Poems* (1977). Waggoner pronounces the volume "a thick book of dull, tired
poems that prompt us to wonder, does Ammons write too much?"[30] *The
Snow Poems* appeared too late for consideration by Holder, which is unfortu-
nate, since the ways in which his judgments differ from Waggoner's represent
a larger critical disagreement over Ammons's work.[31] Amidst a swirl of negative reviews, such as Hayden Carruth's ("a dull, dull book"),[32] Bloom has
remained determinedly silent, while Helen Vendler has given the book limited but sympathetic attention: "Ammons has delineated that landscape and
that climate [of Ithaca, New York] for good and all, with an Emersonian win-
triness of voice diluting the ebullience he inherited from Williams."[33]

But most interesting is the welcome reappraisal of *The Snow Poems*
made by Michael McFee after the appearance of *A Coast of Trees* signaled
Ammons's return to the short lyric. Arguing against what he calls the
"popular critical pacifier, as manufactured by Bloom and others, . . . that
Ammons had come into the world to fulfill the Romantic Transcendental
heritage, to realize the promise of Organic Form," McFee makes two significant points. The first is that "as Ammons became more prominent, the

form of his poetry became more conservative, taking on a more orderly and regular appearance." The second is that "the heart of *The Snow Poems* is "Ammons's deep anti-formalism."[34] Both points raise important questions that need further consideration.

The argument that Ammons's form becomes more conservative as it takes on the orderly and regular appearance of uniform stanzas has two problems. The first is that it reduces poetic form to mere format, or the typographic shape of a poem on the page. Williams often veered dangerously close to the same error, sometimes even committing it, but Ammons never does. For Ammons, "form" is far too large and suggestive a term to let itself be contained within the boundaries of a stanza shape. Any account of his poetic forms must also reckon with rich phonemic configurations, syntactic patterns, rhetorical figures, and occasional metricality, as well as with the larger contours of his characteristic meditative habits. The second problem is that the term "conservative" does not accurately describe what appears to be Ammons's devoted guardianship of the traditional stanza. In Ammons's hands, the stanza format is an instrument of humor, parody, playfulness, figuration, self-description, and poetic revision. The irreverent liberties he takes with his stanzas should disabuse his readers of any notion that his growing fame has caused him to think twice about formal experimentalism. As Ammons's more recent work has shown, especially "The Ridge Farm," he can take or leave the stanza with no trouble at all.

But the second point, that the heart of *The Snow Poems* is a deep antiformalism, leads to a larger debate about Ammons's work. To support his contention, McFee quotes part of the poem "One at One with His Desire":

> this stanza compels
> its way along: a
> break will humble it
>
> form consumes:
> form eliminates:
> form forms the form
> that extracts of the elixir from
> the passage of change:
> well, we mustn't let this
> form reverse itself
> into an opposite
> though parallel
> largely similar insistence:
> must we?

(SP 169)

McFee then concludes that Ammons "endorses the 'hellish paradise' susceptible to shit and wind change, not the artificial order of a stanza." Yes, a break will humble the stanzaic compulsion to repeat and rescue Ammons from the fear of overbearing form he expresses in "The Ridge Farm." But the subsequent lines about form consuming, eliminating, and extracting do not necessarily mean only that form constructs "inflexible structures which drain the elixir vitae of motion."[35] The sequence of consumption, elimination, and extraction also suggests the digestive processes of an organism. In other words, although form may threaten to assume an autonomy of its own, and so must be humbled if creator is to retain control over creation, still that form does have a life of its own. In fact, "the form / that extracts of the elixir from / the passages of change" performs a kind of alchemy, as it rescues from the rush of impermanence and dissolution a precious essence that remains. When this passage joins with a long one preceding it, the full complexity and pathos of Ammons's ambivalence toward his stanza, and toward abstractions of form it represents, emerges:

> art's
> nonbeing's
>
> dark consolation:
> what a nice stanza! imagine just going
> on: I think I've invented
>   rooms to walk through
>   or stand amazed
>   or lie sleepy in:
> it is no place, though,
> to rehearse the flesh
> of the beloved,
>   it is no place to touch
>   or taste
>   enter or leave:
>
> it is dry delight, whatever
> service remains when
> the church closes:
>   the sweepstakes of
>   no desire
>   whole as fulfillment:
> the sweetest passer of time
> scheduled for emptiness:
> the drug that makes erasure
>   bliss: an illusion some
>   of the uneasy can cover
>   misery with:
>
> still when you think of the
> nourishment of such delight as
> over starvation,

what a numb pale
paradise! how constant
the music
dwelling among the constant
bushes, the deathlessness only
lifelessness can know
one not at one with his
desire still has to desire
so much more than nothing.
(*SP* 168–69)

This is not the voice of one who hates form. Instead, it is the deep, moving confession of a man who realizes that he finds himself shut out from rooms where life goes on immediately and unconsciously, shut out from the places where his desire can be fulfilled. As a result, the rooms that stanzas build, and the poems for which they stand as synecdoches, provide the only places for him to dwell. He is fully, radically disillusioned about the "numb pale / paradise!" form encloses, its druglike power that makes erasure bliss, or the misery "the uneasy" use it to cover. This last phrase recalls the "uneasy pleasures" Ammons identifies in the passage about sonnets and free verse in "The Ridge Farm." But he sees no alternative. Life may be preferable to form, but form is the dark consolation of lifelessness. Against the background of these stark choices, the familiar figure of epanalepsis, "desire still has to desire," looms with uncanny power. Like the line below it, "form forms the form," in which repetition threatens to hollow "form" of its substance and meaning, this self-enclosed, self-mirroring line figures both the entrapment of desire and the poetic self-consciousness that gives desire form, if not fulfillment. Ammons gives the repetition of *desire* a twist, as he uses the word first as a noun and second as an infinitive, binding a state or condition to the process that generates it. These nuances may not be much, but they are so much more than nothing.

3

If stanzas, form, and poetry amount to a dark consolation for Ammons's sense of exclusion, that sense of exclusion also has its national dimension. When it comes to America, there are two Ammonses. The first, more familiar to readers who know his work primarily through anthologized selections, appears to be a man without, or beyond, a country. In his compressed fables or his careful annotations of natural phenomena, the operations of history, the pressures of politics, and the awareness of actual America play almost no part. This apparent reticence about, or repression of, America and Americanism associates Ammons with Dickinson and Bishop, or at least with the versions of Dickinson and Bishop that have emerged in much critical writing about their work. But if one comes away from a narrow sampling of Ammons's work with the sense that he has denied, escaped, or transcended nationality, the anthologizers are not entirely to blame, for, as the three editions of his *Selected Poems* make clear, Ammons has chosen to turn this side of himself to the light.[36]

Meanwhile, another Ammons lives in the longer poems, especially in poems that are out of print (*Sphere*) or uncollected ("Summer Place" [1977]). This Ammons explicitly identifies himself with America, alternately celebrating and scolding his country in ways that associate him more with Whitman and Pound than with Dickinson and Bishop. This duality in Ammons's work mediates between extremes in both contemporary American poetry and contemporary American criticism. It also corresponds to a duality in Ammons's formalism, which mediates between the prescriptive fictions of poets like Whitman or Pound and the more internalized fictions of poets like Dickinson or Bishop.

In *Sphere* Ammons considers the nature of his own Americanism in the self-justifying tone of an *apologia* responding to his readers:

> I can't understand my readers:
> they complain of my abstractions as if the United States of America
> were a form of vanity: they ask why I'm so big on the
>
> one:many problem, they never saw one: my readers: what do they
> expect from a man born and raised in a country whose motto is *E
> pluribus* [sic] *unum:* I'm just, like Whitman, trying to keep things
>
> half straight about my country: my readers say, what's all
> this change and continuity: when we have a two-party system,
> one party devoted to reform and the other to consolidation:
>
>   123
> and both trying to grab a chunk out of the middle: either we
> reconcile opposites or we suspend half the country into
> disaffection and alienation: they want to know, what do I
>
> mean *quadrants,* when we have a Southeast, Northeast, Southwest,
> and Northwest and those cut into pairs by the splitting
> Mississippi and the Mason-Dixon line I figure I'm the exact
>
> poet of the concrete *par excellence,* as Whitman might say:
> they ask me, my readers, when I'm going to go politicized or
> radicalized or public when I've sat here for years singing
>
> unattended the off-songs of the territories and the midland
> coordinates of Cleveland or Cincinnati.
>
>   (*S* 65)

In its assertion of nationality and its association of aesthetic ideology with political ideology, this passage foreshadows the dedication of *The Snow Poems,* published three years after *Sphere:* "for my country." On one level, Ammons is fooling around here, easing his sense of isolation by staging a debate between himself and an imagined readership. That the debate represents a piece of ventriloquism becomes apparent when he admits that he has been "for years singing / unattended the off-songs of the territories." If he is truly unattended, then he has no readers, a possibility he considers a few lines later: "My readers are baffling and / uncommunicative (if actual)" (*S* 65).

But on another level, the debate is a profoundly serious one, for it amounts to a psychomachia between two sides of Ammons's consciousness. One side tells him that his poems have national significance and political implications; the other side, displaced onto his imagined readers, taunts him with evading social and political responsibilities. Parts of *Sphere* were published in 1973, the year the United States formally committed itself to removal from Vietnam, and the entire poem appeared in 1974, amidst the Watergate hearings and the resignation of Richard Nixon. Against this background, the lines "they ask me, my readers, when I'm going to go politicized or / radicalized or public" suggest a troublesome anxiety on Ammons's part, one that recalls the experience of many American writers during the thirties, when a public political commitment appeared both appropriate and fashionable.

Ammons negotiates his way out of this impasse by allegorizing his own aesthetics in political terms and by appealing to Whitman, who often does the same. The "one:many problem," the cornerstone of Ammons's ontological musings, aligns itself with the American motto "*E / pluribus unum,*" an enjambment that frames the Latin words for "many" and "one" at the same time that it disrupts the continuity Ammons is asserting. Meanwhile, the passage maps the principles of change and continuity, by means of which Ammons habitually reconciles the impermanence of physical phenomena with his own religious impulse toward what he names the Most High throughout *Sphere,* onto the American political system, identifying the former with the Democratic party and the latter with the Republican. This last strategy recalls the description of the two-party system in Emerson's "Politics" (1844): "Of the two great parties which at this hour almost share the nation between them, I should say that one has the best cause, and the other contains the best men" (*W* 3:209). In its historical context, Emerson's oversimplification allows him both to affirm the reformist impulses he associates with the Democratic party and to distance himself from the "destructive and aimless" radicalism he associates with Jacksonianism and its aftermath (*W* 3:210). Like Emerson's, Ammons's formulation effectively neutralizes the differences between the two parties by presenting them as necessary complements of one another.

Whitman provides Ammons with an alternative to what he sees as the limitations of commitment and partisanship (although, particularly in his early career, Whitman was a staunchly loyal Jacksonian Democrat). Admittedly, Ammons's presentation of Whitman in *Sphere* is not without its ironies and implicit criticisms. The statement "I figure I'm the exact poet of the concrete *par excellence,* as Whitman might say" pokes fun at Whitman's penchant for Gallicisms such as embouchure, en masse, and ensemble, while a subsequent mock-exhortation, "O comrades! of the / seemly seeming" (*S* 67), parodies Whitman's compulsive apostrophizing. Furthermore, in an ambiguous moment, Ammons claims, "I want, like Whitman, to found / a federation of loveship, not of queers but of poets, where / there's a difference" (*S* 66), affirming Whitman's vision of a nation welded by adhesiveness but also qualifying that affirmation in language some might reject.

Nevertheless, Whitman's example provides the precedent Ammons needs, as it shuttles him between potentially divisive oppositions: oppositions between parties, oppositions between the politically committed and uncommitted, and oppositions between those in power and those suspended in "disaffection and alienation." This last group, the disaffected and alienated, Ammons, like Whitman, is particularly anxious to incorporate into his vision of America, for the existence of disaffection and alienation threatens to subvert his dream of national balance and inclusiveness, represented here in terms of the fourfold symmetry of American geography. Another of the conceptual pairings Ammons establishes early in *Sphere* is that of center and periphery (*S* 12), and it serves him in this context, along with those of one-many and change-continuity: "When I identify my self, my work, and my country, you may / think I've finally got the grandeurs: but to test the center / you have to go all the way both ways" (*S* 66). On the periphery, figured geographically as the "territories" (a Whitmanian archaism for a poet in the late twentieth century), are the disaffected and alienated; if Ammons can link them to the center, as Whitman attempts to link a prostitute with a president, he can identify himself with America in good conscience and, he hopes, without a debilitating egotism.

But disaffection and alienation prove to be more difficult for Ammons than the passage from *Sphere* suggests. In "Summer Place," first published in the *Hudson Review* in the summer of 1977, he looks back at *Sphere,* "my last fallacy of imitative form, my book on / roundness," and admits that it "disappointed me some (oh, yes, it did)."[37] Ammons's disappointment in the earlier poem, which won him the Bollingen Prize and which "a lot of people have / bought . . . reading it or not" (*SPl* 173), arises from his wanting to write a poem "standing recalcitrant in its own nasty massiveness, / bowing to no one, nonpatronizing and ungrateful" (*SPl* 173). Although one might question Ammons's disappointment in *Sphere,* he is right; it is not a recalcitrant, nasty, massive, unbowed, nonpatronizing, and ungrateful poem. But in a passage that Ammons is echoing here at the opening of "Summer Place," *Sphere* contemplates such a poem:

> I don't know about you,
> but I'm sick of good poems, all those little rondures
> splendidly brought off, painted gourds on a shelf: give me
>
> the dumb, debilitated, nasty, and massive, if that's the
> alternative: touch the universe anywhere you touch it
> everywhere.
>
> (*S* 72)

This passage, published in 1974, prophesies the changes to come in the writing of 1975–76. According to internal evidence, Ammons composed "Summer Place" between July 4 and July 21, 1975, on the New Jersey coast near Corsons Inlet. The poem did not appear, however, until two years later, by which time Ammons had also composed and published *The Snow Poems,* which follows "Summer Place" in the order of composition but precedes it in the order of publication.

Although in many ways *The Snow Poems* fulfills Ammons's vision of a nasty and massive poem, one from which both he and his critics appear subsequently to have retreated, "Summer Place" represents the transition between the neat tercets of *Sphere* and the nastiness of *The Snow Poems.* It embodies Ammons's urge to write "a / complaining poem" and "a big gritty poem that would just stand / there and spit" (*SPl* 174). Of course, Ammons realizes that "nothing turns people off like complaining, they get / enough of it doing their own" (*SPl* 174), a realization that may explain his decision not to include "Summer Place" in any of his subsequent volumes, including *Selected Longer Poems* (1980), which contains a chronological list of Ammons's longer poems revealing that "Summer Place," although about the same length as "Hibernaculum," is the one long poem under book-length he chose to omit.[38]

Both "Summer Place" and *The Snow Poems* come out of a difficult period in Ammons's career, one during which he seems to have been struggling with the ambiguous aspects of his success as a poet (the Bollingen Prize was preceded in 1973 by a National Book Award for *Complete Poems*). "Summer Place" contains numerous complaints about the chores and burdens of being famous in America, or at least famous among American poets: the letters of recommendation to be written, the manuscripts sent by unknown poets hoping for encouragement and advice, the appeal from a bookstore owner in Arkansas who wants Ammons to sign a stack of bookplates to help move her stock, a review that compares him unfavorably with Stevens. It also contains many statements about how meager and qualified the rewards for poetic fame and power are compared to other kinds of fame and power in America:

> thank goodness, I'm the very
> peakstone of something, a mt [mountain], though I don't know how high

it is: it is not as high as General Motors or even
Anaconda Copper or Kennecott: it's about as high as
up to here: anyhow, I'm sitting on it: it feels good:

bowling champions make twelve times as much as poetry
champions: pool sharks about ten: tennis, fifty, etc:
poetry is a range of ridges which, however, rises.

(SPl 185)

In addition to these complaints about money and the uncharacteristic references to corporate America, "Summer Place" contains many complaints
about desire and the paucity of opportunities for satisfying it, complaints that
fill the poem with the same kind of erotic bitterness Stevens wrestles with in
"Notes toward a Supreme Fiction."

Although the complaint is an ancient and venerable subcategory of
poetry, many readers, as Ammons apparently realized, may have limited
patience with the griping of a forty-nine-year-old man who only a few
years after the publication of "Summer Place" became one of the first
recipients of the lucrative MacArthur Fellowships. But to read "Summer
Place" as nothing more than the venting of crankiness is to miss its larger
ambitions:

I guess I

should forget the grandiose, and all distant approaches
to it, and just say how I feel: well, I feel lousy:

I feel lousy, though, mainly because I can't get through
to do anything good for my country: it matters how
your relations with your wife are holding up, how great a

father you are, whether you're making progress with
the oedipal situation or learning how to mosey with
your peers: but the local effect does not suffice:

profound emotions of allegiance and patriotism (the most
profoundly selfless emotion, probably) are with us,
if not now much in the wear.

(SPl 197)

Not only a personal complaint, "Summer Place" is also an American jeremiad. Begun on the fourth of July, the poem meditates on America not, as in
Sphere, from the perspective of one who identifies himself with his country,
but rather from the perspective of one who finds himself, in spite of his successes, among the disaffected and alienated. In fact, if anything, his successes
irritate Ammons, for instead of bringing him the influence and power necessary to improve his country, they merely confirm his own social and political
impotence:

what *is* it I want to do for my country: I mean, as a
poet: that is, if I could get anybody to read the
stuff: as if reading about something would make it come

true: that is, if I could come up with something worth
coming true: Dean Martin has more effect on this
country in a minute than I have in a lifetime.

(*SPI* 196)

But Ammons does not limit his criticism of America to resenting that
the country does not listen to its famous poets. Instead, he embarks on the
more ambitious project of describing why the America he loves "is hardly / in
prevalent view":

yesterday
was Independence Day: someday we will have to call a

Day Interdependence Day: neither sincere nor serious,
I hesitate to engage anything above the level of a
broken bottle for fear of being, in a free state,

misunderstood or investigated: questioned closely, I
would have to admit that the America I love is hardly
in prevalent view so it must be somewhere hiding around

weeds, fencerows, windowboxes, railsidings, and abandoned
roads.

(*SPI* 184)

The distinction between independence and interdependence recalls
Ammons's pairing of the one and the many. Independence guarantees the
individual's right to life, liberty, and the pursuit of happiness, whereas interdependence entails the recognition that each individual's independence qualifies and compromises the independence of all other individuals. Appropri-
ately, Ammons sets his meditation on interdependence not in the isolated
natural scenes most of his readers will associate with him but rather in the
hot, crowded, noisy streets of Ocean City, New Jersey, a locus of American
democracy at its most vivid and concrete.

In formulating a distinction between independence and interdepen-
dence, and in arguing that the former without the latter is incomplete,
Ammons restates Whitman's version of what he calls in a late note "An
American Problem" (*Specimen Days and Collect* [1882]):

One of the problems presented in America these times is, how to combine one's
duty and policy as a member of associations, societies, brotherhoods or what
not, and one's obligations to the State and Nation, with essential freedom as an
individual personality, without which freedom a man cannot grow or expand, or
be full, modern, heroic, democratic, American. With all the necessities and

benefits of association, (and the world cannot get along without it,) the true nobility and satisfaction of a man consist in his thinking and acting for himself. The problem, I say, is to combine the two, so as not to ignore either. (*PW* 2:540)

It is no less a problem for Ammons in the 1970s than for Whitman in the 1870s, and in coming to understand that the America he loves, an America that acknowledges interdependence as much as independence, is not in prevalent view because it has been pushed toward a peripheral realm of weeds and abandoned roads, the later poet retraces a pattern inscribed by the earlier.

Ammons may be thinking of Whitman's dismissal from the Bureau of Indian Affairs by Secretary of the Interior James Harlan (1865), as of Pound's indictment for treason (1943) or Williams's investigation by the Civil Service Commission, the Federal Bureau of Investigation, and the Library of Congress Loyalty Board (1952–53), when he admits the "fear of being, in a free state, / misunderstood or investigated." Nevertheless, despite disclaimers such as "neither sincere nor serious," "my pure country trash platitudes" (*SPl* 193), and "my trouble as a propagandist" (*SPl* 194), he proceeds to engage a good deal "above the level of a / broken bottle," this last image recalling the broken bottle of Williams's short poem "Between Walls" (1938).

Specifically, Ammons identifies himself with the American periphery, claiming that on the beach surrounded "by all the bathing beauties and bathing boys, / and by the older folks in good houses, . . . I feel like / a bit of country trash" (*SPl* 181). After a trip to the local "library to / look up *trash* in the unabridged . . . / . . . including the *white*" (*SPl* 191), he moves beyond his own rural North Carolina origins and expands his feelings of trashiness into a larger vision of the disaffected and alienated in America:

> take the old geezers and other rest-home spindly drifts of
> flesh: now, that's *trash:* or how about all
> the mentally retarded or disturbed children or old folks:
>
> lesbians and queers of all varieties: migrant workers,
> not getting anywhere: strung-out guitar pickers at
> hopeless junction so and so: aging hookers and johns who
>
> helped with the tide: retired persons: little old
> ladies floated up in Florida, no husband, no home
> no children who want them, and not enough to eat:
>
> we should call this The Republic of Barrels of Trash: we could
> now be entering the bicentennial year of The United States of
> Barreling Trash: "pretty soon the people on welfare gone

be richer than working people": The United States of
Shining Garbage from Sea to Greasy Sea: the litter
glitter: all that remains of free enterprise is if

you fail you deserve it: the land of the hopeless case:
the land of the biggest lobby: we know what is right:
when are we going to make it right.

(SPl 192–93)

Many of the figures in Ammons's grim catalogue appear at various points in
Whitman's poetic inventories and prose memoranda, but nowhere in Whitman's *Leaves of Grass* (1891–92) or *Complete Prose Works* (1892) are they concentrated into such an unmitigated vision of American social and economic
failure. This is the nadir of Ammons's meditation on interdependence, and it
contrasts sharply with the passage about America in *Sphere*. "Summer Place"
attempts to modulate the harshness of this vision by adopting the optative
mood ("we need to sustain the / fallen and extend opportunity to the fallen
who can / rise" [*SPl* 193]), but the poem has arrived at a verdict which it cannot unsay: "it is not a great country that grinds along on / the spills and
breakage of the weak" (*SPl* 193).

Whether or not Ammons will return to such direct scrutinies of America
remains to be seen, but for the moment he has shifted away from them
toward more familiar apolitical ground.[39] This shifting has met with consid-
erable approval (*A Coast of Trees* won the 1981 National Book Critics Circle
Award for Poetry), approval that, in its contrast to the reception of *The Snow
Poems,* may keep Ammons away from the long complaint or jeremiad. Still,
America may not have vanished entirely from his poems, as this poem from
Sumerian Vistas (1987) suggests:

> Another day promised for forty
> come and gone, and we're
> still below freezing: but, at least,
> the trees heavy with ice, it's
> been calm: now, the gray deep
> afternoon is turning windy, and
>
> the thicket snaps like a fire,
> ice creaking and jamming but
> holding, an occasional splinter
> at a crack flicking free:
> another night enameled ghostly!
> yesterday afternoon the sun broke
>
> out late and the trees, perpendicular
> to the light, lit up strict white

> ice-lights at the fractures: tiny
> stirs winked some: others held, red, blue
> glows, water-clear: tonight, we
> have nothing to go on but continuance.
>
> (*SV* 61)

This poem reads like so many of Ammons's observations of natural phenomena, which begin in literal description of the mundane, detach themselves into figurative possibility or parable, and conclude with a statement that is at once banal and prophetic. After the deliberately flattened weather summary, the shimmering into metaphor begins with the enjambment "the gray deep / afternoon," which renders "deep" momentarily nominal and throws the poem toward a vast, wintry abyss that is at once physical and metaphysical, external and internal. The second stanza unleashes a wind as an agent of apocalyptic violence, both destructive and liberating, and the third follows with a sudden illumination, or rather the memory of sudden illumination, that ignites the depressingly gray deep and constitutes the kind of intermittent epiphany that, the poem suggests, rewards and justifies the grim stoicism of the final lines.

But then there remains the matter of the titling, both of poem and of volume. Ammons titles this poem "20 January," a title that pushes the poem toward the mode of the poetic journal and recalls his *Tape for the Turn of the Year* (1965), which begins with "6 Dec:" and ends two hundred pages later with "10 Jan:." Ammons's use of a date as title here may simply represent an intention to associate the later poem with its earlier precedents. But "20 January" is the only date-title in *Sumerian Vistas* or in any of the four books following *The Snow Poems,* which contains a poem called "It's April I." Furthermore, since the Twentieth Amendment to the Constitution was ratified in 1933, the twentieth of January has become a fixture of the American political calendar: "The terms of the President and Vice President shall end at noon on the 20th day of January . . . and the terms of their successors shall then begin." Both January 20 and July 4 mark inaugurations, but the latter marks an inauguration of political change, whereas the former marks an inauguration contained within political continuity.

In this context, Ammons's nature poem, and its final statement "Tonight, we / have nothing to go on but continuance," gather new meaning. Other details in the poem hint at the national resonances of "20 January." First, Ammons's use of "we," rather than the far more prevalent "I," involves a wider community and acknowledges if not interdependence, at least interrelatedness. Second, like Whitman, Dickinson, Pound, and Bishop, Ammons narrows that interrelatedness to a community that has special associations with the colors red, white, and blue, all three of which are hung out at the ends of lines in the third stanza, associating them typographically with "we" and "continuance."

As a political fable, "20 January" moves toward a middle ground some-where between the positive vision of *Sphere* and the negative vision of "Sum-mer Place." Although Ammons may have written the poem long before its book publication, the timing of its appearance in print would link it to either, or both, of the inaugurations in 1981 and 1985. The phrase "the gray deep / afternoon" recalls the commencement of the new presidential term at noon on January 20 at the same time that it suggests a metaphor for America in the eighties. The violent imagery of the second stanza doubles as both a prophecy of and a wish for radical change. The remembered illumination of the third stanza, and the implicit wait for its return, fulfills Ammons's state-ment in "Summer Place" that "if one cannot improve things, one must improve one's / view of things" (*SPI* 200). Somewhere between the confi-dence of *Sphere* and the despair of "Summer Place," Ammons realizes that the only chance for either improvement or an improved view of the unimproving lies in simple continuation.

The act of viewing is implicit in the title *Sumerian Vistas,* which returns Ammons to his earliest poems, several of which are set in Sumer, an ancient country of Mesopotamia.[40] The remoteness in time and place of Sumerian culture would appear to distance Ammons from the actual America of the late twentieth century, as it does distance him in the early Sumerian poems; yet the title of his volume inevitably recalls Whitman's *Democratic Vistas* and intimates that by way of Sumer Ammons may be taking the long view of his own time and place. In any event, "20 January" also has Whitmanian reso-nance, as it recalls "November 8, '76," the only note of *Specimen Days* that takes the date of a particular day as its title: "The forenoon leaden and cloudy, not cold or wet, but indicating both. As I hobble down here and sit by the silent pond, how different from the excitement amid which, in the cities, mil-lions of people are now waiting news of yesterday's Presidential election, or receiving and discussing the result—in this secluded place uncared-for, unknown" (*PW* 1:135). The ambiguity of this passage, which opens with a description of weather similar to that of "20 January," resides in the after-thought following the dash. Is it the natural setting of Timber Creek that is indifferent to the contest between Rutherford B. Hayes and Samuel Tilden, which led to the disputed Compromise of 1877 and the election of Hayes, or is it Whitman himself? Is Whitman aligning himself with the indifference of nature or contrasting the indifference of nature with his own inescapable interest, an interest without which he would never have written this note?

Either way, Whitman, who despite the notes from Timber Creek is not a nature poet in the same way as Ammons, uses the distinct realms of natural phenomena and American politics much differently from the way Ammons does. To Whitman, they are completely separate; to Ammons, they are images of one another. For this reason, reading "20 January" in a national context does not exclude reading it in a natural one. Furthermore, both the political and the apolitical readings accommodate a third and final reading, one that takes the poem as yet another *ars poetica.* In this context, the key word is "continuance," which pertains simultaneously to the succession of the seasons, the duration of human life, the persistence of actual America, and the perpetually extended movement of Ammons's verse, regulated by the colon, a mark he has made his as Dickinson made the dash hers and Whitman, at least in the 1855 *Leaves of Grass,* made the ellipsis his. Like Ammons's inclusive vista, the colon connects, joins, and splices what at first appear to be separate phenomena, all the while insisting that closure, or the approximation of closure, be suspended until the genuine end.

Notes

1. A. R. Ammons, *Sumerian Vistas* (New York: Norton, 1987), 28. All subsequent references to this edition will appear in the text as *SV.* This poem appeared originally in *Hudson Review* 36, no. 1 (Spring 1983): 75–110.

2. A. R. Ammons, foreword to *Ommateum* (Philadelphia: Dorrance, 1955).

3. A. R. Ammons, *Collected Poems, 1951–1971* (New York: Norton, 1972), 260. Subsequent references to this edition will appear in the text as *CP.* In *CP* Ammons shortens the title of this poem to "Summer Session."

4. See definitions in both the *Oxford English Dictionary* and *Princeton Encyclopedia of Poetry and Poetics.* In naming this device *epanalepsis,* I am aware that I am modifying these definitions somewhat.

5. A. R. Ammons, *Lake Effect Country* (New York: Norton, 1983), 8. The didactic tone of the passage from "The Ridge Farm" is characteristic of much of Ammons's poetry. See Willard Spiegelman's clarifying chapter "Myths of Concretion, Myths of Abstraction: The Case of A. R. Ammons" in *The Didactic Muse: Scenes of Instruction in Contemporary American Poetry* (Princeton: Princeton University Press, 1989), 110–46.

6. A. R. Ammons, *The Snow Poems* (New York: Norton, 1977), 203. Subsequent references to this edition will appear in the text as *SP.*

7. See Justus Lawler, *Celestial Pantomime: Poetic Structures of Transcendence* (New Haven: Yale University Press, 1979), 53, 59.

8. Hollander, *Vision and Resonance,* [New York: Oxford University Press, 1975], 230–31. Although phonemically linked by Ammons, the words *rigid* and *ridge,* like *error* and *eros,* are etymologically unrelated.

9. Harold Bloom, "A. R. Ammons: 'When You Consider the Radiance,' " *The Ringers in the Tower* (Chicago: University of Chicago Press, 1971), 257.

10. In *Corsons Inlet* and *Selected Poems, 1951–1977,* these last three lines read "so that I make / no form of / formlessness." The absence of "of" in *Collected Poems* is a printer's error.

11. Bloom, *Ringers,* 275. William Carlos Williams, *Selected Essays* (New York: New Directions, 1954), 286. Subsequent references to this edition will appear in the text as *SE.*

12. As in the nod to Williams in "Essay on Poetics," discussed below, Ammons's direct engagement with Williams is indisputable. He plays on the image of a poem as a "machine made of words," a phrase from Williams's "Author's Preface" to *The Wedge* (1944), revising it in *SP* to "a poem is a machine made out of worlds" (43). Also in *SP,* he closes the poem about his fiftieth birthday (February 18, 1976) with this echo: "A half-century inscribed / birthday cake, promises / of presents, a wheelbarrow / (red, rained on) and stereo!" (157).

13. Although he does not treat these particular lines this way, Alan Holder would argue, if I read him correctly, for this paraphrase; *A. R. Ammons* (Boston: Twayne, 1978). Setting up two groups, or clusters, that "constitute the poles between which Ammons's sensibility oscillates," he associates formlessness with the One (Unity) and form with the Many (Multiplicity). See 68. For a discussion of "Corsons Inlet" as an example of the "walk poem," see Roger Gilbert, *Walks in the World: Representation and Experience in Modern American Poetry* (Princeton: Princeton University Press, 1991), 212–24.

14. A. R. Ammons, *Sphere: The Form of a Motion* (New York: Norton, 1974), 16. Subsequent references to this edition will appear in the text as *S.*

15. Pagination differs in various printings of *Paterson* (New York: New Directions, 1963). In the fourth, for example, this passage appears on 65, in the twelfth, on 50.

16. *The Collected Poems of William Carlos Williams, Volume I: 1909–1939,* ed. A. Walton Litz and Christopher MacGowan (New York: New Directions, 1986), 339.

17. Hoffman, *Harvard Guide* [*to Contemporary American Writing,* ed. Daniel Hoffman (Cambridge, MA: Belknap Press of Harvard University Press, 1979)], 576.

18. These pieces appeared respectively in *Poetry* 102 (June 1963): 202–3; and in *Epoch* 33, no. 1 (Fall-Winter 1983): 38–39. The second has been reprinted in David Lehman, ed., *Ecstatic Occasions, Expedient Forms* (New York: Macmillan, 1987), 1–2. See Holder's bibliography (*A. R. Ammons,* 171) for citations of other prose before 1978.

19. " 'A Place You Can Live': An Interview with A. R. Ammons," *Manhattan Review* 1, no. 2 (Fall 1980): 11.

20. Williams makes this statement in "The Tortuous Straightness of Chas. Henri Ford," first published in 1939; yet the year before, in a letter of January 23, 1938, Williams writes James Laughlin that the sonnets of Merrill Moore have "given me the lie." See Hugh Witemeyer, ed., *William Carlos Williams and James Laughlin: Selected Letters* (New York: Norton, 1989), 25–26.

21. *Tape for the Turn of the Year* (New York: Norton, 1972), 32. Subsequent references to this edition will appear in the text as *T.*

22. The figurative meanings Ammons sees in the typography of his poems receive their clearest statement in "The Limit," grouped in the 1966–71 section of *CP* (266–67) and included in *Briefings.*

23. Hollander, *Vision and Resonance,* 229; [Donald] / [*: Device and Modernity* (Berkeley: University of California Press, 1980)], Wesling, *Chances of Rhyme,* 1–2. For a lucid account of previous discussions of organicism, as well as for Wesling's own original contribution to them, see 12–18.

24. Hyatt Waggoner, "On A. R. Ammons," in *Contemporary Poetry in America: Essays and Interviews,* ed. Robert Boyers (New York: Schocken Books, 1974), 334.

25. Holder, *A. R. Ammons,* 122.

26. Henry Sayre, *The Visual Text of William Carlos Williams* (Urbana: University of Illinois Press, 1983), 53.

27. See Paul Fussell, *Poetic Meter and Poetic Form,* rev. ed. (New York: Random House, 1979), 155.

28. This, at least, is Pound's formulation in his "Treatise on Metre," *ABC of Reading,* 199–200.

29. Bloom, *Ringers,* 283.

30. Waggoner, *American Poets {from the Puritans to the Present Day* (Boston: Houghton Mifflin, 1968)], 622–23.

31. Waggoner applauds *Tape for the Turn of the Year,* calling it "good Emerson," but doesn't "much like" "Summer Session." Holder ranks "Summer Session" "among Ammons' most interesting poems," while in *Tape* he finds "egregious examples of the imitative fallacy," "verbal doodling," and tastelessness. Waggoner, "On A. R. Ammons," 334, 338; Holder, *A. R. Ammons,* 118–20, 123.

32. Hayden Carruth, "Reader Participation Invited," *The New York Times Book Review,* Sept. 25, 1977, 30.

33. [Helen] Vandler, *Part of Nature,* [*Part of Us* (Cambridge, MA: Harvard University Press, 1980)], 370.

34. Michael McFee, "A. R. Ammons and *The Snow Poems* Reconsidered," *Chicago Review* 33, no. 1 (Summer 1981): 32, 35.

35. Ibid., 36.

36. A. R. Ammons, *Selected Poems* (Ithaca, N.Y.: Cornell University Press, 1968); *The Selected Poems, 1951–1977* (New York: Norton, 1977); *The Selected Poems: Expanded Edition* (New York: Norton, 1986). In *Selected Poems, 1951–1977,* for example, Ammons includes two poems that appear consecutively in his *Collected Poems,* "Mountain Talk" and "Loss." However, in *Collected Poems* these two poems follow "Belief," which bears the dedication "for JFK" and focuses its meditation on Kennedy's funeral in November 1963. Of course, Ammons is entitled to select any poems he chooses, but the relative placement of these three poems demonstrates that his two sides coexist at a given moment in his career; it also suggests that the widely anthologized "Loss" may benefit from reading in a larger context.

37. "Summer Place," *Hudson Review* 30, no. 2 (Summer 1977): 173. Subsequent references to this printing will appear in the text as *SPl.*

38. See acknowledgments in *Selected Longer Poems* (New York: Norton, 1980).

39. Although not as explicit a meditation on America as the passages from *Sphere* and "Summer Place," Ammons's long poem "Garbage," written in 1989, signals his return to the long poem, a return made more dramatic by the appearance of *The Really Short Poems of A. R. Ammons* (New York: Norton, 1990). As the title "Garbage" suggests, the meditation on trash, which opens in section 129 of *Sphere* and continues through "Summer Place," extends Ammons's attention to the present realities of actual America. "Garbage" appeared in *American Poetry Review* 21, no. 2 (Mar.–Apr. 1992): 36–41.

40. See Holder, *A. R. Ammons,* 22, for a brief discussion of what he calls Ammons's "Mesopotamian posture."

A. R. Ammons:
Ecological Naturalism and
the Romantic Tradition

Donald Reiman

A first-rate poet—that is, a poet sensitive enough to grasp and intelligent enough to express the deepest issues of his or her time and place—is always a mass of contradictions. Even if we call Shakespeare's acknowledged universality an exception, Milton was a Puritan, a revolutionary, a Christian, a humanist, a traditionalist, a defender of the New Science, an idealizer of women, a misogynist. Shelley was an Academic Skeptic, a Platonist, a radical, an agrarian reactionary, a feminist, and a misguided user of women. The examples can be multiplied. One mark of poetic greatness is an ability to entertain and mediate between seemingly contradictory rationalistic statements of belief. For one of the components of poetic, as opposed to scientific, discourse is its capacity to accommodate contraries.

Therefore, in calling A. R. Ammons an "ecological naturalist" I do not deny that his poetry may encompass other philosophical orientations. Obviously a person writing and publishing poetry (rather than, say, meditating in a cave or spinning a prayer wheel) must be in some sense a humanist; he is, in Wordsworth's truism, a man speaking to men. But I believe that what differentiates A. R. Ammons and a number of other contemporary poets (including, prominently, Gary Snyder and Galway Kinnell) from their Romantic and modernist predecessors is that their primary philosophical orientation—the ground of their values—does not reside in an evanescent supernatural source of inspiration (a Spirit of Intellectual Beauty) or in the highest powers of the human mind (the Imagination) but in what Shelley called "the everlasting universe of things"—the nonhuman, unself-conscious operations of natural processes. Ammons' triumphs by finding the words and the images to express the awareness, growing since the time of Galileo and Copernicus, that the Taoists, the pre-Socratics, and Lucretius may have given us a clearer picture of man's place in the knowable universe than did the Sophists and St. Augus-

Originally published in *Twentieth Century Literature* 31.1 (Spring 1985): 22–54. Reprinted by permission.

tine: that the geocentric, homocentric, egocentric view of the nature and destiny of man may be at best a wishful and sometimes a dangerously hubristic misreading of the evidence. At the same time, Ammons follows neither the Stoics, Spinoza, nor other thinkers who sought harmony with Nature/God by joyfully submerging their own identity in the One, nor does he emulate ascetics of various denominations who attempt to reduce the self to a nonentity so as to have no regrets when life ends. Rather, his poems hold in tension the uniqueness of individualities and the ineluctable power of leveling, unifying natural processes. I term the underlying philosophical perspective "Ecological Naturalism"—*Naturalism,* because unself-conscious Nature, rather than an intelligent God (theism or deism), Mankind (humanism), or the self (egoism), provides the ultimate ground of values; and *ecological,* because every creature is accorded its own identity and value within the economy of Nature.

I

In Philip Fried's remarkable interview with Ammons in the second issue of *The Manhattan Review,* Ammons insists (against Fried's humanistic objections) on "the difference between words and things," between the human consciousness and "actuality itself." He declares:

> I'm not sure you can change actuality. On the fate side, we may recognize that we have to accept those limitations and the incarnation imposed upon us. So already, the imagination has had to step down a couple of spaces and what we can change, it seems to me, is the structure we make that we think represents things and is our fiction. We can change our fiction and we can change the way we feel about the fiction we make. But we can't really change actuality.[1]

In an earlier interview by David I. Grossvogel, published in the special Ammons issue of *Diacritics,* Ammons had emphasized his humanistic mission to find an audience, to give people through his poetry "energy" to live their lives, to find his place both within the hierarchy of poets and in human society. But there, also, Ammons emphasized the influence on his own thinking of

> Indian and Chinese philosophy which, when I was younger, I read a good deal, finally coming to Laotse, whom I mentioned earlier. That's my philosophical source in its most complete version. . . . Emerson looks derivative to me of certain of those oriental traditions in the same way as I am derivative of them. In an immediate sense, my forebears are Whitman and Emerson, but in a larger sense my source is the same as theirs.[2]

Ammons' poetry (or his compulsion to write it in the quantities he does) obviously springs both from his keen, often-expressed search for reconciliation with a human community from which he feels alienated and from his need for consolation in the face of death, which has traumatized him at least since May 1930, when his infant brother died.[3] Ammons has ultimately sought comfort by viewing human sorrows as neither illusory or trivial *sub specie aeternitatis;* rather, he attempts, with a notable record of poetic successes, to combine his limited ego-perspective with other perspectives within the same poem or group of poems so that he sees his (any person's) individual fate both from within and from the imagined vantage point of other creatures and of the processes of nature. The self-consciousness remains, but the ego-assertiveness is chastened and modified by the counter-assertions of other "I's" or other "eyes." This I/eye pun was surely in Ammons' mind when he named his first volume of poems *Ommateum,* a word meaning literally "a compound eye."[4]

In the poems from *Ommateum* that Ammons reprinted in his *Collected Poems, 1951–1971,* the chief method of compounding his "eye/I" is to frustrate the expectations of the Judeo-Christian prophetic/poetic voice that the first poem designates as "Ezra."[5] The theme of the volume parallels that of one of Stephen Crane's aphoristic poems:

> A man said to the universe:
> "Sir, I exist!"
> "However," replied the universe,
> "The fact has not created in me
> A sense of obligation."

In "So I Said I Am Ezra," the wind and the sea (the younger Ammons' two favorite embodiments of the processes of Nature) remain unimpressed by the self-assertion of the poet: "I listened to the wind / go over my head and up into the night" and "there were no echoes from the waves / The words were swallowed up / in the voice of the surf. . . ." Finally, after traversing "bleached and broken fields," the poet is left with the unsympathizing forms of nature:

> I am Ezra
> As a word too much repeated
> falls out of being
> so I Ezra went out into the night
> like a drift of sand
> and splashed among the windy oats
> that clutch the dunes
> of unremembered seas
>
> (*CP,* p. 1)

The key word here is "unremembered." For the obvious question raised in the reader's mind is, "unremembered" by whom? No one would be there to "remember" the seas, once "Ezra," symbolic of human self-consciousness, "went out into the night." The poet does not himself ask the question directly, as Shelley does in "Mont Blanc":

> And what were thou [Mont Blanc], and earth, and stars, and sea,
> If to the human mind's imaginings
> Silence and solitude were vacancy?

The question raised by Ammons' poem cannot be rhetorical, and it can have no positive answer. The seas will be unremembered because, once mankind goes "out into the night," there will be (so far as the poet knows) no consciousness to remember anything.

"So I Said I Am Ezra" both sets the problem and carries with it a set of limitations upon the answers that are explored in the poems that follow. "In Strasbourg in 1349" (*CP*, pp. 2–3) shows the futility of a certain narrow religious attitude toward death and natural disaster. The Christian inhabitants blame a plague on "the Jews" and burn them. The poet, presumably rejecting this policy of scapegoating some distrusted minority, "walked up into the air," and "When morning came / I looked down at the ashes / and rose and walked out of the world." The senselessness of such parochial quarreling is reemphasized in "I Went Out to the Sun," where the sun becomes angry with the moon and the poet urges them not to quarrel, "since all at last must be lost / to the great vacuity" (*CP*, pp. 6–7).

But there are limits to the possibilities of reconciliation. In many of his attempts to find companionship in the universe, the Ezra-poet fails because he tries to engage the nonhuman on purely human terms. In "Turning," he attempts to court and mate with a lioness, but (like the lady who went for a ride on the back of a tiger) ends up fumbling "about in the darkness for my wings" (*CP*, pp. 11–12). In "With Ropes of Hemp" he lashes his "body to the great oak / saying odes for the fiber of the oakbark / and the oakwood saying supplications / to the root mesh . . . while eternity / . . . waited with me patient in my experiment"; though the poem ends with the poet "in the night standing saying oaksongs / entertaining my soul to me" (*CP*, p. 14), we are to judge the experiment as a noble failure, I think, on the same plane as Shelley's attempts, by making his "bed / In charnels and on coffins," to force "some lone ghost / . . . to render up the tale / Of what we are."[6] In these poems from *Ommateum*, Ammons is rejecting not only the Judeo-Christian humanism that would see man as being made in the image of a self-conscious God and having "dominion . . . over all the earth," but also an easy pseudo-Romantic pantheism or "con-theism." The lioness follows the nature of lionkind and the oak its querculian nature, both quite independent of, and generally unaffected by, human thoughts and words.

If the higher forms of animal and vegetable nature are thus unresponsive to human desires, how much greater is the indifference of the fundamental manifestations of what Shelley's Demogorgon calls "Fate, Time, Occasion, Chance, and Change." Several early poems treat the dissolution of the individual amid unknowing, uncaring surroundings. In "Chaos Staggered Up the

Hill," chaos, in passing, "engulfed me / and I couldn't know dissolving / it had rhizobia [i.e., nitrogen-fixing soil bacteria] with it / to make us green some other place" (*CP,* p. 6). The key word here is "us," implying that a fundamental community links the conscious self that dissolves into chaos and the material elements that recombine into new forms of life. In "Consignee," one of the earliest poems in the canon, but first published in 1965 and collected in *Northfield Poems,*[7] the individual who is "consigned" to "death, the diffuse one," "quarreled and devised a while / but went on / having sensed a nice dominion in the air, / the black so round and deep" (*CP,* p. 8). Here the surroundings are still oblivious to the fate of the self, but again, the imagination—though powerless to "change actuality"—has (as Ammons declared that it could) changed "our fiction and . . . the way we feel about the fiction we make." Instead of resisting fate to the bitter end, in the manner of Byron's Manfred, Goethe's Faust, or the aging Yeats, Ammons changes the myths of death into a return to the "nice dominion" of a comforting, womb-like peacefulness.

In "Whose Timeless Reach" (*CP,* p. 33), "Ezra" resists the easy logic of "the frozen mountain" that tells him "death does / not take away[:] it / ends giving [,] halts bounty"; Ezra's mind freely associates the word "Bounty" with "ships / that I might take and helm right / out through space / dwarfing these safe harbors and / their values"—in short, that he might avoid the limitations imposed on thought "by bones" and, instead, glide "eternally." But in this and other poems, such free association obviously comes to no more than a wishful attempt to evade actuality.

In the long reach of Ammons' early vision, even art and human artifacts possess no ultimate, lasting value. At the death of the greatest human intellect—one that has probed alike the secrets of interstellar space and those of the catacombs—"no one knew / that he had ever flown / he was no less / no more known / to stones he left a stone" ("Having Been Interstellar," *CP,* pp. 19–20). And in "Coming to Sumer," Ezra, who here represents human imagination turned into mere greed for wealth and fame, "rifled the mud and wattle huts," looking among the graves for artifacts of "recent mournings"— "gold leaves and lapis lazuli beads / in the neat braids loosening from the skull"; finding nothing, he sets fire to the huts and abandons "the unprofitable poor" to move on, "casual with certainty" toward the tombs of "king and priest" in Sumer (*CP,* p. 22).

Finally, "In the Wind My Rescue Is" states unequivocally that the poet's hope lies not in the assertion or preservation of his own identity, not in stone monuments to the self, which would merely be eroded by time or ravaged by imaginative spoilers from some future civilization. Rather his "rescue" lies in the wind as process, the force of natural change that continuously transforms the land and stirs up the waters. By identifying with the process of change itself, the poet imaginatively attaches himself to that which is truly eternal. The poem reads, in full:

In the wind my rescue is
in whorls of it
    like winged tufts of dreams
bearing
   through the forms of nothingness
   the gyres and hurricane eyes
the seed safety
    of multiple origins

I set it my task
to gather the stones of earth
    into one place
the water modeled sand molded stones
  from
    the water images
    of riverbeds in drought
from the boundaries of the mind
from
    sloping farms
    and altitudes of ice and
to mount upon the highest stone
a cardinal
chilled in the attitude of song

But the wind has sown loose dreams
in my eyes
    and telling unknown tongues
drawn me out beyond the land's end
    and rising in long
   parabolas of bliss
borne me safely
from all those ungathered stones[8]

    If one reads this poem in the truncated version published in *Selected Poems* (1968) it seems to stand as a counter-piece to a poem written in 1956 and published in 1958 (Wright, p. 87), Ammons' "Apologia pro Vita Sua." There the poet "started picking up the stones / throwing them into one place" until he had built a cairn that, even after his death, remains a human artifact amid an alien nature, "a foreign thing desertless in origin" (*CP*, p. 38). In these early poems, Ammons defines the central issue of his poetry: Man is one among many creatures, and all his self-consciousness, imagination, and creativity have no power to hold back the inexorable forces of time and change that will swallow up mankind and all traces of human existence. Yet he remains alienated from other natural creatures by apprehending the fact of death and by feeling sorrow amid the joys of sensory experiences because of their foreseen ending.

II

The tension between the intellectual acceptance of the "actuality" of death and the reality of man's emotional longing to achieve permanence, either for the individual identity or for the values that the individual espouses, has been a central issue for all Romantic, Victorian, Modernist, and Postmodernist poets. And the melancholy of the human being who is unable to submerge himself in the sensual pleasures of merely natural creatures has been the theme of poems at least from Horace and the *Pervigilium Veneris* onward.

Ammons for years refused to accept the skepticism toward the findings of science with which the Romantics had protected their hopes and their idealism. Shelley could write at one time that the only reason for the human idea of immortality is a psychological variant of the physical law of inertia: "This desire to be for ever as we are; the reluctance to a violent and unexperienced change, which is common to all the animated and inanimate combinations of the universe, is, indeed, the secret persuasion which has given birth to the opinions of a future state."[9] But he could sufficiently doubt the logic of such reasoning and the evidence of the senses to assert his "modest creed" that "in this life / Of error, ignorance and strife— / Where nothing is—but all things seem, / . . . that death itself must be, / Like all the rest,—a mockery."[10] Byron, who sometimes relied on Pyrrhonist Skepticism, at the end of *Childe Harold's Pilgrimage* undercuts his praise of human artistic achievements by reminding his readers that in the face of the "deep and dark blue ocean" ("the image of Eternity"), man and all his achievements are transitory and trivial: "He sinks into thy depths with bubbling groan, / Without a grave, unknell'd, uncoffin'd, and unknown." But Byron can then immediately claim some affinity with the monster, expressing a feeling of trust toward this awesome power: "And I have loved thee, Ocean! . . . 'twas a pleasing fear, / For I was as it were a child of thee, / And trusted to thy billows. . . ."[11] Thoreau, Emerson, and Whitman looked to a similar harmony between human nature and the underlying spirit of the universe. But Wordsworth, Coleridge, Tennyson, Browning, Eliot, and Auden ultimately put their faith in a God beyond and at odds with mere mortality, while a number of writers of the Victorian and modern periods on both sides of the Atlantic—including, at moments, Mark Twain, Hardy, James Thomson ("B. V."), and Hemingway—saw the hostility between the highest human values and the ordinary course of nature and societies, without finding any way to resolve the dichotomy because they could not believe in a supernaturalist solution.

Algernon Swinburne was one of the few English writers of the later nineteenth century to deny the traditional hopes for either immortality or the divine redemption of humane values without succumbing to either bitter irony or despair. And he did so in the spirit of Lucretius and the pre-Christian Graeco-Roman philosophers: death is a natural part of life and the absence of any afterlife frees human beings from fears that the deeds of their restless, limited, imperfect selves will bring them to a judgment that, under the standards of perfection, they are incapable of passing unscathed. If the Good Shepherd, the personal God of pity and mercy, is removed from the cosmic vision, death can be seen as a better option than an eternal life that merely extends infinitely the existence of mortal limitations, doubts, and fears.

> From too much love of living,
>   From hope and fear set free,
> We thank with brief thanksgiving
>   Whatever gods may be
> That no life lives for ever;
> That dead men rise up never;
> That even the weariest river
>   Winds somewhere safe to sea.[12]

In order to be comfortable with such a view of human destiny, the poet must keep his eye firmly on mortal limitations—those moments of dissatisfaction with identity and its surroundings that, at times, oppress even the most orthodox religious poets, as in the "terrible sonnets" of G. M. Hopkins:

> I am gall, I am heartburn. God's most deep decree
> Bitter would have me taste: my taste was me;
> Bones built in me, flesh filled, blood brimmed the curse.
>   Selfyeast of spirit a dull dough sours. I see
> The lost are like this, and their scourge to be
> As I am mine, their sweating selves; but worse.[13]

In order to rest human hopes in the necessity of dissolution, the poet must emphasize, not life's "moments of vision" but its "satires of circumstance" (to use the titles of two of Hardy's poetic volumes). Keats's "To Autumn," which some have read as a positive acceptance of mortality, resolves itself, when seen in the context of Keats's life and poetry, into a last-ditch stand at a naturalistic fall-back position after his humanistic hopes had been overrun by the grim reality of deaths past and death to come. And Wallace Stevens' positive naturalistic declarations in "Sunday Morning" and the rest of *Harmonium* were to be undercut by the dissatisfactions with mortality voiced in *Ideas of Order* and subsequent volumes, complaints not to be fully silenced until Stevens' very last poems returned to accept "Not Ideas about the Thing but the Thing Itself."[14]

In Stevens' case, his two phases of naturalism may index three stages of his development, passages of life now recognized as being as important to the psychology of the adult as to that of the child. Ammons' career exhibits a similar development that may explain certain shifts in the emphases of his poetry over the years. Although the evidence is far from complete, I think that there have been thus far three major phases and one important smaller development in Ammons' poetic career. First, in the poems written between 1951 and the end of 1963, Ammons pursued the gnomic and prophetic styles of the "Ezra" poems that I have quoted. The poet's desires are sharply stated and just as sharply answered by voices representing either other natural creatures or the universe at large. Beginning with *Tape for the Turn of the Year* (1965; written December 1963–January 1964), the style loosens, becoming much more colloquial and confessional, presumably under the influence of William Carlos Williams and the generation of Lowell, Roethke, Berryman, Ginsberg, and their admirers. This opening up of Ammons' style does not, however, mark a major thematic development, because he included in each subsequent volume through *Briefings* (1971) poems that he had written from the very earliest period of his published poetry (1951–1955).[15] And I find no sharp break in his worldview through the first twenty years of his poetic production.

With the publication of *Sphere: The Form of a Motion* (1974), a new Ammons clearly emerges. And looking back into the earlier work from the perspective of *Sphere,* I see the beginning, in such poems as "Summer Session 1968" (*Uplands*), of what may have been Ammons' major mid-life crisis. Ammons worked through this crisis in *The Snow Poems* (1977), thereby freeing himself to move on to an entirely new—and what seems to me his richest— vein of poetry in his recent volumes *A Coast of Trees* (1981), *Worldly Hopes* (1982), and *Lake Effect Country* (1983), as well as in "The Ridge Farm," a major poem published in the thirty-fifth anniversary issue of *The Hudson Review* (36 [Spring 1983], 75–140).

III

If *Ommateum* sets the assertiveness and, occasionally, the ruthlessness of human individuality against the indifference of nature, *Expressions of Sea Level* (1964) shows the poet adapting his psyche and his myths to the actuality that "Ezra" had found so depressing. In "Raft," the first and keynote poem in this carefully wrought volume, the poet "called the wind" and, after he had empathetically "vanished into the beauty / of any thing I saw / and loved" along the shore—"pod-stem, cone branch, rocking / bay grass"—he sets sail on a round reed raft, at first poling out from shore and then giving himself joyously to wind and wave.[16] The theme continues in poems with titles such as "Risks and Possibilities" and "Terrain"—"The soul is a region without definite boundaries: / . . . it floats (self-adjusting) like the continental mass"—and through such positive images of death as that in "Bridge," where the poet watches people "go over the steep moonbridge at the pond's narrows," their fleshly reality at first "rising on the bridge" above their images, and he then sees them "descend into the pond, / where bridge and mirror-bridge merge / at the bank / returning the images to themselves."[17]

When in "Unsaid" (toward the middle of *Expressions of Sea Level*), the poet asks his reader, "Have you listened for the things I have left out? / . . . the non-song / in my singing," we are reminded that throughout this important volume of Ammons' young manhood, the only expressions of human love are for "Nelly Myers" (pp. 14–17), a woman of limited intellect, more a part of nature than a rational being, "not a member of the family" who "came to live in the house I was born in" and who cried real tears "as I left / to go back to college (damn all colleges)"; for his hog "Sparkle," butchered at the end of "Hardweed Path Going" (pp. 50–53); and for his mule "Silver" (pp. 57–58). The rest of the poems keep their distance from sympathetic emotions, to lose the self in identifications with wind, sea, and other natural phenomena. The final poem, "Nucleus," which is the only one in the volume to show the adult poet in his social relations (as a businessman, traveling to Montreal to look over a factory that his company may buy), is the most distanced and alienated poem of all. Absent—"unsaid"—in these poems and in Ammons' other early work, is a clear statement of the place of the individual in the social nexus—man as a lover, householder, breadwinner, or citizen, who is responsible to others as well as to his own destiny. In this respect, the early Ammons is a true heir to the tradition of T. S. Eliot and Wallace Stevens, a poet of metaphysical and epistemological meditation, writing an involuted poetry about the dilemmas faced by the poetic individual. The same concentration (or limitation) characterizes Ammons' next two miscellaneous volumes, *Corsons Inlet* (1965) and *Northfield Poems* (1966). But between these two, Cornell University Press also published, in May 1965, Ammons' first extended poem in a much different style.[18]

Tape for the Turn of the Year is openly written on experimental formal principles. Drafted from 6 December 1963 through 10 January 1964, just as *Expressions of Sea Level* was coming off the press,[19] *Tape* represents Ammons' progress from the "pastoral" scope of his early short poems toward the epic scope that validates the emergence of major poetic talents. As with Ammons' earlier rejections of traditional modes of pastoral, so he casts his "epic" in a mode designed to frustrate conventional expectations. Yet, like Byron's *Don Juan*, *Tape for the Turn of the Year* fulfills many of the conditions of the "primary epic," as C. S. Lewis applied that term to *The Iliad, The Odyssey,* and *Beowulf.*[20] Ammons' poem openly plays off *The Odyssey*. He addresses the Muse (p. 1) and contrasts the idea of 10,000 years, so tiny when viewed as part of geologic time, with the magnitude that 10,000 years represent in terms of human history—taking us back before Troy and Sumer (pp. 5–7). Ammons writes:

> I wish I had a great
> story to tell: . . .
> . . . but
> I can't tell a great

> story: if I were
> Odysseus, I couldn't
> survive
> pulling away from
> Lestrygonia, 11 of
> 12 ships lost
> with 11 crews: I couldn't
> pull away with
> the joy of one
> escaped with his life:
>   (pp. 8–9)

And then Ammons realizes that he *does* have a story to tell: "how / a man comes home / from haunted / lands and transformations"—not literal, but ideological and psychological hauntings and transformations that have alienated him from Nature:

> bring the man
> home, to
> acceptance of his place
>   and time,
> responsibilities and
> limitations: I mean
> nothing mythical—
> Odysseus
> wandering in ghost-deep
> background—I mean only
> or as much as
> restoration
> which takes many forms &
> meanings:
>   (p. 10)

Throughout *Tape,* Ammons emphasizes his efforts to reconcile both himself and his readers to the values of the quotidian world, unburdened by great goals or ulterior aspirations. At one point, near the middle of the poem, he comes to question even why he as a poet needs "to throw / this structure / against the flow / which I cannot stop?" And he recommends (though without fully practicing) "acquiescence, acceptance: / the silent passage into / the stream, going along, / not holding back" (pp. 88–89). At this point, Ammons defines his work as poet "to transfigure these / days / so you'll want to keep / them" (p. 89). Later, after examining the limitations of human understanding, he suddenly announces:

> Lord, I'm in your
> hands: I surrender:

it's your will
and not mine:
you give me
singing shape
& you turn me to dust:
(p. 141)

And there Ammons asks how he can praise "the Maker"—asking if the best he can do with his "long thin song" isn't "to be / simply & completely / human?" (pp. 141–42). Like the other creatures of Nature, human beings should "leave structure / to the Maker / & praise / by functioning" (pp. 142–43). Still later in the poem, Ammons links the doctrine of accepting reality to creativity:

they say creation is
thwarted unless
a man accepts & realizes
himself, stands open
& finished
as a flower:
(pp. 157–58)

Ammons demonstrates the miscellaneous character of the reality whose flow he seeks to transfigure by the subjects he chooses to treat in *Tape*. The poem is a heightened diary of Ammons' mental and emotional life, as well as a record of his impressions of external events for all but three of the days from 6 December through 10 January.[21] Having allowed the shape and length of the poem to be governed by the width and length of the adding-machine tape on which he typed his draft, Ammons allows the contents of his poem to be generated by the flow of events and emotions that occupy his mind between the time he put the tape in the typewriter and the time he filled it with words. Thus the form and contents echo the poem's theme: humanity must be content to go with the flow and to renounce—or downplay—systems and structures, rational constructs, in favor of untutored reality.

There are at least three other points to be made about the style of *Tape*. First, its very use of the physical materials—the length and breadth of an adding-machine tape to give shape to the poem—is not original in either the epic tradition or in modern literature. The Homeric epics themselves were apparently shaped originally into episodes of a length convenient to dramatic recitation and then, during later Alexandrian redactions, were divided into twenty-four books on the basis of the then-standard lengths of the papyrus rolls onto which they were being copied about the first century B.C.[22] More recently, Gertrude Stein divided such works as *Stanzas in Meditation* into sections, the varying length of which was determined by the number of pages of the French schoolchildren's blank copybooks in which she drafted her work.[23]

In this practice, Stein—like Ammons—exercised considerable powers of choice. She wrote on every other line; sometimes she would use two copybooks to make up a section, just as Ammons chose the width and length of the particular roll of tape he purchased.

The second point is that Ammons, far from really "going with the flow," made a large number of aesthetic choices that produced a work of art rather than a collection of random jottings or graffiti. Besides choosing to write "a long / thin / poem," rather than one jotted randomly to fill blank spaces on backs of envelopes, letters, and advertising circulars, or whatever flowed onto his desk—or one scratched on stones and logs during his walks—Ammons also carefully chose, for their thematic values, what subjects were to be included and what excluded. (He mentions some representative meals, not others; urinating, but not defecating; having sex with his wife, but not the substance of conversations with his friends or business associates.) In *Tape* Ammons follows the lead of William Carlos Williams and of the generation of Auden, Lowell, Roethke, and Berryman in breaking away from the tight, thematic reticence of the high Modernists. He gives up the mode of symbolist poetry that, in the words of W. D. Snodgrass, ignores "matter and external reality" and becomes "a search for a state of Being, a rejection of that world of Becoming in which we are born, grow, and die."[24] Thus, though not part of the movement into "confessional poetry" that centered around Lowell and Berryman, Ammons reflected the reemergence of the Whitmanian tradition that included at one end the "confessionals" and spanned a wide range of poets through the Black Mountain group and Gary Snyder to Allen Ginsberg and the "Beats."

In one important passage in *Tape for the Turn of the Year,* Ammons declares, *"ecology* is my word: tag / me with that: . . . that's the door: here's / the key: come in, / celebrant / to one meaning / that totals my meanings" (p. 112). Three pages later, he provides two instances of ecological modes of life:

> the plains Indians centered
> their lives
> on the chase: rooted in
>   a moving herd
>   of buffalo!
>   a center
> stabilized
> in instability:

>   or the reverse: the
> barnacle
> on a rock, stationary,
>   depends on the sea,
> to bring it food:
>   (p. 115)

After adding the word *"provisional"* to *"ecology"* (p. 116), Ammons exhorts his readers not to "establish the / boundaries / first, / . . . and then / pour / life into them" but rather to "let centers / proliferate / from / self-justifying motions!" (p. 116). At the end of *Tape*, Ammons answers the question, "how does one come / home:" in these words:

> self-acceptance:
> reconciliation,
> a way of
> going along with this
> world as it is:
>
> nothing ideal: not as
> you'd have it:
>   (p. 203)

IV

By the time Ammons wrote *Sphere: The Form of a Motion,* he had apparently changed his perspective. For there he seems to provide a predetermined shape, to "establish boundaries first . . . and then pour life into them," both formally and in content. Visible in *Sphere* is the influence of Harold Bloom and other humanistic critics—many of them *ephebes* of Bloom—who contributed to the special issue of *Diacritics* devoted to Ammons, in which were first published the initial ten sections of *Sphere*.

The poem's structure appears, superficially, to be as formal as that of *Tape* was random: besides the introductory poem "For Harold Bloom," *Sphere* contains 155 sections, each consisting of four unrhymed tercets (à la Stevens) with lines of approximately equal length. But closer examination reveals a surging antiformal spirit that kicks against this apparent symmetry. Just as *Tape* fulfilled its epic intentions partly through its rejection of stereotyped epic conventions, so *Sphere*'s superficial adherence to the formalities and thematic concerns of Stevens' brand of Modernism turns out to underline Ammons' fundamental differences from that tradition. For the subjects treated in *Sphere* are roughly the same as those in *Tape,* with the flow covering a longer span of time, the rapid turn of more than one seasonal cycle: In section 19, "it's spring"; by section 29, on Halloween "spirits / loosen from the ground . . . there's a lit door: / hello: we're pirates" (p. 23), leading thence to winter snow (#33–34) and a renewal of spring (#37).

Ammons, moreover, replicates not only the flowing, time-bound mode of *Tape,* but at various points he restates the same ideals:

> . . . to be saved is here, local and mortal:
> everything else is a glassworks of flight: a crystal
> hankering after the unlikely: . . .
>
> (#33; p. 25)

> redemptions despise the reality: when may it not be our
> task so to come into the knowledge of the reality as to
> participate therein: wherever the imagined lands it's

> likely to brush up against a thorn and pop or get hit by
> a bus on the freeway or at the minimum be thought flatulent:
>
> (#59; pp. 36–37)

> . . . I sought out peaks and stars and at my cost
> sang them high and bright: you don't have to be superhuman
> to survive—let go and let your humanity rise to its natural

> height, said the star, and you will in that smallness be as
> great as I: so I sat down and sang and mountains fell and
> at last I knew my measurable self immeasurable. . . .
>
> (#111; p. 60)

Man should accept his mortal, limited humanity and be careful in submitting to his dreams or aspirations.

Yet aspirations toward the supermortal definitely shape the superstructure of *Sphere* in a way they did not affect most of the work brought together in *Collected Poems, 1951–1971*. Man feels his separation from merely natural creation through his *longing* to reach beyond mere nature. As Ammons puts it in the introductory poem "For Harold Bloom":

> I do not speak to the wind now:
> for having been brought this far by nature I have been
> brought out of nature
> and nothing here shows me the image of myself:
>
> (p. [5])

And in *Sphere,* more than in most of the earlier poems, the role of the *past* is seen to be central to the human condition. Ammons attempts to escape his fear (if not the reality) of death through word-games, of which the many puns and anagrams scattered through the poem—e.g., "scared / sacred" (#104) "acme came" (#109), and "big ditties" (#135) are *low* instances and of which manipulation of language to create the poem itself is a *high* example. Portraying himself as magician, the poet, with his "hocus focus" (p. 21), "hocus pocus" (p. 59), or "magnum hokum" (p. 77), seeks a way to transform his control of "the life of words" into control of life (#109; p. 59). Ultimately he fails, but at the poem's end, in the best tragic-humanistic tradition, there are assertions, reinforced by heavy-handed echoes of Wordsworth and Shelley, that man's unsuccessful attempts to reach beyond his grasp elevate human consciousness—and even America and its astronauts—above the mortal sphere into some kind of demigodic Valhalla.

Yet *Sphere* as a poem cannot, finally, validate the most blatant humanistic aspirations tacked on in the final sections. While *Tape,* with its understated and limited affirmations, drawn from the honest grappling with the stream of experience, rose beyond its ostensible form to the status of an epic of modern consciousness, *Sphere* sinks into bathetic anti-epic under the weight of its unstable mixture of factual reportage and unsupported (and only half-believed) assertions. In *Sphere,* Ammons pretends to observe our little sphere, the Earth, from a cosmic perspective, with the poet-magician's consciousness serving as the arbiter of values, creating through its "magnum hokum" illusions of imaginative order. Repeatedly, the poet asserts that "though nothing shaped stays," "the imagination, / though bodiless, is shaped . . . and so can dwell in nothingness" (#108, p. 58). Not only does civilization, finally, depend on the creative magic of poetry, but each person in order to give meaning to his life must become a poet. When Ammons tries to reassert Whitman's call for an America of poets, the passage reeks of forced, insincere emotion and, in fact, noticeable embarrassment:

> . . . I didn't mean to talk about my poem, but
> to tell others how to be poets: I'm interested in you, and
> I want you to be a poet: I want, like Whitman, to found
>
> a federation of loveship, not of queers but of poets, where
> there's a difference: that is, come on and be a poet, queer
> or straight, adman or cowboy, librarian or dope fiend,
>
> housewife or hussy: (I see in one of the monthlies an astronaut
> is writing poems—that's what I mean guys): now, first of
> all, the way to write poems is just to start: it's like
>
> learning to walk or swim or ride the bicycle, you just go
> after it: . . .
>   . . . O compatriotos,
> sing your hangups and humiliations loose into song's
> disengagements (which, by the way, connect, you know, when
> they come back round the other way): O comrades! . . .
>   (#125–26; pp. 66–67)

Clearly, Ammons did not have his heart in this kind of bombast, which was mixed with a stand-up-and-salute-the-flag patriotism in adjacent passages that seems to reflect his reaction to protests against the Viet Nam War. If Ammons inherits Whitman's mantle, it is not basically as a proselytizer for every man a poet, but as an expounder of the relation of quotidian experience to his own inner being. Ammons' expounded self, unlike Whitman's, exposes isolation and loneliness, rather than a sense of community and love. The condescension inherent in the passage I have quoted from *Sphere,* #125–26, is totally foreign to Ammons' better poetry, which grapples with his own fears and doubts, rather than patting the rest of mankind paternally on the head.

Ammons superficially adopted the doctrines of the Bloomian humanists in *Sphere,* I believe, because the existential angst that had fueled his poetry from the beginning was compounded during the late Sixties and early Seventies by the common mid-life crisis that strikes men when they realize that they are growing old and may never achieve the goals they have set for themselves. On the verge of such a crisis in 1963–64 (as *Tape* suggests), Ammons had postponed its impact by changing jobs and through the success he enjoyed in publishing four volumes of poems in three years (1964–66) and then winning consecutive fellowships from the American Academy of Arts and Letters and the John Simon Guggenheim Memorial Foundation. But though the conventional signs of success and recognition were there, Ammons was still reaching out toward his audience, trying to awaken in others (in Shelley's words) "a community with what we experienced within ourselves."[25]

Ammons seems, from the evidence of the poetry, to have turned his eyes toward the kind of youthful feminine beauty he celebrates in "Guitar Recativos,"[26] perhaps the students he describes at the end of "Summer Session 1968" as "the 18-year-old / seedbeds." But he declares that "knowledge is to be my insemination: / . . . with my trivia / I'll dispense dignity, a sense of office, / formality they can define themselves against: / the head is my sphere!"[27] The purpose for which Ammons chose to exploit his magisterial authority was to inculcate a doctrine of life to his students and readers. As his earlier poems clearly indicate, however, he had (and has) a deep distrust of all doctrines and dogmas. Supported by praise of the humanistic aspects of his works and by the critical recognition that resulted from Bloom's enthusiasm for his poetry,[28] Ammons, probably subconsciously, tried to turn his mid-life doubts about his own achievements and powers of communication into a positive message for younger and future generations as Shelley, at a comparable moment of self-doubt, advocated in "Ode to the West Wind."[29] Whereas *Tape* exhibits honest self-doubt, *Sphere* suffers from a superfluity of assumed bravado.

The same is true of the middle-length poems that lead up to *Sphere*— "Summer Session 1968," "Essay on Poetics," "Extremes and Moderations," and "Hibernaculum."[30] Though each of these four poems shows Ammons' mature command of language and his mastery of his own ideas, they suffer from the obvious effects of pressures—both internal and external in origin— to write poems in the tradition of Wallace Stevens' later meditations, thereby fulfilling the preconceptions of Ammons' academic critics.

V

The Snow Poems volume (1977) reveals what students of Byron's poetry in our age of Freud-conscious criticism will recognize: the psychological trauma underlying Ammons' pervasive sense of alienation from others originated in the fear and hostility his father had aroused in him during childhood. Ammons' early love of books and language and his sympathy (expressed in *Expressions of Sea Level*) for the mistreated mule Silver, the slaughtered hog Sparkle,[31] and the feebleminded Nelly Myers all seem—in the light of *The Snow Poems*—to originate in a revulsion against a bullying father who "sure was a mess," but with whom Ammons at the age of fifty can now identify and even confuse himself.[32] In a gloss-passage to "When in early / December," Ammons recalls his father saying to him: "some day / your mouth will / get you in trouble" and "you'll be a preacher, / like your uncle"; to this Ammons the poet now replies, "close enough, in that / I try to give the / word life." Then he adds:

> oh, my father,
> I am one of the few
> left to miss you
> I do not miss you much[33]

Later in the volume, we discover (perhaps as the poet himself first recognizes) that the origins of Ammons' filial hostility resided in his father's gratuitous sadism. In "My Father Used to Tell of An," he writes: "what my father enjoyed / most—in terms of pure, / high pleasure—was / scaring things."[34] If we put the evidence of these poems together with the report that when Ammons' father lost his own farm during the Depression, he supported his family by serving as a court officer or sheriff's deputy whose job it was to dispossess other debtors (a task at which he excelled because everyone was afraid of him), we have a picture of someone who had the power to turn a sensitive, imaginative child toward books and the rewards offered by supportive teachers. Ammons begins one of the most powerful of *The Snow Poems*: "When one is a child one lives / in helplessness, in terror / of arbitrary force, and in the / fear of death" (p. 180). Even the memories of his childhood attempts to identify with his father have soured upon recollection: "I carved my father's / initials and my own in / a treetrunk and 1937: / I would not want to see that / work again" ("Arm's Length Renders One," p. 233). Yet he needs to be reconciled with the father his hatred of whom drove him toward poetry, the "dud / dad" (p. 156) who "was so / strong he could carry me and / my sister, one leaning to / each shoulder, with our / feet in the big wooden slop bucket," but who "died with not a leg / to stand on" (p. 230).[35] Finally, though he concedes the impossibility of such reconciliation across the grave, Ammons admits that he finds his father in himself:

My father, I hollow for you
   in the ditches
O my father, I say,
and when brook light, mirrored,
worms,
     against the stone ledges
     I think it an unveiling
or coming loose, unsheathing
of flies
O apparition, I cry,
     You have entered in
     and how may you come
     out again
     your teeth will not
     root
     your eyes cannot
unwrinkle, your handbones
may not quiver and stir
O, my father, I cry,
are you returning:
I breathe and see:
it is not you yet it is you

            (p. 276)

Ammons' confession in *The Snow Poems* of his deep emotional ambivalence toward his father seems, in part, to have liberated him from a primary aspect of his existential obsession—his feeling of separation from other human beings. In the midst of *The Snow Poems,* Ammons cries out: "I have become so lonely / that only the word / is free and large enough to take my / mind off / the world going day / by day over the brink / used up but unused" (p. 191). But by the end he can write, with a conviction that rings true:

I am myself:
I am so scared and sad I can
hardly bear to speak
and yet delight breaks
falls through me
and drives me off laughing
down a dozen brooks:

     . . . . .
I am free:
I feel free, I think:
my chains have healed into me
as wires heal into trees

the saving world
saves by moving,

lost, out of
the real world
which loses all

(p. 287)

And most significant is the character of the incident that leads to this affirmation. Ammons has, on his walk, stopped to pet a neighbor's "frizzled schnauzer," whom he terms "the old fellow, friend" and of whom he declares: "he knows me: we were / friends last fall: / *I am myself*" (pp. 286–287, italics added). Nobody who has ever encountered in Gertrude Stein's writing a similar test for identity—"I am I because my little dog knows me"[36]—can doubt the significance of Ammons' affirmation. Ammons starts to reknit the genuine community of identity and love, ruptured during his childhood, not by proclaiming a fellowship of poets all over America, but beginning with the humble old schnauzer "stretching up toward my face" (p. 286). Now that he is free to be himself—"FARM BOY MAKES GOOD," "REDNECK . . . UNDER TOTEM / WASP"[37]—he turns against "the lords of volition," who have littered his property with beer cans and other refuse, to embrace those who glide with, and who even facilitate, the flow of nature by picking up after those self-indulgent ones to maintain "a neat ditch with clipped banks" ("They Say It Snowed," pp. 291–92).

Contemporaneous with parts of *The Snow Poems* are several of the thirty short poems that Ammons published in an expensive limited edition entitled *Highgate Road* in July 1977. Eight of these poems had been printed earlier in periodicals (one as early as 1965, the others between 1974 and March 1977) and "For Doyle Fosso" had been issued in a single printed sheet in sixty copies at Winston-Salem, N.C., in June 1977.[38] But the twenty-one previously unpublished poems join these to form a volume that evidences Ammons' developing sense of freedom and self-confidence and growing warmth toward those around him. The collection, "dedicated to my son, John, with all my love" (words that Ammons paralleled in the dedication of *SLP* in 1980), also contains poems "For Louise and Tom Gossett" and "For Doyle Fosso" which reflect Ammons' friendship with two professors of English at his alma mater, Wake Forest, where he spent his sabbatical year from Cornell (1974–75) as Poet-in-Residence. The thirty poems range from the clever sophistication of "North Street" ("I tipped my head / to go under the / low boughs but // the sycamore mistook / my meaning and / boughed back") to the homespun, laconic wisdom of "Handle":

Belief is okay
but can do
very little for
you unless you
would kill for

> it in which
> case it is
> worth too much
> to have or not
> worth having.

But with most of the poems apparently occasional in origin and the longest of these "briefings" reaching only nineteen short lines ("Significances," p. 4), this minivolume is too elliptical to indicate clearly the direction in which the poet intended to set his course after *The Snow Poems.*

That direction emerges unequivocally in Ammons' next volume, *A Coast of Trees,* published by Norton in 1981, which underscores his positive attitude toward both nature and the human community around him. Dedicated simply "for Phyllis" (his wife), as *Expressions of Sea Level* had been, the volume is keynoted by the deep composure of its first short poem, "Coast of Trees." There the question, "how are we to find holiness" is answered by a faith in acceptance and a humble giving up of "all mechanisms of / approach" (p. 1). The poem concludes in the Taoist realization "that whatever it is it is in the Way and / the Way in it, as in us, emptied full." In "Continuing," the poet resumes his habit of questioning "the mountain." After seeing that the leaves of yesteryear are beginning to decay, he asks, "what becomes of things: / . . . one / mourns the dead but who / can mourn those the dead mourned"; he receives an answer (quite gentle, coming from one of Ammons' mountains) that "most time . . . lies / in the thinnest layer: who / could bear to hear of it" (p. 4). And as the poet scoops up the sandy soil that remains from the decay of earlier generations of leaves, he seems to accept the mountain's final thought: "it / will do for another year."

In *A Coast of Trees,* Ammons exhibits an entirely new interest in using poetry itself—rather than simply dedications—to commemorate those who have been important to him personally. (The fourth poem, for example, is entitled "In Memoriam / Mae Noblitt.") Ammons' recurring questions about death and human significance also assume a new form. Instead of centering on the facts of death and dissolution, he inquires about the nature of love and of the grief that attends bereavement:

> is love a reality we
> made here ourselves—
> and grief—did we design
>
> that—or do these,
> like currents, whine
> in and out among us merely
>
> as we arrive and go:
>
> (p. 7)

His answer, too, assumes a new form. The limitations of the earthly milieu that we can comprehend with our physical senses yield to a faith in a higher "reality we agree with, / that agrees with us," which "arrives / to touch, joining with / us from far away" (p. 7).

If this hint of supernaturalism surprises Ammons' readers, they have only to recall his continuing distrust of all philosophical and logical systems, as well as the strong element of religious quest throughout his work. Ammons follows the lead of Wordsworth, who in *The River Duddon* first portrays the life of man naturalistically in terms of a stream that ultimately winds somewhere safe to sea, but then has an "After-Thought" in which he distinguishes between the river (which "was, and is, and will abide") and all human individuals: "the brave, the mighty, and the wise / We Men, who in our morn of youth defied / The elements, must vanish;—be it so!" Wordsworth then, in the final lines of the sonnet, asserts that men can live truly human lives only if they have hope that the significance of their lives can, in some way, go beyond the limits of their physical being:

> Enough, if something from our hands have power
> To live, and act, and serve the future hour;
> And if, as toward the silent tomb we go,
> Through love, through hope, and faith's transcendent dower,
> We feel that we are greater than we know.[39]

This hopeful feeling, going against the grain of rationalistic and scientistic dogmatisms, also sustained Shelley in his elegiac duty in *Adonais,* where Keats/Adonais "wakes or sleeps with the enduring dead; / Thou [the cruel reviewer] canst not soar where he is sitting now" (lines 336–37); the young poet/martyr's significance is transmitted, through his poems, to the beauties of Nature he celebrated (e.g., the moon and nightingales) and through the example of his career, which is present wherever "lofty thought / Lifts a young heart above its mortal lair" (lines 392–93). Thus Ammons in *A Coast of Trees* moves closer to—though he does not quite join—the Romantics, whose philosophical Skepticism enabled them to trust the heart's single eye more than the thousands of flickering lights that spangle Reason's darkness.

The best *and* most important single poem in *A Coast of Trees* is "Easter Morning," not, I think, because it outshines the rest of the collection (as Helen Vendler seems to imply in her sensitive *New Republic* review),[40] but because it epitomizes and utilizes the new psychic freedom that Ammons had won for his poetry at such cost in *The Snow Poems*—a freedom that is evident throughout *A Coast of Trees.* "Easter Morning," set at the North Carolina cemetery where most of his relatives lie buried, treats the same theme as Henry James's "The Jolly Corner": "I have a life that did not become, / that turned aside and stopped, / astonished" (lines 1—3; p. 10). In *The Snow Poems,*

A. R. Ammons saw in himself traces of the "redneck" East Carolina dirt farmer that he might have become, had he not rebelled so fiercely against his father's tyranny and had not the U.S. Navy and the G.I. Bill made it possible for him to postpone going home again. In "Easter Morning," Ammons attempts to weave together the threads of his torn experience, to bind age to age in natural piety, in conscious opposition to Wallace Stevens' joyful sundering of Modernist humanism from its roots and traditions in "Sunday Morning."

In "Easter Morning" Ammons revisits his "home country" to contemplate the graves of his baby brother, his "trinket aunts who always had a little / something in their pocketbooks" for him, uncles, schoolteachers, and "mother and father there, too," "collected in one place waiting, particularly, but not for me" (pp. 19–20). Recalling that when, as a small child, he stood "by the road / . . . crying out for / help," the "great ones . . . / could not or did / not hear," he now realizes that their failure to answer his cries has, in part, cut him off from "my place where / I must stand and fail" (p. 21). Yet, returned there on "a picture-book, letter-perfect / Easter morning," he sees "two great birds, / maybe eagles," flying from south to north, who stop and circle, "looking perhaps for a draft" and then turn to continue their journey northward. From this omen he draws a moral:

> . . . it was a sight of bountiful
> majesty and integrity: the having
> patterns and routes, breaking
> from them to explore other patterns or
> better ways to routes, and then the
> return:
>
> (p. 22)

The purposeful flight of the "great birds" that ends "Easter Morning" contrasts with closing images in Keats's "To Autumn" (in which "gathering swallows twitter" sadly before their seasonal flight south) and Stevens' "Sunday Morning," where at the end of the diurnal cycle "casual flocks of pigeons make / Ambiguous undulations as they sink, / Downward to darkness, on extended wings." The poetic analogue to Ammons' "great birds" that springs first to mind, however, is Hopkins' "Windhover," in which the poet's "heart in hiding / stirred for a bird" that "Rebuffed the big wind" of circumstance. Flying north, against easy acceptance of the cycles of mortality, Ammons (with his mate), broke from his predetermined "patterns and routes" to "explore other patterns or better ways," but he has now returned to claim his roots and traditions.

Those traditions include the web of care and concern for kinfolk, and "neighbors"—including "Ann Pollard's pine" tree, "cracked off in high wind," that "ivy has / made . . . an ivy tree" (in "Neighbors," p. 27), the "clear-eyed / babies gumming french fries" in "Sunday at McDonald's"

(p. 40), the "small white-headed man" who "unloads the wheelchair" into which he lovingly places his "wife, snow white" to roll her "through the hospital doors" in "Sweetened Change" (p. 41), a husband (the same one?) watching his wife sink into near-obliviousness in "Parting" (pp. 42–43); and the courageous "man whose cancer has / got him just to the point / he looks changed by a flight of stairs" but who "is like a rock / reversed"—"he shakes / in body only / his spirit a boulder of light" ("An Improvisation for the Stately Dwelling," pp. 47–48). The traditions Ammons reclaims also include allusions to the key images of earlier poets without embarrassed, self-conscious swervings or sweating *agon* to conform to critical theories, but with proper respect both for the greatness of the father-poets and for the integrity of his own poem. The most notable allusions of this type in *A Coast of Trees* are Ammons' adoption of symbolic birds to represent the poet. Besides employing the "great . . . eagles" of "Easter Morning," he identifies himself with a "hermit lark" (pp. 16 and 45) to suggest both his isolation (à la Whitman's "hermit thrush") and his more-than-natural aspirations (à la Shelley's "sky-lark"), while maintaining the integrity of his own choice of specific characteristics and habitats—bare fields and shorelines—and migratory range.[41] Ammons is no longer afraid of expressing either his affection for other people or his indebtedness to the poetic tradition that drew him beyond the limits of his native place.

Ammons' recent poetry, in *A Coast of Trees, Worldly Hopes* (1982), *Lake Effect Country,* and "The Ridge Farm" (both 1983), shows him giving up many of the quirks of style with which he screamed for attention in the volumes from *Tape for the Turn of the Year* through *The Snow Poems.* He has abandoned to *some* extent his idiosyncratic system of (non)punctuation, now utilizing commas regularly and even introducing a few periods and an exclamation point and one query to mark the end of some poems. Moreover, he has (again with qualification for exceptions) regained the sense of decorum that he had, strangely, discarded during his mid-life phase.[42] In the longer poems, such as "Easter Morning" and "The Ridge Farm," where he relies on what the Australian poet A. D. Hope has characterized as "the discursive mode," Ammons has returned to the style that needs to be cultivated in order to restore the ecology of poetry in the twentieth century.[43] But he also revives a more gnomic and imagistic or symbolic mode. In short, Ammons is again using the English language, not as a toy or to illustrate theories, but as an expressive instrument over which he displays a total yet comfortable mastery.

Until we know the precise order in which Ammons' smaller poems were written, we cannot be sure that *Worldly Hopes* is not largely made up of occasional pieces written between the publication of *Diversifications* and *The Snow Poems.*[44] One poem that seems to be new is "Hermit Lark," which extends the analogy between the "sky bird" and Ammons:

> . . . I learn my real
>
> and ideal self from you, the right to sing
> alone without shame
> . . . . .
> I learn from you and lose the edginess I speak of
> to one other only, my mate, my long beloved, and
> make a shield . . .
> . . . . .
> . . . how
> hard to find the bird in the song!
>
> (p. 25)

"Hermit Lark" and an amusing analysis of "The Role of Society in the Artist" (pp. 21–22) are two of the more discursive poems in the volume, which contains many "briefings"—some of them Oriental moods-of-a-moment that seem just right without internal or terminal punctuation. Their forms, in fact, clearly reinforce the thematic message expressed by the words themselves. "Epistemology," for example, is left as fragmentary as the "bit-of-truth" one person tells another and its incompleteness is as irritating as "the bit / untold / avoided" that festers (p. 19). Ammons himself comments on this poetic development in "Progress Report":

> Now I'm
> into things
>
> so small
> when I
>
> say boo
> I disappear
> (p. 16)

But there is no suggestion here that the poet is being driven into a corner by society or by his own anxieties (as he was in "Lion::Mouse," *CP*, p. 203). Rather, the general sense conveyed by the recent publications is that the poet, having struggled for years to establish his "Worldly Hopes" and achieved most of those goals—now finds that "the toy life" (p. 49) he set out to grasp is not what he really values. Death, therefore, does not hold the same terrors as it did in the earlier poetry. In "Volitions," after a day of being turned "round and round" by "the wind," he asks the sky to "drive me / into the / ground here, / still me with the ground" (p. 45).

With a prolific poet like Ammons, now in the midst of a five-year MacArthur Fellowship, it is difficult to predict the scope or direction of his future work. But of his achievement to date there can be no doubt. A. R. Ammons has engaged the fundamental metaphysical and psychological issues of twentieth-century man—concerns about the relationships of the individual with the Universe and with his own familial and social roots—and he has shown us a way to triumph without relying on dogmatisms or on mere palliatives. Finally, after making peace with his father in *The Snow Poems,* he has made his peace with the inexorable and, possibly, inimical forces of "Fate, Time, Occasion, Chance, and Change," not by denying them or by pretending to out-shout them, but by accepting them as being at least as significant as his own subjectivity. His clarity of perception and the courage of his acquiescence appear strikingly in "Rivulose," the final poem in *Worldly Hopes:* "You think the ridge hills . . . / hold on to you, if dreams / wander, give reality recurrence . . . / but then you realize" that, in terms of the span of geologic time:

> not only are you not being held onto but where
> else could time do so well without you,
> what is your time where so much time is saved?
>
> (p. 51)

VI

In the *Manhattan Review* interview, which took place in late June 1980, four years after completing *The Snow Poems* and three years after he wrote "Easter Morning,"[45] Ammons told Philip Fried that he turned to the study of science partly because it provided "a pagan way of associating yourself with universals rather than with the coming and going of mortal things." He explained this by saying:

> if you think of the pagan societies as rather carefully paying attention to what the natural forces were around them and then trying to identify with and, as it were, listen to what that force was and appease it, and know something about it, learn its nature, then science does the same thing today.
> It puts aside, for the moment, its personal interest in things and tries to know what is the nature of the thing out there. I regard that as a very high value. The humanities often feel opposed to that because that attitude obviously puts human things secondary, whereas the humanities have often claimed that man is the center of everything and has the right to destroy or build or do whatever he wishes.
>
> (p. 7)

Ammons' concern for the environment—"ecology" in the conventional sense—is clearest, perhaps, in "Extremes and Moderations," a poem that I have scanted as being written while Ammons was most influenced by the humanist critics. There he calls upon human beings to stop their pollution of space-ship Earth, if only for reasons of their own self-interest: "if contaminated water forces me to the extreme purification of bottled or distilled/water, the extreme will be costly" and (the final line of the poem) "in an enclosure like earth's there's no place to dump stuff off" (*SLP,* p. 66). But in returning to the "ecological naturalism" of the earlier volumes, Ammons' most recently published poems once again question even man's very capacity to desecrate nature. Whereas the humanist Robert Frost regretted that in the process of change, "Nothing gold can stay," Ammons reads the positive obverse of the coin in a poem entitled "Providence," which asserts that nothing tarnished can stay:

> To stay
> bright as
> if just
> thought of
> earth requires
> only that
> nothing stay
> (p. 46)

And, again, the closest poetic analogue is found in the work of Gerard Manley Hopkins, S.J.: though "generations have trod" and "all is seared with trade,"

> . . . for all this, nature is never spent;
> There lives the dearest freshness deep down things;
> And though the last lights off the black West went
> Oh, morning, at the brown brink eastward, springs—

We may never find A. R. Ammons adding to his title "Providence" Hopkins' conviction that the diurnal cycles move "Because the Holy Ghost over the bent World broods with warm breast and with ah! bright wings."[46] Yet, as we have observed in charting his development, he has brought his "ecological naturalism" to the point where its spirit approximates that of the supernaturalism of his childhood heritage, but with greater emphasis on the brotherhood of all creatures. Just as students of Spinoza can debate whether to describe him as an atheist or as the "God-intoxicated" philosopher, so we can finally discard all labels and realize that the poetry of A. R. Ammons provides us with a unique and important perspective and that, without attempting to provide easy answers, it conveys hopefulness and courage for the future of a world in which there is a central place for mankind just as long as human beings take their limitations and responsibilities as seriously as they do their volitions.

Notes

1. *The Manhattan Review,* 1, no. 2 (Fall 1980), 20–21. (Available from Philip Fried, editor, 304 Third Avenue, Apt. 4A, New York, NY 10010.) For suggestions on preliminary reading for this essay, I am grateful to Jerald Bullis and John Benedict; for suggestions on the text of the essay itself, I thank Philip Fried, Jerald Bullis, and Andrew Kappel.

2. *Diacritics,* 3 (Winter 1973), 51.

3. See Ammons' short autobiographical sketch in New York *Times Book Review,* January 17, 1982, pp. 13 and 19.

4. For Ammons' comment on the "I/eye" pun see *Sphere: The Form of a Motion* (New York: Norton, 1974), 36:8. The full title of the first volume is OMMATEUM with DOXOLOGY. For a facsimile of the title page, see Stuart Wright, *A. R. Ammons: A Bibliography, 1954–1979* (Wake Forest University, 1980), p. 2 (hereafter cited as "Wright"). I quote the early poems from Ammons' *Collected Poems, 1951–1971* (New York: Norton, 1972). This edition is hereafter cited as *CP.* Throughout this paper, Ammons' poetry is quoted by permission of the author and W. W. Norton & Company.

5. Given Ammons' interest in etymology, it may be significant that in Hebrew Ezra means "help."

6. *Alastor,* lines 23–29; see also "Hymn to Intellectual Beauty," lines 49–54.

7. See Wright, pp. 104, 21; *Northfield Poems* (Ithaca: Cornell Univ. Press, 1966).

8. *CP,* pp. 23–24. When Ammons first reprinted this poem in *Selected Poems* (Ithaca: Cornell Univ. Press, 1968), p. 22, he dropped the first stanza and the poem began—and was retitled—"I Set It My Task." In *CP,* however, he returned it to the original form it had in *Ommateum.* When I wrote to ask him about the poem, he replied on April 30, 1982: "I really like beginning with the imaginative action in stanza two, leaving out the preparatory speculations of stanza one—but then I began to think that formally or structurally the framing was necessary, its reverberation with the last stanza perhaps the best part."

9. "On a Future State," in Shelley, *Complete Works,* ed. Roger Ingpen and Walter E. Peck, VI (London: Ernest Benn, and New York: Scribners, 1929), 209.

10. "The Sensitive Plant," *Shelley's Poetry and Prose,* ed. Donald H. Reiman and Sharon B. Powers, 3rd printing corrected (New York: Norton, 1981), p. 213.

11. Byron, *Complete Poetical Works,* ed. Jerome J. McGann, II (Oxford: Clarendon Press, 1980), 184–86.

12. "The Garden of Proserpine," penultimate stanza, quoted from Swinburne, *The Collected Poetical Works* (London: Heinemann, 1917), I, 171.

13. "I wake and feel the fell of dark, not day," quoted from *A Hopkins Reader,* ed. John Pick (New York: Oxford Univ. Press, 1953), p. 27.

14. See Donald H. Reiman, "Keats and the Humanistic Paradox," *Studies in English Literature,* 11 (1971), 659–69, and "Wordsworth, Shelley, and the Romantic Inheritance," *Romanticism Past and Present,* 5, no. 2 (Dec. 1981), 1–22.

15. That earliest grouping, besides providing the contents of *Ommateum,* was drawn on for three poems in *Corsons Inlet* (1965), three in *Northfield Poems* (1966), one in *Uplands* (1970), and three in *Briefings* (1971). Of volumes published before *Collected Poems, 1951–1971,* only *Expressions of Sea Level* (1964) relied entirely on material later than 1955.

16. Ammons, *Expressions of Sea Level* (Columbus: Ohio State Univ. Press, 1964), pp. 3–7.

17. *Ibid.,* pp. 19–20.

18. Ammons had earlier, apparently, thought of building a long poem through accretion. "Ten Poems" that appeared in *The Hudson Review* issue of Autumn 1960 (13: 350–63) included six that were titled "Canto 1," "Canto 7," "Canto 8," "Canto 10," "Canto 12," and "Canto 17," respectively. In 1960 Ammons also published "Canto 13" in *Accent,* 20 (Autumn

1960), 199–200, and "Canto 24" and "Canto 29" appeared in *Impetus,* no. 7 (Spring 1963), pp. 15–18. Of these poems, "Canto 24" was never reprinted; the other eight, given new titles, reappeared in *Expressions of Sea Level.* See Wright, pp. 91–92, 95.

19. See the references to "my book" on 11 and 13 December, pages 39, 56.

20. In *Romantic Poets and Epic Tradition* (Madison and Milwaukee: Univ. of Wisconsin Press, 1965), Brian Wilkie demonstrated that literary history teaches the paradox that the epic poet's "partial repudiation of earlier epic tradition is itself traditional" (p. 10). See also Lewis, *A Preface to "Paradise Lost"* (1942; London: Oxford Univ. Press, Paper-back, 1960), pp. 13–32, and Donald H. Reiman, *"Don Juan* in Epic Context," *Studies in Romanticism,* 16 (1977), 587–94.

21. The days for which there is no record are 24 and 25 December, presumably dedicated to the celebration of Christmas, and 29 December, which (as he tells on 30 December) he "gave to the memory of / William Carlos Williams" by attending a reception for Mrs. Williams in New York (p. 129).

22. John Van Sickle, "The Book-Roll and Some Conventions of the Poetic Book," *Arethusa,* 13 (Spring 1980), 9.

23. See Ulla E. Dydo, "How to Read Gertrude Stein: The Manuscript of 'Stanzas in Meditation'," *Text: Transactions of the Society for Textual Scholarship,* 1 (New York: AMS Press, 1984), 271–303.

24. W. D. Snodgrass, "A Poem's Becoming," in his volume of essays *In Radical Pursuit* (New York: Harper & Row, 1975), p. 52.

25. Shelley, "On Love," *Shelley's Poetry and Prose,* ed. Reiman and Powers, p. 473.

26. Ammons, *Uplands: New Poems* (New York: Norton, 1970), pp. 26–29; first published in *The Hudson Review,* 21 (Spring 1968), 106–08.

27. *Uplands,* p. 68, cf. pp. 58–59, 61–63. Ammons' use of "sphere" in "Summer Session 1968" develops the significance of the word beyond its rather limited or negative associations in Ammons' early poem entitled "Sphere" (written 1956–1960; first published in *Chelsea* [#14, January 1964, 51] and collected in *Northfield Poems* [1966], pp. 47–48). In that Freudian poem, "Sphere" is the womb, "A warm unity, separable but / entire, / you the nucleus / possessing that universe" (*CP,* pp. 97–98).

28. Bloom was one of three members of the committee that chose Ammons' *Collected Poems, 1951–1971* to receive the National Book Award for Poetry in 1973.

29. Compare with Shelley's "Ode," these lines from *Sphere:* "history uprights, sways to the give and take in / a touchy balance . . . : / . . . fire . . . god / of a kind, traveling wave of the imagination . . . / that gives destruction's ash to the future," (#148; p. 76). Ammons changes Shelley's image from unextinguished sparks lighting new fires to the fertilizing qualities of ashes and the room given in the burned-out area for future growth in the forest.

30. These four poems have been collected, together with "Pray without Ceasing" (Ammons' sensitive reaction to the mid-life crisis of America, as exemplified by its free use of napalm on children in Viet Nam), in *Selected Longer Poems* (New York: Norton, 1980); this edition is hereafter cited as *SLP.*

31. In *The Snow Poems* (New York: Norton, 1977), there are two references, on pages 4 and 16, to the killing of hogs such as Ammons earlier had bemoaned in "Hardweed Path Going" (*CP,* pp. 66–68).

32. "My Father Used to Bring Banana," *The Snow Poems,* p. 12.

33. Pp. 30–31. Ammons' use of the vertical gloss as subtext seems, like other technical innovations in *The Snow Poems,* to grow out of his interest in the experimental poetry of John Ashbery and, possibly, in the criticism of Derrida and the French deconstructionists.

34. "My Father Used to Tell of an," *The Snow Poems,* p. 229.

35. In his notes to the first draft of this paper, Jerald Bullis wrote: "This is literally true. His father's legs were amputated during the final stages of the diabetic illness that killed him. See 'The Run-Through' (*CP,* pp. 285–286) and 'Motioning' in *Lake Effect Country,* which will be

published by Norton." The latter poem appears on pp. 44–45 of *Lake Effect Country* (New York: Norton, 1983).

36. Stein first quoted this sentence from *The Spirit of Modern Philosophy* by her teacher Josiah Royce in "Saving the Sentence," part of Stein's *How to Write* (Paris: Plain Edition, 1931), p. 19. (I am grateful to Professor Ulla E. Dydo for this information.)

37. "I'm the Type," pp. 234–36.

38. For this poem, see Wright, p. 59; for *Highgate Road,* see Wright, pp. 61–62.

39. Wordsworth, *Poetical Works,* ed. E. de Selincourt and Helen Darbishire, III, 2nd ed. (Oxford: Clarendon Press, 1963), 261.

40. Helen Vendler, *New Republic,* 25 Apr. 1981, pp. 28–32.

41. One interesting sidelight of this choice (given Ammons' care as a student of nature) is that, since the meadowlark is not a true lark but a type of blackbird, the reference is to the only true lark in the Western Hemisphere—the horned or shore lark (a relative of the European skylark), which has a migratory range that includes North Carolina only in winter, but New Jersey and New York all year long.

42. Apparent exceptions are a poem in *Worldly Hopes: Poems* (New York: Norton, 1982), entitled "Shit List" (pp. 27–29), and section 15 of "The Ridge Farm" (*Hudson Review,* 36 [Spring 1983], 83). The first, however, maintains its own low style, while the passage on "shit" in "The Ridge Farm" is so elemental and earthy in its thought that to use any but the plain term would falsify the tone. Neither of these uses produces the shock effect exploited in passages of "Essay on Poetics" (*SLP,* p. 47), "Extremes and Moderations" (*SLP,* p. 57), or those I have already alluded to in *Sphere* and *The Snow Poems.*

43. See "The Discursive Mode: Reflections on the Ecology of Poetry," in Hope's *The Cave and the Spring: Essays on Poetry* (Chicago: Univ. of Chicago Press, 1970), pp. 1–9.

44. Only eight of the forty-three poems in *Worldly Hopes* had appeared in print by the fall of 1979, the terminus ad quem of Stuart Wright's *A. R. Ammons: A Bibliography.*

45. "Easter Morning" was written, Jerald Bullis tells me, in April 1977. It was first published in *Poetry,* 134 (April 1979), 1–4 (Wright, p. 134).

46. The concluding two lines of Hopkins' sonnet entitled "God's Grandeur" (*A Hopkins Reader,* p. 13).

Myths of Concretion, Myths of Abstraction: The Case of A. R. Ammons

Willard Spiegelman

After the publication of *The Excursion,* Coleridge wrote a letter to Wordsworth laying out his hopes and fears about the relationship between poetry and philosophy, and, more important, about Wordsworth's presumed capacity to write the first genuinely philosophical poem. Sensing the affinities between his friend and collaborator and a distant Roman who is our first major didactic poet, Coleridge makes a rigid distinction that he then proceeds to dismember:

> whatever in Lucretius is Poetry is not philosophical, whatever is philosophical is not Poetry: and in the very Pride of confident Hope I looked forward to the Recluse, as the *first* and *only* true Phil. Poem in existence. Of course, I expected the Colors, Music, imaginative Life, and Passion of *Poetry;* but the matter and arrangement of *Philosophy*—not doubting from the advantages of the Subject that the Totality of a System was not only capable of being harmonized with, but even calculated to aid, the unity (Beginning, Middle, and End) of a *Poem.*[1]

Coleridge was, of course, to be disappointed in his hope, but in his distinction between philosophy and poetry he established the grounds for the prejudice in favor of the short lyric that defined most Romantic and post-Romantic tastes from Edgar Allan Poe through Cleanth Brooks. Ironically, he set up at the same time an alternative hope for modern poetry: the ability to encompass grander worlds, meanings, and abstractions than the tiny lyric will permit. Poetry's reach has always exceeded its grasp, and one measure of the poetry of the past two centuries is the variety of means it uses to bridge the gap between the two. One might call the "passion of Poetry" and "the matter and arrangement of philosophy" the Coleridgean equivalent of Horace's *delectare* and *prodesse,* especially since both critics suggest the hopeful possibility for a marriage between the two, the creation of a tertium quid.

Originally published in *The Didactic Muse: Scenes of Instruction in Contemporary American Poetry* (Princeton: Princeton University Press, 1989), 110–46. Reprinted by permission.

The will to epic and the impulse to lecture apparently go hand in hand: when poets think big they also think philosophically, and length of utterance usually comes with seriousness and depth of purpose. To put the matter somewhat differently, when poets wish to write a long poem (rather than a medley of the sort favored by essentially lyric poets like Tennyson, Berryman, and Robert Lowell), they have two avenues open to them: they can write either a narrative, following the traditional path of epic, or a philosophical, meditative work, tracking the path of post-Renaissance poets. To explain the world poets either tell a story or make an examination. The way of narrative and of etiology are older but the way of analysis may be more congenial to contemporary explicators, who distrust history as a possible guide to truth. Didactic poets, by definition, wish to explain things. A more recent appreciation of Lucretius reminds us of that Roman's modernity and also of his usefulness as a model for a didacticism that takes science, a normally "untenable" area for poetic thought, as its major subject: "Poetry is not poetical for being short-winded or incidental, but, on the contrary, for being comprehensive and having range." Thus, Santayana on Lucretius's appropriation of what the philosopher-critic calls "the workshop and busy depths of nature, where a prodigious mechanism is continually supporting our life."[2]

As an explainer, A. R. Ammons is without peer. He constantly tells where he is going, taking retrospective glances when necessary at where he has been. He surveys his terrain, a landscape composed partly of the world around him and partly within the confines of his meditating mind. Even the physical universe includes both what can be seen with the naked eye and what is either cosmic or subatomic. And the entire process includes, as well, the relationship of word to line to page that we come to know as the poem that we read and upon which he is commenting even in the process of composing it. World, mind, their inscriptions within each other, and the consequent inscription made by the creative intelligence imposing itself upon its material: such is the perpetual arena in which Ammons stakes his claims, makes his discoveries, and teaches his lessons. It is, moreover, an arena in which science provides both a source of metaphor, figuration for our emotional and mental lives, and also a subject matter: Ammons shares Auden's and Nemerov's interest in scientific discovery and James Merrill's impulse to present "poems of science," explanations of worldly reality whose primary subject matter is biochemical, ecological, and geological.

Among the poets discussed in this book Ammons stands out not by virtue of his subject matter or of his technique (a poetry that Helen Vendler with some exaggeration calls bereft of adjectives and the presence of human figures),[3] but because he seems, from the very beginning, to have known himself and his interests. His poetry neither develops nor changes, formally or technically, in any significant ways.[4] Reading through thirty years' worth of poetry one can see a quantitative distinction between the longer poems and the short lyrics, but aside from this (and the quirks of punctuation that have come to define Ammons's streaming longer efforts), little else separates the nominally simple and easy lyrics from the meandering, expansive ruminations. Ammons tells us over and over that his main theme, perhaps his sole one, is the relation of the one and the many, and this old pre-Socratic dichotomy, along with variants (inside versus outside, up versus down, center versus periphery, freedom-verging-on-entropy versus stability-turning-into-imprisonment), is his obsession. To these older concerns he brings a modernist's self-consciousness about the role and nature of language, how it fits into the various ways of conceiving the world and how it also creates those very ways.

"Motion" succinctly presents Ammons's creed about the relationship between language and poetry. Words, he says, are "tags, labels"; language, arbitrary by its nature, is

> the
> method of
> distinguishing,
> defining, limiting:
> poems
> are fingers, methods,
> nets,
> not what is or
> was:[5]

Ammons shares the didactic habits of repetition and listing with Allen Ginsberg and Adrienne Rich. What separates Ammons, in addition to the seemingly lazy charm of the short lines, arbitrarily divided, broken by his colons, is the insistent depiction of language at work attempting to explain itself: no other poet gives such self-consciously measured degrees of figuration in his work. The metonymic "tags, labels" and then "methods" and "nets" as means of defining poetry (Ammons relies heavily on the "x is y" formula for both simple and abstract acts of clarification) are deliberately different from the prosaic gerunds, which may still remind us of certain figurative associations, primarily through their etymologies (to define is to limit, after all). And both metonyms and gerunds seem less figurative than the more genuinely metaphoric "fingers," which punningly resonates when we consider its own relation to the Greek dactyl (i.e., finger) as a way of measuring or defining a block of verse.

Ammons continues by describing the music (rather than the meaning or substance) of poetry by professing a theory of pure meaninglessness through a negative formulation: poetry "traps no / realities, takes / no game" (although one may recall that by such logic poetry *is* a game); at last, in an old-fashioned simile, he tells what poetry is *like:*

> but
> by the motion of
> its motion
> resembles
> what, moving, is—
> the wind
> underleaf white against
> the tree.
>
> (*CP,* 147)

The last three lines stand out like an imagist poem or a pseudo-haiku, a piece of pure description to which the poem has progressed after several steps of moving away from "what is" to what the motion of poetry's motion resembles. Resemblance, not identity, is all one can get, however; even the "motion of its motion" ambivalently moves one both closer to (in the direction of a Platonic idea) and farther away from (as the motion of the motion is an echoic, subsidiary force, not a primary one) the nature of the true subject. The most characteristic touch comes in the phrase "what, moving, is," which brings mere being into a collision with motion and simultaneously defines being as the product of motion ("whatever is *is* by virtue of perpetual motion") and asks readers to hear, by an aural removal of commas, the participle become a gerund, and so the entire phrase become a deeper act of definition within the larger, surrounding ones: "what is the nature of moving?" he seems to be asking, as throughout his work questions and conundrums often wear the grammatical guise of statements.

The tension between participle and gerund noted above opens up a dimension of conflict throughout Ammons's work. Like Lucretius, who describes a world in which stasis and movement provide the poles for understanding, Ammons seems perpetually torn between a sense of fidelity to the onrushing change of atomic and cosmic nature and a wishful, almost nostalgic, belief that poetry, or language itself, can furnish suitable acts of definition. In the early, lovely "Gravelly Run" (*CP,* 55), he begins by pretending he could become like Wordsworth's Lucy, herself "rolled round in earth's diurnal course, / With rocks and stones and trees":

> I don't know somehow it seems sufficient
> to see and hear whatever coming and going is,
> losing the self to the victory
>   of stones and trees,
> of bending sandpit lakes, crescent
> round groves of dwarf pine:

"Whatever coming and going is" reverses normal syntactic expectations and allows us to hear a phrase doing double duty: Ammons wants to know whatever is coming and going in the sway of natural circumstance, but he also wants to know the nature of "coming and going," that peculiar, doubled abstraction the understanding of which might also ensure a self-understanding. Beneath the charm of Ammons's naturalistic poems lurks an impulse toward abstraction, in phrasing and in substance.

Ammons's poetry, again like Lucretius's, has as its two characteristic, excessive flaws the dullness of prosaicism and the airiness of abstraction. He is well aware of both, and both are the necessary risks of a scientific, discursive poet. He acknowledges his dilemma just as he begins to settle into smug contentment with the blocked and well-defined stanzaic units he has made for himself:

> how handsome the stanzas are
> beginning to look, open to the total acceptance, fracturing into
> delight, tugging down the broad sweep, thrashing it into
> particulars (within boundaries): diversity, however—as of
>
> the concrete—is not ever-pleasing: I've seen fair mounds
> of fine-stone at one end or the other of highway construction
> many times and been chiefly interested in the "hill": but
> abstraction is the bogey-boo of those incapable of it, while,
>
> merrily, every abstractor brings the concrete up fine: one,
> anyway, as Emerson says, does well what one settles down to:
> it's impossible anyone should know anything about the concrete
> who's never risen above it, above the myth of concretion
>
> in the first place:
>
> ("Extremes and Modulations," *CP*, 329)

Concrete furnishes the concrete example of "the concrete" upon which all abstractions, the hills that develop from fair mounds and then flatten out into roadbeds, are built; Ammons nods soberly toward the very "myth of concretion" that he has constructed and then rises above it, passing it by. The fun, as Robert Frost knew, is in how you say the thing.

Along with Merrill, Nemerov, and Auden, Ammons has realized the famous prophecy from the preface to the 1800 *Lyrical Ballads,* in which Wordsworth looks forward to the day when Science "shall be ready to put on, as it were, a form of flesh and blood," and "the Poet will lend his divine spirit to aid the transfiguration, and will become the Being thus produced, as a dear and genuine inmate of the household of man."[6] Ammons shares with Nemerov a concern with intricate ecological and mental dependencies and with philosophical debates between unity and multeity, or nominalism and realism. The fragile strength of webs and nets glimmers through the lines of both: there is a similar breezy alternation between colloquial speech (the kind that a real "flesh and blood" person might use) and exact scientific nomenclature. Both poets have a knack for self-irony that modifies the heaviness of the prophetic mantle they occasionally wear. Ammons even pays implicit homage to Nemerov's blue swallows, those birds whose tails are dipped into an invisible ink, which we attempt to read:

> O calligraphers, blue swallows, filigree the world
> with figure, bring the reductions, the snakes unwinding,
> the loops, tendrils, attachments, turn in necessity's precision,
> give us the highwire of the essential, the slippery concisions
>
> of tense attentions! go to look for the ocean currents and
> though they are always flowing there they are, right in place, if
> with seasonal leans and sways:
>
> ("Extremes and Modulations," *CP,* 334)

At least two habits separate the sophisticated city boy who turned to nature late and the countrified scientist, both of which are evinced by the homage above. The shape of Ammons's poems on the page, their visible presence riddled with colons that stand as marks of equation and subordination, connection and separation, is unlike the well-wrought wares of Nemerov.[7] More significant is Ammons's view of the world, borrowed from Emerson but more horrifying, a Lucretian vision of potential chaos sufficient to wither and overwhelm man's dreams and his very place. Ammons fears inundation from nature and language (compare "a word too much repeated falls out of being" with Nemerov's "Man's greatest intellectual pleasure is to repeat himself").

Ammons's encyclopedic lists, like Whitman's catalogues but often without their ringing enthusiasm, expose the dangers of openness. As in *Tape for the Turn of the Year,* Ammons's greatest failing is the tedium of indiscriminateness. Like John Ashbery and Allen Ginsberg, Ammons wants to get everything in: "I'll have to say everything / to take on the roundness and withdrawal of the deep dark: / less than total is a bucketful of radiant toys" ("Cut the Grass," *CP,* 288). Reading Ammons, one often wishes to tell him to get on with it, to avoid the simple detail ("ants ran over the whitish greenish reddish / plants"), the philosophical repetition ("the precise and necessary worked out of the random, reproducible, the handiwork redeemed from chance"), and the enthusiastic banality ("The wonderful workings of the world: wonderful, / wonderful"). But these are the price and correlative of the magical visions:

> earth brings to grief
> much in an hour that sang, leaped, swirled,
> yet keeps a round
>   quiet turning,

> beyond loss or gain,
> beyond concern for the separate reach.
>
> ("Saliences," *CP,* 155)

The simple monosyllables open up at "quiet turning," a little phrase whose ambiguity (is "quiet" a noun, "turning" a participle, or does the adjectival "quiet" modify the gerund "turning"?) assures at least a minor consolation in a world that ignores our individual fates. Even the delicately delivered half-rhymes ("brings," "grief," "leaped," "reach") that sound the common fate of human aspiration are poised within a framework of the alliterative *r*'s throughout the lines, which steady and mollify our existential fears.

Like Nemerov in his more fearful moments, Ammons is generally an antipastoral poet. For all his fascination with the details of the natural world, and despite his precise attempts to capture its dappled, Hopkinsesque grandeur, Ammons often seems alone and uncomfortable out of doors. In God's house there may be many mansions, but Ammons usually picks one without apparent walls. "I chose the wind to be delivered to": his desire to be part of a general Emersonian unity is countered by inevitable feelings of loss, as in "Gravelly Run," which denies animism and insists with Blake that there is no natural religion. Although the "cedars' gothic-clustered / spires could make / green religion in winter bones," one is not at home in this wintry scape. The mitigations of *could* are too soon made solid. Ammons marches to the verge of natural contentment and containment, and then backs away:

> no use to make any philosophies here:
> I see no
> god in the holly, hear no song from
> the snowbroken weeds: Hegel is not the winter
> yellow in the pines: the sunlight has never
> heard of trees: surrendered self among
> unwelcoming forms: stranger,
> hoist your burdens, get on down the road.
>
> (*CP,* 56)

The typical Ammons landscape, whether a south Jersey shoreline or an Ithaca mountain lake, is bare, wintry, or unappealing in conventional ways: gravel, gullies, roils, mud, and dunes attract him most. In them he is most, because least, at home.

This potential for a Lucretian alienation amid the fragmentary atomistic world produces the singular hallmark of Ammons's poetic diction—its poly-syllabic and abstract words laced with jaunty colloquialisms. Lucretius, too, was comfortable with the arcane, the archaic, and the manufactured many-sided word. A line like Ammons's "multifilamentous chains / knobbed with possibility" joins abstraction to physicality, and the tongue-twisting appeal of long words is cemented by a single Germanic monosyllable, [CP, 76]. The balance between polysyllabic perversity and commonness corresponds to the tension within the external world, which is threatened by "discontinuities" and "disoriented chains," "motions building and tearing down," entropy tearing at order. Potential terror threatens the mind everywhere:

> after these motions, these vectors,
> orders moving in and out of orders, collisions
> of order, dispersions, the grasp weakens,
>
> the mind whirls, short of the unifying
> reach, short of the heat
> to carry that forging:
> after the visions of these losses, the spent
> seer, delivered to wastage, risen
> into ribs, consigns knowledge to
> approximation, order to the vehicle
> of change, and fumbles blind in blunt innocence
> toward divine, terrible love.
>
> ("Prodigal," *CP,* 77)

The divine love, Ammons's approximation of Dante's love that moves the sun and the other stars, is terrible precisely because he so seldom apprehends it except through an occasional direct reference, as above, or through other "approximations" of knowledge and poetic assurance.

One of Ammons's recurrent themes is "the possibility of rule as the sum of rulelessness" ("Corsons Inlet"), but *only* the possibility. If Ammons had not existed his advocate Harold Bloom would have had to invent him as a contemporary model who swerves away from Shelley, Emerson, and Whitman by siphoning them through the instruments of Lucretius, his true precursor. Ammons combines the visionary chaos in Lucretius's atomic particles with the visionary, microcosmic auguries of Blake (who hated the atomism of Newton and Democritus). Blakean energy erupts in Ammons's exclamations—"errors of vision, errors of self-defense! / errors of wisdom, errors of desire!" ("Jungle Knot"); Blakean contentment in his reflective quietude— "the talk of giants, of ocean, moon, sun, of everything, / spoken in a dampened grain of sand" ("Expressions of Sea Level"). Like Nemerov on trees, Ammons on spiderwebs traces the imagery of philosophical possibility in the world ("Identity"): there can be neither total genetic coding, eliminating differences and possibilities for how a single spider builds its web, nor total freedom, destroying the patterns in the webs of a single species. The truth resides somewhere between the two. Even as Lucretius perceives harmony as a balance between the destructiveness of Mars and the creativity of *Venus genetrix,* with an accompanying balance in his hexameters between long, convoluted paragraphs and pithy epigrams, concise summaries, so does Ammons chart chaos and order with comparably varied language and by the alternation of longer poems with shorter ones.

The relentless account making in Ammons's ecological ledger is usually leavened by his wit; in this, at least, he is full of surprises. No one else but Emerson, but without the same touch, talks to mountains, and to no other living poet do mountains talk back. No one else would so wryly entitle a poem "If Anything Will Level With You, Water Will" (the title alone gives a new meaning to that other title, cited above, "Expressions of Sea Level"), and certainly no one else as prone to large, meandering forms has so keen an instinct for the miniature:

> The reeds give
> way to the
>
> wind and give
> the wind away
> ("Small Song," *CP,* 222)

Whittling away at, or riffling, his peripheries, and accumulating, shoveling, or amassing detail in the hope of either distilling an essence or accounting for everything, Ammons always arrives at "the bumfuzzlement—the impoverished diamond" in finding an arc line, inside which there is nothing and outside which there is also nothing. The amplitude of his language, its fluctuations between the abstract and the colloquial, demonstrates both that nature is inevitably alienating, since it will not accommodate itself to the categories of human longing, and that every walk is a new walk, a new linguistic and perceptual beginning. Vision is beyond him and so he settles for clear seeing. Unity is provisional; the odd assortment of linguistic shards corresponds to the discrete, radiant objects of fear and desire that surround him.

Ammons's longer poems (almost anything more than two pages qualifies as "long") provide object lessons in poetic organization—his own odd ways of effecting the transitions or turns that Wordsworth said constituted the major odal qualities of "Tintern Abbey"—and, more important, testify to his rightful place among today's pedagogically minded poets. At the start of this chapter I suggested that one cause of the genesis and the ongoing popularity of the philosophical-meditative poem since *The Prelude* has been the displacement of narrative and the machinery associated with epic by the self-conscious monologue of a mind contemplating the world (or "the dialogue of the mind with itself," in Matthew Arnold's famous phrase). Ammons's first book-length poem, *Tape for the Turn of the Year* (1965), begins with a timid discussion of its own possible subjects and, like *The Prelude,* glances at classical epic with a nostalgic sigh before pressing on to more immediate concerns:

> I wish I had a great
> story to tell: the
> words then
> could be quiet, as I'm
> trying to make them now—
> immersed in the play
> of events: but
> I can't tell a great
> story: if I were
> Odysseus, I couldn't
> survive
> pulling away from
> Lestrygonia, 11 of
> 12 ships lost
> with 11 crews:
>
> (*TTY*, 8–9)

Ammons gives two new twists to the standard trope of unreadiness or the unwillingness to follow conventional epic tales. First, he implies a qualitative difference between the "quiet" unself-conscious words of Homer and the noisier prattle of the modern poet wrestling vociferously with his own ineptitudes. And second, he equates his inability to tell Odysseus's story with his failure to be anything like the epic hero himself. Not only is he not Homer but, more important, he is not the Prince of Ithaka nor was meant to be. Ammons is canny enough to realize that his own poetry has, in fact, an Odyssean theme—the effort of a modern man to discover a cosmic home for himself—but he also knows that "it doesn't unwind / into sequence: it stands / still / and stirs / in itself like / boiling water / or hole of maggots." (There is a further Homeric note in that during the composition of the poem he is awaiting a letter from Ithaca, New York, with an invitation to teach at Cornell.) The centripetal reaching for home, an acceptance of and by the universe, is rendered anew by the literal twistings of this poem, composing itself by unrolling and recoiling: the poet places an adding machine tape into his typewriter and, as it unwinds from a wastebasket on the floor, he records upon it the sequence of days from 6 December to 10 January. "Unwinding and unwound, it / coils again on / the floor / into the unity of its conflicts." The wry philosopher gives a new meaning to the organicist's dream of the wedding of form and content: his poem literally twists as it metaphorically tropes upon its epic and meditative predecessors.

Whereas Wordsworth, or a contemporary like Robert Lowell, memorializes the past by revisiting and revising it, Ammons preserves the present moment by adhering to the random tentativeness of experience. *Tape* carries the diary to a foolishly logical inevitability, but in so doing it replaces narrative, epic or romantic, with a grab bag of vignettes and, increasingly as Ammons discovers his true metier, with minilectures on the nature of things. Both the form and the content share an organizing principle:

> if
> structure without life is
> meaningless, so is
>   life without structure:
> we're going to make a
> dense, tangled trellis so
>   lovely & complicated that
> every kind of variety will
> find a place in it or on
> it:
>
> (44–45)

So, in addition to commenting on the weather and other changing details of life in southern New Jersey, the poem remarks the process of its own composition. It is provisional (a term Ammons himself applies to his work) in both senses of that term: it seems temporary and of the moment, but it also provides the sustenance necessary for survival. In the small lines forced upon him by the size of his paper, Ammons discovers rapidity and richness:

> safe in these cages, I
> sing joys
> that never were
>   in any thorough jungle:
>
> but betimes & at times
> let me out of here:
> I will penetrate into the
> void
> & bring back
> nothingness
> to surround all these
>   shapes with!
>
> closing in
>   without closing:
>   running through
> without filling:
> opening out
>   with walls:
>
> (63–64)

The itemized responses to the world's details produce a double effect: a positive accumulation of things, and a negative, icy sense of the isolation of meaningless facts, Ammons's rendition of Pascal's silent eternal spaces:

                    so many people
        with bodies only:
                    so many bldgs with
                    mere addresses:
                    buses, subways, cabs,
        somebody everywhere:

        fragments: faces never to
        be seen again: isolations:

        poets, peeks of need,
                    loose cold
                    majesties,
        sizing heights, cut off
        from the common
        stabilizing ground of their
        admirers:

                            (129–30)

Lost in the city (he is recalling a visit to New York to attend a reception for
Mrs. William Carlos Williams), Ammons contemplates the anonymity of
contemporary life, a theme that recurs throughout this Odyssean poem in
counterpoint to the details of a life with wife, hearth, and home. Approaching the end of his poem, Ammons yearns for a surcease to weariness and
frustration. He has bludgeoned the reader, he says, "with every form of
emptiness," as the tape and time are running out as well as running
through.

    Ultimately the poem is a list of its own making. The poet reconciles
himself with what he has got and given: "I wrote about these / days / the way
life gave them." Ideally, however, he would

                be like a short poem:
                that's a fine way
                to be: a poem at a
        time: but all day
        life itself is bending,
        weaving, changing
        adapting, failing,
                    succeeding:

                            (204)

Taking his leave, Ammons thanks us with a reminder of his bequests: he has
given us, he says, "my emptiness," with no revelation (what Virginia Woolf
used to call the "cotton wool" of ordinary life).[8] From start to finish it has
been a long journey:

                I've given
        you my

emptiness: it may
not be unlike
    your emptiness:
    in voyages, there
    are wide reaches
    of water
    with no islands:

I've given you the
interstices: the
    space between
    electrons:
    I've given you
    the dull days
when turning & turning
revealed nothing:
I've given you the
sky,
uninterrupted by moon,
bird, or cloud:
    I've given
you long
uninteresting walks
so you could experience
vacancy:

old castles, carnivals,
ditchbanks,
    bridges, ponds
        steel mills,
        cities: so many
interesting tours:

the roll has lifted
from the floor &
our journey is done:
thank you
for coming: thank
you for coming along:

the sun's bright:
the wind rocks the
    naked trees:
    so long:
        (204–5)

Bequests, summations, the legacy of accomplishment—the poem lists things and blanknesses, the interesting and the uninteresting together, and the road remains open although the poem is closed, cluttered and curled, on the floor.

Tape is a nervously experimental poem. Ammons is at a literal and figurative turning point: waiting for his job letter from Cornell; concerned as he reaches the male climacteric with the possibility of sexual failure; frustrated with all kinds of "cagings." The short lines correspond to a relatively short attention span, and to an emotional giddiness as he seesaws between childish wonder at the workings of the universe and insomniac fears of annihilation. He acknowledges his plight as Odysseus's in a parenthetical aside: "(if you were / sitting on a / distant strand, / longing for home, / you'd have to / conjure up things to / occupy the time, / too)" (136), but by the end of the poem he comes to rely on the salvation of art as the only possible relief from his anxiety. The salvation is unsurprising. Ammons is philosophically old-fashioned, in spite of both his concern with contemporary scientific discoveries and his seemingly cranky stylistic novelty. His crackpot antisocial gruffness, his cracker-barrel stances, his "good ole boy" southern diction (when he feels like reverting to it) conceal but barely a true conservative. Like most genuine eccentrics, Ammons is ordinary, and the lessons he preaches are the perennial favorites.

This is especially true when one considers his poetics, a subject to which he gives more than passing attention in *Tape* and in his other long poems. He is an unabashed, Coleridgean organicist ("unity & diversity: how / to have both: must: / it's Coleridge's / definition of a poem" [185]), and a worshipper at the modernist shrine of art: "poetry has / one subject, impermanence, / which it presents / with as much permanence as possible" (145). But language claims us and deceives us, disappointing where we most demand its complicity. In the universe, boundaries push to the edge of entropy, and the making of boundaries deadens or at least inhibits freedom; Ammons asks for an endless proliferation of centers. Likewise, "definition is death: / the final box: / hermetic seal" (171). Ammons's self-fulfilling and self-cancelling statement demands our simultaneous assent and refusal. It is a performative utterance, with colons taking on the job of equalizing the surrounding elements, the coffin itself hemmed in by the opening proposition and the concluding label; but since "definition" is by definition deadly, our impulse is to spurn even as we accept it. Who would choose to murder to dissect? Moreover, the definition is a logical impossibility, given Ammons's other stated and implicit judgments about the nature of language and its relation to reality: "there's unity, / but objects don't / describe it: / nor do words" (167). Where does this leave us?

It leaves us with the naturalist-bard's constant effort to press his mind against an external reality of which he is a part but from which he receives ample resistance. Ammons loves to make statements, to perform acts of definition, which provoke the semi-assent that we can vouchsafe only to poetic truths. "Poetry" (he says) "has no use, except / this entertaining play: /

passion is / vulgar when not swept up / into the cool control / of syllables" (178–79). In a theory about the sway and genesis of poetry that comes half out of Shelley's "Defence" and half out of other statements of romantic primitivism, Ammons insists that language contains a fire, constantly renewable through the joint acts of concentration and inspiration. Not for nothing is the poem in part a lengthy address to a muse, who is herself a Lucretian *Venus genetrix* figure to the poet obsessed with the specifics as well as the general nature of all sexual behavior, beginning with his own. The old bard, Ammons boldly declares, depended only "on mead & word" (177) for his creations. For "mead" read external stimulus, for "word" read the conscious manipulation of his inherited language, capturing an isolated perception, relating it to others, transfiguring all into some unity, however transient, by the capture of "word & / image in surprise."

It is no novelty to think of poems as made things, although it seems somehow inconsistent with the apparent randomness of much of Ammons's work to revert to neoclassical rhetorical doctrine. (In *Sphere* he actually confesses that "I'm sick of good poems, all those little rondures / splendidly brought off, painted gourds on a shelf" [72]). Nevertheless, Ammons's conservatism inhabits his pages: "poetry is art & is / artificial: but it / realizes reality's / potentials" (177). The aphorism literally opens up (and opens one to) the linguistic truths it contains: *art*ificiality derives from art, just as *real*ity demands *real*ization. The "cool control of syllables" creates the poem's meaning through the resonant harmonies of its music. In *Tape* more than in the other long poems, these harmonies are varied and playful, owing largely to the visible presence of the poem as a continuous short-lined and swiftly moving congress. Ammons's obsessive horror of boundaries appears here playfully in his ability to "honor a going thing" (his opening command in his most Hopkinsesque poem, "Mechanism" [*CP,* 77–79]).

There is an additional twist to the causes and effects of Ammons's verbal shapings. In the visible fashioning of his poems one can literally *see* his playfulness, of course, but also his determination to produce a poetry that resembles (in this if in nothing else) that of e. e. cummings. Current literary wisdom holds that all literature gives prominence to the *lisible,* because language is inscriptive. No priority is granted to voice, transcendent reality, or "world" because language itself creates, commands, and precedes the meanings that it inscribes, submerging its "referents" more and more deeply into a scribal palimpsest. I do not wish to tackle, let alone refute, Derridean orthodoxies, any more than I would choose (as might seem appropriate to poets like Ammons and Nemerov) to open an older linguistic can of worms, the debate between realist and nominalist theories of language. Still, it seems legitimate to credit Ammons with having created a poetry, like that of William Carlos Williams, that is genuinely unhearable. Any spoken rendition, as by a poet at a public reading, limits the possible insinuations of the poem, in the way any performance of a dramatic text must choose among opposing emotional or intellectual possibilities within it. And it also falsifies the effect and meaning inscribed by the appearance of lines snaking across and down a page. Even the matter of Ammons's famous punctuation forces one to consider his poems as "more inscribed" than, say, those of Nemerov, or Ginsberg, or James Merrill (the sacred books virtually demand to be read aloud in order to distinguish among the considerable cast of human characters—who are of course themselves distinguished through the means of literary characters on the page, but this is another story).

Looking at the last page or so of *Tape,* quoted earlier, one can see that Ammons' poetry works visually, in spite of all his claims for bardic music and syllabic sounds. He gives "sky" as he says he gives it, untouched by the literal objects that succeed it. Its presentation on the page reminds one that what he has in fact offered is "sky" rather than sky; he thus proves the accuracy of poststructuralist definitions of language's representational capacity. He gives "interstices" on pages where what is inscribed is embedded within white vacancies. He gives "uninteresting walks," but then literally surrounds the objects of his interest ("old castles" etc.) with a re-appraisal ("so many interesting tours"). One might ask as well whether that list is meant to constitute the experience of vacancy that the colon before it seems to promise (the colon as an act of equalizing the two items it separates) or, to the contrary, the substance of "interesting tours" that it precedes. What lineation and punctuation suggest in this case (and I take this example as a model for what Ammons does on virtually every page) is the way the mind in the act of proposing, and the reader in the act of viewing, the inscribed data, can reinterpret the substance of experience. The mere listing of places, in other words, effects a reevaluation: what initially seemed uninteresting becomes, through the intervention of several colons, a magical mystery tour.

Even closure is both resolved and questioned, in part by the punctuation, in part by the repetitions in diction. Poet and poem complete their journeys simultaneously, the paper literally levitating and symbolically disappearing, at least from the writer's blindered view of his typewriter. In a poem that has dealt frankly with sexuality, one can't help hearing in "thank you / for coming" a suggestion of climactic release (especially because the poet addresses himself in swift succession, sometimes at the same time, to reader, muse, and poem), a grateful sigh to both the adding machine tape and the indulgent reader for their patience. And in the amplified repetition of a polite formula ("thank / you for coming along") one hears a reminder of the length of the poem (and of the "long / uninteresting walks" it and we have made) and a preparation for the terminal cliché that promises both a farewell and a weary sigh (as if Ammons is saying "it's been so long" since . . . we might imagine what). "So long, it's been good to know you," "vaya con dios"— Ammons allows readers to supply whatever handy truth leaps to mind. One summons a cliché, almost by definition, to render an arbitrary ending when nothing more seemly or powerful is available. Here the ending has been both arbitrary and foregone: the poem will stop when the raw material, the blank paper, is run through. But like this trite farewell (which will ring hollow to any reader of Ammons's most anthologized piece, "Corsons Inlet," the great contemporary "pedestrian" poem, ending with a summary tautology, "tomorrow a new walk is a new walk"), the final inscribed mark is neither a period nor an open-ended blank, but the favored colon, which promises and denies everything and therefore nothing.

A voice could never do justice to the multiple sounds implicit in that colon: the slightly raised pitch that suggests reluctance; the flatter, conclusive sound a period might enforce; a monotone for two mono-syllables that calls all tone, like all hypotheses and all philosophy, in doubt. By giving form to his own sexual, intellectual, and poetic anxieties, *Tape* confirms Ammons in his resolve and his capacity to write longer poems. Increasingly, in "Essay on Poetics" and *Sphere,* Ammons employs his conceptual machinery in the service of his interest in literature itself: for all his fascination with external nature, visible or not, Ammons has turned himself into a member of an imaginary philosophy department, lecturing his students not only on natural causes but also on aesthetics. Typically the two concerns coincide. Ammons gives a short run-through in "Summer Session" (much as a summer course miniaturizes and condenses materials from lengthier terms), a document of what he observes in the world of Ithaca, in and out of the classroom, and of what he must do to and for the undergraduates in his writing class. Planting and sowing; reading and writing; production and excrement: Ammons makes his usual pairings:

> in my yard's more wordage than I
> can read:
> the jaybird gives a shit:
> the earthworm hoe-split bleeds
> against a damp black clump:
>
> the problem is
> how
> to keep shape and flow:
>
> (*CP,* 248)

He accepts with generous irony the whole process of distilling or instilling knowledge, a process comparable to and at the same time vying against more basic hormonal urges:

> here are the 18-year-old
> seedbeds & the
> 19-year-old fertilizers:
> they have come for a summer session:
> knowledge is to be my insemination:

> I grant it to them as one grants flesh
> the large white needle:
> what shall I tell those who are
> nervous,
> too tender for needles, the
> splitting of iridescent tendons:
> oh I tell them nothing can realize
> them, nothing ruin them
> like the poundage of pure self:
> with my trivia
> I'll dispense dignity, a sense of office,
> formality they can define themselves against:
> the head is my sphere:
> I'll look significant as I deal with
> mere wires of light, ghosts of
> cells, working there.
>
> (*CP*, 260)

Like the physician in Lucretius, coating his bitter pill with honey, or like any other temperamentally didactic poet, Ammons *signifies* by looking significant, investing himself with pedagogic authority even though he realizes that the students naturally resist his lessons, which are, at best, only clever rehashings of clichés. Teaching "creative" writing, a fate of many contemporary poets, is a pleasant, harmless enough way of earning the necessary time to write one's own poetry: it also encourages Ammons to consider the organic nature of his own material. When referring to teaching, we naturally endow the verb with a double object, one direct and the other indirect: one teaches students, one teaches poetry. What Ammons increasingly considers is the how and why of teaching poems *to* students; in other words, a primary concern as he develops it in "Essay on Poetics" and *Sphere* is the nature and use of poetry, and its place in education.

His hypothesis comes literally as a conclusion to his various investigations: "the poem / is the symbolical representation of the ideal organization" (*CP*, 315). Ammons has said this before, but in "Essay on Poetics" (*CP*, 296–317) he arrives at his end after a meditative ramble through other notions borrowed and revised from romantic commonplaces. He acknowledges at the start a perceptual bias: "the way I think is / I think what I see: the designs are there: I use / words to draw them out—also because I can't / draw at all: I don't think: I see" (298). I take this as a thinly disguised version of Wordsworth's confession at the start of "Tintern Abbey": "I cannot paint what then I was," and a reliance upon the basic techniques of Lockean observation that the Romantic nature lyric confirmed for English poetry. As it happens, however, Ammons's homage to empiricism also contains the punning germ of his pedagogic concerns: "draw [i.e., lead] them out" is etymologically what educators do to their students.

He begins with a speculation about lyric as the mode that processes information, becoming a synthesis of bits, and as a shape that seems most to aspire to roundness ("all saliences bend to the same angle of / curve and curve becomes curve, one curve, the whole curve" [296]). As a model of assimilated wholeness, the lyric also permits "another wholeness, / another lyric, the same in structure" and Ammons is off and running with a contemplation of the "one/many" mechanism that everywhere enthralls him. An imaginary landscape with cows, copses, paths, and the possibilities of knowledge inferable through inscriptions of weather (a sort of "Tintern Abbey" of the mind) pulls him up short when he considers how the "blades of reason," stopping upon any word or any element in this imagined landscape, will destroy the whole picture:

> for language heightens by dismissing reality,
>
> the sheet of ice a salience controlling, like a symbol,
> level of abstraction, that has a hold on reality and suppresses
> it, though formed from it and supported by it:
>
> (298)

What Wordsworth, referring to the relation of mind and nature, terms in *The Prelude* an "ennobling interchange . . . of action from without and from within," Ammons here symbolizes through the image of an ice sheet pressing down against a medium resistant and supportive. Later he makes the same point, differently: "the reality under / words (and images) is too multiple for rational assessment and / that language moves by sailing over" (301). He updates Wallace Stevens's configuration of reality and imagination as interdependent, equal rivals, by picturing reality as that in which we find and admire infinite "centers." We wish, however, to inhabit the limits, peripheries, or high suasions that these centers infinitely lead us toward. We have the earth; we aspire to the place "where phenomena / lose their drift to the honey of eternity" (300). Such transcendent escape is as impossible linguistically as it is religiously.

The blades of reason will destroy an icy reality, that is, when we attempt to "define" by cutting through, by dividing, by clarifying through making boundaries. The way of analysis, as Ammons always allows, has its particular charms and failures; to these he adds the other way of "definition," the acceptance of "the multiplicity of synthesis," by seeing steadily and whole: "the grandest / clustering of aggregrates permits the finest definition" (302). Poetry works exactly in both ways together: "to heighten the crisis and pleasure of the reconciliation" it considers the etymology of "tree" (which comes from "true"), and it also considers the very elm in the backyard, the growth, shape, and progress of which Ammons then describes for several pages, reminding us of both Wordsworth's "single tree" in the Intimations ode, the one representing the many, and Yeats's chestnut tree, a whole greater than the aggregation of its constituent parts. Truth, Ammons decides, is a high assimilation of specific details and also a reduction, or distillation, of data into and by means of symbols. The point is to keep the mind open to variety:

> "no ideas but in
>
> things" can be read into alternatives—"no things but in ideas,"
> "no ideas but in ideas," and "no things but in things": one thing
> always to keep in mind is that there are a number of
>   possibilities:
>
> whatever sways forward implies a backward sway and the mind
>   must
> either go all the way around and come back or it must be
>   prepared
> to fall back and deal with the lost sway
>
> (308)

Having established the resilient openness of his mind, and having also exemplified his principles through references to external nature, in fact to his own backyard, Ammons is now ready for another appropriation, the poem's central definition-through-symbolizing. He pictures poetry as a landscape in a lengthy, charming fantasy that mingles details from Shelley's "Mont Blanc" with his own perverse undermining of the classically sanctioned generic ladder.

Ammons assembles a geography of poetic genres from the top down: "I would call the lyric high and hard," he announces, reminding us of his opening depiction of lyrics as atomic particles—hard, firm, lucid and, within the boundaries of form, reproducible. Like Shelley gazing at his Alpine landscape (and using it as a figure for his own "separate phantasy," wedding mind and matter), Ammons begins at the summit and declines. The poet who would historically ascend from eclogue to georgic to epic finds himself faced with a different perspective. One glances at the top, and

> then there is the rush,
>
> rattle, and flash of brooks, pyrotechnics that turn water white:
> poetry is magical there, full of verbal surprise and dashed
> astonishment: then, farther down, the broad dealing, the smooth
>
> fullness of the slow, wide river: there starts the show of genius
> . . . .
> genius, and
>
> the greatest poetry, is the sea, settled, contained
>
> (309)

From the "snowline melt of individual crystalline drops" to the brook, the river, and the "orientationless, but perfectly contained" ocean, Ammons's visionary eye moves like Shelley's scanning the Alpine scene from the inaccessible heights to the viewless ocean. The difference is that Ammons's application is a purely literary one: each of the genres (there seem to be four, of which only lyric is labeled) has its distinctive "uses and special joys." The content, Ammons assures us, updating Thales' cosmology, is a constant: water.

As water to the landscape, so (one infers) is language to poetry: the element of composition, always moving, always containable: "the verbal moves, depends there, or sinks into unfocused / irreality: ah, but when the mind is brought to silence, the / non-verbal, and the still, it's whole again to see how motion goes" (310). A poem, like a landscape, can be known and traveled around in: one can measure the motion of physical nature or of language and afterward, having reduced it to stillness, one can see it entirely. No poet has so neatly and correctly applied the Heisenberg laws of measurement, aligning them with Shelley's earlier effort to discover reality in the interacting processes of mind and nature. This application leads Ammons to one of his characteristically plain yet paradoxical definitions: "poems are arresting in two ways: they attract attention with / glistery astonishment and they hold it: stasis: they gather and / stay: the progression is from sound and motion to silence and / rest" (310).

Ammons is not producing a new theory of poetry but rather a startlingly old-fashioned (and therefore almost new) justification for teaching it. A poem is both part of our natural order and *like* part of the natural order: "poems, of human make, are / body images, organisms of this human organism." His figurations seem at times conventionally metaphorical (lyrics are like atoms, or hard, clear crystals), but at other times startlingly literal (the actual progress of a poem is from sound to silence). Working out of Coleridgean organicism and applying the sexual language for poetry that becomes common coin within his poems, Ammons returns to the most conventional defense for poetry: pleasure. He insists that the normal way of discussing poems— through history, meaning, and influence—is a pedantic evasion of the sexual processes that describe a poem's thrust and drive and the sexual pleasure ("superior amusement," he mockingly phrases it with his own parentheses) readers derive—actually? analogically?—from poems:

> organisms, I can tell you, build up under the thrust to

> joy and nothing else can lift them out of the miry circumstance:
> and poems are pure joy, however divisionally they sway with
>   grief:
> the way to joy is integration's delivery of the complete lode:
>   (313)

Poems present themselves as symbols of integration, harmony, and the relationship between "high levels of oneness and the / numerous subordinations
and divisions of diversity" (315). Ammons's conclusion, delivered with firm,
even rhythms that seem virtually prosaic and that follow two excerpts from
biology texts about the cooperative nature of matter within all ecosystems,
asserts the helpfulness of poems in strengthening the mind, allowing it to
organize its own energy and letting "the controlled / flows occur" (an example, here, of literal influencing) within the perceiving subject.

Ammons strikes, at last, a civic note, one that has no real source, I think,
in either his Romantic or his native American forebears. Poetry produces
patriotism:

> I used to wonder
> why, when they are so little met and understood, poems are
>   taught
> in schools: they are taught because they are convenient
>   examples
>
> of the supreme functioning of one and many in an organization
>   of
> cooperation and subordination: young minds, if they are to
>   "take
> their place in society" need to learn patience—that oneness is
>
> not useful when easily derived, that manyness is not truthful
>   when
> thinly selective—assent, that the part can, while insisting on
> its own identity, contribute to the whole, that the whole can
>
> sustain and give meaning to the part: and when these things
> are beautifully—that is, well—done, pleasure is a bonus
> truth-functioning allows: that is why art is valuable:
>
> (315)

And so from analogies with biology and geology, from the observation of
domestic detail and the invention of a figurative landscape, Ammons lands
squarely not just in his own backyard (he has composed the poem, he says, to
help him get through a snowstorm) but in his own nation. The transcendental and organic dimensions of poetry have been seen before—they are cultural
commonplaces by now—but Ammons's political version of natural harmony,
although it derives from a Lucretian image of a cosmos in which politicized if
not fully human particles engage in mutual combat and support, has a surprising lesson to teach all Americans living in an active commonwealth.

Like trees, children suffer and profit from both nature (their genetic
code) and nurture (the effects of environment, individual circumstance, and
choice) to produce their distinctive destinies. What children, unlike the trees

they might observe, can learn is patience, a lesson necessary for individual and political health. Patience, a reader of Ammons would surely argue, is also the virtue necessary for reading his poems, especially the long, meandering ones that circle around and back to favored spots, ideas, or metaphors, repeating, amplifying, proving, testing, including the smallest banalities of life and diction within the confines provided by a text. But at the same time, those banalities, along with deeper and more "salient" passages, create that very text that confines and (to speak as Ammons might) liberates them to flow so easily. Ammons has distinctly, if unintentionally, united the civic-mindedness of Allen Ginsberg or of the more measured, Horatian Robert Pinsky, with the all-inclusiveness of Frank O'Hara and his "I do this, I do that" poems. His worst sin, like O'Hara's and Ginsberg's, is non-exclusion, but every so often the apparent wandering points to the rhyming potential, actual or implicit, of words and the things they represent (a trait learned from Hopkins and shared with the English poet Charles Tomlinson): "I've been at this / poem or prose-poem or versification or diversification for three / or four days," he says at one point in "Extremes and Modulations," and even the very pairings invite us to hear or see "prose-poem" as both the opposite of "poem" and its result, coming as it does syntactically out of a prior state. Likewise, "diversification" is merely an extension of "versification" (a 1975 volume is entitled *Diversifications;* having made his pun in an earlier context, Ammons went on to profit from it), the same thing but longer and more varied, adding a syllable but rendering a rhyme, proving that poetry allows us to see more vividly than anything else the collusion of the one and the many.

Sphere, Ammons's 1974 Lucretian epic, embodies all the mental and stylistic habits of the poems discussed here, and might provoke the same kind of response that *The Excursion* did in Coleridge. Beginning with a nod in the direction of *De Rerum Natura,* the poem makes a simple statement: "The sexual basis of all things rare is really apparent." Its main subject, however, turns out not to be sexuality but the way sexual language allows us to understand the "intermingling of parts," a version of the standard one-many dilemma. Although his principles of organization are different from James Merrill's, Ammons takes as his major concern an idea that is central to *The Changing Light of Sandover* as well: shapeliness, centers, and boundaries are all versions of limited visions. When trying to encounter "the highest god," one is thwarted; indeed, one may never meet this "essence out of essence, motion without motion," which exists only peripherally, although one can catch occasional glimmers of it. The real subject of *Sphere* (as well as its shape) is Ammons's attempts to catch those fleeting glimpses—just as Merrill's, in the sacred books, is the effort to hear the sacred voices, channeled through a hokey medium.

The biological apparatus in *Sphere* allows Ammons to continue his earlier interest in education, specifically the role of poetry in education, throughout this various poem. In the fifteenth and sixteenth sections he develops an elaborate analogy (another reminder of his debt to the Shelley of "Mont Blanc") between our minds and anthologies of words ("good sayings") that are the genes, and poems and stories that are the chromosomes: "gene pool, word hoard." Critic and teacher examine and foster the relationship between the capacious anthology and possible additions, always checking to see whether the "new thing" might find an attachment in and with the anthology, an energy source that would flow between it and the store already accumulated. If not, "it dies, withered away from the configuration of the people: / but if it lives, critic and teacher show it to the / young, unfold its meaning, fix its roots and extend its reach" (17). The teacher now becomes a husbandman. Ammons cannot resist the delicious duplicity of "roots" to relate a literary scholar's activity to a gardener's. With the poet and critic, the teacher performs a function at once natural and civil:

> the anthology is the moving, changing definition of the
> imaginative life of the people, the repository and source,
> genetic: the critic and teacher protect and reveal the source
>
> and watch over the freedom of becomings there: the artist
> stands freely into advancings: critic and teacher choose, shape,
> and transmit: all three need the widest opening to chance
>
> and possibility, so perceptions that might grow into currents
> of mind can find their way: all three are complete men,
> centralists and peripheralists who, making, move and stay:
>
> (17–18)

Although the distinction between critic and teacher is arbitrary and never explained, it fits into Ammons's aesthetic and pedagogic schemes to imagine a triumvirate of guardians for his updated version of Yeats's "book of the people" who will encourage its growth and spread its currents: a trio who inhabit comfortably both the centers (where stability, coding, and knowledge reside) and the peripheries (the outlands, the saliences, the spaces of widest uncertainty) of the imagined garden within the literary, genetic, or cosmic sphere. The balance between one and many, or center and arc, is neatly epitomized in the last line above with its dramatic enacting of a definition through the syntax and sounds of its language: "move and stay" are possible only by virtue of "making," a word that literally combines them through rhyme—as if Ammons wants to press upon readers the way *making* combines the consonant of "moving" with the long vowel of "staying" and thus resolves the apparent paradox of the phrase.

Such resolution of oppositions is the consistent scheme as well as the subject of *Sphere.* As always, Ammons is tempted by the clarities of definitions, whether those of others or of his own making, but always backs away from them, understanding their limiting and potentially dangerous effects.

As teacher and poet himself, he must both move and stay; one demonstration is the organization of the poem into 155 twelve-line stanzaic units, ongoing but never fully stopped or resolved until the concluding period. An obsession with division and openness is, I think, another, far from fortuitous, inheritance from Wordsworth and Lucretius, two didactic forebears. Observing a wintry landscape, Ammons makes of the image of pheasants walking out of snow thickets into and between a "white paling fence" an occasion to contemplate a favorite problem:

> it's hard to draw a line, the careful,
> arrogant, arbitrary imposition, the divider that blocks off
> and sets apart, the arising of difference and distinction:
>
> the discrete a bolus of slowed flux, a locus of depressed
> reaction rates, a boned and fibered replication: slowed
> but not stopped (heightened within its slows):
>
> (24)

Such joint mingling and separation derives, within the Romantic tradition, from the opening landscape in "Tintern Abbey," in which Wordsworth paints a picture of a landscape plotted and divided by "hedgerows," which he then modifies by denying them ("hardly hedgerows, / Little lines of sportive wood run wild"), and in which "one green hue" colors details that are otherwise separate. In other words, the unity and multeity of a visible scene give philosophical poets ample inspiration to make comparable divisions and unifications while recollecting their own lives. Elizabeth Bishop makes the same sort of gesture in "At the Fishhouses," her updating of "Tintern Abbey," but we can see the differences between her more reticent poetic temperament (one less prone to the kind of didacticism treated in these pages) and a more aggressively discursive one by comparing Ammons's continual leaping into a scene for philosophical applications and Bishop's reluctance to do more than imply her conclusions. That Wordsworth himself may have inherited his wish to picture a landscape both unified and distinctive from Lucretius, as well as from the more immediate precedents of eighteenth-century locodescriptive verse, only increases the possibility for establishing bonds among the three poets. In fact, in *A Guide through the District of the Lakes,* Wordsworth commends a passage in Lucretius as evidence that poetry captures better than nature itself the beauty of vines and olive trees; it is a passage that might remind us, once we have made the necessary arboreal adjustments, of the opening lines of "Tintern Abbey": "a grey-green belt of olives might run between the vineyards to mark the boundaries, stretching forth over hills and valleys and plains; just as now you see the whole place mapped out with various charms, laid out and intersected with sweet fruit-trees, and fenced around with fruitful shrubs" (*De Rerum Natura,* 5.1370–78).

It may be "hard to draw a line," but that is what teachers, whether poets or critics, love and have to do. All definition is a form of closure, and since "closure ends all shows, the plain strict and the frowsy / brilliant" (#42), one can understand the risk involved in any attempt, and a poet's reluctance to commit himself. But, proceeding *pedetemptim,* "step by step" (Lucretius's self-evaluation), Ammons everywhere complements his reluctance to dash to peripheries with his sometimes resigned, sometimes daring, realization that he must, even if like a pedestrian, hazard his definitions: "we might as well make as much distinction / here as we can." To keep possibility open, his turnings often include a variation on a dialectic habit, inherited from Romanticism's appropriation of Socratic dialogue. In stanzas 54–55, one sees in miniature Ammons's technique, here applied to a common fixation:

> how to make the essential fashionable is the
> problem without promoting boredom for there is little variation
> day to day in the essential and, worse, when the fashionable
>
> hangs on it loses the quality of the fashionable: of course
> we are sure that the fashionable relates only peripherally
> to the essential so that it is nearly certain that to be
>
> fashionable is not to be essential: there is the aspect,
> though, of change that it is constant so that always to be
> fashionable is to participate in the lasting: problems
>
> problems: the essential without specification is boring
> and specification without the essential is: both ways out
> leaves us divided but so does neither way: unless—and here
>
> is the whole possibility—both essential and fashionable can
> be surrounded in a specified radial essential, which is difficult:
>
> (34–35)

Having built an intellectual structure, which identifies two logical possibilities (call them *A* and *B*), Ammons neatly summarizes and synthesizes the opposing elements (since change is constant, "to be fashionable is to participate in the lasting"). Such dialectic maneuvering, as always in Ammons, resolves nothing in itself, but occasions still further reflective possibilities. He resumes his stance, taking two possibilities (now *A* stands for the boredom of "the essential without specification" and *B* for the boredom of "specification without the essential," phrases whose very resemblance suggests a possible exit from logical difficulties), and somewhat more gently arriving at a new solution—admittedly a "difficult" one—that both "essential" and "fashionable" be included in a tertium quid, which he inelegantly labels the "specified radial essential."

Ammons inherited his dilemma from the American and British Romantics: it has a double edge, linguistic and religious. When attempting to allow a single item or image to stand for an entire class, one is overinvesting its boundaries. This is the sin (Ammons does not say this, but it is clear) of synecdoche and metonymy. This is, however understandably, asking the item to "do" a lot of work. But if one moves beyond the level of paradigm to that of larger classes, then "matter is a mere seed / afloat in radiance," and the individual is lost. This is the sin of universal predication. Just as one item standing for all loses its individual charge and falls beneath its own weight, so an abstraction that ignores boundaries immerses particulars within the total radiance. The religious application of the problem deals of course with the identity of the Most High, whatever one chooses to call it, which both comprehends and obliterates distinct particularities, the atomies of existence. Here is where poems come in: all movement themselves, they also move us, to a conclusion of silence (from sound) and stasis (from their joint activity with us): "the purpose of the motion of a poem is to bring the focused, / awakened mind to no-motion" (40).

Poets, then, like the poems they have created, push out diversely into linguistic and experiential realms, assimilating greater degrees of the unexpected into their expectations, and adjusting their expectations to shadings of tone and meaning. Ammons's image, borrowed jointly from Shelley and Wordsworth, returns to the poet a quasi-natural function in his pedagogic efforts:

> if raindrops are words, the poet is the cloud whose
> gathering and withholding overspills generously and unmissed
> from a great keeping: (depression, low pressure area): the
>
> false poet is a white wisp that tries to wrest itself into
> a storm: but the true storm moseys on with easy destructions
> like afterthoughts: how else but by greatness can the huge
>
> presence exist between the gifty showers, twists and blow-outs:
>
> (43)

And on he goes, detailing the short nonsense poem he has just composed en route from Northfield, everywhere spreading his own largesse, a poetic consciousness working from a center and relocating that center as his forces gather and spill themselves beneficently onto the page. A separate study might describe the ramifying, associative structures throughout Ammons's work, the most thoroughgoing example in contemporary poetry of the way an older empiricism (of Locke and Wordsworth) has been joined, via William James's "stream of consciousness," to the different kind of associationism that might be called Freudian. Suffice it here to say that the poem develops within itself a rhythm that allows passages of abstract definition to be followed by

others of specific detail, ideas giving over to daily life, definitions to enact-
ments, theory to application. Although Ammons says at one point that "the
work of the staying mind is to burn up or dissolve the day's / images" (53), he
also proves that the mind never stays anywhere for long. "Nothing shaped
stays and shapelessness is dwellingless" (58), so where can one dwell? Everywhere and nowhere at once. Ammons *thinks* about travel, like Wallace
Stevens, another famous stay-at-home, and unlike Elizabeth Bishop, who
both questions it and participates in it, but for him the act of focusing the
mind suffices, because what really interests him is the relation between theory, or rigid abstraction, and practical affairs. Since he acknowledges a basic
temperamental difference between himself and his obvious American epic
forebear ("I am not a whit manic / to roam the globe"), he ends up often
sounding like a less precious Stevens, substituting for Stevens's opulence the
rich linguistic arcana of science itself. "Can we make a home of motion" (76)
is his large question, but since he refuses question marks, it is also a statement. We can.

One reason that we can is Ammons's serious, and virtually literal, acceptance of Whitman's famous pronouncement that "the United States themselves are essentially the greatest poem." Ammons explores the philosophical
and poetic applications of this metaphor. Since a poem by definition is the
clearest example of the one-many problem, incorporating literally (i.e., visibly) multiple parts and saliences within the formal limits imposed by shape
and page, it follows that one can be both at home and traveling in poetry
(cf. Keats's "On First Looking into Chapman's Homer," Dickinson's "There is
no frigate like a book"), *and,* by virtue of an American birthright, that one
can apply the principles of poetic organization to a political entity:

> I can't understand my readers:
> they complain of my abstractions as if the United States of
>   America
> were a form of vanity: they ask why I'm so big on the
>
> one:many problem, they never saw one: my readers: what do
>   they
> expect from a man born and raised in a country whose motto is
>   E
> *plurishus* [sic] *unum:* I'm just, like Whitman, trying to keep things
> half straight about my country: . . .
>   .   .   .   .
>   my country: can't cease from its
> sizzling rufflings to move into my "motions" and "stayings":
>
> when I identify my self, my work, and my country, you may
> think I've finally got the grandeurs: but to test the center
> you have to go all the way both ways: from the littlest

> to the biggest: I didn't mean to talk about my poem but
> to tell others how to be poets . . .
>
> (65–66)

And he continues his lessons with a "How-To-Write-A-Poem": as in learning to ride a horse or a bicycle, one's got to fall off a few times and learn the balance between forces before ultimately sailing right along. The jaunty, confident side of Ammons's temper, the obverse of the dark, brooding, fearful side, comes out in these playful renditions of advice giving: mind—his own, that of his readers, and the greater Emersonian oversoul (when he is in a mood to credit that one)—resembles the U.S., and both resemble a (or *the*) poem, the one under construction before one's eyes. Everyone can be a poet in a democracy, especially one that counts itself a melting pot. The unabashedly Romantic conception of mind and of poetry as congregations of conflicting and harmonizing forces preoccupies Ammons on virtually every page. He shares, however, the political application of this figuration with Ginsberg and Whitman, and surprisingly with Robert Pinsky, whose *An Explanation of America* begins with the identical premise that one may lay the nation open to the grandest possible *explication de texte*.

The conclusion of the poem (roughly its last twenty-three sections) vigorously repeats and readjusts the moods, tones, and messages of the whole: the hopeful and the despairing, the confident and the weary, the abstract and the fastidious sides of Ammons' personality have one final moment in which to express themselves. He starts this stretto of the piece with a question that affirms his debts to both American populism and Wallace Stevens: "what are my hopes: / it's hard to tell what an abstract poet wants" (69). He is abstract insofar as he is concerned with abstractions and because by this point he has identified himself with *the* American poet as a composite of all the single ones: *e pluribus poetis unus*. His answers to his own self-questioning summarize his natural, ecological, and cosmic concerns:

> my hopes
>
> are for a context in which the rosy can keep its edges out of
> frost: my hopes are for a broad sanction that gives range
> to life, for the shining image of nothingness within which
>
> schools of images can swim contained and askelter: my hopes
> are that the knots of misery, depression, and disease can
> unwind into abundant resurgences:
>
> (69)

Such attention contains its own undoing, or at least its requisite dangers. Praying too much, one might forget to shop for dinner, Ammons thinks; likewise, "if the abstract poem goes out and never / comes back, weaves the highest plume of mind beyond us," it acquires a bitter, deathly spirit: "we have so many ways to go wrong / and so often go wrong" Ammons confesses, that abstraction, turning to airiness, calls us *from* the things of this world (rather than, in Richard Wilbur's famous phrase about love, calling us *to* them), creates our gods and enables us to "float in plenitude rather than in / starved definition."9 As Merrill does in the sacred books, Ammons imagines order and chaos a twinned configuration, like the visible and the invisible, the coherent and the incoherent. The question remains: to which will he pledge his primary allegiance?

Physical facts and his own occasional darker moods tend him toward the periphery, the outer darkness where light is finally defeated; Ammons's dreams of reenacting a Dantean journey through the stars are thwarted by entropy and his own desert spaces; science and autobiography conspire:

> I have dreamed of a stroll-through, the
> stars in a close-woven, showering bedazzlement, though
> diamond- or ruby-cool, in which I contemplated the universe
>
> at length: apparently, now, such dreams, foolish anyway,
> must be abandoned and the long, empty, freezing gulfs of
> darkness must take their place: come to think of it, though,
>
> I'm not unfamiliar with such gulfs, even from childhood, when
> the younger brother sickened and then moved no more: and
> ahead lies a gulf light even from slow stars can never penetrate,
>
> a dimension so endless not even the universal scale suits it:
> the wise advice, don't get beyond yourself into foolish
>   largeness,
> when at my step is a largeness the universe lies within:
>
> (72–73)

On the one hand he turns aside from the well-made poems, those that take no risks and prefer the potential deadness of small completions to the spaciousness of astronomical assimilations; on the other, he understands that pioneering journeys to the periphery end in a complementary deadness, a dispersal rather than a petrifaction. What is a poet to do? Ammons goes over in his mind the details of another habitual day, and significantly ends his poem with a double gesture: a lecture, a piece of advice to an importuning student ("another youth anxious for fame and sorry he doesn't / have it") and a vast, suicidal release that responds to the gesture of Shelley at the end of "Adonais," a precursive poem (though without the epic and scientific apparatus of *Sphere*) that also ends with a minilecture on the proper way to achieve immortality.

Death is the one event for which no preparation is possible, no repetition likely. (It is the opposite of the way one sexual experience prepares one for the next.) Nowhere does Ammons paint a bleaker picture of the vanity of human wishes and the little profit that worldly experience can bring:

> who knows
> whether in the middle years, after the flashing passions
> seem less like fountains and more like pools of spent flood
>
> metal, one may not keep on partly because of that black sucker
> at the end, mysterious and shiny: my skull, my own skull
> (and yours) is to be enclosed—earpits, eye sockets, dangled-
>   open
>
> mouth—with soil, is to lie alone without comfort through
> centuries and centuries, face (if any) up, as if anticipating
> the return of the dream that will be only the arrival of
>
> the nova: how sluggish consciousness, when in death
> the nova is a wink away!
>
> (74–75)

By such grim standards, the epic adventures of Whitman will serve not a jot: Ammons would agree with Horace that "caelum, non animum, mutant qui trans mare currunt" ("those who fly across the sea change their skies, not their souls"). Ammons prefers for himself a Horatian sufficiency: "I dream of a clean-wood / shack, a sunny pine trunk, a pond, and an independent income: / if light warms a piney hill, it does nothing better at the / farthest sweep of known space." Or so speaks one side of his mind. Suddenly, however, and subtly, he begins a new tack, specifically a nautical one. "We move and see but see mostly the swim of / motion" he announces in stanza 146 (75). Such language accords with his own flux and the images for it, but as he contemplates motion within the swim of time, he begins to consider the human attempt to balance opposing forces (one is always forced to go below and check one's metaphorical ballast) and he does so with an increasingly clarified image from sailing:

> a wind may come up subtle or sudden and persist and you may
>
> have to go down and change the ballast, only to find when the
> wind does cease that uprightness in an imbalance is imbalance:
>
> (76)

And once again the opposing forces of the universe place us in their midst, buoyantly supporting us, both as individuals and as a collective mass; "we are alone in a sea," he asserts in one of his most beautiful and daring stanzas, that

> shows itself nowhere in a falling surf but if it does not
> go on forever folds back into a further motion of itself:
> the plenitude of nothingness! planets seeds in a coronal

> weaving so scant the fabric is the cloth of nakedness:
> Pluto our very distant friend skims a gulf so fine and far
> millions and thousands of millions of years mean little to—
>
> how far lost we are, if saving is anywhere else: but light,
> from any distance or point we've met it, shines with a similar
> summation, margin affirmational, so we can see edges to the
>
> black roils in the central radiances, galaxies colliding in
> million-year meetings, others sprung loose into spiral
> unwindings: fire, cold space, black concentration:
>
> (77)

From "the plenitude of nothingness" and "the cloth of nakedness" Ammons receives energizing excitement rather than immobilizing fears. Adjusting his own intellectual and emotional balance to a cosmic and marine harmony of the tidal sways in which he locates his poetry, he brings the poem to its end, the sphere of its own motion having been amply clarified by an earlier image: "this poem is an elongated cylinder / designed to probe feeling, recognition, and realization, / to plunder the whoozies of the world sensationally and cause / to come to bear what is and may be" (75).

The effort to consolidate polar opposites finds an analogue in Ammons's political aspirations, as both an application and a variant of his Lucretian vision. Steering a middle course between "differences" and "the common tide of feelings," he hopes for the "specific congruence of form and / matter" in the creation of

> a united, capable poem, a united, capable mind, a united
>   capable
> nation, and a united nations! capable, flexible, yielding,
> accommodating, seeking the good of all in the good of each:
>
> (79)

Ammons's political slogans, his Fourth of July exclamations, are less original than his coupling of scientific language to his central metaphoric purposes, but they are no less a part of his didactic program, just as Whitman's rancorous mumblings are the inevitable result and also the cause of his democratic vistas. His ending, which is also the new beginning to which "Corsons Inlet" had testified at its conclusion, embodies what he had earlier called his "magnum hokum" in a uniquely American image, which itself metamorphoses out of and then back into the spiritual bark with which Shelley alights to follow the beckoning light of Keats at the end of "Adonais":

> to float the orb or suggest the orb is floating: and, with the
> mind thereto attached, to float free: the orb floats, a bluegreen
> wonder: so to touch the structures as to free them into rafts

that reveal the tide: many rafts to ride and the tides make a
place to go: let's go and regard the structures, the six-starred
easter-lily, the beans feeling up the stakes: we're gliding: we

are gliding: ask the astronomer, if you don't believe it: but
motion as a summary of time and space is gliding us: for a
    while,
we may ride such forces: then, we must get off: but now this

beats any amusement park by the shore: our Ferris wheel, what
    a
wheel: our roller coaster, what mathematics of stoop and climb:
    sew
my name on my cap: we're clear: we're ourselves: we're sailing.
                                        (79)

The stanza floats between the vagueness of infinitive phrases, which seem to
extend from the preceding stanzas without truly clarifying them (but which
may actually be, retrospectively, infinitives of result: "in order to float the orb
. . . let's go and regard the structures") and the assurances of present tense
declaration ("we're gliding . . . we're sailing"). Likewise, the globe of the preceding stanza ("a united nations") turns into the floating orb of this one,
which itself then metamorphoses into the floating but less spheroid rafts that
he sets adrift.

    Ammons' childlike wonder ("we *are* gliding") finds a temporary justifica-
tion in external authority ("ask the astronomer if you don't believe it"), but
since everything in this stanza seems provisional, one tone or image quickly
supplanting another, we cannot be surprised that the kid in him takes over
for a moment as it would in any adult reliving childhood pleasures and fears
in an amusement park. The stanza undergoes so many metamorphoses that
the dizzying movements of the Ferris wheel ride have their stylistic implications for our own experience. The orb, for example, seems initially to be the
product of our moving it, but it then floats freely, "with the / mind thereto
attached." Just as soon as rafts have become land structures, lilies, or bean
poles, Ammons returns us to wavy gliding motions, as if preparing us
metaphorically with a proof of his succeeding hypotheses that motion summarizes space and time together, thereby enabling such deft transferences,
and that space is gliding us, rather in the way that the mind, at the start of
the stanza, was implicitly floating the imagined orb. But as soon as he
acknowledges that motion glides us, he reverses if only for a moment his
grammatical and cosmological priorities by suggesting that "we may ride
such forces." The final roller coaster ride embodies all of the jumpy peri-
pateias that this stanza, the poem in miniature, has been making. The "this"
of the penultimate tercet reminds us that what we are riding at last is a mental roller coaster not in any littoral (or literal) amusement park but in a Coney

Island of the mind. The final setting out exists only because the poet has subsumed his image, at last, within the clear dimensions of an imagined, internalized geography. It is appropriate that the poem comes to its one and only full stop on an assertion of perpetual motion. Even the choice of the progressive present tense ("we're sailing") uplifts us from temporality into a virtually infinite condition just at the moment when we might long for stillness. The period—itself an inscribed sphere—leaves us in full, giddy possession of Ammons's circularities. In his ending he demonstrates his earlier question/assertion: he *has* made a home of motion.

Notes

1.   E. L. Griggs, ed., *The Collected Letters of Samuel Taylor Coleridge* (Oxford: Oxford University Press, 1959), 4:969.

2.   George Santayana, *Three Philosophical Poets* (Cambridge, Mass.: Harvard University Press, 1944), 14, 25. I have dealt with the problems of philosophical poetry in "Some Lucretian Elements in Wordsworth," *Comparative Literature* 37 (1985): 27–50.

3.   Helen Vendler, *Part of Nature, Part of Us* (Cambridge, Mass.: Harvard University Press, 1980), 330.

4.   Harold Bloom, "A. R. Ammons: the Breaking of the Vessels," in *The Ringers in the Tower* (Chicago: University of Chicago Press, 1971), 257–90. Bloom reads the poetry chronologically, detecting a break after "Corsons Inlet," which abandons the hope for transcendence.

5.   *Collected Poems 1951–1971* (New York: W. W. Norton, 1972), 146, hereafter cited as *CP.* Other poems are from *Tape for the Turn of the Year* (New York: W. W. Norton, 1965), hereafter *TTY,* and *Sphere: The Form of a Motion* (New York: W. W. Norton, 1972).

6.   *The Prose Works of William Wordsworth,* ed. W.J.B. Owen and Jane Worthington Smyser (Oxford: Clarendon Press, 1974), 1: 141.

7.   In his latest book, *Sumerian Vistas* (New York: W. W. Norton, 1987), Ammons uses very few colons. In the two long poems, "The Ridge Farm" and "Tombstones," each section ends punctuationless, except the last section of the former, which has a period. The remaining, short lyrics in the book all end with periods. Ammons's punctuation implies his ideas about the differences between long and short poems.

8.   Virginia Woolf, *Moments of Being: Unpublished Autobiographical Writings,* ed. Jeanne Schulkind (New York: Harcourt Brace Jovanovich, 1976), 70–71.

9.   Richard Wilbur, *The Poems of Richard Wilbur* (New York: Harcourt, Brace & World, 1963), 65. Wilbur's poems from the fifties and sixties, like "Love Calls Us to the Things of This World," embody the various traits that Robert von Hallberg associates with the predominant "suburban" temperament of our major poets, a modification and extension of the opulent side of Wallace Stevens.

Symbol Plural:
the Later Long Poems of A. R. Ammons

CARY WOLFE

For years now, Ammons criticism has in general followed Harold Bloom's reading of the poet out of the American transcendental—Bloom's "Emersonian"—tradition. Bloom's readings have been instructive, often exciting (and make for a compelling version of literary history); his work on Ammons and on other contemporary poets (Strand and Merwin come to mind) constitutes a fascinating thematics of what it is to be an American poet. In terms of poetics, however—and here I mean how a given poet *constitutes* his subject—Ammons needs to be examined in light of his highly ambivalent relationship with those writers who provided the poetic machinery for the transcendentalists in the first place—I refer, of course, to the English romantics.[1] Here, I will replace Bloom's "Emerson" with the Coleridgean "symbol" and the romantic notion of the organic—though I hope to avoid what Frank Lentricchia has called the Bloomian "spirit of revenge."[2] Rather, I want to argue that the romantic symbol must, for a poet like Ammons, be dealt with in the realm of poetics in much the same way that Emersonianism must be confronted as a kind of thematic bedrock for later American poets.[3] The fact that Ammons's later poetry is highly discursive—I mean this in relative terms, as compared with, say, the work of James Wright—makes this sort of approach all the more imperative for Ammons criticism.[4] Furthermore, I want to argue that Ammons's significant modification of romantic poetics constitutes a re-situating of the ideological role of poetic writing and of the "aesthetic" as traditionally conceived.[5]

Bloom has dubbed Ammons "a poet of the Romantic Sublime" ("Vessels" 194), yet in a fundamental sense Ammons's sublime is both postromantic and post-Emersonian; for this one-time biologist, oneness with nature is a brute (and brutal) fact, a "one-sided extension" ("Essay" 42)—as much a curse as a blessing—which is (in Emersonian terms) finally not a

Originally published in *Contemporary Literature* 30:1 (Spring 1989): 78–94. Reprinted by permission.

fullness but an emptiness, a lack of common ontological ground that makes knowledge possible.

Part of the reason Ammons is able to embrace nature (sometimes in terror) while at the same time avoiding the appropriations of the romantics is that from the "Essay on Poetics" on he adopts a different model of nature, one fundamentally different from the talking wind and mountains of the early poems. Drawing his new model from cybernetics, Ammons emphasizes the becoming, rather than the Being, of nature—the processes rather than the fixity of a *logos* which drives them (Buell 210–11). It is important to note just how strong the connection is between the nature of the "Essay" and that of cybernetic theory. In its very first line we find the melding of literary and cybernetic diction ("lyric information") that runs throughout the poem. Ammons is attempting here to deal with the questions of how nature can in some sense be known and how poetry can have anything to do with that knowledge. By adopting the cybernetic model, Ammons achieves a distinctive modification of the romantic idea of organic form, largely because in the new context the idea of the organic is itself redefined. We might say, following Lentricchia's assessment of Northrop Frye in *After the New Criticism* (10ff.), that Ammons's new organic opens outward, is centrifugal rather than the centripetal "innate" form of Coleridge.

It may be helpful at this point to offer a few key concepts of the cybernetic model drawn from Gregory Bateson's landmark essay "Cybernetic Explanation." The cybernetic universe is above all relational and formal; communication is a product of redundancy and repetition of pattern (the usual figure for this concept is the signal-to-noise ratio—the signal is recognizable pattern, the noise, the unidentifiable random). Pattern, in turn, is closely wedded to predictability: "To guess, in essence, is to face a cut or slash in the sequence of items and to predict across that slash what items might be on the other side. . . . A pattern, in fact, is definable as an aggregate of events or objects which will permit in some degree such guesses when the entire aggregate is not available for inspection" (407). In cybernetic explanation, "information and form are not items which can be localized" (409) because they are relational correspondences (between message and referent, item and context) which resemble the ideas of contrast, frequency, symmetry, congruence, conformity, and so on—they are "of zero dimensions" (408). The difference between a piece of paper and a cup of coffee, for example, is not in the paper, nor is it in the coffee—the contrast (and subsequent information) cannot be localized. Cybernetic epistemology posits a concept of mind which is organic but not organicist: "The individual mind is immanent, but not only in the body. It is immanent also in pathways and messages outside the body; and there is a larger Mind of which the individual mind is only a subsystem. This larger Mind . . . is . . . immanent in the total interconnected social system and planetary ecology" (461). A final and important point from cybernetics is this: "All that is not information, not redundancy, not form and not restraints—is noise, the only possible source of *new* patterns" (410).

The cybernetic model goes a long way, I think, in helping to explain the similarities and differences between the nature of the "Essay"—and to a large extent of all the later long poems—and that of the romantics. The opening of the "Essay," in both diction and conception, shows clearly the shaping presence of a cybernetic kind of thinking; the poem aspires to express something like immanent mind through "information actual / at every point // but taking on itself at every point / the emanation of curvature, of meaning" (30). The nature of the "Essay" is a "bit-nature" where each instance of wholeness and form is "internally irrelevant to scope, / but from the outside circumscribed into scope" (31). Eighteen lines into the poem we come upon the crucial passage, the critical "but," which clearly distinguishes the cybernetic character of Ammons's view of nature from that of the romantics:

> but then find the wholeness
>
> unbelievable because it permits
> another wholeness,
> another lyric, the same in structure,
>
> in mechanism of existence
>
> (30)

"Wholeness" is presented in the "Essay" not as the purified essence of existence but as a *condition* of existence, not as *either* one or many but as "a one:many mechanism" (31).

Frederick Buell calls Ammons's new model a "partial humanization of nature" (210); I believe what Ammons recognizes and what Buell is trying to get at is that nature is for us always already conceptualized, symbolized, abstract:

> I wonder if I'm really talking about
> the economy of the self. . . .
> . . . .
> we never talk about anything but ourselves,
> objectivity the objective way of talking about ourselves
>
> ("Extremes" 59)

Ammons's shift to a "bit-nature," a nature not of Being but of evidence becoming information, "saliences," is not so much a willful move to humanize nature as it is a recognition of the abstract as a precondition of existence and of knowledge ("the manageable rafters of salience"); the attempt to deal only in the concrete results in the sort of dilemma discussed midway through "Hibernaculum":

                    nature seems firm with casual

certainties (one could say a steel spike is a foot
long) but pressed for certainty breaks out
in bafflings of variability, a thousand close

measurings of the spike averaged out and a thousand
efforts to average out the variables in the instruments
of measure or in the measuring environment

(room temperature, humidity, the probable frequency
the door to the room is opened): recalcitrance is built
in perfectly, variations thereon perceived as possibility
                                                    (88)

This passage clearly echoes the cybernetic idea that conceptual "noise" (the recalcitrant, the as yet unpatterned or unassimilated) is the source of new patterns—variations on recalcitrance perceived as possibility. At the same time, the other end of the problem, so to speak—that of extreme abstraction—is constantly threatened with gaseous evaporation:

                                        the swarm at the
subatomic level may be so complex and surprising that it puts
quasars, pulsars and other matters to shame: I don't know:

and "living world" on the other hand may be so scanty in its
information as to be virtually of no account
                                            ("Essay" 46)

We can see, then, that Ammons is being playful but also exercising a very concentrated economy of expression (underscored by the echo of "tree" in "true") when he writes, "true, I really ought to know where the tree is: but I know / it's in my backyard" ("Essay" 38). The organic becomes for Ammons a question of limits and perimeters. In contrast to *a* center, the location of "the primordial egg of truth" ("Hibernaculum" 89), Ammons offers a mobile universe of which wholeness is an abstract condition, a beginning rather than a closure:

a center's absolute, if relative: but every point in spacetimematter's

a center: reality is abob with centers: indeed, there is
nothing but centers
                                            ("Essay" 33)

A center is, of course, an abstract matter; like form and information, it cannot be located but is rather the product of relational processes, as Ammons indicates in his grappling with the concrete particulars of trying to locate the tree in the back yard:

I assume the fixed point would have to be
   the core center of the planet, though I'm perfectly
prepared to admit the core's involved
   in a slow—perhaps universal—slosh that would alter the
   center's position

                                                 ("Essay" 38)

Ammons's argument with the traditional idea of organic form is that it isn't organic enough; its organicism is based on an idea of closure and completion rather than on an ability to maintain an open, functioning relationship with the accidental and haphazard—an ability to translate "noise" into "signal":

                                 I am not so much
arguing with the organic school as shifting true organismus from
the already organized to the bleak periphery of possibility,
an area transcendental only by its bottomless entropy

                                      ("Essay" 51)

Coincidental with Ammons's criticism of the closure of organic form as traditionally conceived is a similar attitude toward its analogues of symbol and lyric; the "already organized" is a condition for knowing which provides a "disposition" toward the unassimilated but can be changed by new data. The ontological point is of course that the "disposition" depends on the mechanism, and the sort of knowledge one derives depends upon both. The problem with the lyric is precisely its inflexibility as a mechanism for knowing; not open to the possibilities and potential waiting in the coincidental and the unassimilated, its intolerance gives the lyric its expressive power—its small explosion—but renders it, like some sort of exotic poodle, unfit for survival. The lyric is a "slight completion" (in both senses): "to be small and assembled! how comforting: but how perishable!" (*Sphere* 73). A similar distrust marks Ammons's attitude toward the idea of symbol. If anything, the symbol isn't abstract *enough:* "and the symbol won't do, either: it differentiates flat / into muffling fact it tried to stabilize beyond" ("Extremes" 54). The point Ammons is making is de Man's in "The Rhetoric of Temporality": by holding that some things are concrete and others abstract, and by then privileging a kind of concrete abstraction, the traditional idea of symbol draws us into a pseudodialectic of subject and object (198). For Ammons, the concrete as such is a myth but is valuable as a function, a nexus of localization in the "one:many mechanism":

      it's impossible anyone should know anything about the concrete
      who's never risen above it, above the myth of concretion

      in the first place

                                        ("Extremes" 54)

For Ammons, the particulars of nature are not of value primarily because they are concrete but because they are *evidence* (see Jacobsen 34)— and evidence only makes sense, has meaning, within a larger framework of abstraction kept honest, so to speak, by new evidence. Ammons's empirical observation (as in, for example, sections 75–76 of *Sphere*), and his knowledge and use of the language of science, is unsurpassed in American poetry, yet almost always these empirical forays end in a questioning, a dizzying explosion into a new realm of complexities. Empirical observation pushed far enough dissolves, in one sense, into a question of the one and the many— finally, he writes, "a problem in rhetoric" which cannot be reconciled in language ("Hibernaculum" 86). (His discussion of "division" versus "differentiation" in "Hibernaculum" is helpful here.) Ammons's playful and prismatic variation upon Williams's "No ideas but in things" clarifies the point that the relationship between one and many, subject and object, symbol and symbolized is multivalent, always leaving an opening because always leaving something out:

> the symbol apple and the
> real apple are different apples, though resembled: "no ideas but in
>
> things" can then be read into alternatives—"no things but in ideas,"
> "no ideas but in ideas," and "no things but in things": one thing
> always to keep in mind is that there are a number of possibilities
> ("Essay" 43)

(Ammons characteristically underscores the point by the casual statement "one thing to keep in mind"—rather than "one *idea* to keep in mind.")

Ammons brings this sort of attitude to his discussion of the tree as paradigm of organic form, begun in the "Essay" and returned to regularly and finally as the oblique subject of *The Snow Poems*. What he refers to sarcastically as "the transcendental / vegetative analogy" is too tidy as an "analogy" and too simplistic as "vegetative." The "point of change" makes him realize that "actually, a tree / is a print-out: the tree becomes exactly what the locked genetic // code has pre-ordained—allowing, of course, for variables" ("Essay" 50). But Ammons goes on to consider the fact that the "locked" code is "apparently based on accidence, chance, unforeseeable distortion" (51)—like his center, it is absolute, but relative. The problem of identity as a paradigm of organic form persists:

> if I back off to take the shape of a tree
> I gather blurs: when does water seeping into the roothairs
> pass the boundary after which it is tree
> (*Sphere* 21)

Ammons's symbolism is of a very different order; the tree becomes as much a symbol of difference and otherness—of all that it cannot contain—as it is a paradigm of identity and order.

The shift from tree as organic paradigm to tree as print-out is telling in a number of ways. The "point of change" can be expressed by the tree but cannot be located there, is not *in* the tree. If I examine the tree at different points over time, it will be each time, considered as a concrete thing, a different tree. I can induce change—its motion and perhaps its "drift"—from the variations, but the change is not in the tree, nor is it "between" one examined tree and another. The tree, in this sense, is like a frame of film; it has meaning only insofar as it is traced or inscribed with aspects of the frames which precede it and insofar as it serves to intimate some sense of predictability about the frames to follow.

The elm tree of *The Snow Poems* functions as a locus "to show change by reflecting light differently in a series of exposures" (Harmon 11). (It is worth noting here that Saussure used in his notes and lectures the terms "historical," "diachronic," and "cinematic" interchangeably to suggest that change or evolution is always an operation of abstracting change and continuity out of discontinuous items.) Ammons's shift to the print-out is, I believe, a movement away from the closed space of self-contained organic form which "partakes" (as Coleridge put it) of transcendent substance, and toward an emphasis upon the metonymic nature of the tree as a product of the "contiguous" conditions of its environment and of our perception of it. The form is thus not finished but open to the accidental and haphazard (and thus to new information and patterning). The crucial difference is that Ammons goes out of his way to present his metonymies *as* metonymies, to remind us that, in his readings of parts of a world for the whole, it is the *mechanism* and not the substance that informs the meaning of the organic. I emphasize the metonymic nature of Ammons's symbol to point out how it is resolutely untranscendental, "local and mortal." As Kenneth Burke has written, "Viewed as a sheerly terministic, or symbolic function, that's what transcendence is: the building of a *terministic bridge* whereby one realm is *transcended* by being viewed *in terms of* a realm 'beyond' it" ("Machinery" 187). And, Burke adds, "*beyond* the here and now" (191). It is Ammons's openness and inclusiveness which gives his symbol—in contrast to Coleridge's—a kind of centrifugal character (this is, I think, in part what is suggested by "the emanation of curvature" of "one curve, the whole curve" at the beginning of the "Essay"). Ammons's symbol is "translucent," but to its own provisionality. Poetry achieves the greatest scope of meaning not by exclusion of all that is not organic form but by inclusion of all that might be. Ammons's unique brand of symbolism is in part his strategy for dealing with the dilemma described by Geoffrey Hartman (and we should think here of Stevens's variation upon Williams's "El Hombre"):

The aura of the symbol is reduced even as its autonomy is strengthened. It is ironic that, by the time of Stevens, "the philosophy of symbols" (as Yeats called it) confronts the poet with a new discontinuity: the symbols, or romantic relics, are so attenuated by common use that their ground (sky?) is lost. They become starry junk, and the poem is a device to dump them, to let the moon rise as moon. ("Evening Star" 176)

Hartman's "starry junk" is in Ammons countered by the material of the moment—the "worn-outs, stiff-and-thins, the used-up literary" ("Summer Place" 201). The "growing edge to change and surprise" of the poem can turn anything—trash included—into art with its "one:many mechanism" (while, Ammons would hope, retaining the essential "trash nature" of the bits). Unlike the early Ammons, the poet of wind and mountain, the last two long poems care less about the particular material of the poetry—rely less on wind or mountain—and more about making poetry out of whatever is at hand. Indeed, in both poems Ammons seems to gravitate toward the peripheries, away from the tidiness and centeredness of literary diction and lyric organization. We already see the desire for scope, whatever the risks, emerging in *Sphere:*

> I'm sick of good poems, all those little rondures
> splendidly brought off, painted gourds on a shelf: give me
>
> the dumb, debilitated, nasty, and massive, if that's the
> alternative: touch the universe anywhere you touch it
> everywhere
>
> (72)

The key word in all of this is *discontinuity*. Ammons, confronted with the question of how to make poetry possible in a postsymbolist (and in some senses postliterary) context, begins with the "Essay" a new type of writing which emphasizes the discontinuity between word and world, writing and speech, but at the same time has a profoundly orphic dimension.[6]

Ammons began, with the Ezra persona of the early poems, in a mode that presented itself as already an analogue of expression: "*so* I said I am Ezra" has no antecedent in the poem. It can only be interpreted as the result of something occurring before the Ezra persona "speaks"—something "outside" the poem or just before it begins. The poem begs to be read as an analogue of speech, the speech an analogue of the Ezra persona, and the persona, finally, an analogue of a human speaker. Implicit in the idea of poem-as-analogue representation is a continuity across ontological levels: the graphic array of language is an analogue for the acoustic, which in turn is analogous to the verbal, the verbal to the intellectual.[7] A paradigm of analogue representation would be the clock: the movement of the hand is an analogue for the movement of the earth. Analogue representation is based on a real correspondence between real magnitudes—representation is motivated by the nature of its object. It is highly conventionalized and metaphoric in the sense that the nature of the representation is motivated by the nature of its object—the circular movement of the hands by the circular movement of the earth, for instance.

Digital representation, on the other hand, makes a point of its discontinuity with real magnitudes and asserts its abstract and arbitrary conventional nature. It can, unlike analogue, represent, and indeed must make use of, negatives (Wilden 162). Rather than a fixed analogous whole, the disruption of whose syntax would destroy the entire representation, the digital representation is discrete and infinitely divisible. The continuity between 11:57 and 11:58 is so because in the conventions of the system 8 follows 7, not because of its correspondence to the actual magnitude of that which it represents (as in the case of, say, a thermometer). Analogue representation will emphasize accuracy; digital will emphasize *specificity* (the ontological ground for accuracy having been removed). As Anthony Wilden points out, "The digital mode of language is denotative: it may talk about anything and does so in the language of objects, facts, events and the like. Its linguistic function is primarily the sharing of nameable information . . . its overall function is the transmission or sharing or reproduction of pattern and structures" (164).

We see Ammons, from the "Essay" forward, develop a style and form which makes a point of disrupting the idea or impression that his poems are analogue representations. The form makes a point of its own arbitrariness, its discontinuity: the three-line or four-line "stanza" of the later long poems (excepting *The Snow Poems*) runs from margin to margin, the writing structured simply by arbitrary imposition (line breaks do not coincide with acoustic or syntactic breaks or with a sonnetlike "shift of mind" of the speaker). In "Hibernaculum" and in *Sphere,* the arbitrariness is further emphasized by the grouping of stanzas into numbered sections—the more apparent the graphic structure, the less it matters at any other level. The "structure" is there to present a visual array pleasing in itself and not as an analogue of the acoustic or intellectual dimensions. When we move inside the stanza, we find a similar discontinuity emphasized again by Ammons's punctuation; there are no periods ("a complete sentence is a complete thought") but only colons, creating a "closeless" structure. As Robert Pinsky has written, "In movement from part to part, the strings of repeated colons suggest a conflict between the stationary or simultaneous and the developing or sequential; each part explains every other part, with a minimum of the consecutive structuring in which part rests on part as in a building or a tree" (193).

The most apparent structuring device is the "friction" between the "regular" stanzas and the staccato movement of the lines produced by the colon, but it cannot be located in either one. Ammons gives us not a consecutive structuring which builds an analogical whole, but a series of read-outs—

meaning kept up in the air by its use in circulation. Again, the movement is not inward toward closure—a zeroing in on meaning—but is centrifugal, providing a "growing edge to change," "increasing the means and / assuring the probability of survival" ("Essay" 50). Even though the later long poems are linear, they are at the same time primarily nonnarrative, relying not on a principle of consecutive structuring so much as on a kind of accretive activity which oscillates back and forth from center to periphery, from specific to general, and so on. We could say that, although the form on the page is (of necessity) linear, the governing and informing principle is radial, "circling about, repeating, and elaborating the central theme. It is all 'middle,' . . . with apparently interchangeable structural units" (Clancy 5).[8] This is, I think, the logic implicit in Ammons's playful assertion in "Summer Place": "circle around the truth without telling / it and you tell it" (188). The attempt to make the governing principle of form radial is already present in the title and impulse of *Sphere: The Form of a Motion:*

> the essential without specification is boring
> and specification without the essential is: both ways out
> leaves us divided but so does neither way: unless—and here
>
> is the whole possibility—both essential and fashionable can
> be surrounded in a specified radial essential
>
> (34–35)

Ammons's salient interest in arcs and curves gives rise to a desire for "a form to complete everything with! orb" (*Sphere* 38), a form whose center ("disposition") remains intact (because mobile) even as the periphery expands. As Ammons has said in a recent interview, "a poem doesn't exist only in motion, in time. It seems to me that when you know the poem intimately you know it radially and complete. You have a non-linear perception of the whole thing" ("Event" 215).

Still, the poem must, to open outward to such knowledge, insist on its own discontinuity, must be "chocked full of resistance" (*Sphere* 13). Writing of *Sphere* in "Summer Place," Ammons echoes the "recalcitrance built into nature" that resists "casual certainties," and he seems to want a similar resistance in his own work: "I wanted something / standing recalcitrant in its own nasty massiveness" (173), "a big gritty poem that would just stand / there and spit" (174). Underneath the complaining is, I think, a weariness of having the work taken as an analogue, a "fallacy of imitative form" (173) too easily appropriated: "pretty soon you're a nature poet, everybody / saying, lands, something nice to go with dinner" (177).

The Ammons of "Summer Place" and even more so of *The Snow Poems,* having generated a kind of radiant wholeness in the previous long poems, now emphasizes that his universe—as he had been saying all along—is a *dis-*

crete whole (as in this example from the *OED:* "The parts of an animal form a concrete whole; but the parts of a society form a whole that is discrete"). This is, I think, the implicit logic behind much of Ammons's seemingly unpoetic diction of the "economy of the self" ("Extremes" 59); Ammons resorts to terms like "currency," "interest," "account," "expenditure," "overinvestment" (a symbol is "the overinvested concrete"), "balance" ("all identities are imbalances") to speak of a wholeness while at the same time avoiding the ontological pitfalls of the language of organicism.

The discrete whole of society as theme is most explicit in "Summer Place." Concomitant with its patriotic ending and the inscription of *The Snow Poems* as a work "for my country" comes a shift inward toward the poet's own world, toward a poetry more explicitly discrete, separate, and discontinuous. The broad sweep of the earlier long poems is replaced by a more fragmented universe and the more intense internalization of voice of the highly "digital" *Snow Poems:* the work is (based on internal evidence and chronology) a long poem, but broken up into pieces; the titles are not analogues of the "content" of the pieces, but simply read-outs taken from the first lines (which, in a long poem, are not first lines). The voice is a bit more irascible and the verse more recalcitrant toward wholeness, including in its conglomeration "outriders," marginal glosses and counters, and games both typographical and lexical. The material at hand of "Summer Place" becomes here the material conditions of the poet's environment—elm tree, typewriter, dictionary, paper.

At the end of *Sphere* and in "Summer Place" Ammons becomes more overtly concerned with the social and the political; but the essentially liberal polemics here are not, I would argue, the source of Ammons's true political force. Part of Ammons's project has been to dislodge poetry from its closed and rarefied space, to situate it in what he would call a larger "network" of relations, most of them not particularly "aesthetic." If we look at Ammons's writing as a cultural and therefore social act—as his extraliterary and political content begs us to—then what we see is a rewriting of the idea of poetry and of the role of literary culture. To emphasize the making and not the made, the mechanism and not the substance, is to engage a poetics of the centrifugal, to consciously resituate poetry—and, by extension, culture—in a network of relations both biological and social. If, as Lentricchia has suggested in his reading of Burke, "To make metaphor is to violate in one act the status quo of discourse and of society," then we can see how Ammons is attempting to restore and reassert the power of poetry to be something more than "superior amusement," more than the various but marginal repetition of the Beautiful in all its highly allusive forms (*Criticism* 147).[9] I say "restore" because in the above sense poetry is always radical, always a subversion of the language of the marketplace—even, as Burke has argued, antinomian: "Art's very accumulation (its discordant voices arising out of many systems) serves to undermine any one rigid scheme of living—and herein lies 'wickedness' enough" (*Counter-Statement* viii).

Ammons would seek to undermine those habits and institutions that compromise our lived awareness of the "saliences," of "massive suasions." Here again we need Burke to complicate what might seem like an easy holism, a "natural fact": "Any reduction of *social* motives to terms of sheer 'nature' would now seem to me a major error. Naturalism has served as deceptively in the modern world as supernaturalism ever did in the past, to misrepresent motives that are intrinsic to the social order" (xv). What Burke is getting at but does not say is that "nature" masks ideology; indeed, if (as Ammons realizes) we encounter a nature that is always already abstract, how could it be otherwise? Ammons often says, with little or no ironic cover (but with perhaps more than a dash of sentimentality), that his later long poems are "ideal organizations":

> not homogeneous pudding but

> united differences, surface differences expressing the common,
> underlying hope and fate of each person and people, a gathering
> into one place of multiple dissimilarity
>
> (*Sphere* 78)

More important than the vision of genuine community here is the *writing* of it—through a poetics that goes beyond the romantics and thus speaks with special timeliness—into a radically decentered poetics not of Being but of beings, of a heterocosm "local and mortal."[10] Truth then becomes not a metaphysical but a pragmatic matter: what, in the manner of the late William James, it is better for us to believe.

We could do worse than to read Ammons as something of a contemporary pragmatist, and in doing so helping to sharpen the contrast between the ideology of Ammons's work and the Emersonianism that Carlyle so much admired. We are, as Ammons reminds us in his earthbound variation of Emerson, "unmendably integral," and implied here is an imperative for conduct, but not only for the poem (as ideal organization) or the poet (as Emersonian representative man). Ammons's work is often the poetry of constraints and balances, of the local and mortal context; he rails against wastefulness in "Extremes and Moderations," and in *Sphere* would ground the work of mind in the specificity of its objects:

> one terror mind brings on
> itself is that anything can be made of anything
>
> · · · · · · · · · · · · · · · · · · ·
> . . . scary to those who need prisons,
> liberating to those already in
>
> (*Sphere* 61)

Ammons reminds us again and again (and often in oblique reference to the romantic symbol) that "all identities and effects are / imbalances" (*Sphere* 50). Keeping in mind Ammons's linkage of poetics and ideology, then, we can read in the following passage on the symbolic a dark parable indeed:

> when an image or
> item is raised into class representative of cluster, clump,
>
> or set, its boundaries are overinvested, the supercharge is
> explosive, so that the burden of energy overwhelms the matter,
> and aura, glow, or spirituality results, a kind of pitchblende,
>
> radium, sun-like: and when the item is moved beyond class
> into symbol or paradigmatic item, matter is a mere seed
> afloat in radiance
>
> (*Sphere* 39)

The source of the sublime in Ammons is the confrontation between the knowledge that "the mind will forever work in this way" (*Sphere* 39) and the understanding that the larger network of which it is a part cannot, finally, be subjected to such "overinvestment." The effect of what I have called Ammons's metonymic symbolism is to go beyond representation, beyond the romantic symbolic; as Ammons puts it: "when we have made the sufficient mirror will // it have been only to show how things will break" (*Sphere* 31). Ammons's ideal *organization* seeks to unseat the idea of poetry as the polishing of such a mirror, to show us how we might go about things with a full awareness of the local and mortal context, how we might socially be otherwise by coming to terms with the physical, biological network of necessity that can't be otherwise. This is the social message of Ammons, of the poetics not of partaking but of making: "when may it not be our / task so to come into the knowledge of the reality as to / participate therein" (*Sphere* 36).

Duke University

Notes

1.   Daniel M. Fogel, in response to the Emersonian bias of the special *Diacritics* issue on Ammons, has suggested a number of "non-Emersonian rifts" that Ammons criticism could pursue, many of them pertaining to Ammons's relation to the romantics (49).

2.   Lentricchia's discussion of Bloom in *After the New Criticism* (319–46) is particularly acute in pointing out the essentializing impulse inherent in Bloom's version of literary history.

3.   Paul de Man's critique of the ontology of the romantic symbol in "The Rhetoric of Temporality" is particularly acute; as he points out, in the romantic symbol "the substance and its representation do not differ in their being but only in their extension" (207). Such an assimilation entails a challenge to the priority of the subject, resulting in what Peter Thorslev has

called the romantic devaluation of consciousness and self-consciousness—"fallen" man versus the "unconscious" spirit (Wordsworth's "holy plan") of unfallen Nature (86ff.). As de Man phrases it, the self must "borrow" from nature the teleological assurance it lacks (200). The range of critics who have agreed on this point is in itself interesting; see, for example, Babbitt 285 and Hartman, "Romanticism" 54.

4.   Hayden White's introduction to his *Tropics of Discourse* is an interesting discussion of the issues and methods of "tropological" criticism, though White's suggestion of a biological, rather than social and ideological, foundation for what Kenneth Burke called the "Four Master Tropes" partially undermines the shrewd pun embedded in Burke's title and errs, for some critics, in the direction of Jakobsonian reduction; see Lentricchia's "restoration" of the ideological Burke in *Criticism and Social Change*.

5.   This essay was written before the publication of Ammons's most recent long poem, "The Ridge Farm," in his latest book, *Sumerian Vistas*—hence its absence from these pages.

6.   Derrida's critique of writing as an image of speech, and assertion that speech is already a type of writing, is of some use here (46ff.). See also Bruns's discussion of the "orphic" and "hermetic" modes (1–3).

7.   I would like to thank William Harmon for formulating with regard to Ammons the digital/analogue distinction. See Bateson 372–74 for a limited discussion of analogic versus digital communication, and Wilden 155–95 for an extended and expert treatment from the vantage point of cybernetics and information theory.

8.   It is interesting to note one distinction between analogue and digital as formulated by Wilden: digital communication's "combinatorial possibilities depend only upon the PLACING and the ORDERING of its discrete elements, rather than upon their nature or their location as such," whereas analogue maps continuums (162). Although we would not want to push Wilden's precise distinctions too far in an analysis of poetics, Ammons's reliance on terms like "mechanism," "information," and so on invites speculation from the vantage point of cybernetic theory.

9.   Such a move is, for Lentricchia, in the direction of the Burkean sense of Rhetoric, and away from the opposition of rhetoric and the aesthetic, an opposition that marginalizes the aesthetic as it rarefies it.

10.   Contrast Mazzaro's reading of the Ammonsian "heterocosm" (42) with Bloom's use of the term.

Works Cited

Ammons, A. R. "Essay on Poetics." *Selected Longer Poems* 30–52.
———. "Event, Corrective, Cure." Bloom, *A. R. Ammons* 213–19.
———. "Extremes and Moderations." *Selected Longer Poems* 53–66.
———. "Hibernaculum." *Selected Longer Poems* 67–104.
———. *Selected Longer Poems*. New York: Norton, 1980.
———. *The Snow Poems*. New York: Norton, 1977.
———. *Sphere: The Form of a Motion*. New York: Norton, 1974.
———. "Summer Place." *Hudson Review* 30 (1977): 173–209.
Babbitt, Irving. *Rousseau and Romanticism*. Boston: Houghton, 1919.
Bateson, Gregory. "Cybernetic Explanation." *Steps to an Ecology of Mind*. New York: Ballantine, 1972. 399–410.
Bloom, Harold. "A. R. Ammons: The Breaking of the Vessels." *Salmagundi* 31–32 (1975–76): 185–203.
———, ed. *A. R. Ammons*. New York: Chelsea House, 1986.
———, ed. *Romanticism and Consciousness: Essays in Criticism*. New York: Norton, 1970.

Bruns, Gerald L. *Modern Poetry and the Idea of Language: A Critical and Historical Study.* New Haven: Yale UP, 1974.

Buell, Frederick. "To Be Quiet in the Hands of the Marvelous." Bloom, *A. R. Ammons* 195–212.

Burke, Kenneth. *Counter-Statement.* 2nd ed. 1953. Berkeley: U of California P, 1968.

———. "Four Master Tropes." *A Grammar of Motives.* Berkeley: U of California P, 1969. 502–17.

———. "I, Eye, Ay—Concerning Emerson's Early Essay on 'Nature' and the Machinery of Transcendence." *Language as Symbolic Action: Essays on Life, Literature, and Method.* Berkeley: U of California P, 1966. 186–200.

Clancy, Joseph P. *The Earliest Welsh Poetry.* London: Macmillan, 1970.

De Man, Paul. "The Rhetoric of Temporality." *Blindness and Insight: Essays in the Rhetoric of Contemporary Criticism.* 2nd ed. Minneapolis: U of Minnesota P, 1983. 187–228.

Derrida, Jacques. *Of Grammatology.* Trans. Gayatri Chakravorty Spivak. Baltimore: Johns Hopkins UP, 1978.

Fogel, Daniel M. "Response." *Diacritics* 4.1 (Spring 1974): 49–53.

Harmon, William. Rev. of *The Snow Poems,* by A. R. Ammons. *American Book Review* Dec. 1977: 15–16.

Hartman, Geoffrey. "Evening Star and Evening Land." *The Fate of Reading and Other Essays.* Chicago: U of Chicago P, 1975. 147–78.

———. "Romanticism and 'Anti-Self-Consciousness.'" Bloom, *Romanticism and Consciousness* 46–56.

Jacobsen, Josephine. "The Talk of Giants." *Diacritics* 3.4 (Winter 1973): 34–38.

Lentricchia, Frank. *After the New Criticism.* Chicago: U of Chicago P, 1980.

———. *Criticism and Social Change.* Chicago: U of Chicago P, 1983.

Mazzaro, Jerome. "Reconstruction in Art." *Diacritics* 3.4 (Winter 1973): 39–44.

Pinsky, Robert. "Ammons." Bloom, *A. R. Ammons* 185–94.

Thorslev, Peter L. *Romantic Contraries: Freedom versus Destiny.* New Haven: Yale UP, 1984.

White, Hayden. *Tropics of Discourse: Essays in Cultural Criticism.* Baltimore: Johns Hopkins UP, 1978.

Wilden, Anthony. *System and Structure: Essays in Communication and Exchange.* 2nd ed. New York: Tavistock, 1980.

Ammons, Einstein, and the Pathetic Fallacy: A Reading of "Tombstone" Meditation #19

WILLIAM J. RUSHTON

To read of the physical world in the poems of A. R. Ammons is to be thrust to and fro between the despair of alienation and the comfort of common ground. In one poem, Ammons will assail us with time spans that strain the imagination almost to the breaking point: "a pulse in one of earth's orbits / beats once in four hundred thousand years"; in another, he will portray the daunting force that shapes new stars—"the whining, / insisting energy . . . that // sings stuff back together"—in a way that invites credible parallels to our own lives. This oscillating movement is orchestrated nowhere with more poignance and concision than in poem #19 from his series of graveside meditations entitled "Tombstones" (*Sumerian Vistas,* 1987), and nowhere else with such far-reaching implications. For here Ammons coordinates his own insights with those of modern physics to disrupt not only the reader's particular sensibilities but the entire tradition of nature poetry (and nature-gazing in general) since Wordsworth while at the same time deftly aligning poetic utterance even with those ineffable cosmic forces at which today's scientist aims his impossible scrutiny. Here is the poem in full:

19

the things of earth are not objects,
there is no nature,
no nature of stones and brooks, stumps, and ditches,

for these are pools of energy cooled into place,
or they are starlight pressed
to store,

or they are speeding light held still:
the woods are a fire green-slow
and the pathway of solid earthwork

is just light concentrated blind

(*SV,* 50–51)

388

Ammons focuses his attention on the physiology of his subject here in a way that has not been done before in poetry. Whereas the medieval poetic tradition of tomb gazing and *memento mori* (a tradition that carries over into Renaissance poets such as Herbert) emphasized the gravestone's lack of permanence, this meditation grapples with a more disconcerting proposition, one made possible by Einstein's claim that mass was merely a form of energy: the gravestone's lack of substance. Newton's universe was mechanical—fixed objects acted upon by external forces. But the atomism of classical physics, and with it the long history of attempts from Democritus to Newton to reduce matter to discrete components, has yielded to a notion of patterns and probabilities: patterns not of discrete phenomena, but of energy; probabilities not of things, but of interrelations.[1] The notion of "object," though still a necessary myth, has (at least at the level of scientific theory) been laid to rest. Even the electronic age's insistence on a fluid universe has proven inadequate. Indeed, it has been the special genius of our own age to recognize that all such metaphors are inaccurate . . . and yet to recognize, also, that metaphors are all we know and all we can ever know.[2] Particles, fluids, waves, and now the curves, colors, and tastes of quantum physics are merely figures of snow, as it were, thrown aloft Mont Blanc: with whatever certainty they are hurled, they will just as certainly melt under the next epoch's sunrise. The tropological unfolding of Ammons's meditation ("things . . . are pools of energy . . . or they are starlight pressed . . . or they are speeding light held") then imitates the formal promiscuity of matter, or more accurately of energy, in its innumerable and perforce temporary concentrations, and imitates as well the tropological nature of modern scientific description itself. Like both "Mont Blanc" and modern physics, moreover, Ammons's poem is guided by an implicit distrust of any single interpretation of reality that hardens into doctrine.

For Ammons himself the readjustment is, at least in part, empowering. One senses in his poem, in the quickening way analogy spawns analogy, an exuberance of the kind found in Shelley's "Ode to the West Wind" or "To a Skylark," in Whitman's disparate epithets for a blade of grass, or in Stevens's barrage of reimagined pineapples.[3] Derrida, too, celebrates the syntactical progression of "or . . . or," having it stand for the waking of childhood into language:

> The child will know how to speak when one form of his unease can be substituted for another; then he will be able to slip from one language to another, slide one sign under another, play with the signifying substance; he will enter into the order of the supplement, here determined as the human order.[4]

But to recognize a kinship between the play of language and the manner in which the material world itself is structured, the way energy assumes its various incarnations, does more than merely applaud the mind's faculty for metaphor. Emerson says in the late essay "Poetry and Imagination" that

> The poet accounts all productions and changes of Nature as the nouns of language, uses them representatively, too well pleased with their ulterior to value much their primary meaning. Every new object so seen gives a shock of agreeable surprise.

The declaration wins this compliment from Harold Bloom: "Emerson . . . daringly makes of natural change only a series of tropes."[5] No doubt Ammons, too, gains strength from this exercise of theme and variation through which he addresses the tombstones confronting him, reveling in imagined power over their daunting significance, their "ulterior meaning." And yet his rhetorical gesturing, at the same time that it flexes its own imaginative muscle, also offers a credible account of the material reality that constitutes those tombstones—and, moreover, in a style that ingeniously mimics their structure.

To be sure, the inclination to regard Ammons's brazen troping against nature primarily as a fantasy of power (as we do the troping sprees of Shelley, Whitman, and Stevens) remains strong. Indeed, his equation of natural landscape with "pools of energy" eerily parallels the arrogant and cynical posturing of modern industry. Similarly, "starlight pressed / to store" would almost seem to celebrate the kind of hoarding of natural power Heidegger inveighs against (he calls it "standing reserve") in "The Question Concerning Technology."[6] Yet beneath such poetic bravado lie certain ominous warnings the poem implicitly urges us to consider. Mark Edmundson discerns a ratio of power to danger in the relationship Emerson professes to enjoy with "Fate" (in the essay so entitled) that may guide us in our deeper approach to Ammons. Edmundson offers this analysis of Emerson's abrupt assertion that "Fate has its lord; limitation its limits":

> This turning is achieved rhetorically by a sequence of refigurings of Fate until the agency becomes, imaginatively, a function of Emerson's powers of verbal invention. Through the first half of the essay, Emerson shows how Fate can be summoned forward, figured, and dismissed, slain, as it were, in the gap between sentences, then brought freshly to life at the whim of the creator.[7]

True, we may read Ammons's refigurings of gravestones ("pools of energy," "starlight pressed / to store," and "speeding light held still" in this meditation alone) in like fashion: as an attempt to fantasize the barely comprehensible force of universal energy (and death, which the stones signify more directly) to be a mere function of his own verbal powers. Edmundson concludes his discussion of the Emerson passage, however, on a darker note. Such "rhetorical imperialism," he argues, is, in Stevens's phrase, to be stripped of every fiction except one, with Emerson's imagination taking the part of that fiction, the "absolute-Angel." For to trope against Fate is to deprive oneself of defenses; in Freud's terms it is to attempt to use the imagination to demystify the Reality Principle, and the experiential results are likely to be disastrous. (151)

Ammons's poem is about stripping fictions, too, even if it is also (or perhaps because it is also) about imposing them, and the dangers implicit within such privileging of the poetic imagination over external forces are presumably the same for both authors: narcissism, solipsism, madness. And yet a different aspect of the reality principle is being demystified in each case, and the demystification proceeds on largely different grounds. The external force Emerson most often defined himself against was the European intellectual tradition to which he was, however perturbingly, heir. His primary means of ignoring, or at least diffusing, such historical and cultural forces—of struggling, as Edmundson phrases it, "not to be constituted by the lost object" (150)—was to insist on his status as American born anew.[8]

Granted, Ammons, too, is occasionally lured by the prospect of an identity loosed from influence, though he is perhaps more willing than Emerson was to acknowledge the dangers inherent in such freedom. In the short lyric "Uppermost," for example, Ammons imagines profiting from but ultimately transcending his forebears, which yields an exuberance tempered by the expectation of loneliness and psychic instability:

> The top
> grain on the peak
> weighs next
> to nothing and,
> sustained
> by a mountain,
> has no burden,
> but nearly
> ready to float,
> exposed
> to summit wind,
> it endures
> the rigors of having
> no further
> figure to complete
> and a
> blank sky
> to guide its dreaming

(*SELECTED POEMS,* 103)

But the reality one encounters in the majority of Ammons's later poems, and in the tombstone meditations especially, is that of the earth and elements, not culture; and the anxiety over perception and the *Ding an Sich* that he inherits from the Anglo-American philosophical tradition (and poetically from Stevens) is exacerbated tenfold by the precepts of quantum theory and relativity. In Ammons, consequently, what is called into question is not so much the preference of the imagination over reality, as it is in Emerson and Stevens, but the fact or facticity of reality itself. Or, what demystifies reality in Ammons, revealing instability where there had seemed to inhere so much stability, is not poetic will so much as scientific understanding. At any rate, the result is unavoidably, at least in part, psychic ill ease. For if one of the happy functions of reality is, as Freud maintains, to provide external objects onto and against which the self can fix its identity, thereby marshaling its energies outward rather than being victimized by them internally (claustrophobically), then insomuch as reality is now understood to be inherently unstable, those regularizing attachments between self and object (between humankind and nature, say) are put at considerable risk. In a sense, what modern science has actually done is to *re*mystify the reality principle . . . yielding potential effects on the ego, however, that are hardly conservative.

Ammons has often expressed anxiety over the mutability of nature: "the land's a slow ocean," as he proposes from a hilltop in "Delaware Water Gap," for example; "we're floating . . . and a new wave / to finish this one is building up somewhere . . . you and I, / to be drowned, now so sustained and free" (*SP,* 94). Indeed, the way the passage of time in Ammons constantly slips away from any sort of human frame makes it difficult for him to reap psychic advantages of the type Freud presumed external reality to provide. The kind of mutability Ammons explores in "Tombstone" #19, however, where matter is understood not simply as ephemeral but as an illusion, is both more original (time's effect on the material world has always inspired poetic speculation) and potentially more disquieting. Let us turn again to the lines,

> there is no nature,
> no nature of stones and brooks, stumps, and ditches,
>
> for these are pools of energy cooled into place,
> or they are starlight pressed
> to store,
>
> or they are speeding light held still:

At least structurally, the formulation is reminiscent of existentialist narratives, especially those in which characters stumble upon the realization that their humanity is essentially ungrounded (i.e., that while we are free to create a *personal* nature, there is no such thing as a fundamental *human* nature) and are thereby struck by an immense and unsettling freedom to reinvent the terms of their lives.[9] Yet the nervous freedom (and potential *nausée*) behind the presumption of an abyss in or of *Mother* nature, as it were, is of a different order from that which accompanies the existential experience of self. It is one thing to feel that the self is fashioned rather than inherited—we have grown comfortable enough with the idea.[10] It is quite another thing to insist that the external world of objects, which has for so long aided us in the fashioning of ourselves, in fact contains no objects.

We have already considered possible repercussions of this claim for the real (or anticlaim) in Freudian terms: since reality's principle is that it not only limits but also helps stabilize the ego, then whatever diminishes confidence in reality also automatically threatens sanity. Let us now consider how such unreifying of the real fits into the poetic tradition in which Ammons is writing, for the project of affixing ourselves to or aligning ourselves with objects of the natural world (the most self-conscious articulation of such a project, at least) dates from the beginning of Romanticism: in Wordsworth's desire to "fit / Our . . . existence to existing things,"[11] and in the organicism of Coleridge and Emerson. While the majority of Ammons's poetry tends to share ontological premises with the works of these men (Ammons, too, is interested in stable correspondences between humankind and nature), the almost frenetic list of tropes we encounter in #19 threatens to put the psychological comforts we derive, as well as the inspiration poets draw, from organicism in danger. The poem therefore marks an instance of self-overcoming of which Ammons himself was perhaps only partially conscious.

So much of Ammons's poetry offers finely tuned descriptions of trees, mountains, and streams as means through which he strives to unveil some aspect of our internal life. But what does it mean to propose for psychic "investment" (the term is both Wordsworthian and Freudian) such alienating epithets for natural phenomena as pools of energy and stored light? The feeling of speed with which the terms are rattled off is almost enough, by itself, to unsettle the apparatus of mirroring for which we have traditionally looked to nature. In Book I of *The Prelude,* Wordsworth recalls being uncannily moved, while descending from a "stony moor" toward the valley where a murderer was once hanged, by "the visionary dreariness / Which . . . Did at that time invest the naked pool" beneath: moved, but also no doubt relieved, for whatever childhood anxieties composed that "dreariness" (his father's death perhaps among them, which he mentions soon after) would have been purged to some degree, or at least allayed, by their assignment to this valleyscape and moor.[12] But Ammons's landscape of energy pools is not so readily available for cathexis; indeed, the imagery of this poem signals a radical shift away from an alignment between humankind and nature that is as old as the etymological root shared by mother and matter (*mater*), and toward altogether unfamiliar terrain.[13]

To conclude this part of our discussion of meditation #19, I do not mean to suggest that the tone of the poem is one of straightforward despair, for again, Ammons clearly takes delight in such descriptive freedom toward the material world as contemporary physics makes available to an imaginative author. I do want to insist, however, that just as Emerson's pretended authority over Fate not only subtly betrays the extent to which he felt vulnerable but also threatens to dissolve a crucial means of mental security, so Ammons's pretense of calling cosmic energy (which becomes less comprehensible and more alien as the decades unfold) in and out of being by his many and diverse namings signifies psychic instability as much as it does poetic self-confidence. Were Ammons ever fully to renounce the Newtonian physics that undergirds the bulk of his nature poems, such blending of audacity and trepidation as we find (or at least, as we see forecast) in meditation #19 would serve him well for the new poetics.[14]

If one way to negotiate the daunting prospect that physical form is an illusion is to trope against energy (or even better, to assume the role of energy and trope against matter), another way is to align the process by which energy takes shape in the world with some mythic structure that is already familiar. The originary accounts of earthly matter that Ammons presents in meditation #19 stem, of course, from the big bang theory of cosmic origins. This is Lincoln Barnett's description of the "dense flaming core of the universe before it began to expand":

> no elements, no molecules, no atoms—nothing but free neutrons & other subatomic particles in a state of chaotic agitation. When the cosmic mass began to expand, however, the temperature began to fall; and when it had dropped to about one billion degrees the neutrons & protons condensed into aggregates; electrons were emitted which attached themselves to nuclei, and atoms were formed. All the elements in the universe were thus created within the space of a few critical moments in the cosmic dawn. . . .[15]

Envisioning "the things of earth" as "energy cooled into place" corresponds directly to such an account.[16] The imagery of "starlight pressed / to store" and "speeding light held still," however, is rife with other implications as well. Light is only a tiny fraction of the electromagnetic spectrum, which also includes radio and X rays, and is therefore merely one among many manifestations of energy. Yet the privilege afforded to the concept of light throughout literary history makes it a reasonable metonymy for energy; certainly, its association with poetic vision makes it an appropriate choice for Ammons. Indeed, only a small leap of imagination is needed to equate the notion of holding light still with poetry itself, whose aim is to capture and preserve an author's visions in concrete terms, to give the "airy nothing" of his imagination a "local habitation and a name." Moreover, in the *pressing* of a star's light for *storage* (compare, in Dickinson, the storing of a rose's "Essential Oils," which "[b]e not expressed by Suns—alone— / It is the gift of Screws"), a myth of cosmic agency begins to emerge, a cosmic poet-god who must—for the sake of greater appreciation? longevity?—(ex)press his vision in matter. No ideas but in things.

The traditional Christian articulation of this structure focuses on the god's generosity, as in these lines from Milton's "On the Morning of Christ's Nativity," which praise God's willingness to take on earthly shape:

> That glorious Form, that Light unsufferable,
> And that far-beaming blaze of Majesty,
>
> . . . .
>
> He laid aside; and here with us to be,
>   Forsook the Courts of everlasting Day,
> And chose with us a darksome House of mortal Clay.

The Gnostic vision of origins is structurally similar to this, though morally opposed: in Gnosticism, the translation of God into the physical world was caused by forces of evil, rather than generosity, the "good" being perforce ineffable and immaterial.[17] Ammons's focus has typically been more on the formation of *ideas,* however, as in his iteration of this same structure from an early poem called "The Strait":

>   . . . step
> by step into the
>   actual,
> truth descending
> breaks,
>
> reaches us as
> fragmentation
>   hardened
> into words
> (*Corsons Inlet,* 38)

Not surprisingly, the figure who bears this "truth" down into language suffers an anxiety of loss from the translation.

Indeed, the "god" of this poem greatly prefers to dwell among apprehensions so massively general and whole that he deigns to enter into the particulars of our broken experience only, it would appear, when coerced by some fiercely desiring mortal poet. Contrary to Milton's charitable deity, and more in the vein of Gnostic ideals, Ammons's god is niggardly,

> violent to
> overreach the
>   definite:
> why should
> he, who is
> all, commit
> himself to the
>   particular?
> say himself
> into less
>
> than all? pressed
> too far, he
>   leaves
> wounds that are
> invisible[18]

In "Tombstone" #19, though, the vehicle and tenor get reversed. In "The Strait" a fantastic poet-god is summoned in order to illustrate an earthly poetic plight: how to find the best combination of words for an idea, given that any articulation results in compromise; or to reinvoke Shelley, how to begin composition with as little decline in inspiration as possible. Here in #19, by contrast, the idea of a poet is summoned (in almost neo-Platonic fashion) in order to help illustrate the process by which "the things of earth" were originally formed: just as these tombstone poems are a material representation of Ammons's light, so earth itself is a material representation of its own luxurious source. Or more concisely, the tombstones are God's poems as well as Ammons's since the light from both sources is instilled/inscribed there. Thus the conventional fantasy of alliance between poet and divine creator (indulged most earnestly during the Renaissance and nineteenth century) is ingeniously renewed under the lens of modern science.

That Ammons has composed these epitaphic meditations on the surface of what are already poems of God (or of cosmic force) would seem to sanctify at least Ammons's particular craft of poetry.[19] Like "The Strait," however, "Tombstone" #19 also assumes a burden of absence or fallenness, concluding its depiction of the poet/god alignment with images of mutual despair over the loss of energy and presence that unavoidably attend incarnation or representation:

> or they are speeding light held still:
> the woods are a fire green-slow
> and the pathway of solid earthwork
>
> is just light concentrated blind

Not only is the created world fleeing (chemically, the decay of wood *is,* as Frost suggested, very much like fire—cf. the woodpile's "slow burning of decay"; but cf. also the "slow fire" with which "dull Time / Feeds" on the Roman gravestones in Shelley's "Adonais"),[20] but it seems to have paid an even severer price for its very existence: in the fall from *e* to *m,* to put it in Einsteinian terms, "just light" has been "concentrated blind." The earth rolling in its path through space like a blind eye ingeniously coordinates Emerson's "transparent eyeball" with another image soon following in *Nature,* "this green ball which floats . . . through the heavens," as if to cast doubts upon the former bard's claim of unmediated reception.[21] (Ammons's image has some of the brilliance of his precursor's, as well as some of its comic awkwardness.) But Milton's invocation to the sun in *Paradise Lost* III perhaps also looms in the background:

> thee I revisit safe,
> And feel thy sovran vital Lamp; but thou
> Revisit'st not these eyes, that roll in vain
> To find thy piercing ray, and find no dawn; (20–23)

Ammons's figure for poetic despair is a blind planet, Milton's a blind eye, but both poets are anxious about the loss of vision that necessarily ensues from an originating light's descent into material expression. Milton begins his invocation, "Hail holy Light . . . May I express thee unblam'd?" (1–3), and soon proposes the ideal of Christ as the impossible goal toward which he must nonetheless strive: "in him, *all* his Father shone / Substantially express'd" (239–40, emphasis added).[22] While Ammons is not worried about blame particularly, his image of a blind earth does effectively annihilate those vestiges of Ptolemaic self-importance that buoy Milton's posture toward the forces of creation. On the other hand, the sheer breadth of indictment implied by such an image should reduce, or at least moderate, his thirst for full expression, for what reasonable hopes can a poet have for immediacy when his entire planet is a mere representation of something burned up, dead?

Newton's mechanical vision of the universe yielded the metaphor of a cosmic clock. Although the days of such precisely unifying schemes may be behind us, Ammons's suggestion of a cosmic poem (earth as an exuberant, if ultimately failed, attempt to store the vibrancy of its own originating light) does provide an alluring poetic order to a chaotic world without denying the truth of chaos. Yet this vision of earth as poem also shares something in common with pre-Enlightenment conceptions of the created world as God's book: both insist on the need for (and burden of) interpretation and, therefore, on a considerable degree of negative capability ("what does reality stand for?" in the one case; "what *is* reality?" in the other), and both ascribe to nature an unmistakable quotient of danger (savage in the one case, unknowable and alien in the other). My point here has not been to suggest that Ammons's rendition of this myth of incarnation, of energy's descent into matter, provides a uniquely provocative comparison to or illumination of those found in Milton, the Gnostics, or for that matter the Gospel of John (world as word-made-flesh). For whereas theirs are fully belabored strategies aiming to convince an entire populace of some universal truth, Ammons's is the merest insinuation elicited by a few phrases, and its aims are consciously circumscribed within the narrow readership of contemporary verse. On the other hand, the suggestion in "Tombstone" #19 of an unacknowledged modern scientific debt to such cosmic genealogies as may be found in the Christian Bible, its Apocrypha, and its Hebraic and Platonic underpinnings implicitly reassesses Einstein's most stunning declaration as not so much an *ex nihilo* discovery as a brilliant troping of what was already a longstanding poetic convention. Certainly, Ammons's poem reveals an uncanny prescience in those ancient narratives, illuminating, moreover, theoretical correspondences between our own day and antiquity in precisely those areas of speculation (namely, the realms of hard science) where alienation from past models has, for most people, unquestionable currency.[23]

Notes

1. Lincoln Barnett, *The Universe and Dr. Einstein* (New York: Bantam Books, 1948, 1957), 64.
2. Lincoln Barnett, 36.
3. Walt Whitman, "Song of Myself," section 6 (*Leaves of Grass, 1891*); Wallace Stevens, "Someone Puts Together a Pineapple," in *The Palm at the End of the Mind,* ed. Holly Stevens (New York: Knopf, 1971), 295.
4. Jacques Derrida, *Of Grammatology,* trans. Gayatri Chakravorty Spivak (Baltimore: Johns Hopkins Press, 1974), 248.
5. Harold Bloom, *Wallace Stevens: The Poems of Our Climate* (Ithaca: Cornell University Press, 1976) 5; the Emerson passage cited is from this text as well, same page.
6. Martin Heidegger, *Martin Heidegger: Basic Writings,* ed. David Farrell Krell (New York: Harper & Row, 1977), 283–318.
7. Mark Edmundson, *Towards Reading Freud: Self-Creation in Milton, Wordsworth, Emerson, and Sigmund Freud* (Princeton University Press, 1990), 150.
8. Whatever control over *physical* reality Emerson was inclined to fantasize is more than likely also tied to continental thought—to philosophical doubts (bequeathed to his age by skeptics of empiricism such as Berkeley and Kant) concerning the knowability of the object. This is the side of Emerson spurned by writers and scholars of the so-called nature writing school. Emerson's marked preference for ideas over their green referents in the physical world was off-putting to John Muir, for example, as it is to some present-day thinkers.
9. In Donald Barthelme's "A Shower of Gold" (1964), for example, Peterson suddenly apprehends that "the world is absurd" and that "possibilities . . . proliferate and escalate all around us," then he declares fantastically at the story's close, "My mother was a royal virgin

... and my father a shower of gold. My childhood was pastoral and energetic and rich in experiences which developed my character," etc. Donald Barthelme, *Sixty Stories* (New York: G. P. Putnam's Sons, 1981), 22–23.

10.   Current disputes over whether the individual or culture plays the stronger role in such fashioning are relevant here, but any hope of adjudicating between these two positions would lie beyond the scope of this essay.

11.   William Wordsworth, *The Prelude* (1799), I. 387–88.

12.   William Wordsworth, I. 300–327.

13.   To suggest that people have always derived comfort from the mythical association of *material* and *maternal* is at best, of course, over general. The idea of Mother Nature would have seemed friendlier to a nineteenth-century public than to a medieval or Renaissance one, for example, and such comfort as it has given has presumably been appreciated by men more than by women. At any rate, the link screams for historical context. My present interest, however, involves a newer conception of nature that threatens to dissolve any human attachment whatsoever. (The kind of divorce between humankind and matter implied in Ammons's lines would, it seems to me, put men and women on equal ground—or rather, would unground them with equal force.)

14.   The new pose would perhaps return Ammons more fully to the Romantic tradition as understood by Bloom—to a poetry of mind that only in its weaker moments takes nature for its subject. Bloom would presumably be inclined to find the same potential limitation in Ammons that he finds in Wordsworth.

15.   Lincoln Barnett, *The Universe and Dr. Einstein,* 101; it is likely that the matter of our particular planet was born from the emissions of some star (the hydrogen gas swirls of stars occasionally throw out huge particles) so that "the things of *earth*" are actually a bequest once removed from the big bang itself (see also Fritjof Capra, *The Tao of Physics,* [Boston: Shambhala Publications, 1975], 194).

16.   Steven P. Schneider also provides helpful astronomical background for this poem (and others from "Tombstones") in *A. R. Ammons and the Poetics of the Widening Scope* (Cranbury, NJ: Associated University Presses, 1994), 197–205.

17.   See Hans Jonas, *The Gnostic Religion* (Boston: Beacon Press, 1958).

18.   *Corsons Inlet,* 37; for a more recent as well as a more reverential and affecting treatment of the alliance between (nature) poet and the forces of creation in Ammons, see the enchanting "Singling & Doubling Together" (*SP,* 114).

19.   Karen Mills-Court, in *Poetry as Epitaph: Representation and Poetic Language* (Baton Rouge: Louisiana State University Press, 1990), offers a similar reading of Job 19:23–25 ("Oh that my words were now written! oh that they were printed in a book! / That they were graven with an iron pen and lead in the rock forever!"): "the act of writing," she argues, "is analogous to God's inscription of Himself into the world and is, therefore, indirectly validated by Him. . . . Job is suggesting an epitaph and also a palimpsest: his words written over the surface of God's. This 'double writing' would secure the 'truth' of his own presence as congruent with God's" (74). On the other hand, Herbert also feared that writing was inherently transgressive, blasphemous, usurping, etc., so that he shares Ammons's ambivalence toward his vocation. On this aspect of Herbert, see Barbara Lewalski, *Protestant Poetics and the Seventeenth-Century Religious Lyric* (Princeton, NJ: Princeton University Press, 1979), and William Kernigan and Gordon Braden, *The Idea of the Renaissance* (Baltimore: Johns Hopkins University Press, 1991).

20.   See stanza 50; of equal interest in this stanza, Shelley envisions "one keen pyramid" (the tomb of Gaius Cestius) as "flame transformed to marble."

21.   "I become a transparent eye-ball. I am nothing. I see all," is from the opening essay in *Nature* ("Nature"); the second phrase appears a few paragraphs later in the book's second essay, "Commodity." *The American Tradition in Literature, Shorter Edition* (New York: Random House, 1985), 357, 358.

22. Milton is hopeful, ultimately, that what he has lost in sight will be compensated for in vision: "So much the rather thou Celestial Light / Shine inward, and the mind through all her powers / Irradiate, there plant eyes . . ." (51–53).

23. For a more thorough elaboration of this claim made on behalf of ancient Chinese and Indian religious texts, see Fritjof Capra, *The Tao of Physics.*

Index

♦

The Volume Editor

Robert Kirschten holds a Ph.D. from the University of Chicago. He is assistant professor of English at The Ohio State University/Newark. He is the author of *James Dickey and the Gentle Ecstasy of Earth: A Reading of the Poems, "Approaching Prayer": Ritual and the Shape of Myth in the Poetry of A. R. Ammons and James Dickey,* and a book of poems, *Old Family Movies.* He has edited *Critical Essays on James Dickey* and *"Struggling for Wings": The Art of James Dickey.*

The General Editor

D r. James Nagel, J. O. Eidson Distinguished Professor of American Literature at the University of Georgia, founded the scholarly journal *Studies in American Fiction* and edited it for 20 years. He is the general editor of the Critical Essays on American Literature series published by G. K. Hall / Macmillan, a program that now contains over 130 volumes. He was one of the founders of the American Literature Association and serves as its executive coordinator. He is also a past president of the Ernest Hemingway Society. Among his 17 books are *Stephen Crane and Literary Impressionism, Critical Essays on* The Sun Also Rises, *Ernest Hemingway: The Writer in Context, Ernest Hemingway: The Oak Park Legacy,* and *Hemingway in Love and War,* which was selected by the *New York Times* as one of the outstanding books of 1989 and which has been made into a major motion picture. Dr. Nagel has published over 50 articles in scholarly journals, and has lectured on American literature in 15 countries. His current project is a book on the contemporary short story cycle.